D0534642

Flash 5 | H·O·T
Hands-On Training

lynda.com/books

By Kymberlee Weil and Garo Green
Developed with Lynda Weinman

Design: Ali Karp

Flash 5 | H·O·T Hands-On Training

By Kymberlee Weil and Garo Green

Developed with Lynda Weinman

lynda.com/books | Peachpit Press
1249 Eighth Street • Berkeley, CA • 94710
800.283.9444 • 510.524.2178 •
510.524.2221 (fax)
http://www.lynda.com/books
http://www.peachpit.com

lynda.com/books is published in
association with Peachpit Press,
a division of Pearson Education
Copyright ©2002 by lynda.com

ISBN: 0-201-73134-7

0 9 8 7 6 5 4 3 2 1

Printed and bound in the
United States of America

H•O•T | Credits

Original Design: Ali Karp, Alink Newmedia

Peachpit Editor: Cary Norsworthy

Peachpit Project Coordinator: Suzie Lowey

Copyeditors: Paul Potyen, Dave Awl

Peachpit Production: Lisa Brazieal

Peachpit Compositors: Owen Wolfson, David Van Ness, Jude Levinson

Beta testers: Rosanna Yeung, Dina Pielaet, and Chris Tegethoff

Exercise Graphics: Chris Baxter (`www.cbaxter.org`)

Cover Illustration: Bruce Heavin (bruce@stink.com)

Indexer: Steve Rath

H•O•T | Colophon

The preliminary design for the H•O•T series was sketched on paper Ali Karp | Alink Newmedia. The layout was heavily influenced by online communication—merging a traditional book format with a modern Web aesthetic.

The text in Flash 5 H•O•T was set in Akzidenz Grotesk from Adobe, and Triplex from Emigre. The cover illustration was painted in Adobe Photoshop and Adobe Illustrator.

This book was created using QuarkXPress 4.1, Adobe Photoshop 6, Macromedia Fireworks 4, Microsoft Office 2001, and Flash 5 on a Macintosh G3, running Mac OS 9.1. It was printed on 60# Sonoma Matte at Von Hoffman Printing.

Flash 5 | H•O•T_____Table of Contents

Introduction

H•O•T
Flash 5

A Note from Lynda Weinman

In my opinion, most people buy computer books in order to learn, yet it is amazing how few of these books are actually written by teachers. I take pride in the fact that this book was written by experienced teachers who are familiar with training students in this subject matter. In this book, you will find carefully developed lessons to help you learn Flash 5—one of the most powerful animation and interactivity tools for the Web.

This book is targeted towards beginning-level Web developers who need a tool to create creative, powerful, and interactive Web sites. The premise of the hands-on exercise approach is to get you up to speed quickly in Flash, while actively working through the book's lessons. It's one thing to read about a product, and an entirely other experience to try the product and get measurable results. Our motto is, "read the book, follow the exercises, and you will know the product." We've received countless testimonials to this fact, and it is our goal to make sure it remains true for all of our hands-on training books.

Many exercise-based books take a paint-by-numbers approach to teaching. While this approach works, it's often difficult to figure out how to apply those lessons to a real-world situation, or understand why or when you would use the technique again. What sets this book apart is that the lessons contain lots of background information and insights into each given subject, and they are designed to help you understand the process as well as the exercise.

At times, pictures are worth a lot more than words. When necessary, we have also included short QuickTime movies to show any process that's difficult to explain in text. These files are located on the **H•O•T CD-ROM** inside a folder called **movies**. It's our style to approach teaching from many different angles, because we know that some people are visual learners while others like to read, and still others like to get out there and try things. This book combines a lot of teaching approaches so you can learn Flash 5 as thoroughly as you want to.

This book didn't set out to cover every single aspect of Flash. The manual and many other reference books are great for that! What we saw missing from the bookshelves was a process-oriented tutorial that taught readers core principles, techniques, and tips in a hands-on training format.

We welcome your comments at fl5hot@lynda.com. Please visit our Web site as well, at `http://www.lynda.com`.

The support URL for this book is `http://www.lynda.com/products/books/fl5hot/`

It's my hope that this book will give you a strong foundation in Flash and give you the necessary skills to begin developing animations and interactive Web sites. If it does, then we've accomplished the job we set out to do!

–Lynda Weinman

NOTE | About lynda.com/books and lynda.com

lynda.com/books is dedicated to helping Web designers and developers understand tools and design principles. **lynda.com** offers hands-on workshops, training seminars, conferences, on-site training, training videos and CDs, and "expert tips" for Web design and development. To learn more about our training programs, books, and products, be sure to give our site a visit at `http://www.lynda.com`.

About the Authors

Kymberlee Weil

It all started with a Web-development class at UCLA. After attending just a few sessions, Kymberlee fell in love with the technology and decided to pursue a career where she was excited to go to work each and every day. When she was introduced to Flash for the very first time, Kymberlee knew she had found her passion. She states, "Flash is like playing with Play Doh—you can use your imagination to create anything you want and you can have so much fun doing it!"

Currently, Kymberlee runs a small multimedia development firm, VolcanicLab.com, in Santa Monica, CA, which specializes in Flash based projects. VolcanicLab.com is a full service business, offering services from consulting to Web project development to CD-ROM development.

Kymberlee has worked as a conference speaker and as an instructor for lynda.com, as well as UCLA Extension. She has written courseware for lynda.com and been involved in the beta testing of several lynda.com books. Kymberlee has also worked on creating the conference manuals for the first four Flashforward conferences.

In July of 2001, Kymberlee was a featured speaker at Flashforward 2001 in New York. She presented a session on Business Strategy for Flash developers.

After completing her MBA at Pepperdine in December of 2000, Kymberlee added consulting to her bag of tricks. She has recently been selected to work with a team of individuals on several government projects.

When she isn't working on something computer related, Kymberlee can be seen addressing her stress relief during Muay Thai kickboxing training.

Garo Green

Garo Green has been working with wide range of computers since the tender age of 12. Those were the golden days of tape drives and 64k of RAM memory, where all you needed was a double density floppy disk and a hole-puncher. ;-)

Garo has worked extensively in the development of custom curriculum and courseware for software training, and has over six years of teaching experience in both hardware and software applications. He is known worldwide for his enthusiastic, approachable, and humanistic teaching style.

Garo is also the author of the *Dreamweaver 4 H•O•T* book and author of several Web design training CD-ROMs, including *Learning Flash 5* and *Learning Dreamweaver 4*. He has also been a featured speaker at the Web99 and FlashForward conferences.

In his spare time… (well, he doesn't have much of that anymore, but that's OK) he has found that his passion for teaching and sharing what he knows is very fulfilling. He does sneak away, several times a day, to the local Starbucks for a double latte (ok, honestly it's usually a triple shot) with hazelnut. Of course this might explain why he talks so fast!

Our Team

Kimberlee has found the perfect contrast to spending hours behind one of her computers: martial arts. She is seen here during of her Muay Thai kickboxing training sessions.

Garo and Kymberlee take a moment to rest and smile for the camera.

Garo is learning the art of bonsai, and this is his first tree. Good thing you can't see the dozen that came before this one. ;-)

The lynda.com training center offers classes in Flash, Dreamweaver, Fireworks, Photoshop, ImageReady, GoLive, and Web-design principles. Visit www.lynda.com classes for more information.

Acknowledgements from Kymberlee

This book could not have been possible without the assistance and support of many important individuals.

My warmest aloha and mahalo to:

Garo Green, my coauthor. Thank you for the immeasurable hours you spent creating, testing and working on this book to bring it to fruition. Your work ethic and drive are superhuman!

Lynda Weinman, my role model. Thank you for believing in me and giving me this wonderful opportunity to build upon my passion for Flash and create this book. Your positive feedback and encouragement helped drive me to deliver a product that exceeded your expectations.

Chris Baxter, my right-hand man. Thank you for all the countless hours you spent creating and developing exercise files and artwork for this book. Your work helped bring this book to a higher level and I can't thank you enough for your vision, humor and not to mention your patience with me. You da man!

Jason Coleman, my very first Flash instructor. This is all your fault, Jason! (Thank you, though!)

Robert Reinhardt and **Josh Ulm,** my two intermediate and advanced Flash instructors who I look up to and admire for your knowledge and guidance.

Shane Rebenschied and **Tony Winecoff**. Thank you Shane, for always answering my emails and helping me with any needed artwork and exercise files. Tony, thank you for your moral support and for making sure I was always on track!

The beta testers, Thanks for all your hard work, dedication and attention to detail.

Cary Norsworthy, my Peachpit connection. Thank you for all your assistance and support.

The Macromedia Flash Folks . Thank you for creating a product that I can work with every day in some capacity, so that I can truly say I love what I do for a living!

Charles Hollins, my very first Web-related class instructor. Thank you for inspiring me to pursue a career in which I am truly passionate about what I do. I look forward to every new adventure in this industry and I want to thank you for introducing me to this field.

Roy Hernandez, my mentor/"story" partner. Thank you for sharing your humor and business insight with me, along with a few good stories, of course! Thank you also for your strong support all along the way.

John Barron. Thank you for helping me maintain my sanity throughout the book-writing process. Your advice, support and encouragement meant the world to me!

Ray Copeland, my Sifu. Thank you for allowing me to achieve the optimum stress relief for book writing: Muay Thai kickboxing. I would not have made it through without something/someone to take my aggressions out on!

William Arnold. Thank you for your encouragement, understanding and most of all your patience! I truly appreciate your strength and support all along the way.

My Family and Friends: Dad and Sandy, Mom and Phil, Beverly and Joe, Grandpa, Jack and Marie, Dayna, Jackie, and Guy, and all my Volcanic Lab clientele. Thanks to everyone for your patience, continuous support.

Acknowledgements from Garo

This book, and every other book you read, could not have been possible without a strong team of dedicated, enthusiastic, and talented individuals. I was fortunate enough to work, again, with the best.

My deepest thanks and appreciation to:

You, the reader. By deciding to further your education, you are making an amazing investment in yourself. I really hope that my work will add to this investment and help you realize what you set out to accomplish.

My co-author, **Kymberlee Weil.** Thank you for spending so many sleepless nights to ensure that we produced only the best possible book!

My dearest friend, **Lynda Weinman**. Thank you, again, for giving me another opportunity to share my knowledge with others. You have been a dear friend – what more could I ask for.

My beta testers, **Rosanna Yeung, Dina Pielaet**, and **Chris Tegethoff**. I can't thank you enough for spending endless hours going over each exercise. I know it was a long and sometimes challenging task, but this book would not exist without your hard work and dedication. Your technical and grammatical skills amaze me.

Contributing authors, **Jason Coleman** and **Shane Rebenschied**. Thank you for brainstorming with me and setting the groundwork for some of the exercises in this book. It was really helpful.

My dear friends, Flash developers, and instructors, **Jason Coleman**, **Robert Reinhardt**, and **Josh Ulm**. What can I say? You guys give me Flash envy. ;-) Your work continues to inspire me and your friendship is treasured.

My friends at Peachpit, **Nancy Ruenzel, Cary Norsworthy, Suzie Lowey,** and **Lisa Brazieal.** Thank you for supporting and helping us create the H•O•T series. You guys made a long and difficult process so much fun! In fact, I can't wait to do it again! (OK, maybe after a little vacation!) ;-)

My friends at Macromedia, and all of the **Flash team and engineers**. You have managed to produce a tool that not only changed the Web, but so many people's lives, mine included. Rock on!

The entire **lynda.com staff**. You guys make working each day so much fun; what more could a person ask for!

How To Use This Book

Please read this section—it contains important information that's going to help you as you use this book. The list below outlines the information we cover:

- The Formatting in This Book

- Interface Screen Captures

- Mac System Differences

- Sharing Files with Windows Users

- A Note to Windows Users

- Making Exercise Files Editable on Windows Systems

- Making File Extensions Visible on Windows Systems

- Creating New Documents

- Flash System Requirements—Authoring and Playback

- **H•O•T CD-ROM** Contents

The Formatting in This Book

This book has several components, including step-by-step exercises, commentary, notes, tips, warnings, and movies. Step-by-step exercises are numbered, and file names and command keys are bolded so they pop out more easily.

Captions and commentary are in italicized text: *This is a caption*. File names/folders, Command keys, and Menu commands are bolded: **images** folder, **Ctrl+Click**, and **File > Open...** And URLs are in light serif font: http://www.lynda.com.

Interface Screen Captures

Most of the screen captures in the book were taken on a Macintosh. The only time Windows shots were taken was when the interface differed from the Macintosh. We made this decision because we do most of our design work and writing on a Macintosh. We also own and use a Windows system, so we noted important differences when they occurred, and took screen captures accordingly.

Mac and Windows System Differences

Macromedia did a great job of ensuring that Flash looks and works the same between the Macintosh and Windows operating systems. However, some differences do exist. If you are using this book with one of the Windows operating systems, please be sure to read the section titled *"A Note to Windows Users,"* carefully.

Sharing Files with Windows Users

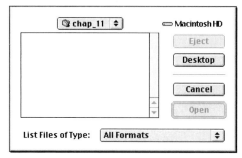

The browse dialog box set to All Formats.
The .fla file is not seen.

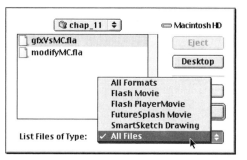

The browse dialog box set to All Files.
The .fla file is displayed.

As you work with Flash, you might need to open a PC-created file on a Macintosh. Because of this, we wanted to make sure you were aware of a little glitch that could cause you some confusion. The Macintosh has difficulty recognizing .fla files that were created on a PC. This means you may not see some .fla files when you use the browse dialog box. You can get around this by changing the **List Files of Type** option to **All Files**. This will display all files in the folder.

A Note to Windows Users

This section contains essential information about making your exercise folders editable and making file extensions visible.

Making Exercise Files Editable on Windows Systems

By default, when you copy files from a CD-ROM to your Windows 95/98/2000 hard drive, they are set to read-only (write protected). This causes a problem with the exercise files, because you need to write over some of them. To remove this setting and make the files editable, follow the short procedure below:

1. Copy the chapter folder from the **H•O•T CD-ROM** to your hard drive.

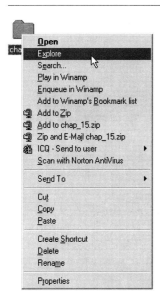

2. Right Click on the chapter folder and choose Explore.

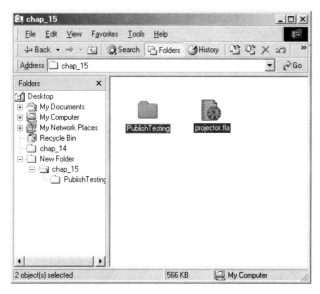

3. Press **Ctrl+A** to select all of the files inside the chapter folder.

4. Right Click on any of the folder icons and choose **Properties**.

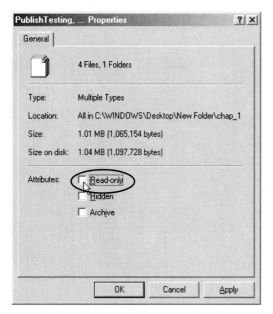

5. Uncheck the **Read Only** checkbox. This will change the setting for all of the files that were selected. If Archive is selected, you can remove that check as well.

6. Click **OK**.

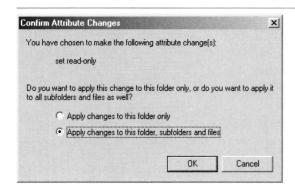

Note: *If there are other folders inside the chapter folder, change the attributes of those folders as well by selecting* ***Apply changes to this folder, subfolders, and files*** *when the above dialog box appears.*

Making File Extensions Visible on Windows Systems

In this section, you'll see three different examples of how to turn on file extensions for Windows 95, Windows 98, and Windows 2000. By default, Windows 95/98/2000 users will not be able to see file extension names such as .fla or .swf. Fortunately, you can change this setting!

Windows 95 Users:

1. Double-click on the **My Computer** icon on your desktop. Note: If you (or someone else) changed the name, it will not say **My Computer.**

2. Select **View > Options.** This will open the Options dialog box.

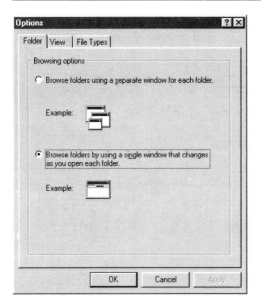 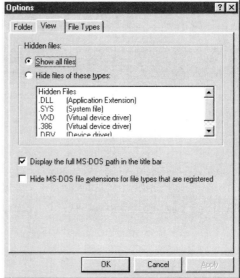

3. Click on the **View** tab at the top. This will open the View options screen so you can change the view settings of Windows 95.

4. Make sure there is no checkmark in the **Hide MS-DOS file extensions for file types that are registered** box. This will ensure that the file extensions are visible, which will help you better understand the exercises in this book!

Windows 98 Users:

1. Double-click on the **My Computer** icon on your desktop. **Note:** If you (or someone else) changed the name, it will not say **My Computer**.

2. Select **View > Folder Options**. This will open the Folder Options dialog box.

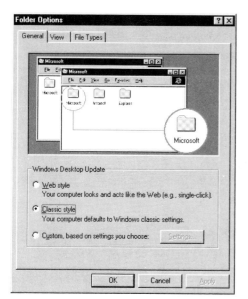 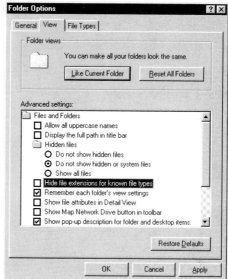

3. Click on the **View** tab at the top. This will open the View options screen so you can change the view settings of Windows 98.

4. Uncheck the **Hide File extensions for known file types** checkbox. This will make all of the file extensions visible.

Windows 2000 Users:

1. Double-click on the **My Computer** icon on your desktop. Note: If you (or someone else) changed the name, it will not say **My Computer**.

2. Select **Tools > Folder Options**. This will open the Folder Options dialog box.

3. Click on the **View** tab at the top. This will open the View options screen so you can change the view settings of Windows 2000.

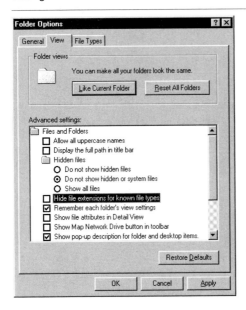

4. Make sure there is no checkmark next to the **Hide File extensions for known file types** option. This will make all of the file extensions visible.

Flash System Requirements

This book requires that you use either a Macintosh operating system (Power Macintosh running System 8.5 or later) or Windows 95/98/2000/Me or Windows NT 4.0/2000. You also will need a color monitor capable of 800 x 600 resolution and a CD-ROM drive. We suggest that you have at least 64 MB of RAM in your system, because it's optimal if you can open Flash and a Web browser at the same time. More RAM than that is even better, especially on Macintosh computers, which do not dynamically allocate RAM like Windows. Here's a little chart that cites Macromedia's system requirements:

Macromedia Flash System Requirements	
Authoring	
Windows	**Macintosh**
133 MHz Intel Pentium processor, Windows 95, 98, NT4, 2000 Professional*, or later	Power Macintosh with Mac OS 8.5, 8.6, 9.x or OS X (classic mode only)
32 MB of free available system RAM	32 MB of free available system RAM
40 MB of available disk space	40 MB of available hard drive space
256-color monitor capable of 800x600 resolution	256-color monitor capable of 800x600 resolution
CD-ROM drive	CD-ROM drive
*On the Windows platform Macromedia Flash performs best on Windows 2000 Professional.	

Macromedia Flash System Requirements

Playback

Windows	Macintosh	Linux	Solaris
Microsoft Windows 95, 98, Me, NT, 2000 Professional, or later	System 8.1 or later	Linux Redhat 6.0 or above (Pentium-based only)	Solaris 2.5 or 2.6 (24-bit color, SPARC only)
Netscape plug-in works with Netscape 3 or later	Netscape plug-in works with Netscape 3 or later, and Microsoft Internet Explorer 3.0 or later	Netscape Navigator 4 or later, with standard install defaults	Netscape Navigator 3 or later, with standard install defaults
Macromedia Flash Player, Java Edition— requires a Java-enabled browser	Macromedia Flash Player, Java Edition— requires a Java-enabled browser		
ActiveX—works with Microsoft Internet Explorer 3 or later (Windows 95 or later, Windows NT)			

What's on the CD-ROM?

Exercise Files and the H•O•T CD-ROM

Your course files are located inside a folder called **exercise_files** on the **H•O•T CD-ROM**. These files are divided into chapter folders, and you will be instructed to copy the chapter folders to your hard drive during many of the exercises. Unfortunately, when files originate from a CD-ROM, the Windows operating system defaults to making them write-protected, meaning that you cannot alter them. You will need to alter them to follow the exercises, so please read the *Note to Windows Users* on pages xxiv–xxix for instructions on how to convert them to read-and-write formatting.

Demo Files on the CD-ROM

In addition to the exercise files, the **H•O•T CD-ROM** also contains a free 30-day trial version of Flash 5 for Mac or Windows. All software is located inside the **software** folder on the **H•O•T CD-ROM**. We have included trial versions of:

- Macromedia Flash 5.0 + (5.0a Update–Macintosh Only)

- Netscape Navigator 4.7

- Netscape Navigator 6.01

- Internet Explorer 4.5 • Internet Explorer 5.0

We also have included several plug-ins on the **H•O•T CD-ROM**. If you don't have these plug-ins installed already, you should do that before working with any exercise in this book that calls for one of them. All of the plug-ins is located inside the **software** folder. We have included the following:

- Flash 5.0 plug-in

- Shockwave 8.5 plug-in

- QuickTime 5.0 plug-in

In addition, Frank Bongers, of SoundShopper.com, was generous enough to donate a huge collection of audio files for you to use with the exercise in this book and your own projects. These files are located inside the **chap_14** folder. There is a folder for Macintosh users, which contains audio files in the .aiff format and another folder for Windows users, which contains audio files in the .wav format. Be sure to visit SoundShopper at **http://www.soundshopper.com** for a huge collection of royalty free sounds. Thanks again Frank!

I.

Background Information

| Why Use Flash? |

| Flash as Project, Plug-in or Projector? |

| File Types Associated with Flash |

| Flash/Shockwave Plug-in | Beyond Flash |

Flash 5

No exercise files.

Most likely, if you've purchased a copy of Flash, you already know why you want to use the program. You might already have experience in building Web pages or using other graphics programs, and you're increasing your software skills for today's job market. However, some of you might not know the benefits of using Flash versus HTML for authoring a Web site. We'd like to take a moment to explain the answer to "Why use Flash?". In addition, we'll also outline some of the ways you can extend Flash content using other technologies such as Generator, CGI and JavaScript. This is a short chapter, so feel free to skim it if you already know some of this stuff. We know you're anxious to get into the hands-on exercises!

Download Speed

For a Web site that contains an abundance of visual content, the users' download speed can be a major problem. As most of you know, nothing can be more frustrating than a slow-loading site. Even liberal use of the compressed bitmap graphic file formats that are used for the Web (GIF and JPEG) can result in slow Web sites that frustrate visitors. Because of this, Web designers are often times forced to change designs to be less visual.

Flash content is often smaller than HTML content because it uses its own compression scheme that optimizes vector and bitmap content differently than GIF or JPEGs. For this reason, Flash has become the delivery medium of preference for graphic-intensive Web sites.

Visual Control!

Another great benefit of Flash is that it frees Web designers from many of the restraints of traditional HTML (HyperText Markup Language). Flash gives you complete and accurate control over position, color, fonts and other aspects of the screen regardless of the platform (Mac or Windows) or browser (Explorer or Netscape) from which it is displayed. This is a radical and important departure from traditional HTML authoring, which requires precise planning to ensure that graphics appear relatively similar on different computers and with different Web browsers. Flash frees designers to focus on design instead of HTML workarounds.

Enhanced Interactivity

While Flash is often known as an animation program, it also provides powerful interactivity tools that allow you to create buttons or free-form interfaces for site navigation that include sound and animation. With the release of Flash 5, powerful, new, and improved scripting makes it possible to create presentations that are far more complex than standard HTML or JavaScript can provide. This book covers interactivity in a number of later chapters.

Combine Vectors and Bitmaps

Most graphics on the Internet are bitmap graphics (GIFs or JPEGs). Bitmap files are measured by how many pixels are contained within a given graphic image. Because of this, as the image size increases, so does the file size and download time. In addition to file-size disadvantages, bitmap images that are enlarged to a size other than the size specified often appear distorted, soft focused, and pixelated.

Graphics that are created within Flash are composed of "vectors." Vector graphics use mathematical formulas to describe the images, unlike bitmaps, which record information pixel-by-pixel and color-by-color.

Vector graphics can offer much smaller file sizes and increased flexibility for certain types of images, such as those with solid color fills and typographic content. Some images are going to be smaller in file size as bitmaps, and some as vectors. The neat thing about Flash is that you can use either kind of image.

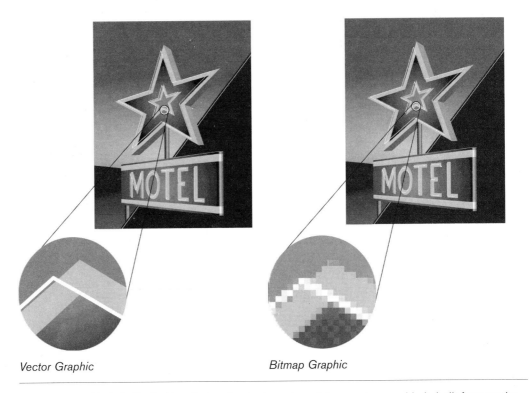

Vector Graphic   *Bitmap Graphic*

A bitmap graphic is built pixel-by-pixel and color-by-color, while a vector graphic is built from mathematical formulas. This means that a vector graphic will be the same file size regardless of its physical dimensions, while a bitmap graphic will grow and shrink in file size depending on how large or small it is. This makes it possible for Flash to create and display large vector images and animations without increasing file size.

Scalability

Because Flash movies can use vectors, they can be resized in any Web browser window and still retain their original scale and relative position. Most importantly, the file size of vector graphics are independent of their display size. This means it is possible to create full-screen vector animations that display on any monitor resolution and that only weigh a fraction of the file size of a comparable bitmap graphic.

Flash content can be set to scale dynamically within the size of the browser window, as shown here.

Does all of this mean you should only use vectors in your Flash movies? Absolutely not. While Flash is known for its vector capabilities, it also supports bitmap images. This means that you can, and often times will, combine bitmap and vector images in your movies. The ability to deliver both bitmap and vector graphics together lets you create movies that look good, scale to different resolutions, and still have a bandwidth-friendly file size. Flash can even be used to convert bitmap images into vectors, which you will learn how to do in Chapter 9, "*Bitmaps*."

Streaming Content

Vectors are not the only way Flash makes itself more bandwidth-friendly. Flash files download to Web browsers in small units. This allows the files to display some content while the rest is still downloading in the background. Ideally, the content will play more slowly than it downloads, so that the viewing experience is not interrupted. This method of playing one part of a file while the rest is still download-ing is called **streaming**, and it differs significantly from the way HTML files are downloaded and displayed in a browser.

Flash is sometimes difficult to understand because of how information is organized within it. With HTML, all content is organized into pages (HTML files). When you load a page, all the parts of its content are downloaded to the browser and then displayed. Flash movies, on the other hand, can be organized in a very different way.

Imagine a Web site with four or five pages. If this were a pure HTML site, every time you traveled from one page to another you would have to wait for the new page to download. Instead, if this was built as a Flash site all of the "pages" could be contained in a single Flash movie. When you visited the site, the first page would download and be displayed. Unlike the HTML only site, while you were reading the first page, the other pages would be downloading in the background. When you clicked on a link to go to another page it would be displayed instantly, with no download wait! This is the real beauty of streaming. When used correctly, it can allow you to build a site that eliminates a lot of the waiting that so many Web users complain about. You'll learn more about how to optimize your Flash content for streaming in Chapter 15, "*Publishing.*"

Flash as Project, Plug-in or Projector?

"Flash" as a term can be confusing. Macromedia interchanges the word to include Flash as an authoring tool, Flash as a plug-in and Flash as a stand-alone player. The following chart should help set the groundwork for understanding the difference between the authoring tool, the stand-alone player and the projector.

Flash Authoring Tool	Creates content for the Web. Flash is the application that allows you to create and edit artwork and animation, add sound and interactivity. The projects that you create using the Flash authoring tool are stored in the .fla file format. You cannot publish the .fla file to the Web it's a file that you use internally to edit and create Flash content. From the .fla file, you can export the .swf file format, which is inserted into an HTML document and published to the Web.
Flash Plug-In	The Flash plug-in must be installed in the Web browser for end users to see Flash content in the .swf file. This plug-in comes pre-installed in current Web browsers and/or can be downloaded from the Macromedia Web site for free.
Flash Projector	Flash content can also be stored in stand-alone projectors that do not require the Web browser in order to play. These files can be distributed on CD-ROMs or on disk, but are not typically distributed over the Web. The file extension for a Flash projector is .exe (Windows) or .hqx (Mac).

File Types Associated with Flash

Flash media can be saved and output in several formats. The most common type of Flash files are project files, movie files, and projector files. The file types can become very confusing, because all of these are commonly referred to as "movies." The following list explains the three most significant Flash formats.

Table Title	
Project File–.fla untitled.fla	The master project file format, which stores all the settings and resources for your Flash project. An .fla file can be reopened and re-edited at any time by the Flash Authoring Tool. (FLA stands for FLAsh.)
Movie–.swf untitled.swf	The movie format that can be embedded in Web pages for Web-based Flash presentations. These files are generally not editable. (SWF stands for Small Web File.)
Projector–.exe (Windows) Untitled.exe **Projector–.hqx (Mac)** Untitled Projector	A stand-alone projector file that can play on any computer a Web browser. Flash writes both Windows and Mac format projector files.

Caution: Plug-in Required!

Flash content is not visible in a Web browser unless either the Flash Player or Shockwave Player has been installed in that browser. In the past, this has been seen as a serious limitation of the format, although over the past two years the number of Internet users who have the plug-in has rapidly increased.

Macromedia has hired an independent consulting firm to maintain an estimate of the number of Flash plug-ins that are in use. At the time this book was printed over 200 million Web users had a version of the one of these plug-ins installed. The Flash Player plug-in comes pre-installed on all new browsers shipped by AOL, CompuServe, Microsoft and Netscape. Additionally, all versions of Microsoft Windows 98 and newer and Apple's OS 8 and newer include the plug-In.

Plug-Ins	
Flash Player:	The Flash Player is used for viewing Macromedia Flash content on the Web. You can download the latest version of the Flash Player at: `http://macromedia.com/software/flashplayer/`. This player installs inside the plug-in folder for your Web browser of choice.
Shockwave Player:	The Shockwave Player is used for viewing Macromedia Director content on the Web. You can download the latest version of the Shockwave Player at: `http://macromedia.com/software/shockwaveplayer/`

Beyond Flash

Flash is an incredibly powerful tool by itself. However, there are a few functions it can't perform. Here are some of the Web technologies you should know about if you want to extend Flash beyond its basic capabilities.

What is Generator?

Generator is a server-based program developed by Macromedia, meaning that it runs on a Web server instead of over a Web browser. Generator is used to create, update, and maintain dynamic graphical content on Web sites. Dynamic content is defined as content that changes and updates on-the-fly. Generator can be used to produce real-time charts, scoreboards, news updates, tickers and any other kind of rapidly changing information.

It can also be used to populate Flash movie templates. This means that you can create a page's look, feel and layout inside Flash, save it as a Generator template, and Generator can then populate the content of the page with data that is pulled from a database. A common use of Generator is to create customized greeting cards. Additionally, you will also see Generator used on investment, commerce, and other business-application sites. Generator instruction and exercises are not covered in this book, although once you have learned Flash, creating Generator templates is not very difficult to master. To create a Generator Web site, you would need additional set up and licenses for a Web server. You may also have to develop a database and CGI scripts (explained in the next section) to hold data and exchange it with the templates.

More information, training, pricing and product specifications about Generator can be found on the Macromedia Web site. While it is outside the scope of this book, many Flash developers use Generator for including real-time, updateable, and dynamic graphic content.

What's CGI?

A CGI (Common Gateway Interface) script is a program that defines a standard way of exchanging information between a Web browser and a Web server. CGI scripts can be written in any number of languages (PERL, C, Visual C, UNIX shells and others). If you plan on creating a complex Web application that requires the use of something like CGI, we recommend you work with a Web engineer who has experience creating these kinds of scripts. Flash can communicate with CGI scripts, although that is a topic way beyond the scope of this book.

For further information on using CGI, please check out the following links:

`http://www.cgidir.com/`

`http://www.cgi101.com/`

`http://www.icthus.net/CGI-City/`

`http://hotwired.lycos.com/webmonkey/99/26/index4a.html`

JavaScript and Flash

Macromedia refers to Flash's scripting language as ActionScript. In Flash 5, ActionScript has been changed from Flash 4, and is based on another scripting language you may have heard of called JavaScript. Although they share a similar syntax and structure, they are two different languages. One way to tell them apart is that ActionScript uses scripts that are processed entirely within the Flash Player, independent of which browser is used to view the file. JavaScript, on the other hand, uses external interpreters that vary according to the browser used.

Additionally, ActionScript and JavaScript can be used together due to the fact that Flash 5 gives you the ability to call JavaScript commands to perform tasks or send and receive data. For many Flash developers, a basic knowledge of JavaScript makes leaning ActionScript easier, because the basic syntax of the scripts and the handling of objects is the same in both languages. However, this is not a requirement of learning ActionScripting.

In Chapter 12, we will introduce you to ActionScripting. That chapter will give you hands on experience working with some of the applications of Flash 5's powerful scripting language. For further information and tutorials about JavaScript and how to use it in conjunction with Flash 5, check out the links below:

`http://www.javascript.com/`

`http://javascript.internet.com/`

`http://www.jsworld.com/`

`http://www.flashkit.com/links/Javascripts/`

`http://www.virtual-fx.net/tutorials/html/jscript_popup.html`

`http://www.macromedia.com/software/dreamweaver/productinfo/extend/jik_flash5.html`

2.

The Flash Interface

Document Window	Timeline
Layer Controls	Stage	Toolbox
Panels	Keyboard Shortcuts

Flash 5 H•O•T

No Exercises Files Needed

If you are like many people, you already want to skip this chapter and jump right to the more exciting and interesting parts of the book. While this works with some software programs, it is not the way we would suggest you learn Flash.

In this chapter, we explain some of the different interface elements you will be working with, starting with an overview of the main components; the Timeline, Stage, Toolbox, Work Area, Zoom Box, and Launcher. Then we will cover each of these elements in greater detail. You will also be introduced to the new panel system in Flash. This will be a relatively short chapter because we believe you will learn how these tools work—and what they are used for—in the course of actual exercises. It is our belief and hope that some exposure to these elements now will make it easier for you to work with them throughout the rest of the book.

The Document Window

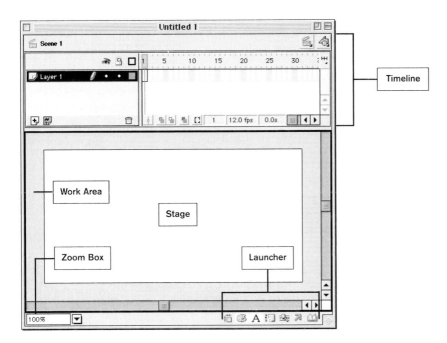

Each time you create a new document in Flash, you will be presented with a new blank document window. This document window can be divided into five main components:

Timeline   The Timeline is where you control the static and moving elements in the project file using the following interface features: Layers, Playhead, Frames, and Status Bar. All are described in detail in the next few pages.

Stage   The Stage is where your animation and images appear. The white area of the Stage represents the visible area of your project. You will learn how to modify the properties of the Stage such as size, color and frame rate, in Chapter 5, "Animation Basics."

Work Area   The light gray area around the Stage is referred to as the Work Area. Nothing in the Work Area will be visible to the end user after you publish your movie. However, you can place objects here until you want them to appear on the Stage. For example, if you wanted to animate a bird flying in from off-stage, you could place the bird artwork off-screen in the Work Area so it would appear to fly from outside the stage area.

Zoom Box   It might seem like a little thing, and maybe it is in size, but the Zoom Box is a handy little drop-down menu that lets you quickly zoom in and out to the contents of your Stage.

Launcher   The Launcher is a row of buttons, just like in Dreamweaver and Fireworks, which gives you quick and easy access to the many panels of the program. Clicking on a Launcher button will display or hide that specific panel, depending on whether the panel is currently displayed on the screen or not.

The launcher items will open the following panels listed above.

TIP | Rulers and Click and Drag Guides

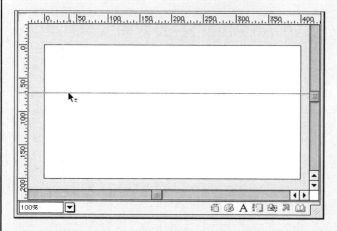

In Flash 5, you can click and drag guides out from the rulers. Much like you can in Fireworks, Freehand, Quark and other tools, these guides can be placed both horizontally and vertically on the Stage. Rulers can be very helpful for placing objects in exact and relative positions. Make sure the rulers are visible (**View > Rulers**) and then click in the ruler area and drag out the guide onto your Stage. To remove a guide, click and drag the guide back into the ruler. You can clear all of your guides by selecting **View > Guides > Edit Guides > Clear All**.

TIP | The Timeline

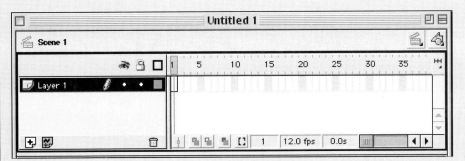

Almost every program you use has a heart. You know, the part of the program that controls the core of everyday tasks. In Flash, the Timeline is the heart of the program. It controls and displays all of the static and moving elements of your Flash projects. This section will address the main elements of the Timeline and point out what you need to know before you begin the exercises. As we cover each of these elements, don't forget that you will get hands-on experience later as you go though the exercises.

Current Scene: Scenes are a way of organizing material for your project if the number of frames in a single Timeline starts to grow too large to manage. The *Current Scene* readout on the upper-left side of the Timeline displays the name of the scene that is currently open on the Stage. As projects get larger, many people use multiple scenes as a form of organizing the content. This visual feedback at the top of the Timeline showing the name of the current scene helps you know which scene is currently in use.

Playhead: The Playhead indicates which Timeline frame is currently displayed on the Stage. You can click and drag on the Playhead to move it to a specific frame, or to scan through the timeline (a process called scrubbing) to quickly preview your animations. You will get a lot of practice doing this in the animation portions of this book.

Layer Controls: This region lets you control the features of the layers. Because there are so many options here, we will break them out in more detail later in this chapter.

continued on next page

TIP | The Timeline *continued*

Status Bar: The Status Bar gives you feedback about the current frame, elapsed time, and frames-per-second (fps) rate of your movie. It also controls some animation tools, such as onion skinning, which you will learn about in Chapter 5, "Animation Basics."

Frame View: This not-so-obvious drop-down menu lets you control the appearance of your Timeline. You can change the appearance of the individual frames and the entire size of the Timeline itself. As you will see, this can be helpful with certain projects.

Edit Scene List: If you work with multiple scenes, this drop-down menu will display a list of all the scenes in your document. You will learn more about how to use multiple scenes in Chapter 16, and get a chance to see this in action.

Edit Symbol List: Symbols are elements that are placed in the Library. The drop-down list will display all of the symbols in your project. This can be helpful for making changes to existing symbols without having to navigate through the Library. You'll learn about symbols in Chapter 7, "*Symbols and Instances.*"

TIP | Docking and Undocking the Timeline

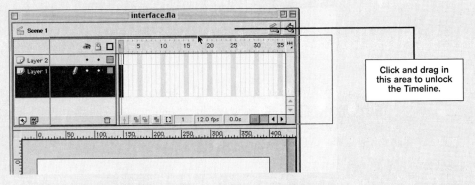

Click and drag in
this area to unlock
the Timeline.

Click at the top of the Timeline to drag it away. A thin outline will appear, indicating that you have grabbed the Timeline and are undocking it.

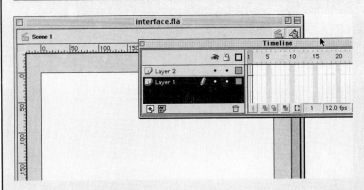

Release the mouse button and your Timeline will be undocked from the document window. If you want to re-dock the Timeline, simply click and drag it back on top of the document window and release the mouse button.

If you have the luxury of working with a large monitor or multiple monitors, then you will be pleased to know that you can easily dock and undock the Timeline from the main document window. This allows you more flexibility in arranging your work environment. For example, you could place the Stage in its own monitor, and stash all the Flash tools on your second monitor, giving you an uncluttered view of your work. By the way, if you find the ability to undock the Timeline annoying, you can disable this feature in the Preferences.

The Layer Controls

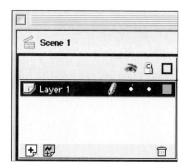

The Timeline's Layer Controls play an important role in your workflow. This is where you add, modify, and delete layers, and where you can hide, lock, and control the appearance of the layer contents.

Layer Name: The default layer names are Layer 1, Layer 2, and so on. Double-click on the name to change it.

Insert Layer: Adding new layers to your projects is as easy as clicking this button. Each time you click, a new layer will be added on top of the layer that is currently selected.

Add Guide Layer: This button will add a guide layer on top of the currently selected layer. You will work with guide layers in Chapter 8, *"Motion Tweening."*

Delete Layer: Not much mystery to this trash can button. Clicking this button will delete the layer that is currently selected. Don't worry, if you click on this button by accident, you can undo this by selecting Edit > Undo. Phew!!

Hide Layer: Clicking on the eye icon will temporarily hide the layer and make it invisible. The layer will still be exported with your movie, just not visible to the end user.

Lock Layer: Clicking on the padlock icon to lock the layer will make it impossible to edit anything on this layer. This can be useful when you start working with multiple layers, especially layers with overlapping content.

Outline View: Clicking on this icon will display all of the layer's contents as an outline view, in which solid shapes are represented as outlined shapes with no solid fill. This can be very helpful when you are working with multiple layers with overlapping content.

TIP | Layer Properties

In addition to the visible ways to control the layers, there are other options available under the Layer Properties dialog box that aren't visible in the Timeline. These additional options are listed below:

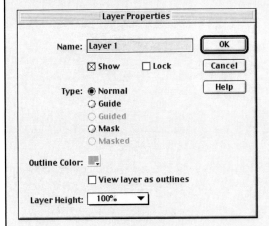

Guide: This option enables you to use the contents of a layer as a tracing image (guide), which helps you create artwork on other layers. Guide layers are the only layers that are not exported with the movie. You will work with a guide layer in Chapter 8, "*Motion Tweening.*"

Mask: Selecting this option will turn the layer into a Mask layer. You will learn more about this layer type in Chapter 9, "*Bitmaps.*"

Masked: Selecting this option will cause the layer to be masked by the Mask layer above it. Don't worry, you will learn how to work with this option as well in Chapter 9, "*Bitmaps.*"

Outline Color: This specifies the color that will be used if you select the *Outline View* option. By default, each layer will have a different color. This just gives you that extra bit of organizational control.

Layer Height: This option makes a layer's Timeline display "taller" when you increase the line height of a specific layer. You can choose 100% (default) 200% or 300%. This feature is especially useful for working with sounds on the main timeline. Allowing the height of the layer with the sound on it to be taller makes it easier to work with the waveforms and synchronize it with your animation. You will try this later in Chapter 14 "*Sound.*"

TIP | The Toolbox

Arrow (V)	Subselect (A)
Line (N)	Lasso (L)
Pen (P)	Text (T)
Oval (O)	Rectangle (R)
Pencil (Y)	Brush (B)
Ink Bottle (S)	Paint Bucket (K)
Dropper (I)	Eraser (E)
Hand (H)	Zoom (M, Z)
	Stroke Color
	Fill Color
Default, None, Swap	
	Tool Options

Tools / View / Colors / Options

As with most drawing programs, the Toolbox contains tools that are necessary when creating and editing artwork. This long vertical bar gives you access to just about every tool you will need to create and modify the objects in your Flash projects. Each of the main tools has an associated keyboard shortcut, which is listed in parenthesis next to the tool name above.

Other than moving the Toolbox around the desktop, there is only one option for the Toolbox. When you hover over the Toolbox icons, a small tool tip will appear with the name and keyboard shortcut for that option. You can disable this feature in the General Preferences, by clicking **Edit > Preferences > General**.

TIP: Docking on Windows vs. Macintosh

There is one minor difference between the Mac and Window operating systems when it comes to docking the Toolbox. On the Macintosh, you can click and reposition the Toolbox freely around the screen. In the Windows operating system, the Toolbox can only be docked along either side of the document window. A minor difference, but one that we thought you'd like to know about.

The Panels

With the latest release of their products, Macromedia has made its first significant movement towards a common user interface. Similarities can now be seen between all of its Web applications, such as Dreamweaver, Fireworks, Freehand, Flash, and UltraDev. In this section, we will address each of these panels and briefly discuss their purpose and options. You will get the chance to work with each of them through the exercises in this book.

You should know upfront that panels are accessed in one of three ways. First, you can select **Window >** **Panels >** then choose panel that you want. Second, you can use the associated keyboard shortcut. Third, you can use the Launcher to open and close the various panels. Which method you use is a matter of personal preference– we suggest that you find one consistent way to work; it makes working in Flash easier.

Most of the panels are set up in default groups, with one panel containing several tabs. Any individual tab can be dragged out of its group to create an individual floating panel. The six major panel groups are listed below:

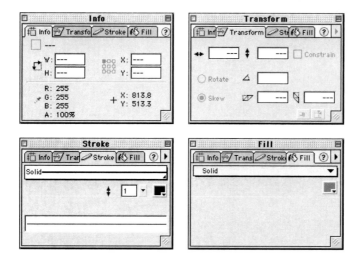

By default, the Info panel is grouped with three other panels, the **Info**, **Transform**, **Stroke**, and **Fill** panels. The chart below describes each of the panels.

Info panel	Contains size, position, and color information about the selected object
Transform panel	Allows you to numerically transform (rotate, scale, and skew) an object
Stroke panel	Allows you to identify and modify the Stroke settings of the selected object.
Fill panel	Allows you to identify and modify the Fill settings of the selected objects

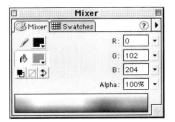 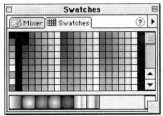

By default, the **Mixer** and **Swatches** panels are grouped together. See the chart below for a description of each of the panels.

Mixer panel	Allows you to select the colors that you will use in your Flash file. It lets you create new colors in one of three different modes—RGB (Red, Green, Blue), HSB (Hue, Saturation, Brightness), or HEX (hexadecimal).
Swatches panel	Displays the default 216 Web-safe colors and lets you select, add, or delete colors.

 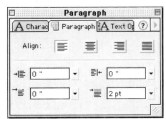 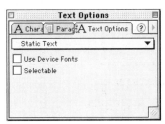

By default, the **Character** panel itself contains three panels, the **Character**, the **Paragraph**, and the **Text Options** panels. The chart below contains a description of each of the panels.

Character panel	Lets you control the various options for formatting text in your project, such as font, style, size, etc.
Paragraph panel	Gives you control over the paragraphs in your document. Allows you to change positioning of paragraph settings, such as alignment, indenting, and line height.
Text Options panel	Allows you to control the type of text that is added in your projects, such as static, dynamic, and input. You'll learn the distinction between these types of text options in Chapter 10, "*Type*."

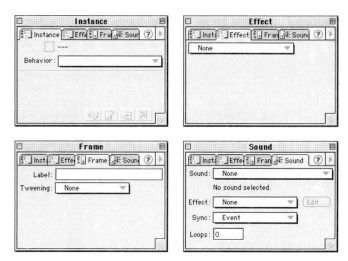

The **Instance** panel by default contains four panels, the **Instance**, **Effect**, **Frame**, and **Sound** panels. Refer to the chart below for a description of each of the panels.

Instance panel	Allows you to edit the behavior of instances, which are copies of symbols that are placed on the stage. You have your choice of three behaviors—a graphic, a button, or a movie clip. You can also name movie clips in the Instance panel.
Effect panel	Lets you apply a number of different effects to instances, such as adjusting its brightness, color, or transparency, which is called "alpha."
Frame panel	Lets you create frame labels, which are very useful for moving to different locations in the Timeline, and create motion or shape tween animations in the Timeline. You'll learn about labels in Chapter 12.
Sound panel	Allows you to adjust how many times you want each particular sound to play in your project, specify the Sync type, and specify any effects, such as fading.

The **Scene** panel is all alone. This panel lets you quickly add, duplicate, delete, or name/rename scenes, if you are using them. It's also a way that you can jump to different scenes in your document.

The **Generator** panel is only active if you have downloaded and installed the Generator Templates. Working with Generator and Generator Templates are outside the scope of this book.

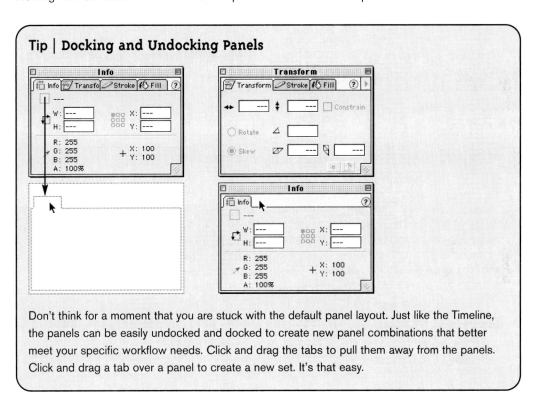

Tip | Docking and Undocking Panels

Don't think for a moment that you are stuck with the default panel layout. Just like the Timeline, the panels can be easily undocked and docked to create new panel combinations that better meet your specific workflow needs. Click and drag the tabs to pull them away from the panels. Click and drag a tab over a panel to create a new set. It's that easy.

Creating Panel Sets

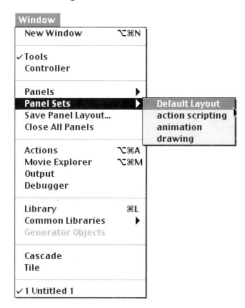

Flash gives you the flexibility to create new panel sets by pulling the tabs apart to separate them or dragging them on top of each other to create new sets. Now, you can save these custom configurations. This means that with the click of the mouse, you can completely modify the layout of your panels. While there isn't a formal exercise to follow here, the following steps will walk you through the process of saving a custom panel set.

Saving Panel Sets

Organize your panels in whatever arrangement you want. For example, you can create different panel sets for different tasks, such as drawing, animation, and working with ActionScripts. This will allow you to quickly organize your workspace for specific tasks.

1. Select **Window > Save Panel Layout**. This will open the **Save Panel Layout** dialog box prompting you to assign a name for this arrangement.

2. Enter any name you want and click **OK**. That's all there is to it.

Changing Panel Layouts

Changing from one panel layout to another is as easy as selecting a menu option. In fact, that's what you have to do to change between your different sets.

Choose **Window > Panel Sets >** and select the layout option you want to display. Your panels will be quickly arranged into that specific arrangement.

Note: Selecting Default Layout will reset the panels to their default positions. This is helpful if you want to quickly restore all of the panels to their default arrangements.

TIP | Deleting Panel Sets

So, what do you do if you create a panel set that you just aren't happy with? While there is no interface for deleting them, it is still a relatively simple process. All of the panel sets are stored in a folder on your hard drive. They are located in the **Flash 5 > Panel Sets** folder. If you want to remove one, just delete the appropriate file from this directory and it will be gone forever.

Custom Keyboard Shortcuts

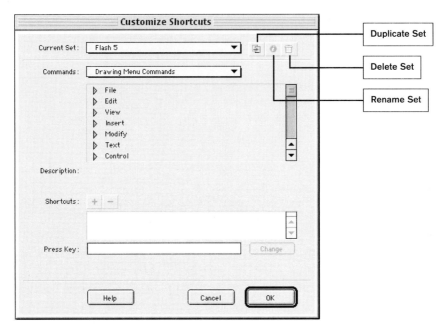

A new and welcome feature to Flash 5 is the ability to create, modify, and delete sets of custom keyboard shortcuts. Macromedia has even designed an entire interface to make this process easy to do. You can even use keyboard shortcuts in Flash that match other programs like Fireworks, Freehand, or Photoshop, or even earlier versions of Flash. While this is more of a power-user feature, we still think you should be aware of it. Besides, you will be a power user in no time.

The steps below outline the process of creating, modifying, and deleting custom keyboard shortcuts. This isn't an exercise you have to complete now; it's meant to serve as a reference for later use.

Creating a New Shortcut Set

1. Select **Edit > Keyboard Shortcuts** to open the Customize Shortcuts (Mac) or Keyboard Shortcuts (Windows) dialog box.

2. Click the **Duplicate Set** button to create a copy of the current set. This will ensure that you are working from a duplicate so you don't mess up the original set.

3. Enter a name for your custom set. You can name it anything you want, however, we suggest you stick to meaningful names that you can recall later. Click **OK**.

4. Click on the left of any of the options to twirl down and display the keyboard shortcuts for that menu. Select the option you want to change.

5. Click the **+** button to add a shortcut (press the—button to delete the selected shortcut.) You can create multiple keyboard shortcuts for one option. (However, that may not be such a good idea.)

6. Press the keyboard shortcut you want to assign to this option. Click the **Change** button to confirm your selection and assign it to the menu item. **Note:** If the key combination you selected is already in use, you will get an error message at the bottom of the dialog box

Well, that's enough of the interface for now. The following chapters are full of hands-on exercises where you will work with these interface elements. So, go ahead and turn the page to get started.

3.

Using the Color Tools

| Using the Mixer | Adding Colors to Palettes |
| Importing Palettes |
| Creating Gradients | Editing Gradients |

chap_3

Flash 5
H•O•T CD-ROM

In this chapter you will learn how to work with the various color tools in Flash, including how to select or customize colors and gradients and how to import and export color palettes. Next, in Chapter 4, "*Using the Drawing Tools*," you will use the color skills you learned in this chapter to edit and create artwork. If you already know how to use basic color tools from your experience in other graphics programs, you can skip ahead to the next chapter. You can always return to these exercises later–just remember that Flash saves a separate palette for each of your files. As a result, any custom palettes that you create are not available to other files in Flash unless you export the custom palette first. You'll learn how to do that and more in this chapter.

What is Web-Safe Color Anyway?

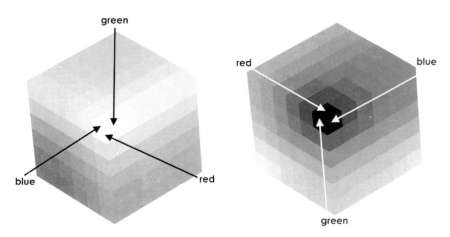

If you've been around the Web for a while, you may have heard the term "Web-safe color." Perhaps you've heard other terms, too, such as browser safe, Web palette, 216 palette, the 6 x 6 x 6 cube, Netscape cube, Explorer colors, Web colors, etc. These all refer to the same 216 colors whose numerical definitions form a mathematical cube.

Browser software defaults to recognizing these specific 216 colors when it encounters an older system that's limited to 8-bit color (256 colors on a Mac or 216 colors on a PC). Most Web developers use these 216 colors so that their presentations will look good on limited color systems. Otherwise, their colors might shift or dither on 8-bit systems.

Its important to point out that more and more people are using computers that display 64,000 colors or more, which makes using the Web-safe palette less of a requirement. In fact, it's hard to get a video card that will display only 256 colors. Whether you decide to use the Web-safe palette or not should really depend on your target audience and the design requirements of your site.

What Is Hexadecimal Color?

When you specify color in HTML, you cannot use decimal values, or the base 10 math that we all grew up learning. HTML requires that you convert the decimal values to hexadecimal values, or base 16. Therefore, the Web-safe RGB decimal values of 0, 51, 102, 153, 204, or 255 need to be converted for use on the Web. This handy chart shows how this conversion works.

RGB Color Translations		
Decimal Value	**Percentage Value**	**Hexadecimal Value**
0	0%	00
51	20%	33
102	40%	66
153	60%	99
204	80%	CC
255	100%	FF

It's easy to spot Web-safe hexadecimal values because they always consist of any three of the pairs 00, 33, 66, 99, CC, or FF in the hexadecimal value range. For example, FF6633 (which is made up of the three pairs FF, 66, and 33) would be a Web-safe color, whereas AB8EFD would not be Web safe.

Flash lets you create colors using RGB and hexadecimal values. Since many Web developers already work with hexadecimal values, it's nice to be able to use them in Flash. Its important to mention that creating hexadecimal colors in Flash is an option, not a requirement.

I. _____Using the Mixer

The **Mixer** is at the core of color creation in Flash. This essential panel helps you create colors and add them to the palette, which you can save for later use. What's so important about that, you ask? Well, it means that you aren't stuck using only the 216 Web-safe colors. You can create any color, using any RGB or HEX combination. In addition, you can adjust the color's level of transparency, called the "alpha setting," to create some pretty cool effects.

In this exercise, you will learn how to create colors and adjust their transparency using the Mixer panel. The Mixer has three color modes: RGB (**R**ed, **G**reen, **B**lue), HSB (**H**ue, **S**aturation, **B**rightness), and HEX (hexadecimal.) You can create custom colors using any of these three modes. For this exercise, we'll be working in the RGB mode, which is the most common mode that you'll work in for Web publishing. To understand why you need to know how to work with the Mixer, you will be changing the fill color of some simple shapes—something you will do many times as you work with Flash.

1. Copy the **chap_03** folder from the **exercise_files** folder on the **H•O•T CD-ROM** to your desktop. This folder contains the files you will need to complete this chapter.

2. Once you have launched Flash, choose **File > Open** and locate the **mixer.fla** file inside the **chap_03** folder. Click **Open**. This file contains three simple shapes: a red square, a blue triangle, and a green circle. You will learn how to create your own shapes in the next chapter.

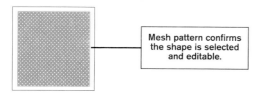

Mesh pattern confirms the shape is selected and editable.

3. Using the **Arrow tool**, click the **red square** to select it. In Flash, when a shape is selected, a mesh appears over it.

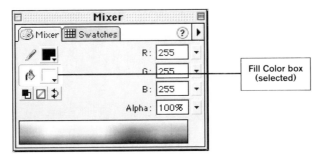

Fill Color box (selected)

4. Make sure the **Mixer** panel is visible and that you have the **Fill Color** box selected. If it's not visible, choose **Window > Panels > Mixer** to make it appear. This is what the Mixer panel looks like in RGB mode.

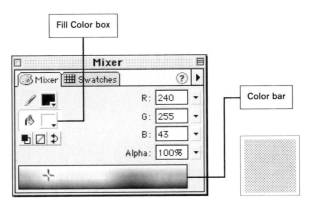

Fill Color box

Color bar

5. Click and drag your mouse in the **Color bar** area of the Mixer. A crosshair appears and the **Fill Color** box changes as you move the crosshair over the Color bar. Select a shade of yellow. When you release the mouse button, the color will be selected and the square will change to that shade of yellow.

It's easy to change the color of an object in Flash at any time using this technique. Isn't it nice to know that you're never locked into an inflexible color choice?

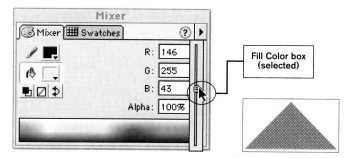

Fill Color box
(selected)

6. Using the **Arrow** tool, click on the blue triangle to select it. In the **Mixer** panel click the **small black arrow** next to the **R:** (Red) field on the right. Drag the slider up until you reach **146**. This changes the triangle to a shade of purple.

You can drag the slider up and down to define the numeric setting for each of the Red, Green, and Blue color values. The total range for each slider is from 0 to 255.

7. Go ahead and experiment with the **G:** (Green) and **B:** (Blue) sliders to see how they work together to create different colors. As you can see, modifying the different RGB sliders is another way you can select colors in Flash.

TIP | Entering RGB Values Manually

You can also type specific RGB values in the Mixer panel. Click in the appropriate field and type the value (from 0 to 255) that you want. This is helpful when you want to create a specific color and you already know the RGB values.

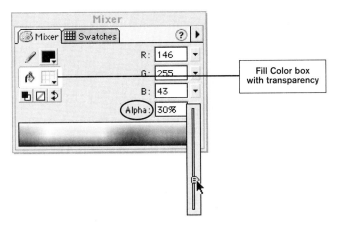

Fill Color box
with transparency

8. Using the **Arrow** tool, click the green circle to select it. Then, in the **Mixer** panel, click the arrow next to the **Alpha** option and drag down until you reach **30%**. Notice the small grid that appears in the **Fill Color** box. This lets you know that the color has been adjusted to be semi-transparent.

In Flash, the term "alpha" relates to the transparency of an object. The Alpha slider adjusts the transparency of the color and has a range from 0% to 100%.

The circle selected without the transparency applied.

The circle deselected with the transparency applied.

9. Click anywhere outside the circle to deselect it. This updates the circle with the new transparency setting. **Note:** You won't be able to see the new setting, or any other settings, until you deselect the shape.

10. Click the **triangle** to select it. Remember that a mesh appears over the shape once it has been selected.

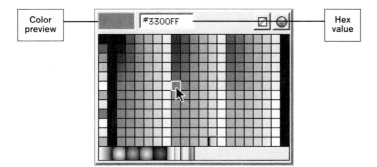

11. Click the **Fill Color** box to display the default color palette for Flash, and move your pointer over the color grid. As you move your mouse over the palette, you see a preview of each color in the upper left corner. The hexadecimal value for that color also appears to the right of the preview area.

TIP | Selecting Specific Hexadecimal Values

You can search for a specific color by entering its six-digit hexadecimal value in the hexadecimal value area at the top of the palette. This enables you to specify colors by their specific numeric value instead of by their appearance.

---

12. Click on any color in the palette. This sets the fill color, updates the selected triangle, and causes the color palette to close. This technique is the easiest way to select color, but it does limit you to only Web-safe colors. **Note:** If you forget to select the object first, select the **Paint Bucket** tool; then you can apply the fill color by clicking the Paint Bucket icon over the object.

---

13. Save and close the file—you won't be working with it anymore.

Now that you have some experience working with the Mixer panel, continue on to the next exercise, where you will use the Mixer to add custom colors to the palette.

2. _____Adding Colors to Palettes

If you completed the previous exercise, you know what the default color palette looks like in Flash. What if you want to add your own colors to create a custom palette? That's exactly what you will learn in this exercise.

You'll use the **Swatches** panel, which works hand in hand with the Mixer. By default, this panel contains a custom arrangement of 216 Web-safe colors organized in six blocks of similar hues, with darker colors appearing along the left side and brighter colors appearing along the right side. You can add and remove colors, save the palette, and reset it to its default state. You can even import Fireworks and Photoshop palettes into Flash and sort them by color, as you'll do in the next exercise. All of these options make working with palettes in Flash a flexible experience.

1. Choose **File > New** to create a new file. Choose **File > Save As** and save this file as **palette.fla** inside the **chap_03** folder. Click **Save**. You must have a file open, even if it's a blank one, to add colors to the **Swatches** panel.

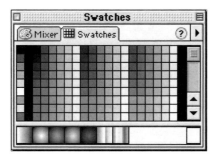

2. Make sure the **Swatches** panel is visible. If it's not visible, choose **Window > Panels > Swatches**, and then scroll to the bottom of the panel to view the currently available color swatches.

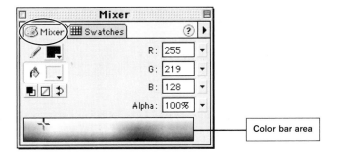

Color bar area

3. Click the **Mixer** tab to return to the **Mixer** panel. Click and drag your pointer in the **Color bar** area to select a color you like. A small crosshair appears as you drag. When you find a color you like, release the mouse. You are going to add this color to the default palette.

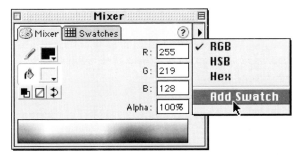

4. Make sure the **Alpha** setting is set to **100%**. Click the arrow in the upper right corner of the **Mixer** panel to access the pop-up menu, and choose **Add Swatch**. This adds the selected color to the default palette, making it much easier to select it again later.

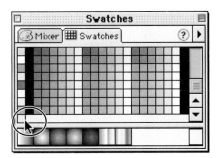

5. Click the **Swatches** tab to return to the **Swatches** panel. Scroll to the bottom of this panel. You should see the new color you've just added at the bottom.

6. Choose **File > Save** to save the change you made to the palette. **Note:** Flash saves the palette information for each file in the source (.fla) file. However, this palette will be available only to this file—and not to your other Flash projects—unless you export it.

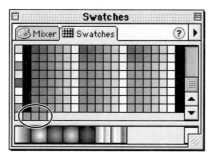

7. Add three more custom colors to the **Swatches** panel as described in Steps 3 and 4. Pick any colors you like.

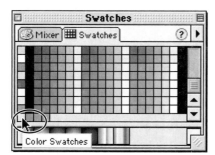

8. Using the **Arrow** tool, click on the very last color at the bottom left of the **Swatches** panel to select it.

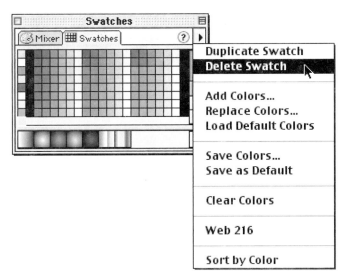

9. From the **Swatches** pop-up menu, choose **Delete Swatch**. This removes the selected color permanently from the color palette for this file.

WARNING | Think Before You Delete

Once you delete a swatch, it is gone forever. You cannot use the Undo command to bring it back. So be certain that you want to remove the color before doing so. Of course, you can always add the color again, but what a headache (and who needs another headache?).

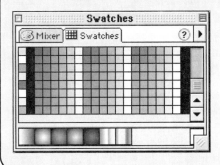

TIP | Resetting the Swatches Panel

Don't panic if you add or remove a color from the palette by accident. You can always get back to where you started by resetting it to the default panel. From the **Swatches** pop-up menu, choose **Load Default Colors**. This replaces the current palette with the default Web-safe 216-color palette. So go ahead and make changes to the palette. You can't break anything. But you should know that you will permanently lose any new colors you have added to the Swatches panel when you choose Load Default Colors.

10. Choose **File > Save** to save the changes you made. Saving the file ensures that the changes you made to the palette are saved properly. You can close this file.

NOTE | Custom Color Palettes Stay with the File

In Flash, color palettes are always saved with individual documents, so if you modify the color palette in the course of working with a Flash file, that custom palette will be saved when you save the file, and the document's custom palette will load whenever you reopen that file.

As long as you leave Flash's default color palette untouched on your hard drive, you can reload it at any time, and when you create a new Flash document, it is the default palette that will load.

3. _____Importing Palettes

In addition to creating and editing your own palettes in Flash, you can import palettes. There are three ways to do this. You can import a Flash Color Set (a palette that has been exported from Flash, having the extension .clr). The .clr file contains all of the RGB color and gradients information for the project file. This format is the only one that holds information about the gradients in your Flash projects. You can also import colors from a Color Table (.act file), a format also used by Fireworks and Photoshop. You can even import all of the colors in a .gif file.

This exercise shows you how to replace the color palette in a Flash file by importing a different color palette. You'll import the three types of files and learn a little bit about each of them.

1. Choose **File > New** to create a new project. Choose **File > Save** and save this file as **import.fla** inside the **chap_03** folder. This file contains the default palette of colors and gradients.

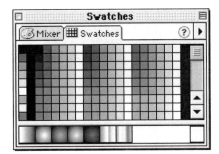

This is what the default palette looks like.

2. Make sure the **Swatches** panel is visible. If it's not, choose **Window > Panels > Swatches** to make it visible.

3. From the **Swatches** pop-up menu, choose **Replace Colors**. This opens a Browse dialog box. **Note:** Choosing **Replace Colors** removes all of the colors and replaces them with the colors you import.

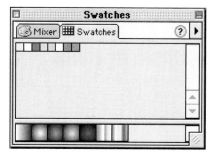

This is what the palette looks like after the colors from the .gif file have been imported.

4. Open the **colors.gif** file located inside the **chap_03** folder. This imports just the colors contained in that .gif file, but it doesn't open the .gif file itself. This GIF image contains eight colors. **Tip:** This is a useful technique if you have graphics—such as logos—that use specific colors and you want to pick up the same color scheme in your Flash movie.

5. From the **Swatches** pop-up menu, choose **Replace Colors**. This opens the Browse dialog box again.

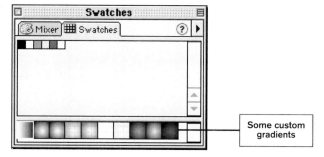

Some custom gradients

6. Open the **gradients.clr** file located inside the **chap_03** folder. This imports all of the colors and gradients in this particular Flash Color Set. Only Flash .clr files allow you to import new gradients. By exporting the .clr file from one project and importing it into another, you can easily share gradients between your Flash project files.

You can create/export a Flash .clr file by choosing the Save Colors option from the Swatches pop-up menu.

7. From the **Swatches** pop-up menu, choose **Clear Colors**. This removes all of the colors except for black and white and one gradient. If you don't do this now, the custom gradients will not be replaced in the next steps.

8. From the **Swatches** pop-up menu, choose **Replace Colors**. This opens a Browse dialog box.

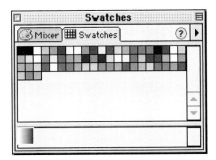

This is what the colors.act palette looks like when it's imported into Flash.

9. Select the **colors.act** file, located inside the **chap_03** folder. Click **Open**. This is a Color Table file that could have been created from either Fireworks or Photoshop. Unlike .clr files, the .act files do not contain any gradient information. **Tip:** Importing an .act file can be useful if you are working with a palette of colors in Fireworks or Photoshop that you want to use in Flash.

TIP | Sorting Your Palettes

From the **Swatches** pop-up menu, choose **Sort by Color**. This sorts the colors from the imported .act file by color. **Note:** You can sort any palette by color to make it easier to see your options.

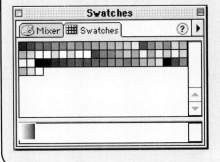

---

10. Choose **File > Save** to save the changes you made to this file. Close the file. You won't be working with it anymore.

4. _____Creating Gradients

Flash comes complete with a powerful gradient editor. Gradients can help you create lots of cool and interesting effects, such as glows, photorealistic spheres, solar flares, and glowing buttons. Flash lets you create two types of gradient fills: linear and radial. In this exercise, you will learn how to create, apply, and change the color of a linear and radial gradient with some shapes in Flash.

1. Open the **newgradient.fla** file in the **chap_03** folder. This file contains a black circle and square. You will be applying gradients to both of these shapes in this exercise.

2. Make sure the **Fill** panel is visible. If it's not, choose **Window > Panels > Fill**.

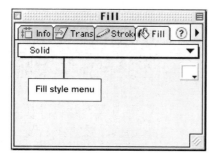 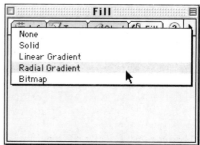

3. Using the **Arrow** tool, click the **black circle** to select it. In the **Fill** panel, click the small down arrow to see the **Fill Style** pop-up menu. Choose **Radial Gradient**. This fills the selected circle with a gradient, using black and white. **Tip:** Radial gradients work well on shapes with rounded edges.

TIP | Hiding the Selection Mesh

A gradient with the selection mesh.

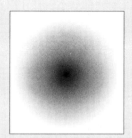
A gradient without the selection mesh.

When shapes are selected, they have a mesh pattern over them. This can make your artwork look like something it really isn't. To hide the selection mesh temporarily, press **Cmd+H** (Mac) or **Ctrl+H** (Windows). **Note:** Remember that the shape is still selected, even though you can't see the mesh, and any changes you make will be applied to it. To show the selection mesh again, press the same keyboard shortcut again. This keyboard shortcut can be very useful when you are creating or modifying shapes in Flash.

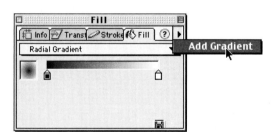
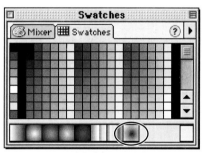

4. From the **Fill** pop-up menu, choose **Add Gradient**. This saves the selected gradient in the **Swatches** panel.

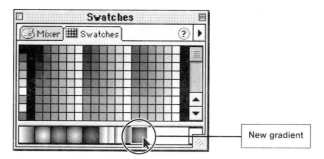

New gradient

5. In the **Swatches** panel, click the new gradient that you added, which is located at the bottom of the panel.

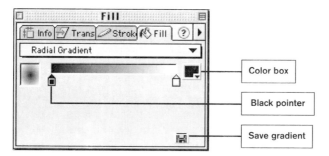

Color box

Black pointer

Save gradient

6. Click the **black pointer** in the **Fill** panel. This selects the black color point of the gradient and causes a Color box to appear on the right side of the panel. This Color box is used to define the fill color for the selected pointer.

7. Click the **Color box** and select a shade of **red** from the palette. This changes the appearance of the radial gradient—instead of ranging from black to white, it will range from to red to white.

8. Next you will make a linear gradient. Using the **Arrow** tool, select the **black square**. **Tip:** Linear gradients work well on shapes that have hard edges, like rectangles and squares.

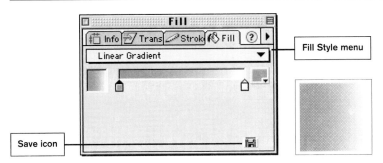

Fill Style menu

Save icon

9. Choose **Linear Gradient** from the **Fill Style** menu. This creates a linear gradient using the same color you used for the previous gradient.

10. In the **Fill** panel, click the **Save** icon in the lower right corner. This saves the gradient at the bottom of the **Swatches** panel.

11. Choose **File > Save** to save the changes you made to this file. Leave this file open; you'll be using it in the next exercise.

TIP | Transparent Gradients!

In addition to adjusting the color of the color points, you can also adjust the Alpha setting for each color in the gradient with the Alpha slider in the **Mixer** panel. Lowering the Alpha setting makes the color more transparent. This can help you make some really interesting effects, such as glows.

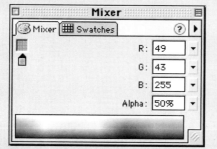

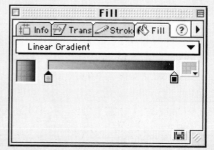

The Mixer panel gives you a nice preview of the Alpha setting being applied to the color.

The Fill panel gives you a preview of the Alpha setting and also shows how it affects the gradient transition.

5. _____Editing Gradients

In the previous exercise, you learned how to create some basic gradients. Now you'll learn how to edit the transition of a gradient from dark to light by adjusting the color points, as well as how to add and remove colors from it.

1. You should still have the **newgradient.fla** file open from the previous exercise. If you don't, open that file now.

2. Using the **Arrow** tool, click the circle shape to select it. **Tip:** Selecting the circle before you edit the gradient will allow you to see the changes you've applied to the gradient immediately. This real-time feedback can be very helpful.

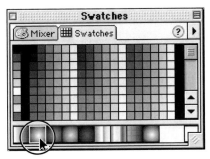

3. In the **Swatches** panel, select the second gradient from the left. This changes the colors in the radial gradient back to black and white.

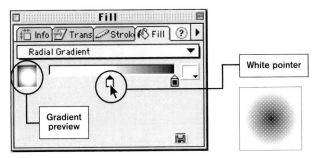

White pointer

Gradient preview

4. In the **Fill** panel, click the **white pointer** and drag it to the middle of the **Gradient Definition bar**. When you release the mouse button, notice that that the circle and gradient preview are updated. The pointers adjust the distance between the colors of the gradient and affect how the colors transition from one to another.

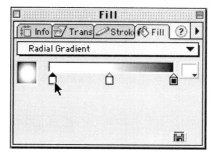

Clicking at the bottom of the Gradient Definition bar adds a new pointer.

5. Click under the far left of the **Gradient Definition bar** to insert a new pointer. This is how you add additional color points to the gradient. New color points default to the currently selected fill color, which in this case was white.

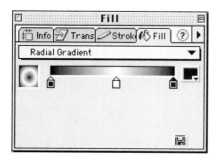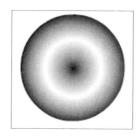

6. Click the **Color box** to the right of the bar, and select the color **black**. This changes the color of the pointer you just added. It also changes the appearance of the circle and gradient in the gradient preview area. Congratulations: you've just created your first black-and-white doughnut in Flash. ;-)

7. Click and drag the various pointers around to see what types of effects you can create. Don't worry; you can't break anything here. Just have some fun.

8. Click the **pointer** on the right, and drag it down and away from the **Gradient Definition bar**. Release the mouse button. This removes the pointer from the gradient. It's that easy.

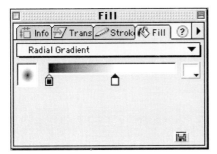

This is what the gradient looks like after the right black pointer has been removed.

9. Choose **File > Save** to save any changes you made to this file. You can close it because you are done with this chapter. Next, you'll learn about making artwork in Flash. Learning to work with color and drawing tools are a precursor to learning animation and interactivity in Flash, so you're well on your way!

4.

Using the Drawing Tools

| Drawing with the Pencil | Modifying Lines |
| Drawing with the Pen | Modifying Paths |
| Using the Oval and Rectangle |
| Using the Brush | Modifying Fills |
| Multiple Objects | Grouping Objects |

chap_4

Flash 5
H·O·T CD-ROM

When most people think of Flash, they think of one thing: Animation. What many people don't know is that Flash comes complete with some really great drawing tools that can help you create the artwork for making cool and interactive animations.

With the introduction of the Pen tool, Flash now has the same precision drawing capabilities as other vector drawing applications such as Macromedia Freehand. It's possible to bring artwork into Flash from Freehand or Illustrator, which will be covered in chapter 16 "*Integration*." However, you will find it is more convenient to draw in Flash for some types of artwork. This chapter exposes you to the unique characteristics and idiosyncrasies of Flash's drawing tools.

The first part of this chapter will introduce you to vector paths as you learn to draw with the Pencil and Pen tools. You'll learn the differences between a line and a fill by working with the Oval and Rectangle tools. Using the Brush, you will learn to draw shapes using only fills. Lastly, you will see first hand some of the unique behaviors of working with multiple objects in Flash.

Drawing Tools Explained

The drawing tools in Flash are very powerful, but they can be somewhat complex as you try to understand their individual behaviors. So, before you jump into this chapter with both feet, take a moment to review the following chart. Don't try to memorize everything here, just read through the different points so when you encounter this material later, you will have some idea of how each tool behaves.

Icon	Name	What Does It Do?
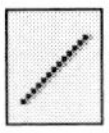	Line	The *Line* tool creates straight lines. Holding down the Shift key with this tool will constrain the lines to 45-degree angles. The lines drawn with the Line tool can be modified with the Ink Bottle and/or Stroke panel.
	Pen	The *Pen* tool creates straight or curved lines. The Pen tool is the only Flash drawing tool capable of creating bezier curves.
	Pencil	The *Pencil* tool creates lines in one of three different modes, Straighten, Smooth, and Ink.
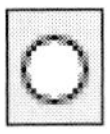	Oval	The *Oval* tool creates circles and ovals composed of fills and strokes, just fills, or just strokes.
	Rectangle	The *Rectangle* tool creates rectangles and squares composed of fills and strokes, just fills, or just strokes.
	Brush	The *Brush* tool creates shapes with fills only. You can adjust the size and style of the brush by adjusting the tool options.
	Ink Bottle	Use the *Ink Bottle* tool to change the color or width of a line, or add a stroke to a shape. The Ink Bottle will never change the fill of a shape.
	Paint Bucket	Use the *Paint Bucket* tool to add a fill inside a shape or change the color of a fill. The Paint Bucket will never change the stroke of a shape.
	Eraser	The *Eraser* tool can be used to remove any unwanted image areas on the stage.

Lines, Fills, and Strokes Explained

In addition to learning how each of the drawing tools behave, you also need to know the difference between lines, fills, and strokes. Understandably, this can be confusing because there is reference to both lines and strokes in the interface. The chart below gives an example and brief explanation of each.

Lines

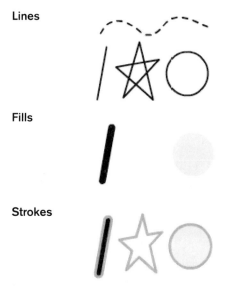

Lines can be created with the Pencil and Pen tools. Lines are independent of any fills, and they are modified using the Ink Bottle and the Stroke panel. The objects created with lines are referred to as shapes.

Fills

Fills are created using the Brush and Paint Bucket tools. Fills can be created with or without strokes around them. They are modified using the Bucket and the Fill panel. The objects created with fills are referred to as shapes.

Strokes

Strokes are always attached to fills; otherwise, they are referred to as lines. Strokes are added to shapes with the Ink Bottle and modified using the Ink Bottle and Fill panel.

About the Pencil

In Flash, the Pencil tool works much the same as the pencil tools in other graphics programs, such as Fireworks. There are, however, some special drawing modes that can help you control the line's appearance. For example, drawing a perfect circle might be really difficult for some of you (especially after that morning coffee!), but with the Straighten mode, it's much easier to create perfect geometric circles. In this chapter, you will get the chance to work with the Pencil tool and each of its modes.

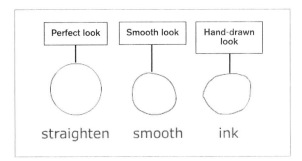

This example shows the result of a circle drawn with the Pencil tool, using each of the three modes.

Below is a brief summary of the different modes and where they might be useful.

Straighten: This name is a little misleading—it will not necessarily straighten lines as you might expect, though it will help you draw a straight line. More significantly, it will also try to recognize the shape you are trying to create and snap your artwork to that shape. For example, if you draw a circle that isn't quite perfect, Flash will snap it to a perfect circle. As you can imagine, this mode is very useful for creating perfect geometric shapes, which no one but a machine is good at producing!

Smooth: This mode will help you draw lines that are smooth. This can be useful when you are trying to draw shapes that need to have smooth curves, but you don't want them to snap to a shape that you don't want. This can be really helpful when you are creating motion guides, which you'll learn about later in Chapter 8 "*Motion Tweening.*"

Ink: This mode is helpful for creating graphics with a real hand-drawn look. You will notice a minor shift in your graphics, but it's not as significant as the Straighten and Smooth modes.

I. _____Drawing With the Pencil

The Pencil tool is one of the easiest drawing tools to use, so let's start with that. This tool behaves much as you would expect a pencil to behave—it will draw a line whenever you click and drag the mouse. By selecting one of the three modes (Straighten, Smooth, or Ink) you can control how the lines are created. In this exercise, you will draw three circles using each of the three modifiers, so you can better understand how each one behaves.

1. Copy the **chap_04** folder from the **Flash 5 HOT CD-ROM** to your hard drive. You must copy the files to your hard drive if you want to save changes to them.

2. Choose **File > Open** and browse to the **pencil.fla** file located inside the **chap_04** folder. Click **Open**. This is just a blank file with stage dimensions set to 400 x 200 pixels. This should be enough space for you to draw some shapes.

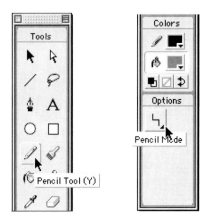

The Pencil Tool   The Pencil Modes are at the bottom of the Toolbox.

3. Select the **Pencil tool** from the Toolbox. If you leave your mouse over the tool long enough, a small tool tip, or name, will appear with the keyboard shortcut for that tool. By default, the Pencil tool will be in **Straighten Mode**.

The circle as you draw
with the Pencil tool.

The circle when you
release the mouse button.

4. On the stage, click and drag with the **Pencil** to create a circle. Release the mouse button when you are finished. Notice that the shape snaps to a perfect circle when you release the mouse button. This is the effect of the Straighten mode as it tries to guess what shape you are trying to create.

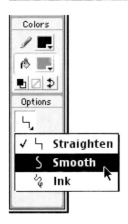

5. In the Toolbox, click the **Pencil Mode** drop-down menu and select **Smooth**. This will change the mode of the Pencil tool.

*The circle as you draw
with the Smooth Mode.*

*The circle when you
release the mouse button.*

6. Using the **Pencil** tool, draw another circle next to the one you just created. When you release the mouse button, notice that while there is a change, it is less significant than when you used the Straighten Mode.

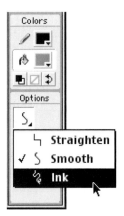

7. Click the **Pencil Mode** drop-down menu and select **Ink**. This will change the mode of the Pencil tool to Ink.

The circle as you draw
using the Ink mode.

The circle when you
release the mouse button.

8. Using the **Pencil** tool, draw a third circle next to the one you just created. When you release the mouse button, notice that there is very little change to the circle you created.

9. OK, enough circles already. Go ahead and try drawing other simple shapes such as squares, triangles, polygons, etc., with each of the different Pencil modes. This will give you an even better idea of how each of them works and how they can help you create artwork in Flash.

*Tip: If you want to clear the stage area for more experimenting, press **Cmd + A** (Mac) or **Ctrl + A** (Windows) to select everything on the stage. Press **Delete** to delete the contents of the stage.*

10. When you are done playing with the Pencil tool, choose **File > Save** and click **Save** to save the changes you made to this file. You can close this file; you won't need it to complete the next exercise.

2. _____Modifying Lines

Now that you know how to use the Pencil tool in Flash, you need to know how to make changes to the lines you create. In this exercise, you will learn how to use the new **Stroke** panel in Flash 5 as well as the **Ink Bottle** to modify the appearance of lines. Both of these tools let you change an object either by adding a line or by modifying the existing line. In addition, you will learn some of the nuances when selecting lines and the reason why you would use the Ink Bottle versus the Stroke panel.

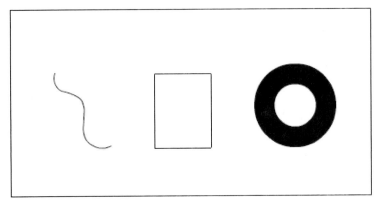

1. Open the **strokes.fla** file located inside the **chap_04** folder. This file contains some shapes created with lines and fills. You will use these shapes to learn to modify lines and add strokes to shapes.

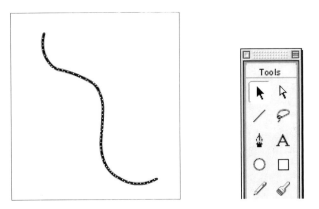

2. Select the **Arrow** tool from the Toolbox, and then click on the squiggle drawing to select it. The line gets a bit thicker and a dotted pattern will appear over it, indicating that the line is selected.

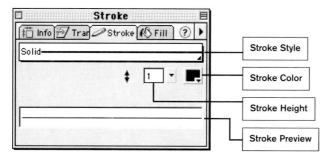

3. Make sure the **Stroke** panel is visible. If it's not, choose **Window > Panels > Stroke** to make it visible. From the **Stroke Style** drop-down menu, select the fourth style from the top, the dotted line style, to change the style of the line from a solid line to a dotted line. Deselect the line by clicking on a blank area of the stage to clearly see the changes.

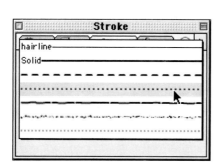
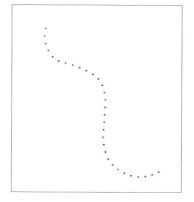

The Stroke panel is new to Flash 5 and is an easy way to modify existing lines. When you have a line selected, the Stroke panel displays the current settings for that line. This is help-ful when you need to know what the line settings are for a particular object. The default stroke settings are for a 1-point, solid, black line.

TIP | Hiding Selections

When lines are selected, it can be very difficult to see the changes you've made. You can press **Cmd + H** (Mac) or **Ctrl + H** (Windows) to temporarily hide the selection mesh so you can see the changes better. Press the keyboard shortcut again to see the selection mesh.

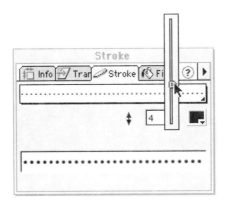
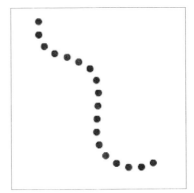
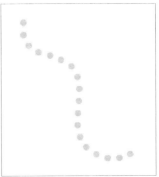
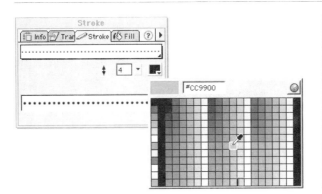

4. From the **Stroke Height** slider, click and drag up until you reach a setting of **4**. This will increase the thickness of the line. The total range of choices is from **0.25** to **10**.

5. From the **Stroke** color box, click and select another color. As you can probably guess, this will change the color of the line.

TIP | Creating Custom Line Styles

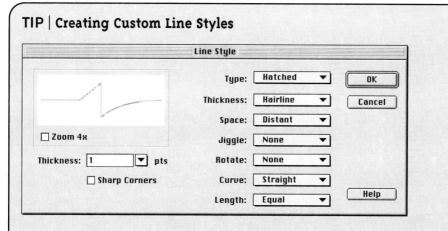

You might be wondering at this point if you can create your own custom line styles. Yes, you can. Click the triangle in the upper-right corner of the **Stroke** panel, and select **Custom** from the pop-up menu (it's the only option.) This will open the **Line Style** window where you can create your own line style using a number of different options. The changes you make to the line style are temporary and the line style will return to its default settings once you quit the program.

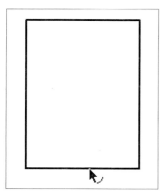

6. Using the **Arrow** tool, move the cursor over the bottom line of the square. Notice that a small, curved icon appears next to the Arrow tool. This is an indication that you are over a line, not a fill.

TIP | Selecting lines and rules in Flash

Unlike other drawing programs, lines with hard angles are broken into separate line objects in Flash. For example, clicking on the bottom line of the square selected only the bottom portion. That's because the square has four hard angles, which have created four separate lines for this object. However, double-clicking on the one of the lines will select the entire square.

7. Deselect the bottom line of the square by clicking on a blank area of the stage. Then, using the Arrow tool, click on the right line segment. Notice that a gray selection mesh appears over that line segment only.

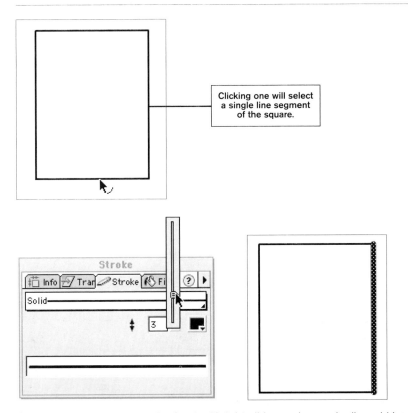

Clicking one will select a single line segment of the square.

8. In the **Stroke** panel, use the **Stroke Height** slider to change the line width to **3**. Notice that only the one selected line segment is changed. In order for a line to be modified, it must be selected before you change the settings in the **Stroke** panel, and in this case, you had only one of the four lines of this square selected.

9. With the line still selected, change the line width back to **1**.

Tip: You can simply enter a line width value in the little text box to the left of the slider when you know the value you want to use.

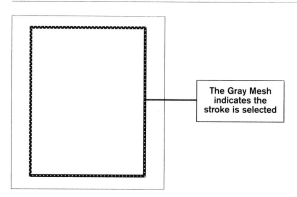

The Gray Mesh indicates the stroke is selected

10. With the one line segment still selected, **Shift + Click** on the three unselected lines. The entire outline of the square should now be selected. Tip: Double-clicking on a line is the quickest way to select the entire outline of an object.

11. From the **Stroke** panel, change the style, width, and color of the selected lines. You can choose any option you like—we just want you to become more comfortable with selecting line styles and preferences from the **Stroke** panel.

Well, now you know how to modify an existing line using the Stroke panel, but what do you do when you have an object that doesn't have a line? You add one using the Ink Bottle tool. That's what you will learn how to do in the following steps.

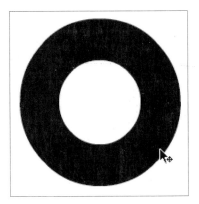

12. Using the **Arrow** tool, click to select the large donut shape. Notice that this shape does not have a stroke applied to it, just a fill. You will add a stroke using the Ink Bottle tool.

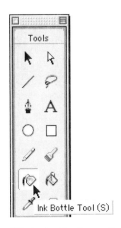

13. In the Toolbox, click to select the **Ink Bottle** tool. The Ink Bottle lets you either add a line around a fill object that has no line or make changes to the color, width, and texture of existing lines.

The Ink Bottle is the tool to use if you want to add a line (also called a stroke) to artwork that contains only a solid fill. This is the only program we know that uses an Ink Bottle icon or term for creating a stroke, so note where it is in the Toolbox and try to remember for future reference. We'll be sure to remind you, too.

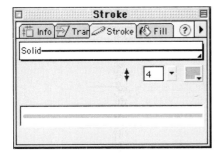

14. In the **Stroke** panel, set the style to **Solid**, the Color to a **light gray**, and the height to **4.**
Your panel should look like the one shown above.

15. Using the **Ink Bottle**, click on the outer edge of the donut shape. This will add a line to
the outside of the shape. Notice that it didn't add a line to the interior of the donut shape.
Flash treats these separated areas as different line objects.

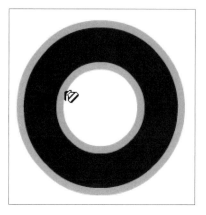

16. Using the Ink Bottle, click on the interior portion of the donut shape. This will add a line to that section.

TIP | The Ink Bottle

The Ink Bottle serves three very important purposes. First, it lets you add a stroke to an object. Second, by shift-clicking on multiple objects, you can use it to add or modify the same line settings to several objects without having to select each line first. This can save you a lot of time when you have several lines to add or modify. Additionally, by selecting the Ink Bottle and observing the Stroke panel, you can preview the stroke settings before they are applied to a line.

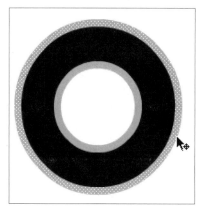

17. Using the Arrow tool, click to select the outer line of the donut shape. The gray selection mesh will appear to confirm you have selected that line.

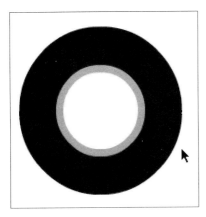

18. Press the **Delete** key. This will remove the selected line. You can use the Ink Bottle to replace the line you just deleted. So, now you know how to add lines to objects and remove lines from objects in Flash.

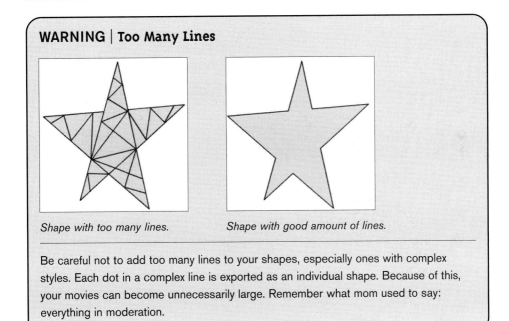

WARNING | Too Many Lines

Shape with too many lines.   *Shape with good amount of lines.*

Be careful not to add too many lines to your shapes, especially ones with complex styles. Each dot in a complex line is exported as an individual shape. Because of this, your movies can become unnecessarily large. Remember what mom used to say: everything in moderation.

19. Choose **File > Save** and click **Save** to save the changes you made to this file. You can close this file; you won't be using it any more.

3.————————**Drawing with the Pen**

The Pen is a drawing tool that's new to Flash 5. It's no longer necessary to use other vector drawing programs, such as Macromedia Freehand, to create complex vector graphics in Flash. However, the Pen tool is still a pen tool and will require a good amount of practice before you become really comfortable with it. In this exercise, we will show you how to use it in Flash by having you draw a few basic geometric shapes. When you are finished with this exercise, you should be a bit more comfortable working with the Pen tool not only in Flash, but in other programs as well. So, lets get started.

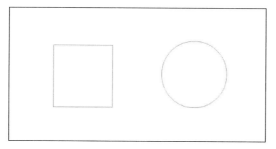

1. Open the **pen.fla** file located inside the **chap_04** folder. This file contains an outline of two separate geometric shapes. **Note:** If you just completed the previous exercise, you might want to set the stroke settings back to their default values (black, solid, 1 pt.)

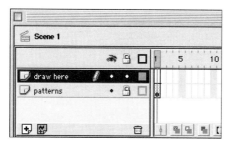

This document has two layers: one for the shape outlines, titled "patterns," and another titled "draw here," which is where you will draw these shapes using the Pen tool. The "patterns" layer is locked so you can't do any damage to the outlines. But have fun drawing on the "draw here" layer.

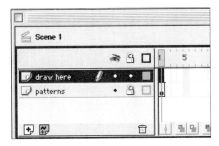

2. Make sure the **draw here** layer is selected in the Timeline. If the **patterns** layer is selected and you try to draw on that layer, you will get an error message asking you to unlock and show that layer.

3. In the Toolbox, select the **Pen** tool.

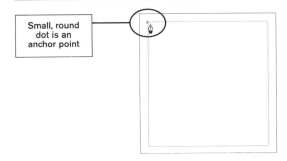

Small, round dot is an anchor point

4. Move the cursor to the upper-left corner of the square outline and click. This will create the first anchor point. Line segments are created between two anchor points.

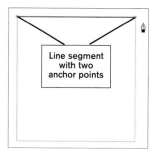

Line segment
with two
anchor points

5. Move the cursor to the upper-right corner and click to add the second anchor point, thus creating a line segment, which only appears after you click. The line segment will appear as a red line with two square anchor points. The line segment color will use the color currently specified in the **Stroke** color box.

6. Move the cursor to the lower-right corner and click. This will create a second line segment between the upper- and lower-right anchor points.

7. Move the cursor to the lower-left corner and click. This will create a third line segment.

8. Move the cursor to the upper-left corner. A small circle appears at the end of the cursor. This is an indication that you will close the path if you click. Click to close the path and complete the shape. The shape will automatically fill with whatever color you currently have selected for the fill color.

TIP | Pen Preferences

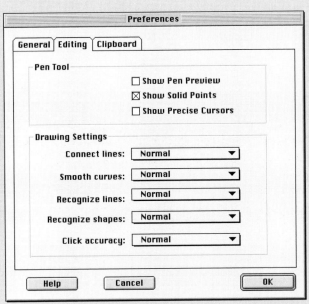

As you learn to work with the Pen tool, there are some preferences you should be aware of that might make your life a bit easier. If you choose **Edit > Preferences** you can access the **Preferences** window. Click on the **Editing** tab, and the Pen preferences will be displayed at the top. There are three preferences you should consider here:

Show Pen Preview (off by default)–this option will let you preview the line segments as you draw with the Pen tool. A stretchy line will appear as a preview of the line segment you will create.

Show Solid Points (on by default)–this option will display unselected anchor points as solid points and selected anchor points as hollow points when you use the **Subselect** tool. (Now, try and say that five times fast! ;-)

Show Precise Cursors (off by default)–this option will cause the pen icon to appear as a crosshair. This can be helpful for precise drawing and works great with the grid feature.

Now that you know how to create a square with the Pen tool, we will show you how to create a circle. This is a bit more complicated and will probably take some time to master, so don't worry if you have to do this exercise a few times before you get the hang of things.

9. Using the **Pen** tool, click at the top center of the circle outline. This will place the first anchor point.

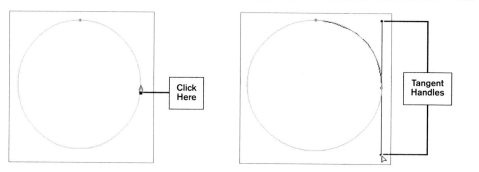

10. Click on the middle-right edge of the circle and drag down to add another control point. As you drag, you will see two tangent handles appear. Move the mouse around and watch how the angle of the line changes as you do this. Don't release the mouse button just yet.

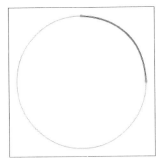

11. Drag down to the bottom right until the line segment seems to match the outline of the circle. Now release the mouse button. **Note:** You don't have to be perfect here; just try to get yourself comfortable working with the Pen tool.

 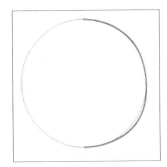

12. Click on the middle-bottom edge of the circle to add another control point. This should complete half of the circle shape.

 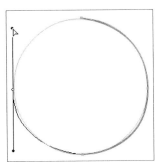

13. Click and drag up on the middle-left edge of the circle to add another control point. As you drag, you will see two tangent handles appear. Don't release the mouse just yet.

14. Drag up the top left until the line segment seems to match the outline of the circle. Release the mouse button.

 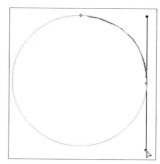

15. Move the cursor to the top of the circle. Click on the first anchor point you created. This will complete the circle and fill it with whatever color you have selected for the fill color.

16. Choose **File > Save** and click **Save** to save the changes you made to this file. Phew, after all that hard work, who wants to lose it! Go ahead and leave this file open for the next exercise. Don't worry if it isn't perfect. You will learn how to modify the shape next.

MOVIE | morepen.mov

If you want to see the Pen tool in action and learn how to create more complicated shapes, make sure you check out the **morepen.mov** movie inside the movies folder on the **H•O•T CD-ROM**.

4. _____Modifying Lines

Now that you know how to create shapes using the Pencil and Pen tools, it's a good time to learn how to reshape them. In Flash 4, you had to use the Arrow tool to make changes to the paths you created. However, in Flash 5, you'll use the new Subselect tool to modify paths using their anchor points, or tangent handles. This exercise will expose you to both tools to give you have a better understanding of how each of these tools works.

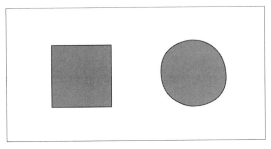

1. The file from the previous exercise should still be open. If it's not, open the **pen.fla** file.

2. In the Toolbox, select the **Arrow** tool.

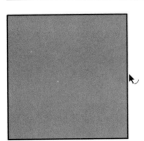

3. Move your cursor over the right edge of the square. Notice that a small curved line appears at the end of the cursor. This is an indication that you are over a line segment.

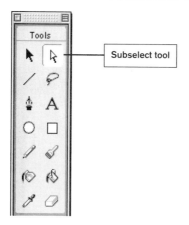

4. Click and drag the mouse to the right. Notice that the shape starts to distort and stretch as you continue to drag the mouse. (Hey, remember silly putty?) Release the mouse button. Notice that both the line and fill have changed their shape.

The Arrow tool offers a free-form way of transforming shapes, and while it can be fun, it can also lack the precision you sometimes need when creating complex shapes. Macromedia recognized this and introduced the Subselect tool in Flash 5, which lets you manipulate the anchor points and tangent handles of paths after you have added them.

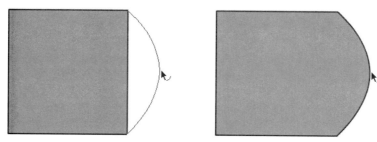

5. In the Toolbox, select the **Subselect** tool.

6. Move the cursor over the edge of the circle shape. A small black square will appear indicating that you are over a line.

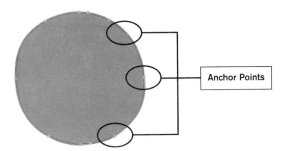

Anchor Points

7. Click on the edge of the circle to select it. Notice that once the shape is selected, the anchor points become visible. The anchor points are represented by small red squares along the line of the circle. **Note**: Flash will add anchor points, if necessary, to create the curve. This is why you might see more than the four anchor points you added.

8. Using the **Subselect** tool, move the cursor over the middle-right anchor point. When you do this, a small white square will appear next to the cursor, indicating you are over an anchor point.

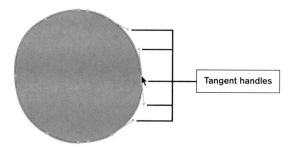

Tangent handles

9. Click to select the middle-right anchor point. When you do, the tangent handles for that anchor point and the ones above and below it will appear. Why? Because all three anchor points work together to create this part of the circle's curve. **Note:** If you don't have as many anchor points as we do in this example then you may not see the three anchor points working together.

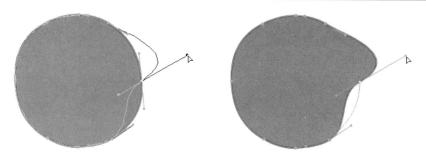

10. Click and drag the top tangent handle of the middle-right anchor point over to the right. Release the mouse button. Notice how the top and bottom portions of the curve change together. This is the normal behavior of tangent handles.

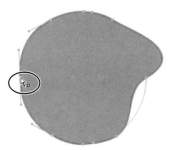

11. Click to select the middle-left anchor point.

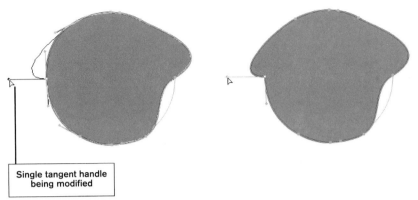

Single tangent handle
being modified

12. Press and hold the **Option** key (Mac) or **Alt** key (PC) as you click and drag the top tangent handle of the middle-left anchor point over to the left. Release the mouse button. Notice
how only the top portion changes. This is how you modify one part of a curve without changing the other.

*Now you know how the Arrow and Subselect tools can be used to modify the lines that
you create in Flash. The Arrow tool can be used to reshape lines that are either straight or
curved. The Subselect tool can help you reshape objects by clicking on and moving the
tangent handles and anchor points in an object. Next, you will learn how to add, remove,
and convert anchor points. Knowing how to do this will give you more control when you
are creating shapes in Flash.*

13. In the Toolbox, select the **Pen** tool. In addition to drawing shapes, the Pen tool lets you
add anchor points to a line.

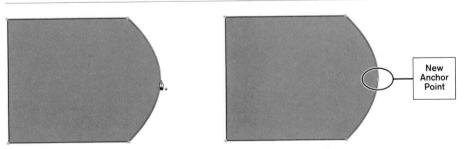

New
Anchor
Point

14. Move the cursor over the rounded side of the square shape. Notice that when you move
over the edge, a small **+** sign (Mac) or **x** sign (PC) appears next to the cursor. This is an indication that a new anchor point will be created if you click. Click to add a new anchor point here.

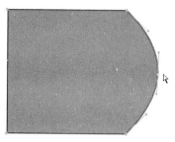

15. In the Toolbox, select the **Subselect** tool, then click to select the new anchor point you just added. Notice that the tangent handles appear. Because the line segment on which you created the anchor point was a curve, Flash knows to give you access to the tangent handles.

Converting curves to straight lines is a rather simple process and one you should know how to do. So, that's exactly what you will do in the following steps.

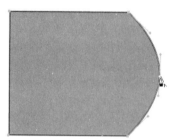

16. Go back and select the **Pen** tool, then, use it to move the cursor over the newly added anchor point. Notice that a small ^ symbol appears at the bottom of the cursor. This is an indication that you will convert the curve point to a corner point if you click.

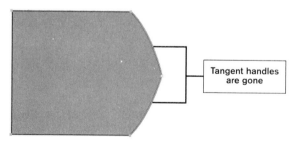

Tangent handles
are gone

17. Click the anchor point. This will convert the curve point to a corner point. The curve will transform into a hard-edge shape, much like a triangle. You will no longer have access to any tangent handles for this anchor point.

Converting a corner point into a curve point is even easier to do.

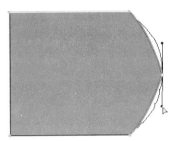 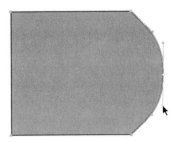

18. Using the **Subselect** tool, **Opt + Click** (Mac) or **Alt + Click** (Windows) and drag the anchor point you just modified up a bit. When you do this, you will convert that corner point into an anchor point. Pretty easy, huh?

Note: Make sure the anchor point is still selected before you Option-drag it. Selected anchor points are white.

Tip: Deleting points is can be done a number of different ways. One of the easiest ways is to select the anchor point with the Subselect tool and press the Delete key.

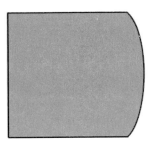

19. With the anchor point still selected, press **Delete**. This will remove the anchor point. Phew!

20. Choose **File > Save** and click **Save** to save the changes you made to this file. You can close this file; you won't need it any more.

Using the Oval and Rectangle

Using the Pencil and Pen to create shapes can be really useful for creating irregular shapes. But they can become somewhat tedious or inefficient for creating simple geometric shapes, such as circles and squares. The Oval and Rectangle tools are here to help with this small dilemma. These tools let you create simple shapes, with lines and/or fills that are independent of each other, quickly and effortlessly. In this exercise, you will learn how to use both the Oval and Rectangle tools.

1. Open the **shapes.fla** file located inside the **chap_04** folder. This is nothing more than a blank file we have created for you.

2. In the Toolbox, select the **Oval** tool. Notice at the bottom of the Toolbox, there are no options for this tool.

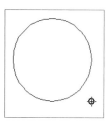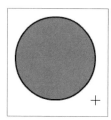

3. On the stage, click and then drag the crosshair cursor to the lower right corner. As you do this, a large thick circle will appear next to the crosshair. This is an indication that you are drawing a perfect circle. Release the mouse button to draw the circle. Notice that Flash uses the current fill and line colors to create the circle.

TIP | Easy Perfect Shapes

When you are using the Oval or Rectangle tools, holding the **Shift** key down while you draw the shapes will force the tool to draw only perfect circles or squares. We just thought we should point that out before you go too far.

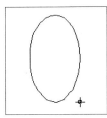 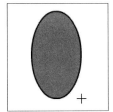

4. Draw another circle, this time in the shape of an oval. Notice that the small circle around the crosshair is smaller and thinner. This is an indication that you are drawing an oval, and not a perfect circle.

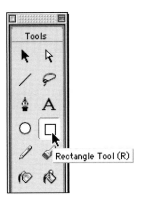 

5. In the Toolbox, select the **Rectangle** tool. Notice at the bottom of the Toolbox, there is one option for this tool. You'll learn about that next.

 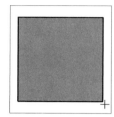

6. Click and drag toward the lower-right corner of the stage. As you do this, a rectangle preview will appear. Notice the "perfect shape" indicator. It's the same as the one you saw on the Oval tool. Release the mouse button to create the shape. Again, Flash used the selected fill and line colors to create this shape.

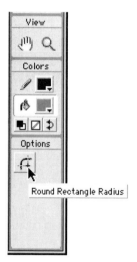

7. At the bottom of the Toolbox, click the **Round Rectangle Radius** button. This will open the **Rectangle Settings** dialog box.

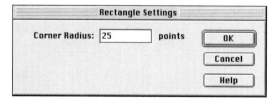

8. Enter **25** for the **Corner Radius** setting. Click **OK**. This will add rounded corners with a 25-point radius to the next rectangle you draw. You can enter any value between **0** and **999**.

9. Using the **Rectangle** tool, draw another rectangle on the stage. Notice that the corners of the rectangle are rounded now. Sweet.

TIP | Round Before You Draw

You can't use the Round Rectangle Radius option after you have drawn the rectangle. So, creating rounded rectangles does require some forethought. However, you can adjust the points as you draw the rectangle. Pressing the **Up** key will decrease the corner radius points, while pressing the **Down** key will increase the corner radius points. Very cool little shortcut.

10. Choose **File > Save** and click **Save** to save the changes you made to this file. You can close this file; you won't be using it any more.

---

6. _____Using the Brush

The **Brush** tool is used to paint shapes. You can create shapes with solid colors, gradients, and even bitmaps as fills. The Brush has several painting modes that are unique to Flash. These modes are covered in detail in the **brushmodes.mov** movie at the end of this exercise. For now, you will learn to use the Brush to create and modify shapes.

1. Open the **paint.fla** file located inside the **chap_04** folder. Once again, this is just a blank file that has been saved for you.

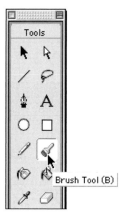

2. In the Toolbox, click to select the **Brush** tool. Notice that there are several options for the Brush tool. You will learn about these options as you complete this exercise.

3. On the stage, draw a circle with the Brush. Notice that it uses the fill color for this shape, and not the stroke color.

4. At the bottom of the Toolbox, click on the **Brush Size** pop-up menu. Select the fourth size from the bottom. This will decrease the size of the next fill that is drawn.

TIP | Adding Lines to Brush Shapes

Because the Brush creates shapes that are fills, you can use the Ink Bottle to easily add a stroke to the shapes you create with the Brush. It's pretty neat; you should try it!

5. Draw a smaller circle inside the large one. Notice that the smaller brush size creates a fill shape narrower than the first one.

6. At the bottom of the Toolbox, click on the **Brush Shape** pop-up menu. Select the fifth shape from the bottom. This will change the shape of the next fill that you draw.

7. Draw another circle on the stage. Notice that it uses the new shape to create the circle. You can produce some pretty cool calligraphy effects using these shapes.

8. Go ahead and experiment with the other Brush shapes and sizes. If you have a tablet, you might want to use it to take advantage of the pressure-sensitive support.

9. When you are done experimenting with the Brush, choose **File > Save** and click **Save** to save the changes you made to this file. You can close this file.

MOVIE | Brush Modes

If you want to learn about the different Brush modes in Flash, be sure to check out the **brushmodes.mov** movie located inside the **movies** folder on the H∑O∑T CD-ROM.

7. —————————————**Modifying Fills**

There are several ways you can change the fill of a shape. You can specify the fill before you create the shape, which is the most obvious way, or you can use the Paint Bucket to fill empty areas of a shape and change the fill of existing areas. The Paint Bucket can also be used to modify bitmap and gradient fills. In addition, the new **Fill** panel lets you create solid, gradient, and bitmap fills, which can then be applied to the shapes you create. In this exercise, you will learn how to use the Paint Bucket tool and the Fill panel to modify the fill of a shape.

1. Open the **modifyfills.fla** file located inside the **chap_04** folder. This file contains a vector graphic of a monkey. And, yes, he has only one eye. ;-)

2. Using the **Arrow** tool, select the left tooth of the monkey. When an object is selected a gray selection mesh will appear over it. In this case it's a tooth.

3. Make sure the **Fill** panel is visible, if it's not, select **Window > Panels > Fill** to make it visible.

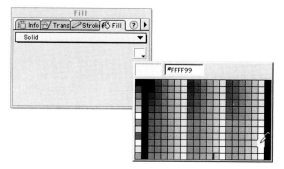

4. From the **Fill Color** box, select a shade of yellow you like. This will automatically change the color of the monkey's tooth to yellow. Yuck!

TIP | Using the Fill Panel

The Fill panel can be a great way to change the solid fill of an object. However, it is important to note that you must have the object selected first if you want to change the fill using the Fill panel. But, you can **Shift + Click** to select multiple objects and change them all at once, this is a great way to make several changes quickly. Also, you can use the Paint Bucket to change unselected fills.

5. Click above the mouth of the monkey to select most of its face. A gray mesh will appear indicating what areas you have selected.

6. Notice that his left ear is not selected yet. **Shift + Click** on his left ear to select that part of the object as well.

7. Zoom in to view the monkey's teeth by pressing **Cmd + =** (Mac) or **Ctrl + =** (Windows). **Shift + Click** again to select the small portion to the left of his left tooth.

8. From the **Fill Color** box, select a different shade of brown. Notice that this changes all of the selected pieces of the monkey. Pretty quick and easy, huh?

9. Click outside the monkey to deselect before you continue. You can also press the **Esc** key to deselect, which is a handy shortcut to remember.

In the following steps, you will learn how to use the Paint Bucket tool to apply a previously selected fill to a shape. In this case, it will be a gradient fill. Then, you will learn how to use the Paint Bucket tool to modify the gradient.

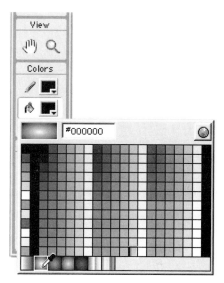

10. At the bottom of the Toolbox, click on the **Fill Color** box and select the black-and-white radial gradient.

11. In the Toolbox, select the **Paint Bucket** tool.

12. Click on the black circle inside the monkey's eye. This will add the selected fill color, a black-and-white gradient, to that shape.

Transform Fill

13. Zoom in on the eye by pressing **Cmd + =** (Mac) or **Ctrl + =** (Windows). With the Paint Bucket selected, click the **Transform Fill** button at the bottom of the Toolbox. A small gradient icon will appear at the bottom of your cursor. This option will let you modify the attributes of the gradient you just added.

 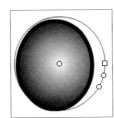

14. Click the eye to select it. When you do, a thin circle with some gradient handles will appear around the eye.

TIP | Gradient Handles Explained

There are several gradient handles available, each with its own purpose. The following diagram explains what each gradient handle will do.

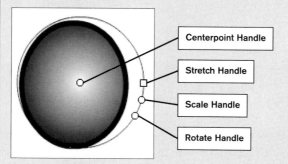

Centerpoint Handle: Dragging this handle moves the center point of the gradient.

Stretch Handle: Dragging this handle stretches the scale of the gradient in one direction.
Note: the Rotate Handle controls the direction of the stretch.

Scale Handle: Dragging this handle expands or contracts the scale of the gradient.

Rotate Handle: Dragging this handle rotates the gradient around the center point.

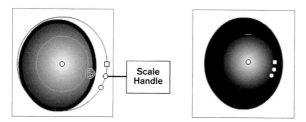

15. Click and drag the **Scale** handle in toward the center of the eye. This will make the gradient smaller, creating a more realistic-looking eye.

16. Choose **View > Magnification > 100%** to return to the normal view of the monkey. There, now the monkey has a good-looking eye.

Tip: To zoom out, you can also use the shortcut keys by pressing Cmd + - (Mac) or Ctrl + - (Windows).

---

17. Choose **File > Save** and click **Save** to save the changes you made to this file. You can close the file.

---

8. _____Multiple Objects

By now you should have a pretty good idea of how to draw within Flash. In this exercise, we want to point out the nuances of drawing in Flash, because it can be really different from drawing in other programs. In this exercise, you will learn how Flash handles multiple and overlapping objects. In addition, you will learn how to protect the artwork from being unintentionally modified.

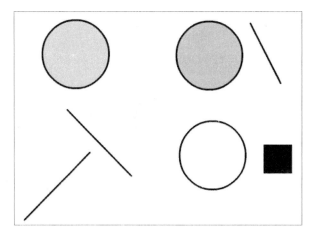

1. Open the **multiple.fla** file located inside the **chap_04** folder. This file contains some simple shapes that you will use to understand the unique drawing behaviors of Flash.

2. Select the **Arrow** tool, and then move the cursor over the line of the green circle. Notice that a small curve appears at the end of the cursor. This is an indication that you will select the line if you click.

3. Click once to select the entire line around the circle. A gray mesh will appear over the line once it has been selected.

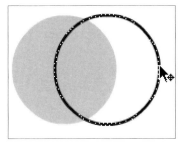

4. Click again on the line and drag to the right. This will pull the line off the circle. As we mentioned earlier, Flash treats the line and fill as separate objects. Because of this, you can easily separate the two.

5. Press **Delete** to permanently remove the line.

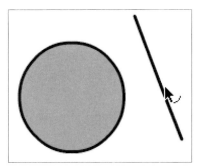

6. Move the cursor over the line next to the blue circle. Again, that little curve will appear at the bottom of the cursor. Click once to select the line.

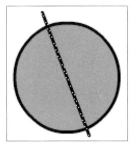

7. Click again on the line and drag it over the blue circle.

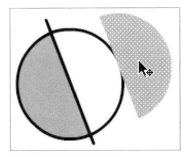

8. Click in the right section of the blue circle and drag to the right. Notice how the line you dragged on top of the circle has cut the fill into different objects.

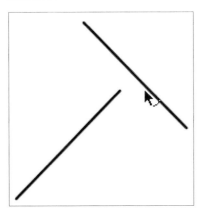

9. Click the line just below the green circle to select it.

10. Click and drag that same line down so that it lies across the other line, then click in a blank area of the stage to deselect the line.

11. Click to select the bottom-right line segment.

12. Click and drag to the right. Notice how the line was split into four segments simply by having two lines intersect. While this might seem a little non-intuitive, it's a great way to create interesting shapes in Flash.

13. Click and drag the small black square into the middle of the yellow circle.

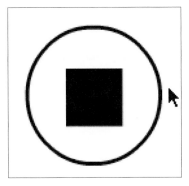

14. Click on any blank area of the stage to deselect the black square.

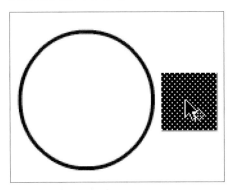

15. Click and drag the square back to its original location. Notice how it left a square hole in the fill of the circle. **Note:** If this square were exactly the same yellow color as the circle, it would have not cut through the circle. Instead, it would have combined with the circle into one shape. Bye-bye square!

16. Leave this file open; you'll need it for the next exercise.

9. ——————————Grouping Objects

Now that you have a good idea of how the drawing features behave in Flash, this exercise will show you how to create shapes that overlap but don't cut or combine into one another. The following steps will show you how to create a grouped object. So don't stop, you are getting to the really good stuff now!

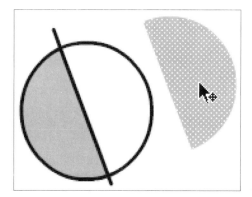

1. Using the **Arrow** tool, click to select the half of the blue circle you separated.

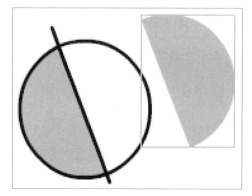

2. Choose **Modify > Group**. When you do this, a thin blue line will appear around the object, which indicates that this is a grouped object, which is protected from intersecting with other objects on the stage.

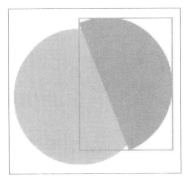

3. Click and drag the blue half circle on top of the **green circle**.

4. Deselect the blue half circle by clicking on any blank area of the stage.

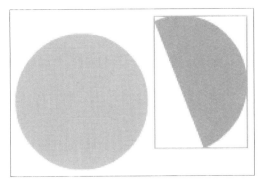

5. Click and drag the blue half circle off of the green circle. Nothing happens. Phew. You see, grouping objects, even single objects, is a quick way of protecting them from being affected by other objects.

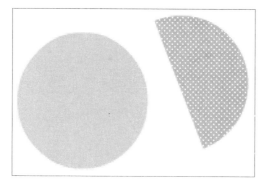

6. With the blue half circle still selected, choose **Modify > Ungroup**. This will ungroup the selected object. You can tell this has been done because the thin blue line goes away and the gray selection mesh returns, both telltale signs that this is a shape in its most primitive form.

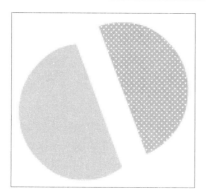

7. Now drag that ungrouped blue shape onto the green circle, deselect and then drag it off again. Yikes! As you can see, grouping objects can be a quick and easy way to protect them from unwanted editing.

8. Choose **File > Save** to save the changes you made to this file. You can close this file because you are done with this chapter!

Well, you made it. By now, you should feel pretty comfortable working with the drawing tools inside Flash. If you aren't quite there yet, please feel free to take some time to play with the different tools. You might try drawing some artwork for a project you want to create in Flash. Nothing will ever replace good old-fashioned practice. It might not make you perfect, but it can make you one heck of a Flash designer. :-).

5.

Animation Basics

The Timeline	Projects and Movies
Movie Properties	Frame-By-Frame Animation with Keyframes
Blank Keyframes and Onion Skinning	Keyframes with Erasing Content
Understanding Frame Rate	Inserting / Deleting Frames
Copying / Reversing Frames	Testing Movies

chap_5

Flash 5
H•O•T CD-ROM

Flash has a reputation as a powerful and robust animation tool. If you know other animation tools, such as Macromedia Director or Adobe After Effects, you might find yourself looking for similarities. It might surprise you that it's actually easier to learn Flash's animation capabilities if you don't know other animation programs, because you have no preconceived notions of how you think it might work. If you've never used an animation tool before, you have an advantage over more experienced animators for this reason!

This chapter introduces you to the Timeline, which is the heart of producing animation in Flash. This is the part of the interface where you will work with keyframes, blank keyframes, frame-by-frame animation, and onion skinning. If these are new terms to you, they won't be for long! This chapter will also cover setting the frame rate, and how the frame rate affects playback speeds. By the end of this chapter, things should really get moving for you, all puns intended ☺.

The Timeline

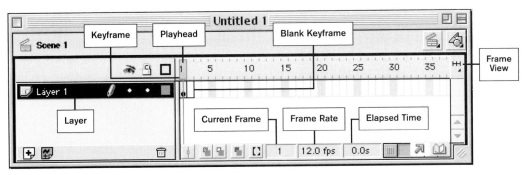

The Timeline is central to all animation activity in Flash. The illustration above identifies the components of the Timeline that you will be working with in this chapter. A more detailed description of each follows.

Layers: Layers are a way of organizing the elements of your animation from front to back, so that one object can move in front of or behind another, or make transitions that are independent of one another. The layer controls for your movie appear in the left-hand column of the Timeline. Each layer has options for hiding/showing the layer, locking it, and displaying its contents as outlines.

Current Frame: Displays the current position of the Playhead and the frame number of the frame that is currently visible.

Frame Rate: Displays the number of frames per second (or fps) at which the movie attempts to play on your end-user's browser or computer. Double-click here is a quick way to access the Movie Properties dialog box.

Elapsed Time: Displays elapsed time from Frame 1 to the current Playhead location at the currently selected frame rate.

Frame View: This pop-up menu gives you several different options for specifying how the Timeline is displayed. Use this if you want to see fewer or more frames on the Timeline. The default view is usually just fine until you start creating a longer animation. At that point, it's great to be able to see more frames as you work.

Blank keyframe: Blank keyframes are empty locations on the Timeline that are ready to have content placed into them. They can also be used to break up or make changes in your animation.

Keyframe: Keyframes define the moment in the Timeline where actions or animation changes occur. Keyframe content display remains unchanged until another keyframe or blank keyframe occurs in the Timeline.

Playhead: The Playhead—a red rectangle with a long red line—indicates the current frame that you are viewing in the Timeline. You can click and drag (scrub) the Playhead back and forth in the Timeline to quickly preview your animation.

Projects and Movies

In Flash, the term "movie" can be used to refer to three separate files—the authoring project file (an .fla file), the Flash content published for the internet (an .swf file), and Flash content published as a stand-alone file (Projector file). This can become rather confusing when you are learning Flash. To help clarify this, we will be using "project" to identify the .fla file, "movie" to identify the .swf file, and "projector" to identify the two projector files. A more comprehensive explanation of these different files is available in Chapter 1 "Background." This chart below helps illustrate the differences between the files:

	Name	Definition
Untitled.fla	**Project**	This file will always have an extension of .fla and is the master authoring file used to create Flash content.
Untitled.swf	**Movie**	This file will always have an extension of .swf and is the only file you will upload to the internet. This is a compressed version of the project file.
Untitled Projector / untitled.exe	**Macintosh Projector** **Windows Projector**	Flash can produce stand-alone projector files for the Macintosh and Windows operating systems. The Windows Projector will have an extension of .exe. The Macintosh Projector will have the word Projector appended to the end of the file name.

I. ——————————Movie Properties

The **movie properties** are general specifications that will affect your entire project. The first thing you should do when you start a new project in Flash is set these properties, which include things like stage dimensions, frame rate, and background color. This exercise will show you how to set them.

1. Copy the **chap_05** folder, located on the **Flash 5 HOT CD-ROM**, to your hard drive. You need to have this folder on your hard drive in order to save files inside it.

2. Select **File > New** to create a new blank movie. By default, your stage dimensions will be 550 x 400 pixels and will have a white background. You'll learn how to change both real soon.

3. Select **File > Save** and save this file as **movie.fla** inside the **chap_05** folder on your desktop.

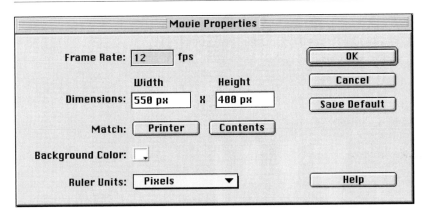

4. Select **Modify > Movie**. This will open the **Movie Properties** dialog box, which contains all the frame rate preferences, movie dimensions, background color, and rule measurements that you can set for your entire movie.

5. Enter **Frame Rate: 22**. This will set the frame rate of your movie to 22 fps (frames-per-second.) This means that for every 22 frames in your animation, one second of time will elapse. We will discuss frame rate in more detail later in this chapter. Keep the dialog box open.

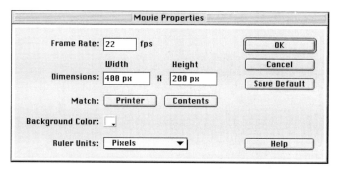

6. Enter **Width**: **400** and **Height**: **200** for the **Dimensions** options. These options control the absolute pixel dimensions of your Stage. You will learn other ways to control the size of your movie when you get to Chapter 15, *"Publishing."*

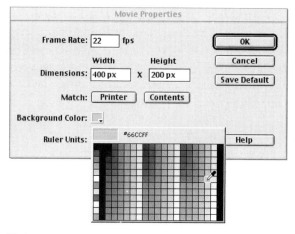

7. Click the **Background Color** box. This will display the default color panel. Select a **light blue** color.

TIP | More Background Colors

If you want to set the background color to something other than the 216 Web-safe colors available in the default palette, you can create a custom color for your background by using the **Mixer**. (Learn more about the Mixer in Chapter 3, *"Using the Color Tools"*, Exercise 1.) Simply create the color you want using any of the Mixer color modes, add that swatch to the palette and it will be accessible to you from the Background Color box in the Movie Properties. In addition, you can use the Eyedropper to pick up any visible color on your screen.

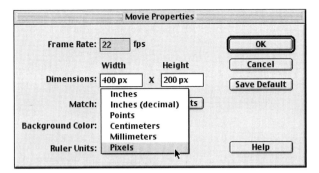

8. Click the **Ruler Units** pop-up menu. The menu will display several different methods for displaying the ruler units on your stage. Make sure you leave this option set to the default of **Pixels**.

9. Click **OK**. The dimensions, background color, and frame rate will be changed to your new specifications. You can return to the Movie Properties dialog box at any point to change these options again. However, you should avoid changing the dimensions of your movie once you have added content to your stage. The reason for this is that if you change the dimension once you've started creating artwork and animation, the position of all your hard work will be offset if you alter the dimensions, and will be difficult to fix.

10. Select **File > Save** to save the changes you made to this file. However, don't close it just yet; you will need it for the next exercise.

TIP | Saving New Default Settings

When you create a new movie, by default, you will get a stage that is 550 x 400 pixels with a white background. This might not be all that convenient when you are working on projects that should have different settings. Good news—you can redefine the default settings so they better fit your needs. Simply change the movie properties to match the settings you need and click the **Save Default** button. Next time you create a new movie, it will have the all the properties you already want. Pretty cool!

What is a Keyframe?

A keyframe is a term that has been used in animation since the early 1900s. It signifies a change in motion, and in Flash, keyframes are displayed on the Timeline. The Timeline represents the passing of time, with each slot representing an individual frame. If you have artwork in Frame 1 and don't change it until Frame 20, the image in Frame 1 will persist until Frame 20. You would need to add a new keyframe in Frame 20 in order to make a change to the artwork. If you have artwork in Frame 1 and change it in Frame 2, you would need to add a new keyframe in Frame 2; therefore you would end up with two keyframes; one in Frame 1 and the other in Frame 2.

The concept of a keyframe might seem abstract to you if you've never worked with keyframes before. This chapter will give you lots of opportunities to work with keyframes, so they won't be alien to you for long.

Keyframes in Flash

Keyframes are located in the Timeline: a keyframe that contains content displays a solid circle in the Timeline, and a vertical line before the frame represents an empty keyframe. Subsequent frames that you add to the same layer will have the same content as the keyframe.

To complicate things a little more, Flash has different kinds of keyframes. They are defined in the following chart:

Frame Types in Flash Defined	
Term	**Definition**
Empty/Blank Keyframe (F7)	An empty keyframe (Macromedia calls this a blank keyframe as well) has no visual representation. It means that there is no artwork on the stage on that frame. By placing artwork on the stage, you will fill an empty keyframe. The Flash Timeline, by default, opens with an empty keyframe. As soon as you put content on the stage, the empty keyframe will change to a keyframe. From that point on, this artwork will be copied to all frames until you define another keyframe and change the content on the stage at that frame.

Frame Types in Flash Defined	
Term	**Definition**
Keyframe (F6)	A keyframe that contains content (meaning that artwork is on the stage at that frame in the Timeline) is represented by a solid circle. A keyframe can also contain actions (covered in Chapter 12, "*Action Scripting Basics*") or sound (covered in chapter 14, "*Sound*"), and is represented by a hollow circle. By default, adding a keyframe in Flash copies the content (except for actions and sounds) from the previous keyframe. In order to make a change, you must alter the artwork on the stage at the point on the Timeline where you have defined the new keyframe. Otherwise, Flash will simply copy the contents from the previous change, and even though you have defined a keyframe, the artwork will not change.
Blank Keyframe (F7)	If you have defined keyframes in your Timeline, you must set a blank keyframe in order to clear the stage of the last defined.
Clear Keyframe (Shift+F6)	To delete a keyframe, you would use the *Clear Keyframe* command. This is used when you want to erase keyframes from your Timeline. It is similar, but different from a blank keyframe. A blank keyframe is used to create a new keyframe without copying the content from the previous keyframe. Choosing *Clear Keyframe* deletes keyframes, and is usually associated with fixing (or clearing) a mistake.
Frame (F5)	The Timeline in Flash looks like it has lots of frames in each layer, which can be a bit deceiving! While it has the slots for frames, you have to specifically define them as frames (or keyframes.) You can do this by clicking in any of the slots and pressing *F5* or select *Insert > Frame*. It's possible to have a different number of frames on different layers. For example, Layer 1 could have 10 frames, while Layer 2 has one frame. It is up to you to set the frames for each layer.
Remove Frames (Shift+F5)	If you ever want to delete frames that you have set, select those frames and press *Shift+F5* or by select *Insert > Remove Frames*.

2. —————————**Frame-by-Frame Animation with Keyframes**

This exercise will teach you how to work with keyframes. A common animation technique is to make a title appear as if it is being written before your eyes. This is very simple to do in Flash using keyframes, because when you insert a keyframe, Flash searches backwards in the Timeline until it finds another keyframe and then copies that content to the newly inserted keyframe. You will learn how to do this in the following steps.

1. Select **File > Open** and browse to the **movieFinal.fla** file inside the **chap_05** folder. We have created this file for you so that you can see the finished version of the exercise.

2. Press **Return/Enter** on the keyboard to preview the animation on the stage. You will notice the word "Home" right before your eyes! You will be creating this same frame-by-frame animation next.

3. Close the **movieFinal.fla** file.

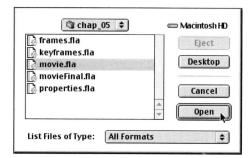

4. You should still have the **movie.fla** file open from the last exercise but in case you accidentally closed it, go ahead and select **File > Open**. Browse to the **movie.fla** you saved inside the **chap_05** folder in the last exercise. Click **Open** to open that file.

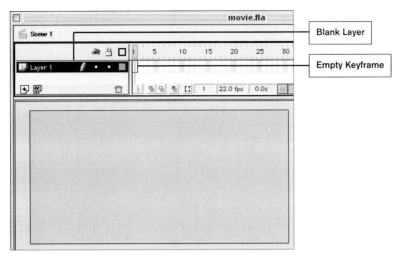

Notice that this document has a single layer, which contains a single empty keyframe. Why? Because every project in Flash has to have a starting point, and this is the minimum that you need to start drawing. The empty keyframe has a line around that frame.

5. Select the **Brush** from the Toolbox. You can use any size, shape, and color you want. You are going to be writing the word "Home," one letter at a time in a series of keyframes.

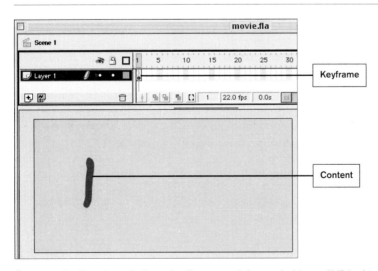

6. Using the **Brush** tool, draw the first part of the capital letter "H" in the left side of the stage just like the picture above. Notice that the blank keyframe in Frame 1 now contains a small black dot, which signifies that it contains content. Frame 1 is now referred to as a keyframe because it is no longer empty. In this case, the content is the line you drew.

In order to make a change on the Timeline, you must have a keyframe where you want the change to occur. Now that you have filled in the first keyframe of Layer 1, you are going to add another keyframe after it so you can draw the second frame of your animation. Adding a new keyframe after the last one will copy all the content from the last keyframe to this new keyframe. You will draw another stroke in this new keyframe in order to create a change in your animation.

7. Select **Frame 2** and choose **Insert > Keyframe** or use the shortcut key, **F6**. (F6 is a keyboard shortcut you should learn right away, because you will be using it often.) This will add a new keyframe to the Timeline in Frame 2, copying all the artwork in Frame 1 and allowing you to continue drawing.

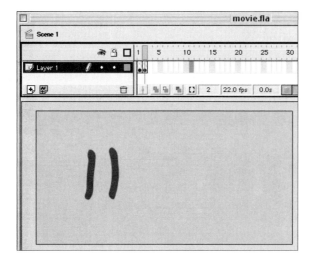

8. Using the **Brush** again, draw the second part of a capital "H" just like the picture above.

9. Select **Frame 3** and choose **Insert > Keyframe** or use the shortcut key, **F6**. This will add a new keyframe to the Timeline in Frame 3, copying all the artwork from the last frame, Frame 2.

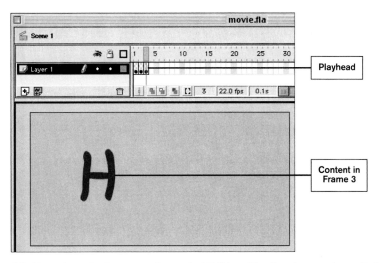

Playhead

Content in
Frame 3

10. Now draw the last part of a capital "H" just like the picture above. Believe it or not, you have already created the beginning of your animation! You can click and drag (scrub) the Playhead back and forth in the Timeline to quickly preview the animation. You will see the "H" being drawn directly on the stage.

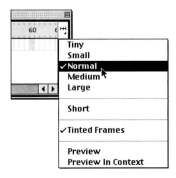

Looking at a Timeline with a bunch of black dots might seem somewhat abstract to some of you. The Frame View menu has several options that help to display the contents of your individual frames right in the Timeline.

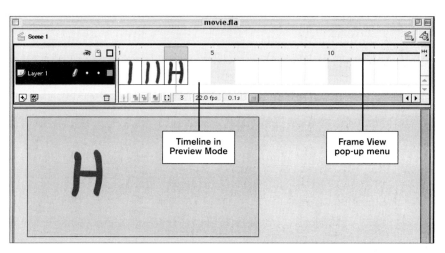

11. From the **Frame View** pop-up menu, select **Preview**. This will change your Timeline so that you see a preview of what is on each frame instead of a bunch of black dots. We find this view of the Timeline very helpful when trying to create frame-by-frame animations.

12. In **Frame 4**, press **F6** to insert another keyframe so you can continue to draw the pieces to spell out word "Home."

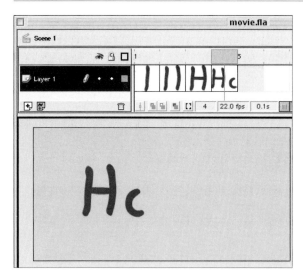

13. Using the **Brush** tool, draw the left half of an "o" on the stage. You should be able to see the contents of your fourth frame appear in the Timeline preview.

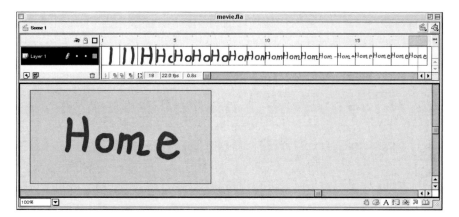

14. Go ahead and continue to spell out the word "Home" by pressing **F6** to add a new keyframe after the previous one and then adding more parts of the letters in each one, using the Brush tool. When you are done, your Timeline should look like the one shown above.

You can get a quick preview of your animation right away using one of two methods. You can drag the Playhead across the Timeline as we mentioned in step 10, or you can press Return/Enter and watch the animation play directly on the stage. So, get out the popcorn and watch your first animation!

15. Press **Return/Enter**. Your animation will play once on the stage and stop at the last keyframe. This time, you are seeing an accurate preview of the frame rate for this movie, which you set in the previous exercise: 22 fps (frames per second). We'll cover frame rate in more detail in the next chapter. Press **Return/Enter** to preview the animation again as many times as you like.

There are other ways to preview your animations, and we will cover those later. For now, let's stay focused on the basics. Save and close this file.

Blank Keyframes and Onion Skinning

Another common animation technique is to make artwork that appears to jitter while it's being viewed. This exercise will teach you a few new techniques. First, you'll learn to use the **Onion Skinning** feature in Flash. This allows you to see a ghost image of the previous frame so you can redraw it in the same location over and over. It will also teach you how to work with the blank keyframe feature, so you can draw something new on each frame. As well, this exercise will also teach you how to use a feature called **Loop Playback**, so you can preview looping animations in Flash.

1. Select **File > Open** and browse to the **jitterFinal.fla** file inside the **chap_05** folder. We have created this file for you so that you can see the finished version of the exercise.

2. Before you preview the animation, choose **Control > Loop Playback**. This will allow you to see the animation repeat over and over when you preview it.

3. Press **Return/Enter** on the keyboard to preview the animation on the stage. You will see the word **jitter** shaking on the stage! In the following steps, you will be creating this same animation technique.

4. Close the **jitterFinal.fla** file.

5. Create a new file and save it as **jitter.fla** inside the **chap_05** folder.

6. Select the **Brush** tool from the Toolbox and choose a purple color.

7. With the **Brush** tool selected, draw the word **jitter** and make a circle around it in the center of the stage. Frame 1 is now considered a keyframe because it now contains a small black dot, which signifies that it contains content.

Now that you have filled in the first frame of Layer 1, you'll add a blank keyframe after it, so you can draw the second frame of your animation. Inserting a blank keyframe in Frame 2 will give you a new empty frame on the Timeline, rather than copying the artwork from the last frame.

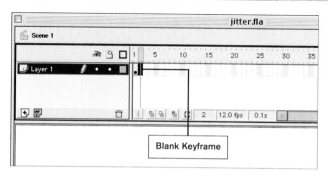

Blank Keyframe

8. Select **Insert > Blank Keyframe** or use the shortcut key, **F7.** This will add a blank keyframe to the Timeline in Frame 2.

A blank keyframe will not copy the contents from the previous keyframe. Notice how the word jitter disappeared. Actually it really didn't disappear, the Playhead just moved to Frame 2 and the artwork was drawn on Frame 1. It's still there.

9. At the bottom of the timeline there is a row of five buttons all grouped together. Click the button that's second from the left. This is the **Onion Skin** button. You will be able to see a faint ghost image of the content that is in Frame 1 on the stage. This is very convenient feature that allows you to see the artwork in the last keyframe and draw over the ghost image in the next frame.

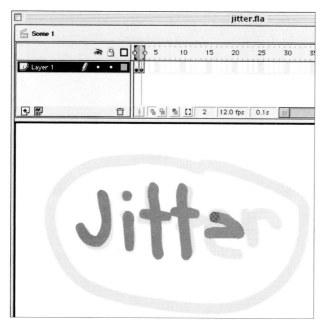

10. With Onion Skinning turned on, use the **Brush** tool again and write the word **jitter** with a circle around it over the top of the onion-skinned ghosted image of the artwork you created in Keyframe 1. It doesn't matter if the artwork doesn't match perfectly. The fact that the artwork is drawn slightly different, in each keyframe, is exactly what causes the jittery animation effect!

NOTE | Onion Skin Markers

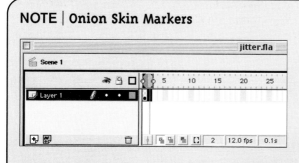

At the top of the Timeline you will notice a gray bar with a draggable bracket on each end appear after you click the Onion Skin button. These are called **Onion Skin markers**. The **Start Onion Skin** marker (the one on the left) is on Frame 1, (the start of your animation) and the **End Onion Skin** marker (the one on the right) is on Frame 2 (the last frame of your animation thus far).

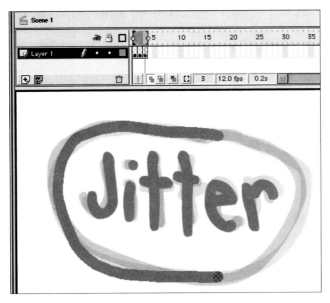

11. Press **F7** to insert another blank keyframe so you can draw the third frame of your animation. With Onion Skinning still turned on, use the Brush tool again and write the word **jitter** with a circle around it over the top of the ghost image you can see from keyframes 1 and 2.

12. Choose **Control > Loop Playback** so that you can see the animation repeat over and over.

13. Press **Enter/Return** to test the movie! You will see the artwork jitter!

Note: *If you click and drag your Playhead to the right or left and let go, the Start Onion Skin slider will move. Basically, Onion Skinning will move along with your Playhead. If you move your Playhead, the Onion Skinning will move too.*

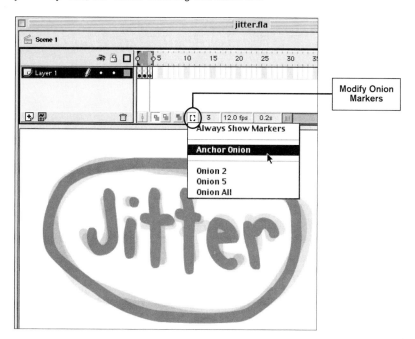

If you do not want the Onion markers to move, you can choose **Anchor Onion** *from the* **Modify Onion markers** *button at the bottom of the Timeline. This will anchor your onion skinning in place and no matter where you move the Playhead, your onion skinning will be locked where it is until you unlock it again or manually drag the Start or End Onion Skinning sliders.*

14. Save and close this file.

4. ——————————Keyframes with Erasing Content

In this exercise, you will work with keyframes again. You'll learn how to create an animation effect by erasing sections of the new keyframe, rather than adding content to it.

1. Open the **keyframes.fla** file located inside the **chap_05** folder. This file has one layer and one keyframe, which contains a drawing of a Simon the cat. Got milk? ;-)

In this exercise, you will insert a keyframe that will copy the contents from the previous keyframe and place that content on the new keyframe. This technique can be useful in situations like this one, where you don't want to draw the entire cat for each frame of the animation.

2. Select **Insert > Keyframe**. This will add a keyframe and place a copy of the cat on Frame 2 of the Timeline. Notice that your Playhead automatically moved to Frame 2.

---

3. Select the **Brush** from the Toolbox. From the **Brush Size** pop-up menu, select the smallest brush size. Make sure you chose an appropriate Fill color for the cat's tongue.

4. Using the Brush, draw a small tongue in the right corner of the cat's mouth. Oh don't worry, he won't bite.

5. Press **F6** to insert another keyframe.

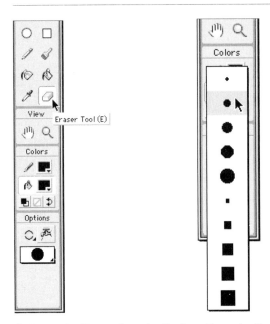

6. Select the **Eraser** from the Toolbox. From the **Eraser Shape** pop-up menu, select the second option from the top. This will give you an eraser small enough to erase just the kitty's tongue.

7. Using the **Eraser**, hold the mouse button down and drag over the kitty's tongue until it is completely gone. You may want to zoom to 200% so you don't accidentally erase his mouth.

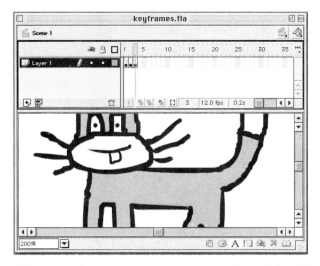

8. Using the **Brush**, draw another tongue in the middle of his mouth.

9. Press **F6** to add a fourth keyframe. Thankfully, with keyframes, you don't have to draw the kitty on each frame. Phew, that would sure create a lot of hairballs!

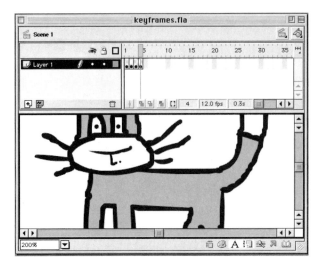

10. Use the **Eraser** again to remove his tongue. No wonder his tongue is so rough, yours would get rough too if you kept erasing it. ;-)

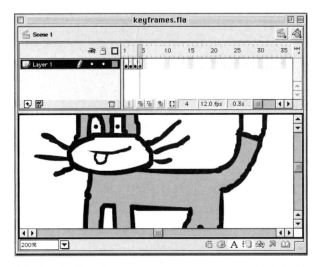

11. Use the **Brush** to create another tongue on the left side of the kitty's mouth. There, now it will look like he is licking his lips.

12. Press **Return/Enter** to preview the animation on the stage. Cute.

13. Save and Close this file. You'll use it later in this chapter.

5. ——————Understanding Frame Rate

Now that you have created a couple of frame-by-frame animations, it's time to better understand what the frame rate of your movie achieves. The frame rate defines how many frames your animation will try to play in one second. We use the word "try" because there is no guarantee that your movie will play back at the specified frame rate. We will explain more about that at the end of this exercise. In the following steps, you will start by opening a file that contains a simple frame-by-frame animation of a mouse moving across the screen (being chased by Simon the cat, of course). You will test the animation to preview the current frame rate and then lower it to see the impact it has on playback speed.

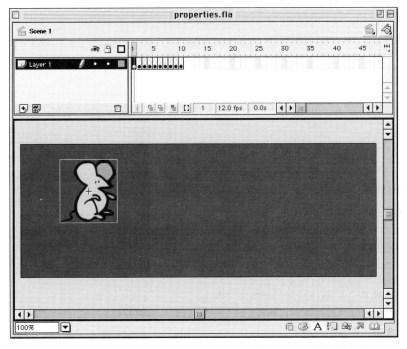

1. Open the **properties.fla** file located inside the **chap_05** folder. This file contains one layer with a frame-by-frame animation of a mouse moving across the screen. Got cheese?

2. Press **Return/Enter** to watch the animation play on the stage. The animation will play at the default frame rate of 12 fps.

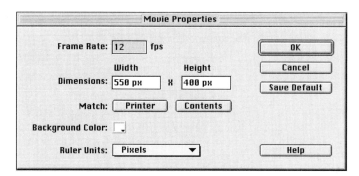

3. Select **Modify > Movie** or **Cmd + M** (Mac), **Ctrl + M** (Windows). This will open the **Movie Properties** dialog box.

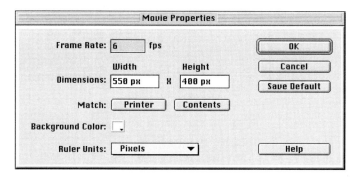

4. Enter **Frame Rate: 6**. This will reduce the frame rate to six frames per second, reducing the speed of the animation by half. Click **OK**.

5. Press **Return/Enter**. Notice how the animation plays much slower and kind of stutters. You are taking twice the time to play the same number of frames. The lower the frame rate, the slower the animation will play.

6. Select **File > Save** to save the changes you made to this file. You can close this file; you won't need it for the next exercise.

What is a Frame Rate?

The frame rate determines the number of frame your movie plays per second. This directly relates to the length of time your animation takes to play.

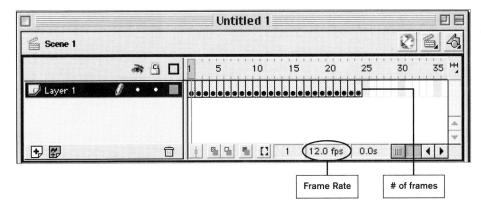

Here's how to use the frame rate to calculate the playback time of your Flash animation. Take the total number of frames in your Timeline and divide that by the frame rate and the result is how many seconds it will take to view your movie.

For example, if your timeline has 24 frames and your frame rate is set to 12 FPS (frames per second), your animation will display in two seconds. The chart below gives you several examples of how frame rate affects the length of time your animation takes to play.

# of Frames	/	Frame Rate	=	Time
24 frames	/	12 fps	=	2 seconds
36 frames	/	12 fps	=	3 seconds
48 frames	/	24 fps	=	2 seconds
72 frames	/	24 fps	=	3 seconds

Recommended Frame Rates in Flash

When you set a frame rate in Flash, you've set the *maximum* frame rate for your movie, or how quickly the movie "tries" to display. The actual playback frame rate is dependent upon several factors, including download speed and the processor speed of the computer viewing the movie. If the frame rate is set higher than the computer can display, the movie will play as fast as its processor will allow. So, if you set your frame rate to 200 (which is really high), the average computer would not display the movie at that rate. Here's another wrinkle: since some Flash frames may have more objects, colors, or transparency than others, they are more difficult for the computer to render. When the computer is having difficulty displaying a movie at a set frame rate, actual frame rate can vary during playback due to the varying rendering requirements from one frame to another.

Based on all this information, we would recommend that you use a frame rate of at least 12 fps and not more than 25 fps, so that the average computer can display your movie as you intended. A frame rate of 22 fps seems to work well most of the time and this is very similar to motion pictures, which typically use a frame rate of 24 frames per second.

6. _____Inserting and Deleting Frames

As you learn to create frame-by-frame and other types of animation, you will at some point want to adjust their speed. In the previous exercise, you learned that adjusting the frame rate will do just that, but it will affect the entire movie. So, in this exercise, we will show you how adding and removing frames to your Timeline can help control the timing of your animation. This means that you can have multiple animations playing at different tempos, even though they all share the same frame rate.

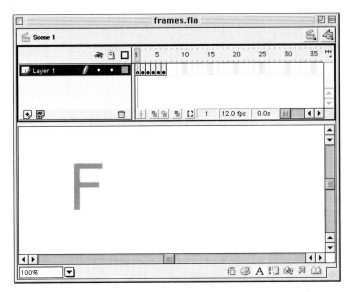

1. Open the **frames.fla** file located inside the **chap_05** folder. This file contains a simple frame-by-frame animation with some text. You'll be learning more about how to use text in Chapter 13, *"Text."*

2. Press **Return/Enter** to preview the animation on the stage. The animation will play pretty quickly. In fact, it's playing so fast that you almost lose the effect of the text appearing one letter at a time.

If you adjust the frame rate to slow down this animation, it would also affect every other animation in this project. This could cause some serious problems if you wanted other sections of your movie to play at a different speed. So, you must find another way to slow down the animation. One way to do this is by inserting frames, at strategic points, to lengthen parts of the animation. That's exactly what the following steps will show you how to do.

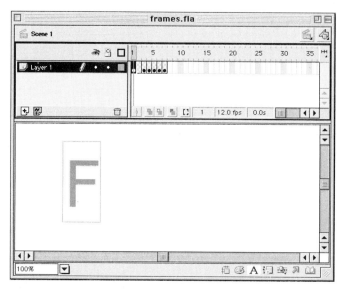

3. Click in **Frame 1** of **Layer 1** and select **Insert > Frame**. This will insert a frame between Frames 1 and 2, extending the Timeline by one frame.

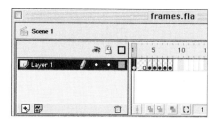

4. Press **F5** to insert another frame. Each time you select **Insert > Frame** or press **F5**, you will insert one frame and extend the Timeline.

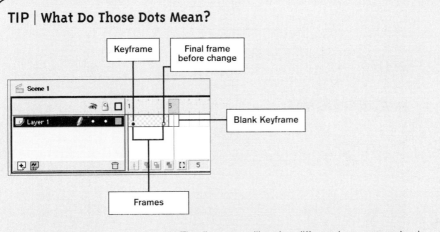

TIP | What Do Those Dots Mean?

Keyframe

Final frame before change

Blank Keyframe

Frames

As you start adding content to your Timeline, you will notice different icons appearing in your Timeline. The black dots indicate keyframes. The light gray frames, after the keyframe, indicate no change in content; the final frame before the next keyframe has a hollow square in the lower corner. The white frame, directly after the frame with a hollow square, is a blank keyframe.

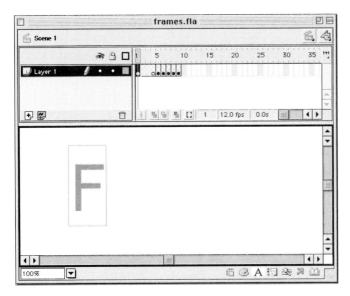

5. Press **F5** again so that you have a total of three additional frames between your first two keyframes. By extending the space between the first two keyframes in the Timeline, you are able to control the timing of the animation, as your image will display for a longer period of time.

6. Press **Return/Enter** to preview the animation on the stage. Now there is a noticeable delay between the letters F and L.

7. Click in Frame 5 of the Timeline. This is where the second keyframe should be located.

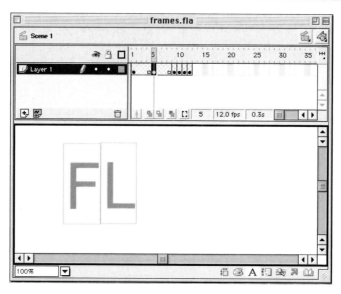

8. Press **F5** three times to insert three frames in the Timeline. This will create a short pause between the letters L and A.

9. Repeat this process for the other letters in the animation. When you are finished, your Timeline should look like the one shown above.

10. Press **Return/Enter** to preview your animation on your stage. See how much slower the entire animation plays, and you didn't have to touch the frame rate for the movie. Nice.

Great, so now you know that you can control the timing of your animations without having to adjust the frame rate of your entire movie. You have just seen that by inserting frames you can slow down an animation, so it should be no surprise that by deleting frames you can increase the timing of the animation. We will show you this next.

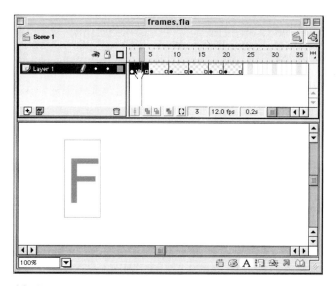

11. Click in **Frame 2** of the Timeline. Notice that a small hand icon appears and selects the range of Frames 1 to 5. This isn't what you wanted to select—you only want Frame 2 selected. We will show you how to do this.

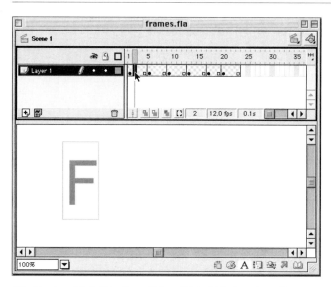

12. Cmd + Click (Mac) or **Ctrl + Click** (Windows) on **Frame 2** of the Timeline. Notice that your cursor becomes an arrow and you select only Frame 2 this time. In order to select a single frame, you must hold down this key as you click. Phew, don't you wish someone had told you sooner! ;-)

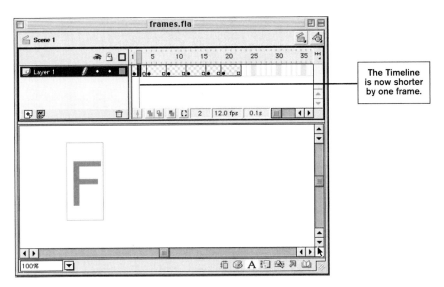

The Timeline is now shorter by one frame.

13. With **Frame 2** selected, select **Insert > Remove Frames**. This will remove the selected frame, shortening your Timeline by one frame and decreasing the amount of time between the F and L letters in your animation.

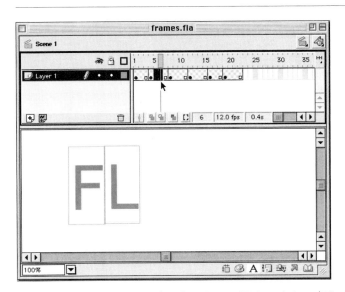

14. Cmd + Click and drag (Mac) or **Ctrl + Click and drag** (Windows) and select **Frames 5** and **6**. Cmd or Ctrl + Clicking and dragging allows you to select a specific range of frames. Make sure you hold the appropriate key down as you click and drag, otherwise you might accidentally move keyframes around.

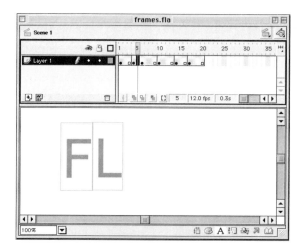

15. With Frames 5 and 6 still selected, press **Shift + F5**, the keyboard shortcut for removing frames. This will remove the selected frames and shorten your Timeline by two frames.

16. Go ahead and use Shift + F5 to remove two frames between each of the keyframes in the Timeline. When you're finished, your Timeline should look like the one shown above.

17. Press **Return/Enter** to preview your animation on the stage. The animation will play much faster than it did before, because there are fewer frames between the keyframes. Now you know at least two ways to speed up or slow down the timing of your animation.

18. Save and close this file.

7. _____Copying and Reversing Frames

Creating a looping animation (one that repeats indefinitely) can be a lot of work if you had to draw all the frames over and over. In Flash, you can quickly and easily copy, paste, and reverse a sequence of frames to create a looping animation. In this exercise, you will develop a looping animation by copying and reversing a sequence of frames.

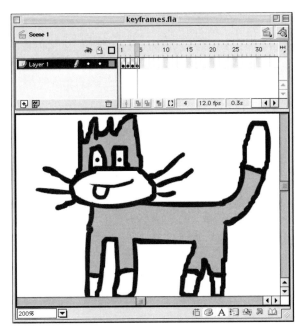

1. Open the **keyframes.fla** file located inside the **chap_05** folder. This is the same file you worked on earlier.

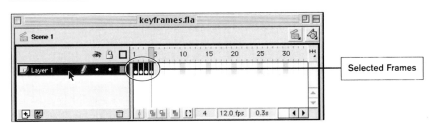

Selected Frames

2. Click to the right of the layer name. This is an easy way to select all of the frames on a layer. Before you can copy a range of frames, you want to make sure you have selected them first.

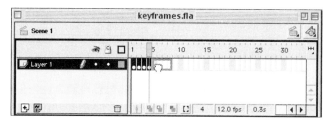

3. Move your cursor over the selected frames. Your cursor will turn into a small hand. Click and drag to the right. But don't release the mouse button just yet! **Note**: the light gray outline surrounding the frames indicates where they'll be moved when you release the mouse button.

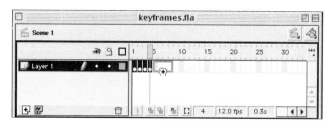

4. While still holding the mouse button down, press the **Option** (Mac) or **Alt** (Windows) key. Notice that a small plus sign appears on the backside of the hand. This indicates that you will duplicate, not move, the frames when you release the mouse button.

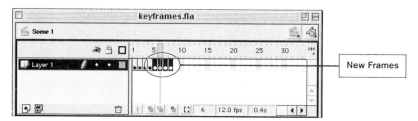

5. Release the mouse button. This will place a copy of the selected frames in Frames 5–8.

6. With the **Frames 5** through **8** still selected, choose **Modify > Frames > Reverse**. You won't see any noticeable reversal in your Timeline, but you will when you test the movie.

7. Press **Return / Enter** to preview your animation on your stage. The cat's tongue will lick from right to left and then left to right, creating a looping effect. **Tip**: If you set **Control > Loop Playback**, you can watch the animation preview loop endlessly.

8. Save and close this file.

8. _____Testing Movies

So far, you've been testing your movies by pressing **Return/Enter** and watching them play on your stage. This is a great way to test the frame rate, but there are other ways to test your work. In this exercise, we will show you how to preview the actual (.swf) file with the **Test Movie** feature and how to preview your movie in a browser with the **Preview in Browser** feature. You will also learn a really easy way to produce the HTML file needed to hold your .swf file. More in-depth instruction on publishing Flash content is covered in Chapter 15, "*Publishing*."

1. Open the **frames.fla** file located inside the **chap_05** folder.

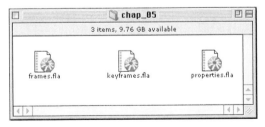

This file should have been saved inside the chap_05 folder. Knowing where your .fla file has been saved is an important thing to know before you use the Test Movie and Preview in Browser features, because as you'll see, Flash automatically generates new files and saves them with your .fla files when you use these features. If you saved your file in a different location, make sure you know where it's located.

Resize Handle

2. Choose **Control > Test Movie.** This will open a new window with a preview of the .swf file that would be exported if you chose to **publish** your movie right now.

Want to see something cool? Click on the Resize handle of the Preview window and drag to make your window larger. Notice that your animation scales with the size of the window. Sweet! A huge advantage of using Flash for your Web graphics is that your content can be scaleable.

TIP | Loop-de-loop

At this point, you're probably wondering why your animation is looping (playing over and over). This is the default behavior of all movies in Flash, although you don't see it when you simply choose **Return/Enter** to preview your work within Flash (unless you set the file to **Loop Playback,** under the Control menu). If you uploaded your published file to the Web, however, it would loop. You will learn to control the looping in your final .swf file later when you learn how to add actions to frames in Chapter 12, *"ActionScripting Basics."* If all this looping is making you dizzy, you can select **Control > Loop** to turn off this feature temporarily.

3. Select **Window > Controller** (Mac) or **Window > Toolbars > Controller** (PC). You'll get a small toolbar on your screen that looks like the front of your VCR or other media player. This handy little gadget helps you control your animation while you are in this Preview window.

4. Press the **Stop** button. As you probably guessed, this will stop your animation.

TIP | Testing at 100%

When you test your movie using the **Control > Test Movie** command, the file you created will be previewed in a new window, but it will display at a size greater than 100%. This can be very misleading if you aren't aware of this behavior. After you select **Control > Test Movie**, select **View > Magnification > 100%** to resize the window to the appropriate size.

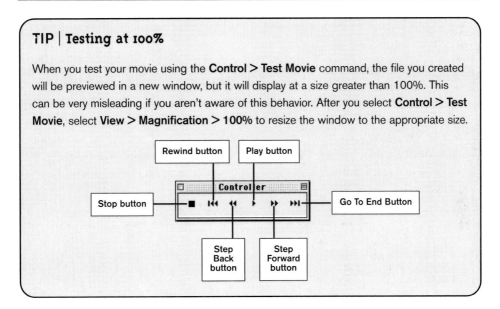

5. Press the **Play** button. Yes, you guessed it; this will play your animation. Go ahead and take a few minutes to play with the other buttons on the Controller.

Something else happened, behind the scenes, when you selected Control > Test Movie. Flash automatically created the .swf file for this movie and saved it inside the same place where you saved your .fla file. Let us show you what we mean.

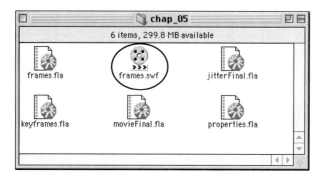

6. Browse to the **chap_05** folder on your desktop. Notice that there is a **frames.swf** file inside this folder. This was automatically generated by Flash. The .swf file is the file that you would add to an HTML page, much like a .gif or .jpg.

7. Return to Flash and close the Preview window.

8. Select **File > Publish Preview > Default – (HTML) F12**. This will launch your default browser with a preview of your .swf file inside the browser window. This is a quick an easy way to see what your .swf files will look like in a browser. We will discuss a more appropriate and formal way of publishing your Flash movies later in Chapter 15, *"Publishing."*

Again, Flash is doing a little something extra behind the scenes. When you preview your Flash movie in a browser, Flash will automatically create an HTML file, and a .swf file if there isn't one already, in the same location as the .fla file. So, make sure you always know where you save your .fla files.

TIP | Why Does Flash Use Netscape 3?

If you have Netscape Navigator 3.0 installed on your computer and you try to preview your movie in a browser. Flash might use Netscape Navigator 3.0 as your default browser. This is just a quirk of working with Flash. If you want to have the Flash content play in a browser of your choice, you can change the default browser to your preferred browser in a few steps. You can find a great explanation on how to do this for either a Mac of Windows machine on Macromedia's web site: **http://www.macromedia.com/ support/flash/** and see techNote 15133.

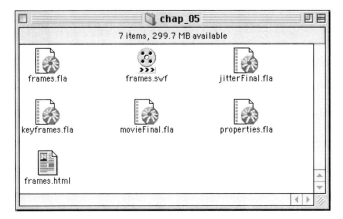

9. Hide Flash for a moment and browse to the **chap_05** folder on your desktop. Notice that there is a **frames.html** file inside this folder. This was automatically generated by Flash to hold your frames.swf file. Now you have everything you need to publish to the Web. How cool is that? ;-)

10. Return to Flash and select **File > Save** to save the changes you made to this file. You can close this file—you are finished with this chapter! It was a long, but essential part of your animation training.

Well, that's about it for the basic stuff. We hope this chapter served as a good introduction to some of the issues and features of working with animation in Flash. The next three chapters deal with more complex and specific issues, such as symbols and instances, motion, and shape tweening. Now would be a great time for a break—you worked through a lot and deserve one!

6.

Shape Tweening

chap_6

Flash 5
H•O•T CD-ROM

Most of you have seen animations on the Web or on television that show an object transforming (or morphing) from one shape into another. You can create this same effect in your Flash movies through learning a technique called shape tweening.

Shape tweening works like this. If you wanted to create an animation that shows the letter X transforming into a circle, you could create the starting point of the animation–the X– and the ending point–the circle–by placing them on separate keyframes, leaving empty frames between them. By setting up a shape tween, Flash automatically generates the art for all the empty frames between the two images. This technique saves a lot of time by not requiring you to draw each frame and also creates a distinct effect of a "morph."

The following exercises offer a thorough introduction to working with shape tweening. After you work through them, you will expand your Flash skill set to include tweening, shape tweening, hinting, animating gradients and multiple shape tweens. Phew, there is a lot of material to get through, so go ahead and get started!

What is Shape Tweening?

In order to describe shape tweening, we need to define a few terms—shape, keyframes and tweening. Here's a handy chart to refer to if these terms are new to you:

Shape Tweening Definitions

Shape

In Flash, a *shape* is a vector-based object, or series of objects. You can create shapes in Flash using any of the drawing tools, or you can bring shapes into Flash from other vector-creation programs, such as Freehand or Illustrator. In order for a shape to be suitable for "shape tweening," it cannot be composed of grouped objects, bitmaps, or symbols (You will learn about symbols in Chapter 7, "*Symbols and Instances*.") Type can be the subject of a shape tween if it is first converted to a shape. This process is called "breaking apart." You will learn how to break type apart later in this chapter.

Keyframes

In traditional animation, a "key" or "lead" animator would draw "extremes," or the important frames of artwork that defined what the motion would look like. If, for example, a cartoon character's arm moved up and then down, a key artist would draw two *keyframes*, the first in an up position and the second in a down position.

In Flash, a keyframe is symbolized in the Timeline by a gray frame with a filled black circle at the bottom. In this example, the first arm would be inside the first keyframe and the second arm would reside in the next keyframe.

Tweening

The term *tweening* is borrowed from traditional cel animation terminology, and is slang for "inbetweening." In cel animation, a job position exists called an "inbetweener." It is the inbetweener's job to take the keyframes that a lead animator created and draw all the frames that go between them that describe the motion. For example, the inbetween artist would take the two keyframes described in the previous description, and would reference them in order to draw a series of images of the arm in various positions between the up and down position.

Flash lets you use shape tweening to animate between lines and shapes and animate the colors and gradients that are applied to them. This process is often referred to as "morphing." The illustration below is a good example of a shape tween:

keyframe 1   *keyframe 2*

The first step in creating a shape tween is to create two unique keyframes.

Flash will then interpolate the difference between the keyframes and automatically generate all of the frames in between. Shape tweening is the only process in Flash that lets you quickly animate from one distinct shape to another. It can also be used to animate from one gradient to another, and/or one color to another, and/or one position to another. As you might imagine, creating this kind of animation by drawing each frame of artwork would be rather tedious. The shape tweening feature in Flash automates this process.

The list below outlines some of the things that can and can't be done with shape tweens in Flash. You'll learn about these in detail in chapter 8, "Motion Tweening."

What shape tweening can do

- Tween the shape of an object
- Tween the color of an object (including a color with transparency)
- Tween the position of an object on the stage
- Tween text that has been broken apart
- Tween gradients

What shape tweening can't do

- Tween grouped objects
- Tween symbols
- Tween non-broken-apart text

I. _____Shape Tweening

In this first exercise, you will learn how to create a very simple shape tween. You will create an animation of a circle changing into a square by creating the beginning and ending frames of the animation sequence. While the results might be a bit simplistic, this exercise is a good introduction to creating shape tweens in Flash.

1. Copy the **chap_06** folder, located on the **H•O•T CD-ROM**, to your hard drive. You need to have this folder on your hard drive in order to save changes to the files inside it.

2. Select **File > New** to create a new blank document. Save this file as **shape_tween.fla** inside the **chap_06** folder.

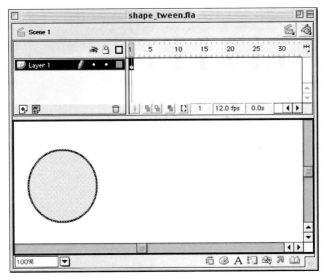

3. Using the **Oval** tool, draw a circle on Frame 1 of Layer 1. This will be the starting frame of this shape tween animation.

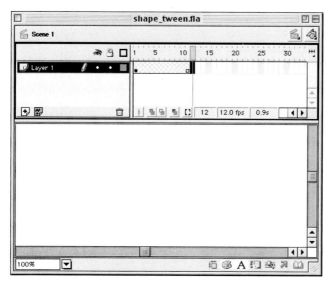

4. Select **Frame 12** on Layer 1 and press **F7** to add a blank keyframe. The circle on your screen will disappear so you have a place to draw the ending frame of this animation.

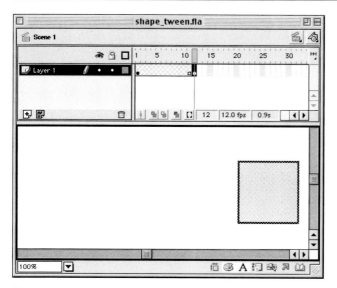

5. Using the **Rectangle** tool, draw a square along the right side of the stage. This will be the ending frame of your animation.

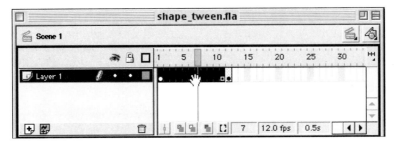

6. Click anywhere in the Timeline between the two keyframes to select that range of frames. You want to make sure you have this selected before you apply a shape tween.

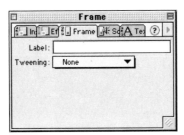

7. Make sure the **Frame** panel is visible, if it's not, select **Window > Panel > Frame** to make it visible.

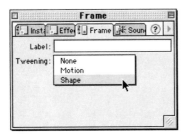

8. From the **Tweening** drop-down menu, select **Shape**. This will create a shape tween between the two keyframes in Layer 1.

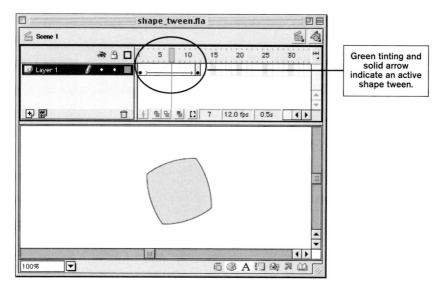

Green tinting and solid arrow indicate an active shape tween.

Once you have applied a shape tween between two keyframes, the Timeline will be shaded green and a long arrow will appear between the keyframes. This is a visual indication that a shape tween is active.

9. Press **Return/Enter** on your keyboard to preview what you have done so far. The circle will gradually turn into a square. See how much easier this is instead of drawing each frame, one at a time?

10. Select **File > Save** to save the changes you made to this file. Don't close this file; you will need it for the next exercise.

WARNING | **Spotting Broken Tweens**

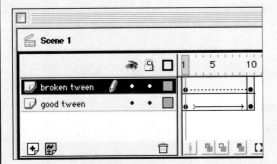

As you work more with shape tweens (and motion tweens in Chapter 8), you may see a broken line (dashed) appear in your Timeline instead of a solid line. Any time you see a broken line in your Timeline, this indicates that the shape tween (or motion tween) is not working properly. This can make it easy to spot problems in your animations.

2. _____Shape Hinting

When working with shape tweening, Flash will automatically determine how to change from one shape to the next. Because this is an automatic process, you don't have complete control over how the tween occurs. Shape hinting is a feature in Flash that helps you regain some control over this process. Primarily, shape hinting is used to fix a shape tween that does something that you don't want it to do. In this exercise you are going to take the shape tween that you created in the previous exercise and add shape hints to better control how your first shape morphs into your second shape.

> **1.** You should still have the file from the previous exercise (**shape_tween.fla**) open. If you don't, go ahead and open it now.

> **2.** Press **Return** (Mac) or **Enter** (Windows) on your keyboard to preview this shape tween.

> *Notice how as the shape tween progresses, the corners of the box appear to rotate to the right? This is how Flash decided to create this shape tween. What if you wanted the shape to change, but you didn't want it to rotate in this direction? In this exercise, you're going to use shape hinting to eliminate the appearance of rotation as the shape changes.*

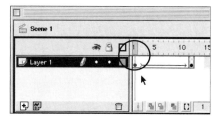

> **3.** Make sure the Playhead is over the first frame. When you add shape hints, you must start on the first frame of your animation.

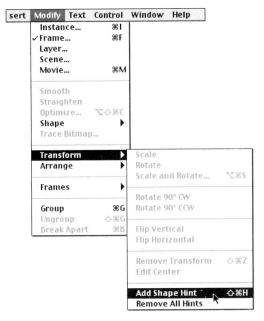

4. Choose **Modify > Transform > Add Shape Hint**.

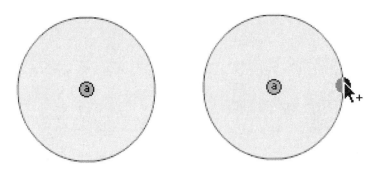

5. A red circle with an "a" will appear in the middle of your stage. This is a shape hint. Click and drag the shape hint to the middle-right of the circle shape. (**Note:** you must use the **Arrow** tool from the Toolbox to do this).

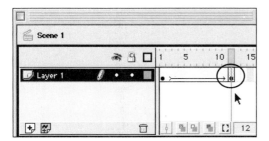

6. Move the **Playhead** to the last frame (**Frame 12**) of your animation.

7. Click and drag the red "**a**" dot that is in the center of your square to the upper-right corner of the square.

When you let go of your mouse, see how the shape hint changes from red to green? Why? This is how Flash lets you know that the shape hint has been accepted and it is a change that Flash can understand. When your shape hint doesn't turn to green on the ending keyframe, it means that Flash didn't understand what you were trying to do. As a troubleshooting tip, try repositioning your shape hint. Sometimes it just takes a small adjustment for Flash to get the hint (no pun intended!).

8. Press **Return/Enter** to preview the effect of changing the shape tween by using shape hints.

Without shape hints—the circle rotates into a square.

With shape hints—the circle makes better transition into a square.

When you add a shape hint to the first keyframe on the right side of the circle and then add another on the second keyframe to the top-right corner of the square, you tell Flash not to rotate the square to match the two points.

9. Try experimenting with moving the shape hints around. By moving the hints even slightly, you can give a completely different look to your shape tween.

TIP | Multiple Shape Hints

If you were to add another shape hint, it would also appear as a red circle but it would have the letter "b" in the middle of it. The next shape hint after that would be "c", and the next would be… I think you see the pattern here. When you get to "z," that's it! You're all out of shape hints. You're given a total of 26 shape hints per shape tween. But don't worry, 26 shape hints should be far too many for most animations. If you find yourself needing more than 26 shape hints, you might want to rethink the complexity of your animation, as by then it is probably putting a lot of strain on the end user's computer processor.

Now that you know how to add shape hints, you should know how to remove them as well. The following steps will show you how to remove a shape hint.

10. Click and drag the **Playhead** back to **Frame 1**.

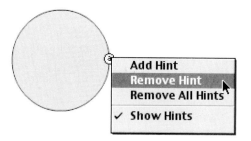

11. Ctrl + Click (Mac) or **Right Click** (Windows) and select **Remove Hint** from the pop-up menu. This will remove the selected shape hint and return the animation back to its original setting.

12. Choose **File > Save**. You might want to look back at your handiwork later. You can also close this file; you won't need it to complete the next exercise.

TIP | Quickly Removing Shape Hints

If you add too many shape hints and really mess up your animation, don't worry. You can remove them all with just a few clicks. **Ctrl + Click** (Mac) or **Right + Click** (Windows) and select **Remove All Hints** from the pop-up menu. You can also select **Modify > Transform > Remove All Shape Hints**. Either option will remove every shape hint from your animation. Thank goodness for this feature.

3. _____Multiple Shape Hints

Shape hinting can work on more than one shape, and is often used by Flash animators who want specific control over how Flash interprets tweens between shapes. This next exercise will demonstrate a common problem of overlapping shapes in shape tweening, and shows how shape hinting can be used to correct this problem.

1. Open the **needhints.fla** files located inside the **chap_06** folder. This file contains a completed shape tween.

2. Press **Return/Enter** to preview the animation.

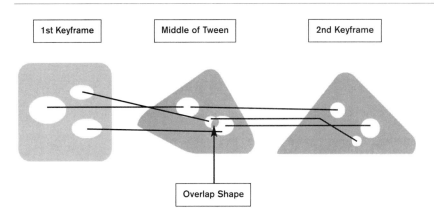

Notice that the shapes cross each other in the middle of the tween. This creates additional shapes in the overlap area that may not be what you expect. Sometimes you might want an effect like this, but the purpose of this exercise is to show you how to control the shape tween and prevent this behavior.

3. Make sure the **Playhead** is moved back to Frame 1 of the animation.

4. Select **Modify > Transform > Add Shape.** This will add a shape hint, with the letter a, to the center of your shape.

*Tip: To add a shape hint, you can also use the shortcut keys: **Shift + Cmd + H** (Mac) or **Shift + Ctrl + H** (Windows).*

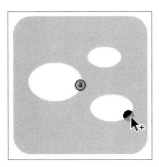

5. Click and drag the "**a**" shape hint to the lower corner of the bottom-right circle. It will automatically snap to the nearest shape. (In this case it was the inside of the circle.) The shape hint is still red because you have not placed the shape hint at the last keyframe.

6. Move the **Playhead** to **Frame 10**. You need to set the shape hint for this keyframe in order for it to function properly.

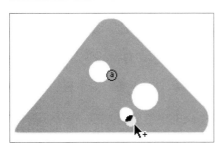

7. Drag the "**a**" shape hint to the lower corner of the bottom circle. Notice that the shape hint turns green when you release your mouse button. This indicates that it is now active.

8. Move the **Playhead** back to **Frame 1**. Notice that the shape hint is now yellow. Active shape hints are yellow on the first keyframe and green on the last keyframe.

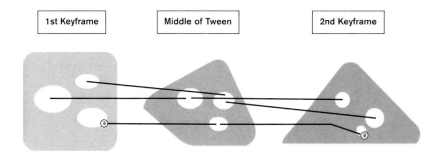

The lines above illustrate which circles on the first keyframe are changing into the circles on the second keyframe. By simply adding one shape hint, it made it easier for Flash to determine which circles changed into which between the keyframes.

9. Press **Return/Enter** to test your movie. The overlapping shape is gone and you have controlled which circle morphs into the other with the shape hint.

10. When you are finished, select **File > Save** to save the changes you made to this file. You can close the file; it won't be used again in this chapter.

Animating Gradients

You can also use the shape tween process to animate gradients. This can produce dramatic lighting effects, such as glows and strobes. In this exercise, you will learn how to modify and animate a gradient.

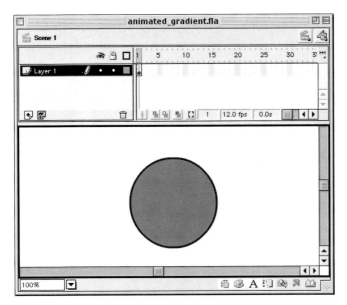

1. Select **File > Open** and browse to the **animated_gradient.fla** file located inside the **chap_06** folder. This file contains a single layer with a blue circle in Frame 1. This is the starting frame of your animation.

2. From the Toolbox, select the **Paint Bucket** tool.

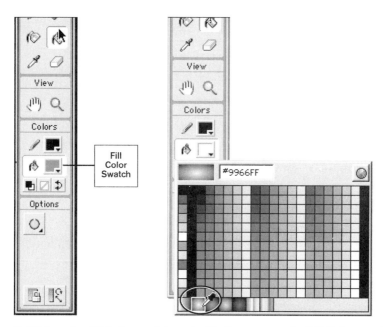

3. Click on the **Fill Color** swatch on the Toolbox to open the **Fill Color** panel. At the very bottom of this panel are some gradients. Choose the black-and-white radial gradient; the one that is second from the left.

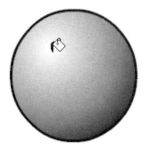

Using the Paint Bucket tool, click in the top-left area of the blue circle. This will fill the circle with a radial gradient. The spot you click defines where the center of the radial gradient is placed. As the radial gradient is white in the center and black on the outside, the area where you click is where the white point of the gradient will be.

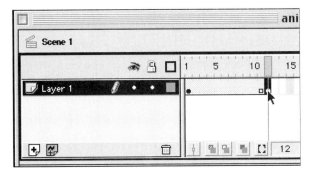

Click on Frame 12 in the Timeline and add a new keyframe by pressing F6. As you might remember from Chapter 5, "Animation Basics," F6 will copy the contents from the previous keyframe and place it on the new keyframe. This can save you from having to recreate entire pieces of artwork, and it's especially useful when you only want to make minor changes.

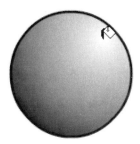

4. Select your **Paint Bucket** tool again and this time click on the top-right of the gradient circle. Now it appears as if a light source is coming from the opposite side of the circle. This is the ending frame of your animation.

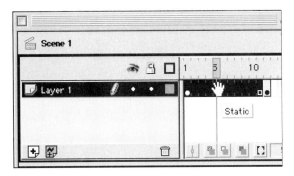

5. Click anywhere between the two keyframes.

6. Make sure the **Frame** panel is visible. If it's not, select **Window > Panels > Frame**.

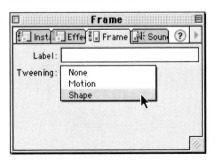

7. From the **Tweening** drop-down menu, choose **Shape** to create a shape tween between the two keyframes.

8. Select **Control > Test Movie** to preview your shape tween. Now it looks like a 3D sphere that is being lit by a moving light source. When you are finished previewing this animation, click the close box to close the preview window.

9. Even though the exercise is complete, it is still possible to change your mind and try something different. From the **Fill** pop-up menu, select a red radial gradient. Move your Playhead to the last keyframe. Using the **Paint Bucket** tool, fill the circle with this new gradient. Test the movie again. Animating the colors of gradients is that simple.

Don't be deceived by the word "shape" in "shape tweening." As you just saw, shape tweens can be used to create animations that don't involve changing one shape into another. In this example, shape tweening was used to animate a gradient.

10. Go ahead and keep experimenting with other gradients. Don't worry, you can't break a thing—just have some fun and try to increase your comfort level in working with gradients.

11. Select **File > Save** to save the changes you made to this document. You can also close this file.

5.———————————**Animated Glows**

In the previous exercise you learned how to animate a basic gradient. In this exercise, you will build on what you learned to create an animated glow. This technique can be useful for creating special lighting effects, such as solar flares, drop shadows, etc.

> **1.** Open the file **animated_gradient2.fla** located inside the **chap_06** folder. This file has a black background and contains a single circle that is filled with a gradient on Layer 1.

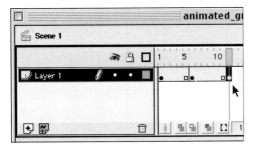

> **2.** Click on **Frame 6** on the Timeline and press **F6** to insert a keyframe. Create a third keyframe on Frame 12 as well.

This time, you'll learn to create a shape tween over three keyframes instead of two. This technique is often used when the first and last keyframe are identical, but a middle keyframe contains a change. In this exercise, the affect of creating three keyframes will cause the glow to start small, get bigger, and then shrink to return to its original size.

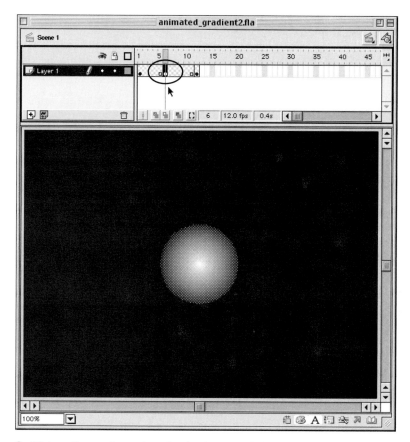

3. Click on **Frame 6** to select that keyframe and all of its content. The selection mesh over the graphics confirms that it is selected.

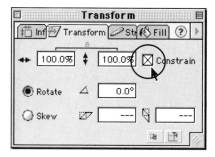

4. Open the **Transform** panel by choosing **Window > Panels > Transform**. Make sure there is a check mark in the **Constrain** checkbox to make your glow resize proportionally. You are going to use the **Transform** panel to make this gradient a little bigger.

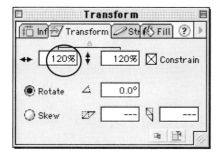

5. In the **Transform** panel, enter **120%** in the **Width** field. Notice how as you type "**120**" into this field, it is also automatically entered in the **Height** field for you too? That's because the Constrain checkbox is selected.

6. Hit **Return/Enter** on your keyboard to preview the animation that you just created. You should see the glow on the stage grow a little bit bigger (20% bigger to be exact).

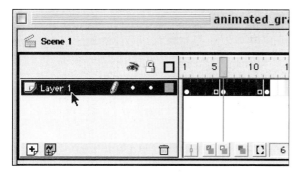

7. Click once on the layer where it says "Layer 1." Clicking once on the layer selects all of the frames on that layer. Now you can turn on shape tweening in the following steps. In Flash 5, you can invoke shape tweens across multiple keyframes in one operation.

8. Make sure your **Frame** panel is visible, if its not, select **Window > Panels > Frame**.

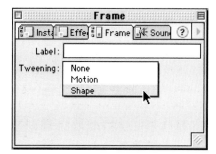

9. From the **Tweening** drop-down menu, select **Shape** just as you did in the last exercise. This time, a shape tween will be created among the three keyframes, creating an animated glow effect.

10. Select **Control > Test Movie** to preview your animated glow.

All you had to do was create three keyframes, change the size of the ball in the middle keyframe, and turn on shape tweening! When you are finished previewing, close the preview window.

11. Select **File > Save** to save the changes you made to this file. Close this file.

TIP | Resizing Objects

When you scale an object using the **Scale** tool (located on the tool bar when the **Arrow** tool is chosen), it resizes the object from the top-left. If you use the **Transform** panel to resize an object instead, it will resize from the center of the object.

6. _____Shape Tweening Text

In many Flash animations, you'll often see typography as the source art used in a shape tween. In order to use text as a source, it first has to be "broken apart." The act of breaking apart converts the text from being editable text into an uneditable "shape." The reason why it is important to break text apart in this exercise is that editable type cannot be the source of a shape tween. It's one of the rules of shape tweening – you can't use grouped objects as source art for this effect. While you might not think of type as a grouped object, by Flash's definition it must be broken apart to become a shape. You will learn more about working with text tools in Chapter 13, "*Text.*" For now, you will work with a file that already contains text so you can focus on learning how to create a shape tween with it.

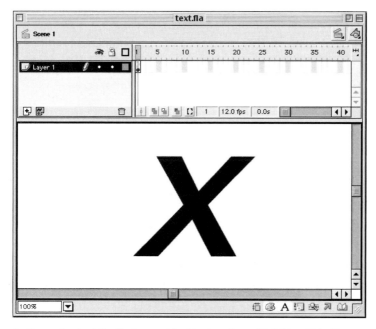

1. Open the **text.fla** file located inside the **chap_06** folder. This file contains a single layer with a large X on Frame 1. The X is still in an editable format, which means you can double-click on it and change the letter to something else.

Next, you will learn how to convert the text into a shape, by using the Break Apart feature in Flash.

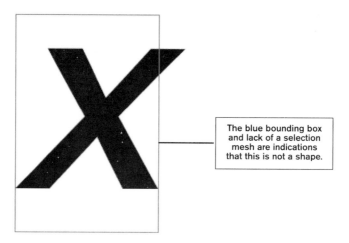

The blue bounding box and lack of a selection mesh are indications that this is not a shape.

2. Using the **Arrow** tool, click to select the large X on the stage. Notice that a thin blue rectangle appears around the text. This is a visual indication that the X is still text, which is editable and not a shape yet.

3. With the X still selected, choose **Modify > Break Apart**. The text will be broken apart and converted into a shape, ready to be shape tweened. The selection mesh over the X is an indication that you are now working with a shape. This will become the first frame of your animation.

4. Select **Frame 10** and press the **F7** key to add a blank keyframe for the ending frame of your animation.

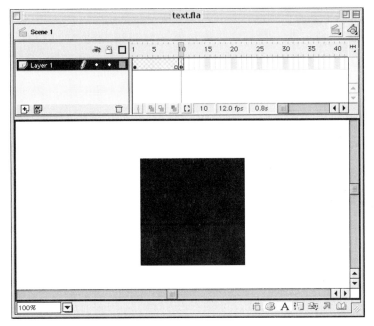

5. Using the **Rectangle** tool, create a large rectangle in the middle of the stage on Frame 10. Since this is already a shape, there is no need to break this apart.

6. Click anywhere between the two keyframes to select that range of frames.

7. Make sure the **Frame** panel is open. If it is not, select **Window > Panels > Frame** to make it visible.

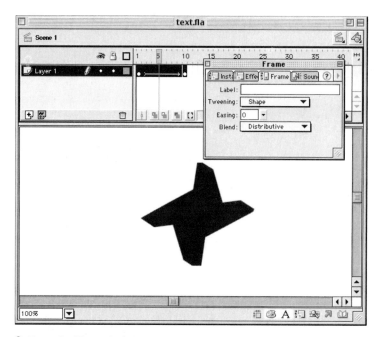

8. From the **Tweening** drop-down menu in the **Frame** panel, select **Shape** to apply a shape tween between the two keyframes. Your Timeline, between Frames 1 and 10, should be shaded green and populated with a solid arrow. This is an indication that the tween is working properly.

9. Press the **Return/Enter** to test your tween.

If you still want further practice with shape hints, this would be a great place to add some, so you can control the way the shape animates. Go ahead—add one, add two—and test different ways to make the letter transform into the box.

10. When you are finished, select **File > Save** to save the changes you made to this file. Go ahead and close this file.

7. _____Tweening Shapes with Holes

Once you start trying shape tweens on source art such as letters, you will probably run into one of the limitations of shape tweening: It doesn't like holes. When you try to tween a shape that has a hole in it, like a letter "O" and a shape that doesn't, like a square, the results are not always what you might expect:

What you expect:

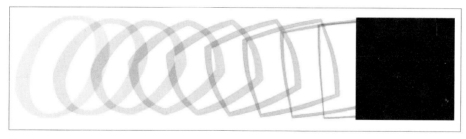

What you get:

In this scenario most people expect to see the hole in the "O" shape contract until it disappears into the solid shape of the square. What actually happens is that the hole expands until the shape looks like it is just an outline and then in one frame, POP; suddenly there is a solid square.

In this exercise, you will learn a technique for shape tweening shapes with holes. The secret to effectively tween objects with holes is to make sure that the start and end objects have the same number of holes. You'll get to try this next.

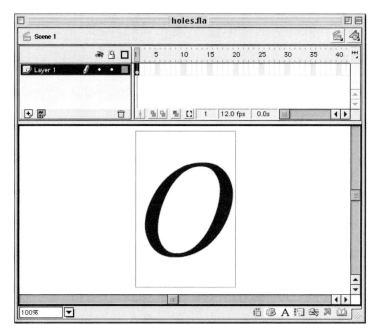

1. Open the **holes.fla** file located inside the **chap_06** folder. This file contains a single layer with a large "O" in the middle of the stage.

2. Using the **Arrow** tool, click to select the large **O**. A thin line will appear around the text to indicate that it is selected.

3. With the letter selected, choose **Modify > Break Apart**. This will convert the text "O" into a shape "O" so that it can be shape tweened. A selection mesh will appear over the "O" to indicate that is in fact a shape.

4. Select Frame 10 and press **F7** to add a blank keyframe to the Timeline.

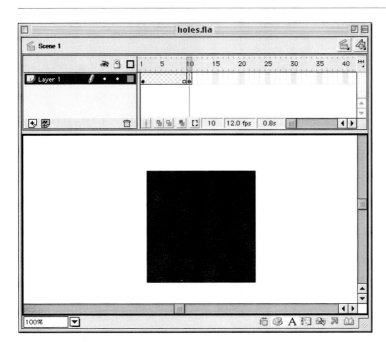

5. Use the **Rectangle** tool to create a large rectangle on the stage. This will be the end frame in the animation.

6. Click anywhere in the Timeline between the two keyframes to select that range of frames.

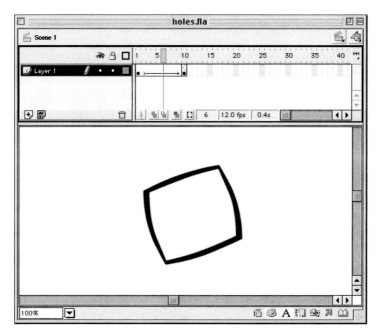

7. From the **Frame** panel, select **Shape** from the **Tweening** drop-down menu. This will automatically generate a shape tween between the two keyframes.

---

8. Press **Return** to see how the tween is working now. Notice that the hole pops to a square between frames 9 and 10. Not a very smooth transition between the two shapes. Why? Because the "O" shape has a hole and the square shape does not. In the next few steps, you are going to change that!

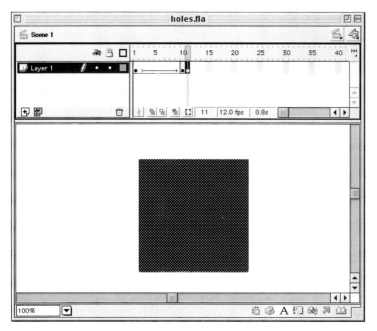

9. Select **Frame 10**. Press the **F6** key to insert a keyframe on **Frame 11**, making an exact copy of what was on Frame 10.

---

10. Move the **Playhead** back to Frame 10.

---

11. Select the **Eraser** tool. Click on the **Eraser Shape** button, at the bottom of the Toolbox, and select the smallest circular eraser. Press the **Esc** key to hide the selection mesh and make it easier to see the square shape.

12. With the **Eraser** tool, click on the middle of the square in keyframe 10 to erase a small hole in the middle of it. Now the square has a hole in the middle of it, just like the "O" shape.

13. Press the **Return/Enter** key to test your tween. Notice that there is a much smoother transition between the shapes. It's pretty amazing that such a little hole can make such a big difference in the animation.

14. Select **File > Save** to save the changes you made to this file. You can close this file.

8. _____Multiple Shape Tweens

So far, you have learned how to create single shape tweens. There will likely come a time when you will want to create more than one shape tween in your project. In this exercise, you will learn how to create multiple shape tweens by placing them on separate layers. Working with multiple layers is the best way to choreograph animations with multiple tweens. As an added bonus, this exercise also teaches you how to use the **Align** panel to align objects!

1. Open the **mutplShpTwnFinal.fla** file located inside the **chap_06** folder. This file contains a finished version of the animation you are about to create.

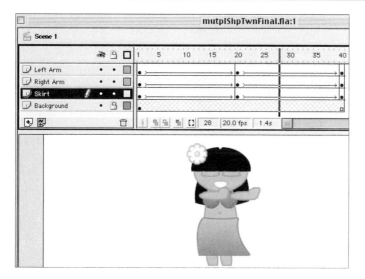

2. Press **Return/Enter** on your keyboard to preview this file. The hula girl does a little dance for you! It might not be apparent, but this dancer was created using shape tweens and multiple layers. Go ahead and close the file. You will learn to create this same animation.

3. Open the file named **mutplShpTwn.fla** file located inside the **chap_06** folder. You will notice it has four layers: one layer named **Background** with the hula girl's body parts that will remain stationary and three more layers where you will apply motion tweens to make her arms and skirt move.

When creating more than one tween at a time, you must separate them on different layers! Each tween must reside on its own layer in order to work correctly.

Artwork on this layer

4. Double-click on each of the layer names to give them new, more descriptive names. Name Layer 1 **Left Arm**, Layer 2 **Right Arm** and Layer 3 **Skirt**. It is important to name your layers so that it is easy to recognize what content is on that layer.

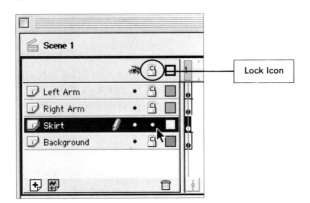

Lock Icon

5. Click the **Lock** icon at the top of the **Layers** panel to lock all the layers at once. Click the **Skirt** layer's **Lock** icon to unlock just that layer.

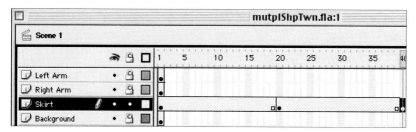

6. On the Skirt layer, press **F6** on **Frame 20** and again on **Frame 40** of the **Skirt** to add keyframes to those frames. This process duplicates the artwork on those specific frames. You should now see artwork on Frame 1 of your **Skirt** layer, representing the beginning of the animation, artwork on Frame 20, which will represent the middle of the animation, and then artwork on Frame 40, which will represent the end of the animation.

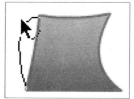

7. Next, make sure your **Playhead** is over **Frame 20**. Since this is where you want the animation to change, you are going to slightly alter the artwork on Frame 20. Move your pointer over the right side of the skirt and notice how the cursor icon changes to a curved line. Go ahead and move the right side of the skirt inward and the left side outward. You should end up with something similar to the picture above. Don't worry if it is not exact—not every hula girl moves the same way!

8. To animate the hula girl's skirt, all you have left to do is to add a shape tween. Click to the right of the **Skirt** layer name to select all the frames on that layer. From the **Frame** panel, select **Shape** from the **Tweening** drop-down menu. This will automatically generate a shape tween between each of the two keyframes.

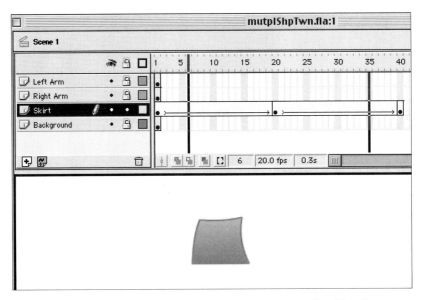

9. Press the **Return/Enter** key to see the shape tween in action. The skirt moves to the left and then returns to its original position.

Notice that you don't see any of the other layers on frames 20 and 40? That's because you only added frames to the Timeline in the Skirt layer. You'll see all the other layers soon enough, as you follow through the other steps.

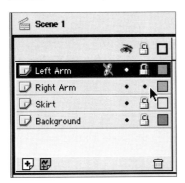

10. Lock the **Skirt** layer and unlock the **Right Arm** layer by selecting and deselecting the lock icons on both those layers. This ensures you are working with the correct artwork on the correct layer and it also ensures that you don't accidentally change other layers that already work properly. You are going to create the shape tween for the right arm next.

11. On the **Right Arm** layer press **F6** on **Frame 20** and again on **Frame 40** to add keyframes to those frames. Just as in step 6, you should now have artwork on Frame 1 of your **Right Arm** layer, representing the beginning of the animation, artwork on Frame 20, which will represent the middle of the animation, and then artwork on Frame 40, which will represent the end of the animation.

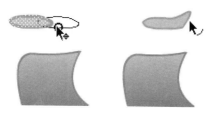

12. Click on **Frame 20** to select all the artwork in that frame. Move the arm slightly to the right, just to the middle of the skirt. Click anywhere on your stage to deselect the artwork and modify the shape by dragging out the right side to make it similar to a bent hand like the picture above. Again, your shape doesn't have to be exact, so don't worry!

13. Now, to add the shape tween, click to the right of the **Right Arm** layer name to select all the frames on that layer. From the **Frame** panel, select **Shape** from the **Tweening** drop-down menu. This will automatically generate a shape tween between each of the two keyframes.

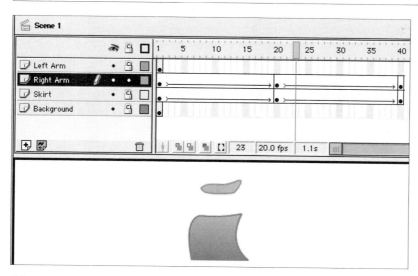

14. Press the **Return/Enter** key to see the shape tween in action. The right arm moves to the right and then returns to the its original position.

15. You are almost done! Lock the **Right Arm** layer and unlock the **Left Arm** layer by selecting and deselecting the lock icons on both those layers. This ensures you are working with
the correct artwork on the correct layer. You are going to create the shape tween for the left
arm next.

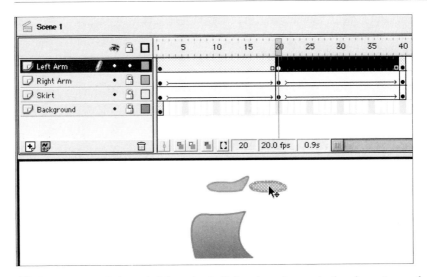

16. Repeat steps 9 through 12 on the **Left Arm** layer to create the shape tween for the left
arm. Be sure to move it slightly right of the existing arm so that you can see them both in the
final animation.

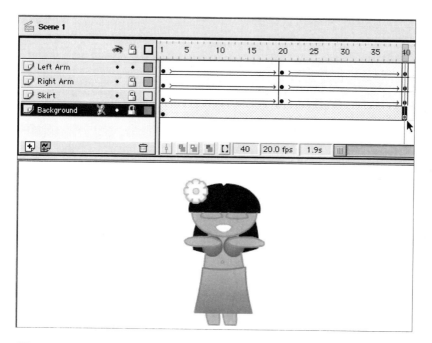

17. On **Frame 40** of the **Background** layer, press **F5** to add frames so that you can see the hula girl's stationary parts throughout the animation.

18. Press **Return/Enter** to test your animation! By using a multiple shape tween, you can have different animations on different layers all happening at the same time.

19. Select **File > Save** to save the dancing hula girl animation. You can close this file.

 MOVIE | hula.mov

To watch a movie of this exercise, open hula.mov from the **Movies** folder from the **H•O•T CD-ROM**.

We hope this chapter uncovered the many secrets and nuances of shape tweening. You started with the simple concepts using simple exercises and progressed to a fairly advanced level with the hula girl exercise. As you gain experience in Flash, shape tweening will likely become a technique you use often for many different types of effects. If you have the stamina, keep pressing forward to the next chapter. There's no rush though; the book will still be here tomorrow. ;-)

7.

Symbols & Instances

Creating Graphic Symbols	Creating Symbol Instances
Editing Symbols	Editing Symbol Instances
Transforming Instances	Animated Graphic Symbols

chap_7

Flash 5
H•O•T CD-ROM

Effective Flash movies, even very simple ones, often rely on fundamental tools in the Flash interface called **symbols** and **instances**. We find that they are also the hardest things to teach and learn, because symbols and instances aren't found in other common graphics, animation, or interactive programs. Chances are, if you haven't used Flash, you've never worked with them before.

You might be wondering what the heck the terms "symbol" and "instance" mean. A Flash symbol is a master document of sorts. You create a symbol once—it can be a simple shape or something very complex—and use it multiple times throughout your movie. Each time you reuse a symbol in your project file, it is called an "instance," which is a "copy" of a symbol.

These concepts may seem a bit abstract at first, but if you plan to do any serious work in the program, it is imperative that you become comfortable with creating, editing, and using symbols and instances. So, if you're thinking about skipping this chapter and coming back to it later, don't do it. The time spent in this chapter will make it possible to learn other essential Flash features, such as motion tweening and working with movie clips.

We are confident that if you try these exercises, you will better understand how to work easily with symbols and instances than if you just read about them. Here's where the premise of a hands-on training book is really worth its weight in gold. For many, trying something and gaining first-hand experience is the key to understanding!

The Symbol and Instance Structure

Just what will symbols and instances do for you? Symbols will enable you to create very complex movies that are faster to download. How? Symbols are downloaded only once; regardless of how many copies (called instances) you have in your movie. For example, if you had a symbol of a star and you added 50 instances of that star to the Stage, the file size would be not be that much larger. However, if you were to instead draw 50 separate stars, the user would have to download all 50 stars and the file size would increase dramatically.

The concept of symbols and instances is the key to reducing the downloading weight of your Flash documents, because the symbol is downloaded only one time, while the instances are simply described in a small text file by their attributes (scale, color, transparency, animation, etc.). This is why instances add very little file size to your final Flash movie. To reduce file size, you should create symbols for any objects that you reuse in your projects. Besides reducing the final file size, symbols and instances can also help you make quick updates to objects across your entire project file. Later in the book, as you learn about more advanced animation techniques, you'll see that symbols and instances play another dramatic role. But that's skipping ahead! This chapter focuses on one concept alone—how symbols and instances are created and manipulated.

There are three types of Flash symbols: graphic, button, and movie clip. In this chapter, you will be working with graphic symbols. Hands-on exercises for creating button and movie clip symbols are covered in later chapters.

Here's a handy chart that explains some of the terms found in this chapter:

Term	Definition
Symbol	A reusable object that serves as a master from which you can create copies (instances). Once a symbol is created, it automatically becomes part of the project file's library.
Instance	A copy of the original symbol. Color, size, shape, and position of an instance can be altered without affecting the original symbol.
Graphic Symbol	One of the three types of symbols. It consists of artwork that can be either static or animated. The graphic symbol's Timeline is dependent on the main Timeline—it will play only while the main Timeline is playing. You'll learn more about this behavior as you work through the exercises in this book.
Effect Panel	Where you edit and store the brightness, tint, and alpha properties of an instance.
Transform Panel	Where you edit and store the scale, rotation, and skew properties of an instance.

Symbol Naming Conventions

As you learn to create symbols and instances in this chapter, you'll need to create names for them. In past versions of Flash, it didn't matter what name you gave to symbols or instances. With ActionScripting in Flash 5 (which you will learn about later in this book), naming conventions are more important than they used to be. This is especially true for movie clip symbols. For this reason, we recommend you get used to naming all your symbols in Flash following the same rules, so you don't develop bad habits that bite you later down the road. Here's a handy chart that explains the rules:

Symbol Naming Conventions	
No spaces	Don't use any spaces. For example, my first symbol should be *myFirstSymbol* or *my_first_symbol*. You can string the words together or add underscores, but don't use spaces.
No special characters	Special characters—such as Δ¨©¢∞£¢¬∂˚Δ˝∑Δ∑´°ø)@#(%$T(%— are forbidden. Some special characters have specific meaning to the Flash Player and can mess up ActionScripting in the future, so be sure to avoid them.
No forward slashes	Forward slashes are often misinterpreted as path locations on a hard drive, instead of the name of an object. So don't name your files like: *my/first/symbol*.
Must begin with a letter	Symbol names that begin with numbers can cause confusion in ActionScripting. For this reason, always start your symbol names with a lowercase letter. Names can contain numbers, but the first character should be a letter.
No dots	Don't put dots in your file names, such *amy.first.symbol*—dots are reserved for ActionScripting syntax.
Capitalization and descriptive names	It is good practice to use descriptive names for symbols. Rather than *symbol6*, you should name it something like *gfxLogoBkgd* so it is more easily recognized. When you use multi-word names for symbols, capitalize the first letter of all words except the first. When you refer to an object in ActionScripting (which you'll get to try in later chapters), you must refer to the symbol with the same capitalization you used in its name.

I. _____Creating Graphic Symbols

Symbols are used for many reasons in Flash. Before you learn hands-on what they're good for, you'll need to learn how to create them. This first exercise will show you one way to create a graphic symbol. You'll learn another way in the following exercise. Later in the book, you'll learn to work with the two other symbol types—buttons and movie clips—which are more difficult.

1. Copy the **chap_07** folder, located on the **H•O•T CD-ROM**, to your hard drive. You need to have this folder on your hard drive in order to save changes to the files inside it.

2. Choose **File > Open** to open the **graphic_symbols.fla** file located inside the **chap_07** folder. This is just blank file that has been already created for you.

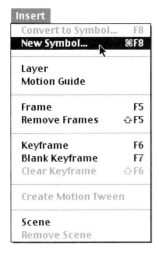

3. Choose **Insert > New Symbol**. This will open the **Symbol Properties** dialog box. There are two things to be decided next: the name and behavior of the symbol.

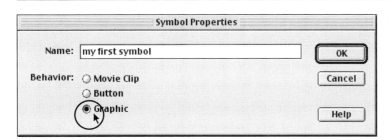

4. For Name, type **myFirstSymbol**, and for the Behavior, select **Graphic**. Click **OK**.

Note: We promise you'll get to learn about movie clips and button symbols in the following chapters. For now, let's focus on graphic symbols only. It's for your own good, we promise!

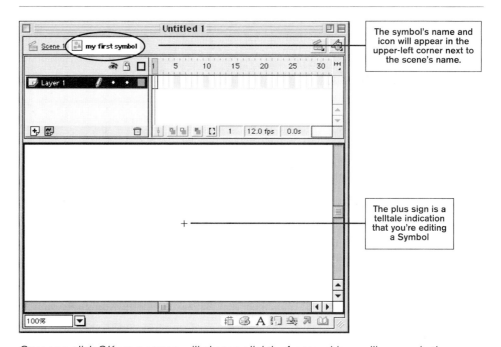

The symbol's name and icon will appear in the upper-left corner next to the scene's name.

The plus sign is a telltale indication that you're editing a Symbol

Once you click OK, your screen will change slightly. A second icon will appear in the upper-left corner of the Timeline. Notice that it has the same name that you assigned to the symbol you named in the previous step. This is an indication that you are now in symbol editing mode (inside the symbol, where you can create or modify its contents) and no longer working on the main Stage or in the main Timeline. Also notice that the gray (work) area around your Stage is gone. When you're in symbol editing mode (inside a symbol) you will not see the work area, unless you are using the Edit In Place feature. There is also a little "plus sign" (+) in the middle of your Stage window. This is the "centerpoint" of the graphic symbol. It acts as a marker telling you where the center of the symbol is. This is an important indicator because it affects how all of the instances of this symbol are rotated and scaled. You will learn how to rotate and scale instances later in this chapter.

TIP | Know Your Location

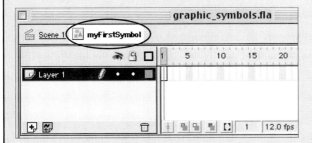

We often see many of our students accidentally creating graphics and animation inside a symbol when they really meant to put them on Scene 1. As you will learn in later exercises, there are several ways to get into symbol editing mode. It's so easy to get yourself into this mode and not even be aware of it, so be constantly aware of where you are doing your work. Keep an eye on the top-left of your Timeline and make sure that you are drawing, animating, or creating in the correct location of your project. If you want to work inside the symbol, the upper-left area of your window will look like what's shown here.

5. From the Toolbox, select the **Line** tool. It doesn't matter what color your line is because you are going to delete it before you are done.

6. Using the **Line** tool, draw a star in the middle of the Stage. You have just created artwork (in this case, a star) inside of the graphic symbol, myFirstSymbol.

7. Using the **Arrow** tool, select and delete each of the internal lines of the star, if you created any while drawing your star.

8. Using the **Paint Bucket** tool, fill the star with a light shade of yellow.

9. Using the **Arrow** tool, select and delete the line around the star.

10. Click on **Scene 1**, in the top-left of your Timeline, to return to the main timeline of this project. That's it! You've just created your first symbol! But wait, where did the star go? Since all symbols are stored in the Library, that's where it has been placed. Only instances (copies of the original symbol) are placed on the Stage.

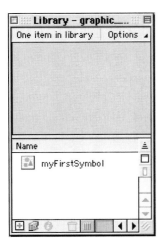

11. Choose **Window > Library** to open the Library for this file. Notice that the file name is displayed at the top of the **Library** panel.

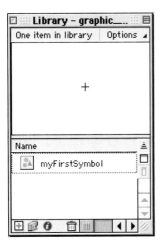

12. Click on the **myFirstSymbol** icon in your Library. A preview of your symbol will appear in the Preview portion of the Library window.

13. Close and save the file.

This process is just one way of creating symbols in Flash. In the next exercise, you will learn another method to create symbols. Which method you choose to use is really a matter of personal preference. Later in this chapter you will learn how to edit these symbols to make several changes quickly. You will also learn how to create and edit instances.

TIP | What is the Library?

The Library is a container where Flash stores and organizes symbols, sounds, bitmap graphics and additional elements such as video and Smart Clips (which you will learn about in later chapters). It is one of the most useful and frequently used interface elements in Flash. The Library is attached to the movie that you're working with. If you give your project file (.fla) to someone else and they open it, they will see the same Library that you see when you have that file open. You can sort the contents of the Library by name, type, usage, and linkage. As your files become more complex, you will find it useful to create folders within your Library to help separate your symbols into different categories. Since you will frequently work with the Library in Flash, it's useful to learn the shortcut to bring the Library to the screen: **Cmd + L** (Mac) or **Ctrl + L** (Windows). You will get an in-depth look at the Library and all its functions in later chapters.

2. ——————Creating More Symbols

In the previous exercise you learned how to create a symbol by starting with a blank symbol and creating artwork inside it. But, what can you do if you have artwork that's already been created? This exercise will show you how to turn a previously created illustration into a symbol in a few easy steps.

1. Select **File > New** to create a new blank document. Save this file as **symbol2.fla** inside the **chap_07** folder.

2. Use the **Brush** tool to create some artwork on your Stage. Go ahead and have some fun here and draw whatever tickles you. If you don't like to be tickled, you can copy the happy face shown above.

3. Press **Cmd+A** (Mac) or **Ctrl+A** (Windows) to select everything on your Stage. You are going to convert the selected object(s) into a symbol.

Tip: If you want to select only portions of a drawing to convert those portions to a symbol, that's no problem. Instead of using the shortcut key Cmd+A (Mac) or Ctrl+A (Windows), which selects everything, you can select individual objects, lines, or fills and those isolated components will become the symbol once converted.

4. Choose **Insert > Convert to Symbol**. This will open the **Symbol Properties** dialog box. You need to give this symbol a name and behavior.

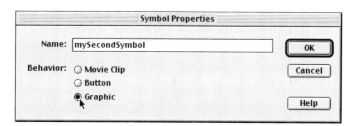

5. For Name, type **mySecondSymbol**, and set the Behavior to Graphic. Click **OK**.

6. Choose **Window > Library** to open the Library for this file. Notice that the file name is displayed at the top of the Library panel.

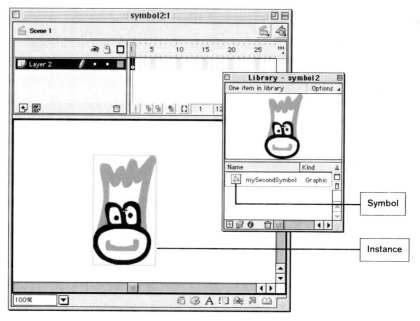

7. Click on the **mySecondSymbol** icon in your Library. A preview of your symbol will appear in the Preview portion of the Library window.

Flash will automatically convert the selected object(s) into a symbol, place the symbol in the Library, and place an instance on the Stage all in one fell swoop. By now, you are probably wondering when you'll learn more about when and how to use instances. You will learn all about them in the next exercise.

8. Save and close this file. You won't need it any more.

3. ———————Creating Symbol Instances

In the beginning of this chapter, you learned the difference between a symbol and an instance and the special relationship that they share. The previous two exercises showed you two ways of creating symbols. In this exercise, you will learn how to create instances from symbols in the Library.

1. Choose **File > Open** and navigate to the **instances.fla** file located inside the **chap_07** folder. This file contains some artwork on two layers and a third blank layer for you to add some stars.

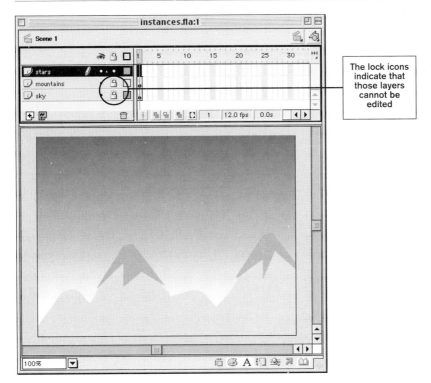

The lock icons indicate that those layers cannot be edited

*The **sky** and **mountains** layers have been locked, so that you don't accidentally change the artwork on those layers.*

2. Make sure the **stars** layer is selected. If it's not, click to the right of the layer name to select that specific layer.

3. Choose **Window > Library** to open the Library for this file. Notice that it contains a graphic symbol of a star. How did the star get there? This star was saved as a Library element in this project file and automatically appears in the Library whenever you open this project file, just like the star you created in Exercise 1.

4. Click on the **star** icon in the Library.

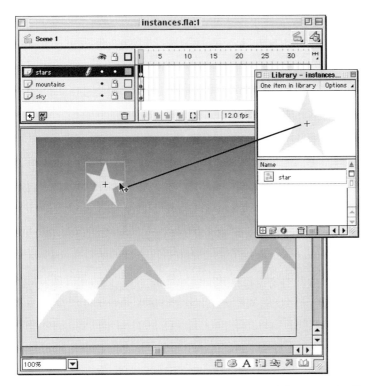

5. From the **Library**, click the preview of the star and drag onto the Stage. When you release the mouse button, an instance of the star will be placed on the Stage.

One key thing to remember here is that symbols are stored in the Library and instances are located on the Stage. From one symbol, you can create as many instances as you want.

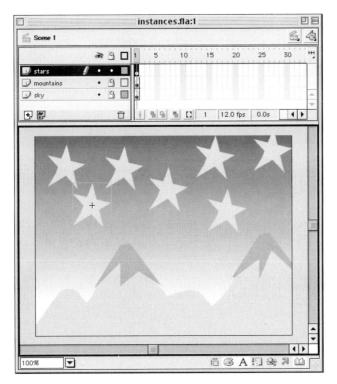

6. Click and drag six more stars from the Library. This will create a total of seven instances on your Stage.

Clicking and dragging from the Library is one way to create instances on your Stage, but you can also Option + Drag (Mac) or Ctrl + Drag (Windows) on an instance on the Stage to create a duplicate of it without opening the Library.

7. Choose **File > Save** to save the changes you made to this file. Keep this file open for the next exercise.

4. _____**Editing Symbols**

The instances on your Stage have a special relationship with the symbol in the Library. This is often referred to in computer programming circles as a parent/child relationship. One of the advantages to this relationship is if you change a symbol in the Library, all of the instances on your Stage will be updated. As you can imagine, this can save you a lot of time when you need to make large updates across an entire project. This ability to make these quick—and sometimes large—updates is one of the powerful advantages of using symbols and instances. In this exercise, you will modify the appearance of the "star" symbol to change all seven instances on the Stage.

1. The file from the previous exercise should still be open. If you closed it, go ahead and open the **instances.fla** located inside the **chap_07** folder.

2. Make sure you have your Library panel open. If it's not, choose **Window > Library** to open it now.

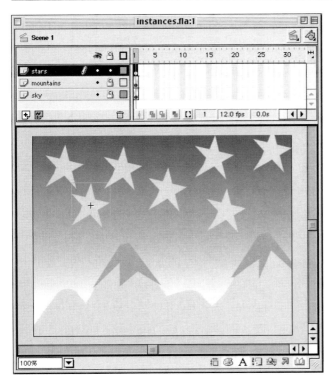

Your Stage should look like the one shown above. If for some reason it does not, refer to the previous exercise to learn how to create multiple instances of the star symbol.

Note: Notice that in this case we have put multiple instances on the same layer? Flash allows this, no problem. There is an important caveat however. If you wanted to create an animation of any of the stars (as you will learn to do Chapter 8, "Motion Tweening"), you would need to put each star on its own layer. It's one of those rules in Flash that can be a gotcha if you don't know it!

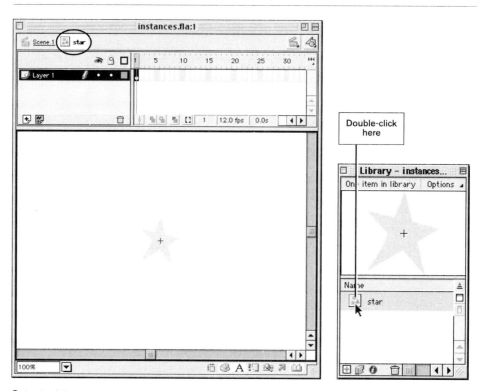

3. In the **Library**, double-click on the small graphic symbol icon to the left of "star." This will change your Stage and take you into the editing mode for this symbol. Notice the upper-left corner of the Timeline has an item called star? This indicates that you are no longer working on the main Timeline, but instead you are inside the "star" graphic symbol.

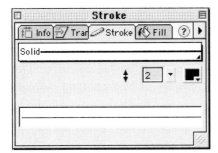

4. If the star isn't already selected, click on the star to select it. Notice that a selection mesh appears over the object, indicating that this is a shape. This means you can easily edit its fill and/or stroke settings.

5. From the **Stroke** panel, select a black, solid stoke, with a width of **2**. Your panel should look like the one shown above.

Note: Although many references use the terms interchangeably, in Flash, lines and outlines are referred to as strokes. You can add strokes to objects that don't already have a stroke applied to them by using the Ink Bottle (as you will do in the next step) and you can also modify an existing stroke by selecting it first, then changing its width and appearance in the Stroke panel.

Ink Bottle Tool

6. Using the **Ink Bottle** from the Toolbox, click on the star shape to add a stroke around it.

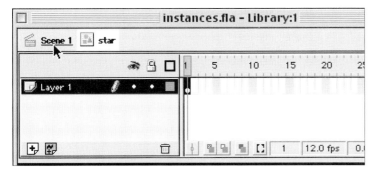

7. In the upper-left corner of the Timeline, click on the underlined **Scene 1** to return to the main Timeline, and you should see the sky and mountain graphics again.

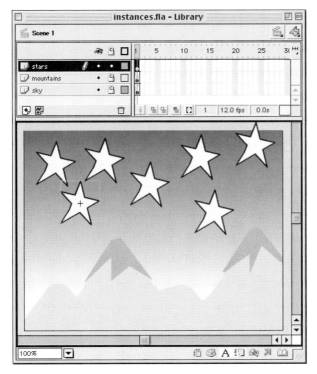

Notice that all of the instances of the star now have a black stroke around them. Every time you modify a symbol, it affects all of the instances you have in your project file, just as you saw here. This can be a very powerful way to make changes throughout your project.

8. Again, double-click on the **star** icon in the Library. This will take you back into the editing mode for this graphic symbol.

9. Using the **Arrow** tool, double-click on the stroke to select the stroke around the entire star. Press the **Delete** key to remove it. Instead of the stroke, you'll make a change to the fill this time. It's easy to change the artwork for the symbol whenever the mood strikes you!

10. Use the **Arrow** tool to select the star shape.

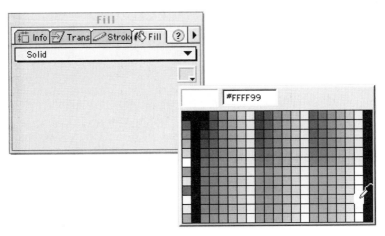

11. From the **Fill** panel, click on the Color Swatch and choose a different shade of yellow. Because the star was already selected, Flash will automatically update the color of the star.

12. In the upper-left corner of the Timeline, click on the underlined **Scene 1** to return to the main Timeline, and you should see the sky and mountain graphics again.

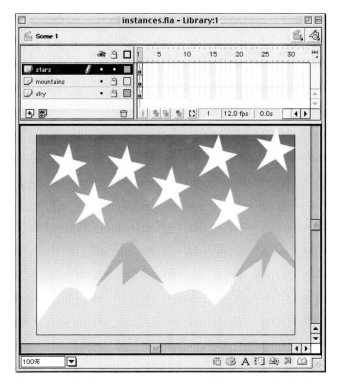

Hey look, all of the stars have changed their color. Again, because you changed the symbol in the Library, all of the instances were updated. This is another example of the parent/child relationship mentioned earlier. Changing the symbol will update all of the instances of that symbol, wherever they exist in your project (even across multiple scenes, which you'll learn about later in the book). Even in this simple example, you can see how much time you saved by not having to change every star one at a time.

13. Choose **File > Save** to save the changes you made to this file. Leave this file open because you are going to use it in the next exercise.

5. _____Editing Symbol Instances

In the previous exercise, you learned how to modify a symbol to make changes to all of the instances on the Stage. But, what do you do if you want to change the color of only one instance, or each instance individually? You use the **Effect** panel to do that. The Effect panel will let you change the tint, brightness, and alpha settings for instances. This is the only way you can change the color values of an instance because the Paint Bucket and Brush tool work only on shapes. In this exercise, you will use the Effect and **Transform** panels to change the appearance of the individual stars. You will also be introduced to the **Scale** and **Rotate** tools, which also modify the appearance of individual stars.

1. The file from the previous exercise should still be open. If it's not, open the **instances.fla** file located inside the **chap_07** folder.

2. Click to select the star in the upper-left corner of the Stage.

3. Make sure the Effect panel is open and visible. If it's not, choose **Window > Panels > Effect** to open it and bring it to the front.

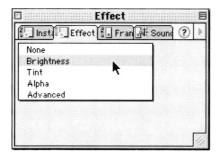

4. From the Effect drop-down menu, choose **Brightness**. The Brightness option controls the brightness value of the instance and has a range of -100% to 100%, with -100% being completely black and 100% being completely white.

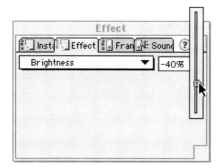

5. Click slider to the right of the pull-down menu and drag it down to **-40%**. Watch the selected star on the Stage. Notice how the star gets darker as you drag down.

6. Click to select a different star on your Stage. You can choose any star you want.

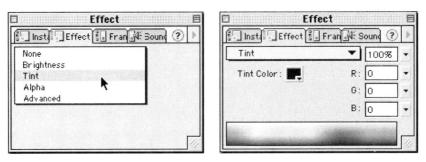

7. In the **Effect** panel, from the drop-down menu, choose **Tint**. The Tint option applies a tint to the base color of your symbol.

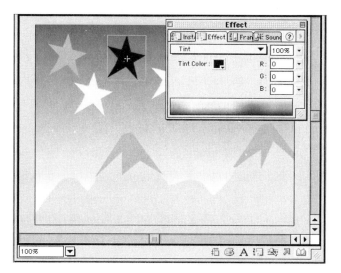

The Tint panel defaults to a Tint Color of black at 100%, which means your selected instance will automatically turn black once you select this option.

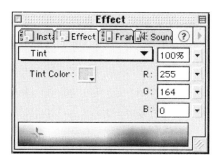

8. In the **Effect** panel, click inside the **Tint Color** pop-up to select a shade of **orange**. Notice how this automatically updates the selected instance on the Stage. It also changes the RGB values in the Effect panel.

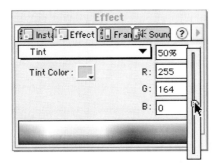

9. Click and drag the **Tint Percentage** slider down to **50%**. Notice that as you drag the slider down, the color becomes more transparent. The Tint Percentage option has a range of 1% (barely tinted) to 100% (fully saturated). Basically, this is changing how much of the Tint Color is applied to the instance.

Note: You control the color of the instance by modifying the percentage of the tint being applied and the individual RGB (Red, Green, Blue) values. The Tint option is the only way you can change the color of an instance. Also, you should know that this option changes both the Fill and Stroke settings. They cannot be changed separately by editing the instance; they can be changed only by editing the symbol.

10. Click to select another star on the Stage. Just make sure you select one that has not been modified yet.

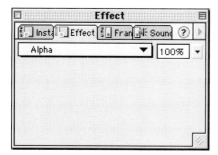

11. In the **Effect** panel, from the drop-down menu, choose **Alpha**. The Alpha option, which has a range of 100% (opaque) to 0% (transparent), lets you control the transparency value of the selected instance.

12. Click and drag the **Alpha slider** down to **0%**. Watch the selected star disappear as you drag the slider down. Return the Alpha slider to **50%**.

In the next few steps, you will learn about the Advanced option in the Effect panel. The Advanced option lets you modify multiple settings for a selected object. For example, you can use this panel to adjust the Tint, Brightness, and Alpha setting of the selected instance.. The best way to learn about it is by using it and that's exactly what you are going to do.

13. Click to select another unmodified star on the Stage.

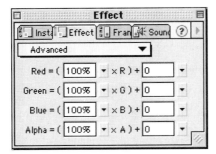

14. In the **Effect** panel, from the drop-down menu, choose **Advanced**.

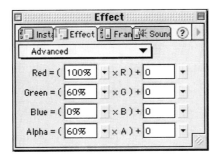

15. Click and drag the **Green** slider down to **60%**. Click and drag the **Blue** slider down to **0%**. Click and drag the **Alpha** slider down to **60%**. The end result should be a star that has a nice shade of orange. *Note: Yours might look a bit different if you didn't select the same yellow for your star symbol as we did.*

16. Go ahead and recolor as many stars as you want. It never hurts to practice!

In this exercise, you gained some experience creating and changing symbol instances. For your reference, we have provided a chart at the end of this chapter that outlines all of the options in the Effect panel.

17. Choose **File > Save** to save the changes you made to this file. Don't close the file; you will need it for the next exercise.

6. _____Transforming Instances

In the previous exercise, you learned how to modify the brightness, tint, and alpha of the instances on the Stage. In addition, you can also rotate, scale, and skew instances. In this exercise, you will learn how to use the Transform panel and the Rotate and Scale tools to modify the instances on your Stage.

1. The file from the previous exercise should still be open. If you closed it, go ahead and open the **instance.fla** file located inside the **chap_07** folder.

2. Click to select any **star** on your Stage. It doesn't really matter which one you select because you will eventually select them all.

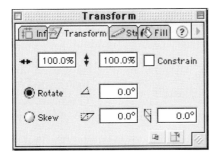

3. Make sure the **Transform** panel is open and visible. If it's not, Choose **Window > Panels > Transform**.

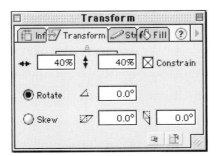

4. Click the **Constrain** checkbox. This will ensure that the width and height options are equal and the object is scaled proportionately. Enter **40%** in either the **width** or **height box**—it doesn't matter which because you are constraining the values. Press **Return/Enter** to accept the changes. The selected star will be reduced to 40% of its original size.

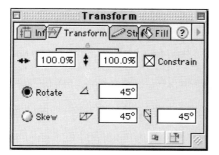

5. Click to select another star on the Stage. In the **Transform** panel, enter **45** to the right of the Rotate radio button, then press **Enter/Return**. This will rotate the selected instance 45 degrees.

While the Transform panel can be great for making exact numeric changes to your instances, the Scale and Rotate tools are a more visual way of making those same changes. The following steps will show you how to use the Scale and Rotate tools to scale and rotate the other instances on your Stage.

6. Click to select a different star on the Stage.

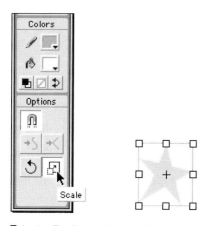

7. In the **Toolbox**, click the **Scale** button at the bottom. Notice that eight white squares appear around the selected star on your Stage. These squares represent the different points that you can grab to scale the star.

8. Click and drag the lower-right square toward the center of the star. This will scale the star proportionately. An outline preview will appear so you can see how small or large the instance will be when you release the mouse button. Make the star about half of its original size. Release the mouse button.

9. In the **Toolbox**, select the **Rotate** button at the bottom. Notice that eight white circles appear around the selected star on your Stage. This is an indication that you are using the Rotate tool and not the Scale tool, which displays white squares.

10. Click and drag the upper-right corner handle downward. This will rotate the star as you continue to drag. Release the mouse button.

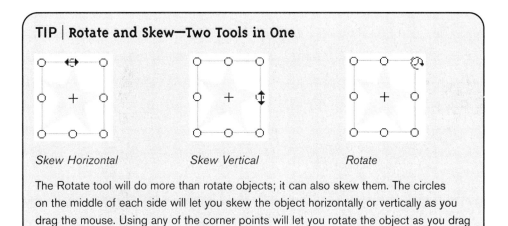

TIP | Rotate and Skew—Two Tools in One

Skew Horizontal   *Skew Vertical*   *Rotate*

The Rotate tool will do more than rotate objects; it can also skew them. The circles on the middle of each side will let you skew the object horizontally or vertically as you drag the mouse. Using any of the corner points will let you rotate the object as you drag the mouse.

11. Go ahead and change the size and rotation of the other stars on the Stage so they are all different. You can use the Transform panel or the Scale and Rotate tools, but use all of them so you get some practice using them all.

12. Choose **File > Save** to save the changes you made to this file. Don't close the file yet; you have one more exercise to go.

NOTE | Edit Center

You might have noticed that the plus sign of an instance serves as an anchor from which position, rotation, and scale originate. It is possible to move the center point if you want to. This technique is used when you want to rotate from a corner or from outside the instance's shape to achieve certain types of animations or appearances. To edit the centerpoint, choose **Modify > Transform > Edit Center**. The plus sign will turn into an outline and you can move it with the arrow cursor to a new location. From then on, any transformations you choose from the Transform panel, or make with the Scale and Rotate tools on the Toolbar, will originate from this new position.

---

7. ——————Animated Graphic Symbols

Up until now you have been working with static graphic symbols. Now you will learn how to create a graphic symbol that contains animation frames. When animated graphic symbols are used in Flash, it's important to understand that the number of animation frames inside the symbol have to relate to the number of frames that are set on the main Timeline. This will make more sense to you after you try it.

In this exercise, you will modify the star graphic symbol and add a simple frame-by-frame animation to its Timeline to convert it into an animated graphic symbol. The end result will be a star that twinkles.

> **1.** The file from the previous exercise should still be open. If it's not, open the **instances.fla** file located inside the **chap_07** folder.

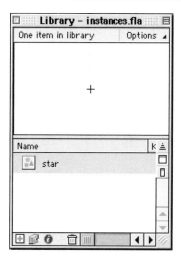

> **2.** Make sure the **Library** is open and visible. If it's not, choose **Window > Library** to open it. The Library contains the one instance of the star symbol.

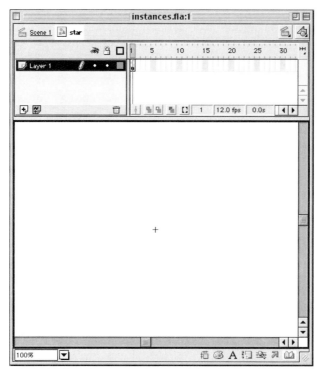

3. In the **Library**, double-click on the small graphic symbol icon to the left of the word **star**. This will take you into the editing mode for this symbol. Notice that the contents of your Stage have changed and that the star graphic symbol icon appears in the upper-left corner of the Timeline.

In the following steps, you are going to create a simple frame-by-frame animation that will make the star look like it is twinkling. Keep in mind that you are creating this animation on your star graphic symbol's Timeline, which is different from the main Timeline in Scene 1.

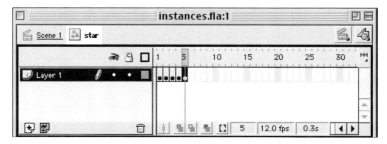

4. Click on the first **keyframe** in the Timeline. Press **F6** four times to create four copies of the star on the next four frames.

5. Click on the second keyframe in the Timeline. This will automatically select the entire contents of that keyframe.

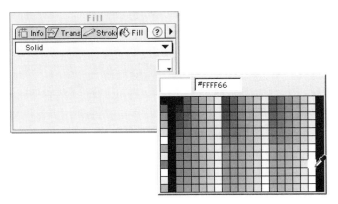

6. With the star selected, use the **Fill** panel to change the color of the star to a slightly different shade of **yellow**. The idea here is to select a color that is just slightly different from the current color. The star should flicker, not act like a strobe light.

7. Repeat this process for the other three keyframes. Each time select a slightly different color of yellow or orange. You can use the same color on more than one of the keyframes, just make sure they aren't right next to each other if you do.

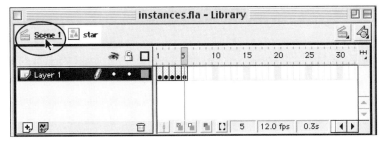

8. When you are finished changing the color of the stars on each keyframe, press **Return/Enter** to get a quick preview of what your twinkle will look like. When you are happy with the twinkle animation, click on **Scene 1** in the upper-left corner of the symbol's Timeline to return to Scene 1's Timeline.

9. Choose **Control > Test Movie**. This will open a new window with a preview of your movie. But wait, the star is not twinkling. Why not? Close the Preview window to return to Scene 1's Timeline and we'll show you how to fix this.

The Timeline of the animated graphic symbol is directly related to the main Timeline (the current scene, in this case, Scene 1) of the project. This means that if the main Timeline is one frame in length, which it is, and the Timeline of the animated graphic symbol is five frames in length, only one frame will be displayed. So, to fix this situation, you need to extend the main Timeline to be at least as long as the Timeline of the animated graphic symbol, which is five frames long.

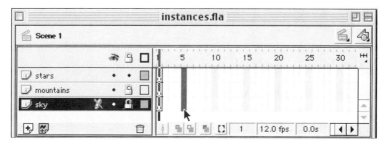

10. Click in **Frame 5** of the **stars** layer and drag down to Frame 5 of the **sky** layer. This will select the range of frames between the layers.

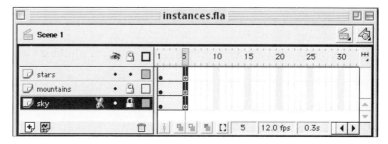

11. Press **F5** to insert frames and extend the Timeline of all three layers to five frames in length. Now the main Timeline is at least as long as the Timeline of the animated graphic symbol, which means you will see the entire animation play. Your stars are about to twinkle!

Note: You just extended all three layers so that the content of these layers is displayed for the same length of time. For example, extending just the stars layer would cause the mountains layer and sky layer to disappear when the Playhead reached Frame 2. By extending them all to Frame 5, it ensures that all of the layers are displayed for the same length of time.

12. Choose **Control > Test Movie** to once again preview your movie. There you go, twinkling stars. Notice that the color changes you made in the Effect panels in Exercise 5, *Editing Symbol Instances,* were not lost.

Notice that the stars are all twinkling together, which doesn't look very realistic. The following steps will show you how to change the starting frames of each animated graphic symbol to create a more natural-looking twinkle.

13. Close the Preview window.

14. Click to select a star on the Stage.

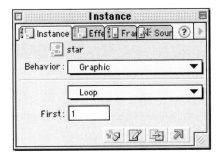

15. Make sure the **Instance** panel is visible. If its not, choose **Window > Panels > Instance** to open it and bring it to the front.

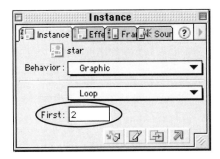

16. Enter any number between **1** and **5** in the **First** field, at the bottom of the **Instance** panel. This field sets the frame on which the animation begins. Since this animation has a total of five frames, you must select a number between 1 and 5.

17. Repeat this process for all the stars on your Stage and enter different start values for each one. By changing the starting frame of each animation, you will change the starting point of each animation and that will produce a more-realistic twinkle effect.

18. Choose **Control > Test Movie** to preview your movie. There you have it, a sky full of twinkling stars. You can go ahead and close the Preview window.

Could this same effect have been achieved using a different method? The answer is yes. In Flash, it is often possible to produce the same effect a number of different ways. However, some ways are more efficient than others. The above example outlines an efficient way of using one symbol to create several instances that look and behave very differently. You could have created and animated each of the stars separately to produce the same effect, but that would have been so much more work.

19. Choose **File > Save** to save the changes you made to this file. You can finally close this file.

Phew, you made it. Congratulations! By now, you should feel a lot more comfortable working with symbols and instances and the role they can play in your projects. But you aren't finished yet. Future chapters on buttons and movie clips will continue this learning process. So, don't stop now, we are just getting to the good stuff.

NOTE | Removing Effects

Earlier in this chapter you added many different effects to the instances on your Stage. If you want to remove all of the effects you have applied to your instances, you can simply choose the **None** option from the Effects panel drop-down menu. This will turn off all of the effects you applied and restore the instances to their original condition. Even better: Try using the **Shift** key to select all the stars at once and apply the None option, or any other option for that matter. One of the benefits of having a separate Effects panel in the interface is that its settings can be applied to multiple instances at one time. Previous versions of Flash didn't have functions such as Effects broken into panels, so this was not possible.

NOTE | Looping

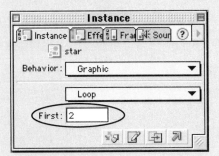

You might have noticed that the five-frame animation of the twinkling stars played over and over again when you tested the movie. This type of behavior is called a *loop*, which is the definition for an animation sequence that repeats over and over. Flash defaults to looping whatever is on the Stage, unless you tell it not to through the use of ActionScript, which you will learn about in Chapter 12, "*ActionScripting Basics*."

The Effect Panel

The chart below explains the different options available in the Effect panel. As you learned in this chapter, the Effect panel is used to change the color and alpha properties of an instance.

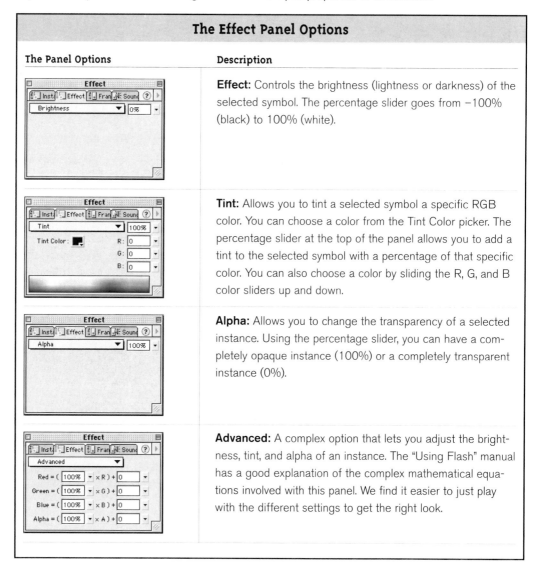

The Effect Panel Options	
The Panel Options	**Description**
	Effect: Controls the brightness (lightness or darkness) of the selected symbol. The percentage slider goes from −100% (black) to 100% (white).
	Tint: Allows you to tint a selected symbol a specific RGB color. You can choose a color from the Tint Color picker. The percentage slider at the top of the panel allows you to add a tint to the selected symbol with a percentage of that specific color. You can also choose a color by sliding the R, G, and B color sliders up and down.
	Alpha: Allows you to change the transparency of a selected instance. Using the percentage slider, you can have a completely opaque instance (100%) or a completely transparent instance (0%).
	Advanced: A complex option that lets you adjust the brightness, tint, and alpha of an instance. The "Using Flash" manual has a good explanation of the complex mathematical equations involved with this panel. We find it easier to just play with the different settings to get the right look.

Important Timeline Vocabulary Terms

In this chapter, you were introduced again to the Timeline. You learned that a symbol has a Timeline too, just like a Scene. Here's a handy chart to read if you want to further understand this distinction among the different timelines.

Timeline Terms	
Main Timeline	You may have noticed that we referred to the "Main Timeline" in this chapter. This is the Timeline that is visible when you're inside a scene. When you open a new Flash document (.fla), it always defaults to showing the Timeline of Scene 1. This is also called the Main Timeline in the Flash documentation. Since other programs don't have a Main Timeline versus other Timelines, we felt this was important to point out.
Graphic Symbol Timeline	As you saw in this chapter, when you edit a graphic symbol, it has a timeline too. This is called the Graphic Symbol Timeline. In the case of graphic symbols, the Timeline of the symbol and the scene in which the symbol is placed must have the same number of frames or the symbol's animation will not play properly. This is important, because movie clip symbols, which you'll learn about later, do not behave this way.
Scene's Timeline	Every Flash project (.fla) has a Main Timeline in the form of Scene 1's Timeline. You'll see in later chapters that Flash projects can have multiple scenes. In those cases, each scene is considered its own Main Timeline. Learning the difference between a scene's Timeline and a symbol's Timeline is one of the key foundations to working successfully with Flash.

8.

Motion Tweening

| Basic Motion Tweening | Tweening Effects
| Editing Multiple Frames | Using a Motion Guide |
| Motion Tweening Text | Exploding Text |

chap_8

Flash 5
H•O•T CD-ROM

In Chapter 6, you learned how to create shape tweens. This chapter covers another type of animation—motion tweening. You should work through the exercises in Chapter 7, "*Symbols and Instances*," to better understand how to create, edit and use symbols before you could graduate to this chapter. That's because motion tweening requires you to work with graphic symbols in most, though not all, situations.

Similar to shape tweening, motion tweening is a method of animation that takes the position and attributes of an object in a *start* keyframe, and the position and attributes of an object in an *end* keyframe, and calculates all the animation that will occur between the two. However, unlike shape tweening, motion tweening requires that you use symbols, groups and text blocks, rather than shapes, to create animation. In addition to position, motion tweens can animate scale, tint, transparency, rotation and distortion. Throughout the following exercises, you will learn much more than simple motion tweening, including how to edit multiple frames and how to use motion guides.

Shape Tween Versus Motion Tween

When you start working in Flash, you might be confused about which type of tween to choose: motion or shape. You may spend unnecessary time trying to figure out why your animation is not working when the solution turns out to be that you simply selected the wrong type of tween. The basic distinction between the two types of tweening is that with shape tweening, you use shapes to create the tweening effect; whereas with motion tweening, you use groups, text, or symbols to create the effect. To further help you, we've provided the chart below as a reference tool:

Tweening Simplified

	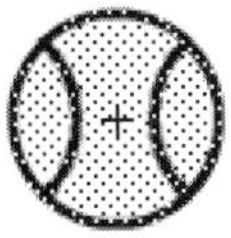	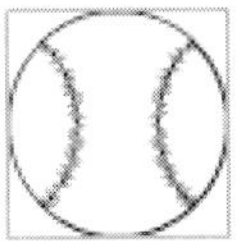	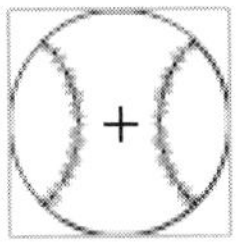	*Play Ball!*	*Play Ball!*
	Shape	**Group**	**Symbol**	**Text Block**	**Broken Apart Text**
Shape Tween	Yes	No	No	No	Yes
Motion Tween	No	Yes	Yes	Yes	No

I. ————————Basic Motion Tweening

This exercise demonstrates how to create a basic motion tween, using a graphic symbol. We've created the graphic symbol for you, but please note that you would need to save your symbols first in your Library if you were creating a motion tween from scratch. Motion tweening itself is very simple, especially once you've learned shape tweening. The big difference is not in technique, but in understanding when to use which type of object: shape, group, symbol, text, or broken-apart text. You may find yourself referring back to the beginning of this chapter often, since remembering the rules of objects and tweening is harder than the process itself.

1. Copy the **chap_08** folder, located on the **H•O•T CD-ROM**, to your hard drive. You need to have this folder on your hard drive in order to save changes to the files inside it.

2. In your **chap_08** folder, open the file **motion_tween.fla** that has been created for you. It has nothing on the Stage, but if you peek in the Library, you'll see that a symbol of a green star has already been created.

3. Open the **Library** for this movie by choosing **Window > Library, Cmd+ L** (Mac) or **Ctrl + L** (Windows). Click **star** to select it. Once it's selected, you will see a preview of it in the preview portion of the Library window.

Note: In Chapter 6, when you were introduced to shape tweening, you saw that your tween had to be from a shape. With motion tweening it is the opposite. When working with motion tweening, the graphic that you're tweening cannot be a shape. Instead, it must be a symbol, text block, or a grouped object.

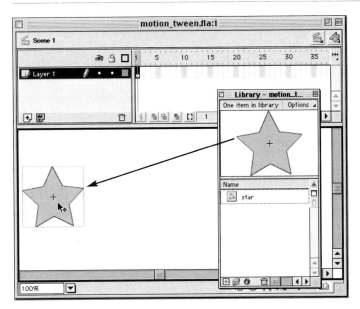

4. Click and drag an instance of the **star** graphic symbol from the Library out onto the left-hand side of your Stage. This is where the star is going to start its animation.

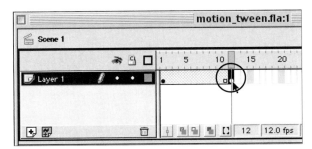

5. Select **Frame 12** and add a keyframe by pressing **F6** on your keyboard.

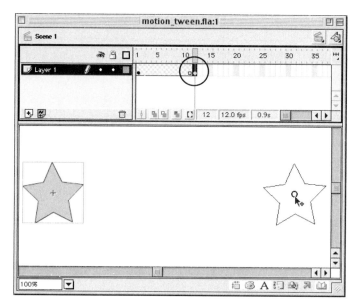

6. Making sure that the **Playhead** is still over **Frame 12**, drag the **star** from the left-hand side to the right-hand side. This will serve as the end-point for your animation.

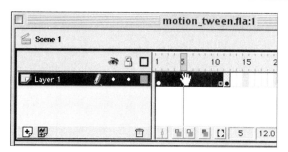

7. Click anywhere between the two keyframes. This will highlight the first keyframe and all of the frames up until the last keyframe. Does this sound familiar? This process is very similar to completing a shape tween.

8. Open the **Frame** panel by choosing **Window > Panels > Frame**, or **Cmd + F** (Mac) or **Ctrl + F** (Windows).

9. From the **Tweening** pull-down menu, choose **Motion**. This turns on motion tweening for the range of frames that you selected in Step 7.

10. Preview your first motion tween by clicking on the Stage, and then pressing **Return/Enter** on the keyboard. The star will move from the left-hand side of the Stage to the right-hand side. All you had to do was set up the beginning and ending points, then turn on motion tweening, and Flash did the rest.

When you apply a motion tween, you can only use it between instances of a single object on a single layer. If you wish to tween multiple items at the same time, you must separate them onto multiple layers. You'll get some practice doing this later in the chapter.

Save this file and leave it open. You will work with it in the next few exercises.

MOVIE | mo_tween1.mov

To see a movie of making this motion tween, play **mo_tween1.mov**, which is located in the folder called **movies** located on the **H•O•T CD-ROM** folder that you transferred to your hard drive.

2. _____Tweening Effects

Surprisingly, a motion tween isn't used solely for tweening motion as its name implies; you can also tween the alpha, color, brightness, size, position, and rotation of a graphic symbol. The next exercise will show you how. This will open the door for you to create a wide range of animated effects–far beyond simply moving an object from one location to another.

1. You should have the file open from the previous exercise, but in case you closed it, we have the previous exercise completed and saved for you. It is in your **chap_08** folder and is titled **mtn_twn_efcts.fla**. Go ahead and open it or work with the file from the previous exercise.

2. Make sure the **Playhead** is over the first frame in the Timeline.

3. Select the **star** on the Stage by clicking on it.

4. Open the **Effect** panel by choosing **Window > Panels > Effect**.

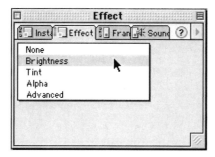

5. From the pull-down menu, choose the first option, **Brightness**.

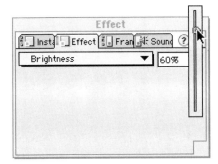

6. To the right of the **Effect** pull-down menu is a small, downward-facing arrow. If you click on it, you are presented with a slider that you can drag up and down. Go ahead and do exactly that. Drag the **Brightness** slider up and down and see what effect it has on the instance of your star. See how it gets brighter and darker as you drag the slider up and down? Choose **60%**.

If you already know the percentage you want, you can also simply type it in the window next to the slider rather than using the slider to adjust the brightness of your symbol.

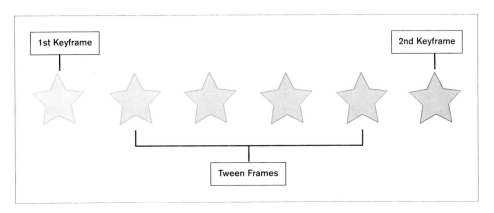

7. Preview the animation by clicking on the Stage, then pressing **Return/Enter** on your keyboard. Notice that the star animation starts out very light and progressively returns to the original color.

You just changed the instance of the star on the first keyframe, but the last keyframe of your animation is unaltered. Since you had motion tweening turned on for this animation, Flash automatically redrew all of the frames in between the two keyframes to accommodate whatever changes you made. This technique would carry through not only to brightness, but to all of the effects that we mentioned at the beginning of this exercise.

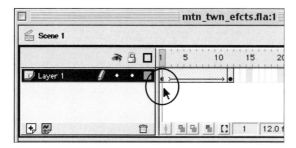

8. Move your **Playhead** back to **Frame 1**.

9. Select the **star** on the Stage by clicking on it.

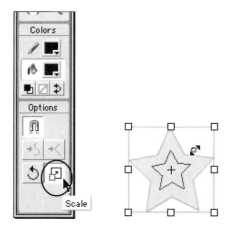

10. Click the **Arrow** tool, then click the **Scale** button at the bottom-right side of the Toolbox. Click on one of the corner resize handles, and drag inward to decrease the size of the star. Release the mouse button.

11. Press **Return/Enter** on your keyboard again to see the changes you've made. Now your star starts off smaller and gets larger as it moves toward the right-hand side of your Stage. At the same time that the size is tweening, the brightness of your star is also changing as it moves! You are now tweening the brightness and scale (not to mention position) in a motion tween. You can take this concept one step further in the following steps.

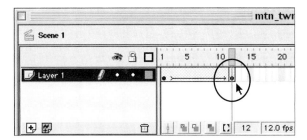

12. This time, move the **Playhead** to **Frame 12**.

13. Select the star on the Stage by clicking on it.

14. Make sure the **Arrow** tool is selected and then click the **Rotate** button located at the bottom-left side of the Toolbox. You are going to rotate the star to the right.

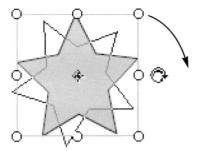

15. Select a rotate handle on the outside corner, and click and drag the star clockwise about 45°. Release the mouse button.

16. Press **Return/Enter** on the keyboard to preview your changes. Now the star also rotates slightly as it moves across the Stage.

17. Save this file and keep it open. You will be using it in the next exercise.

3. ——————Editing Multiple Frames

Suppose you created a motion tween but then decided you would rather have the animation occur across the bottom of the Stage rather than the top. Can you imagine repositioning the items one frame at a time? With the **Edit Multiple Frames** feature, you can bypass that tedious work. The following exercise will show you a method to take the entire animation—including the first and last keyframes—and move them simultaneously.

1. You should still have the file open from the previous exercise. If not, we have a file you can work with. The file is in your **chap_08** folder and is titled **edit_multpl_frms.fla**.

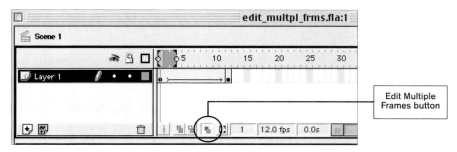

2. Turn on the **Edit Multiple Frames** feature by clicking on the **Edit Multiple Frames** button (located in the status bar of the timeline shown above).

Note: When you click on the Edit Multiple Frames button, you'll notice a gray bar appear on top of the Timeline that looks identical to the Onion Skinning bar, which you learned about in Chapter 5, "Animation Basics." In fact, if you hold your mouse over the end slider bars, Flash's Tool Tips will even say "Start Onion Skin" and "End Onion Skin." Don't be fooled by the similarities, though. Edit Multiple Frames is quite different from Onion Skinning. When working with Onion Skinning, the Onion Skin Range (the gray bar) represents which frames you are seeing at the same time on your Stage. With Edit Multiple Frames, however, the Onion Skin Range represents which keyframes you will be editing at the same time.

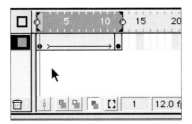

3. Make sure the starting point and ending point of the gray bar (representing your edit multiple frames range) are over **Keyframe 1** and **Keyframe 12**. By doing this you are defining which keyframes you are going to edit simultaneously. In this case you want to take your entire animation and move it up a little on the Stage. Since your animation is composed of two keyframes, (Keyframe 1 and Keyframe 12), these are the keyframes that you want the bar to cover.

4. Click anywhere on the Stage to bring it into "focus." (If you don't, the Timeline will be in focus and Edit Multiple Frames will not work correctly.)

5. Select All by choosing **Edit > Select All**. Notice how you can see the star on the first keyframe and the star on the last keyframe, but unlike Onion Skinning, you won't see all of the frames in between the two keyframes. Also notice that both stars are selected (they have a turquoise border around them), which means you can move them together at one time.

6. Select one of the stars and drag down to the bottom of the Stage. Notice that as you drag, both stars move.

7. Turn off Edit Multiple Frames by clicking on the **Edit Multiple Frames** button again.

It's very important that you turn off Edit Multiple Frames once you have completed your task. If you leave Edit Multiple Frames turned on and continue to work in your Flash movie, Flash will get confused over which frame you're working in and things are your movie will produce unexpected results. But remember, by default you have 100 undo's available to you!

8. Preview the animation by pressing **Return/Enter** on your keyboard. Now the whole animation has been moved to the bottom of the Stage!

Note: The Edit Multiple Frames feature is a great technique to use when you need to move the contents of many frames all at once. By the way, this is the only way to move an entire animation together at one time.

9. Save this file and close it. You won't need it again in this book.

_____Using a Motion Guide

This next exercise shows how to create a motion tween using a **motion guide**. A motion guide is a type of layer on which you can draw a path. With this type of guide layer, the symbol used in the motion tween can follow the position of the path, rather than follow a straight line between two keyframes. This is the only way in Flash to create a curved path, so it is an important technique to understand.

1. Open **motionGuidesFinal.fla** from your **chap_08** folder. This file is a finished version of the file you are about to create. Choose **Control > Test Movie** to view the .swf file. Notice how the leaf moves side to side in a downward direction before reaching the bottom of the screen. Using a motion guide, you will create this same effect next.

2. Close this file.

3. Now, open **motionGuides.fla** from your **chap_08** folder. You will see two layers: the layer with the background image and another layer with a leaf, which is an instance of a graphic symbol.

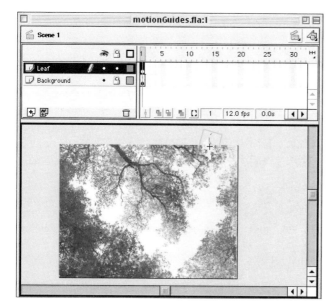

This file serves as a starting point for the next exercise. In the Library for this document, you will see the original symbol called leaf. You will add a motion tween to the leaf instance on the Stage. The difference here is the motion tween is going to follow a line that you will draw.

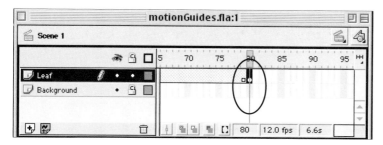

4. Make sure you are on the **Leaf** layer, and add a new keyframe to **Frame 80** by clicking on **80** and pressing **F6** on the keyboard.

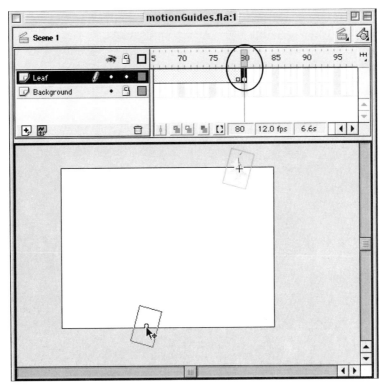

5. Make sure the **Playhead** is over **Keyframe 80**, and click and drag the leaf instance to the bottom of the Stage.

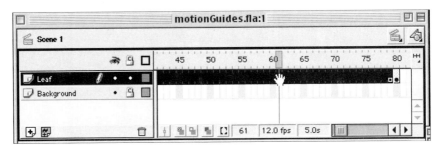

6. On the Timeline, click anywhere in between the two keyframes to select the range of **Frames 1–80**.

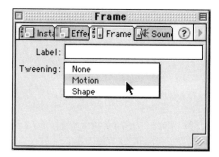

7. Open your **Frame** panel by choosing **Window > Panels > Frame**, or you can press **Cmd + F** (Mac) or **Ctrl + F** (Windows), and turn on motion tweening by choosing **Motion** from the **Tweening** pull-down menu.

You just created a simple motion tween like the one you built in Exercise 1 of this chapter. Now we will show you some techniques to enhance a basic motion tween.

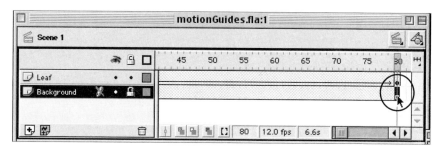

8. To make sure the background shows throughout your animation, you will need to add frames up to the end of the animation. Click on the **Background** layer, then click on **Frame 80**, and press **F5** to add frames up to Frame 80.

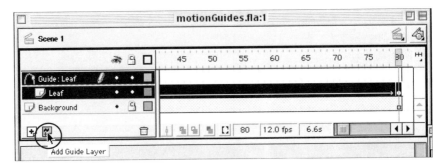

9. Select the **Leaf** layer by clicking to the right of the layer name. Next, you will add a **guide layer** to it. Click the **Add Guide Layer** button once, at the bottom of the Timeline (to the right of the Insert Layer button). This will add a motion guide layer to the Leaf Layer. This new layer has been automatically already named as "Guide: Leaf."

Something else has happened that you haven't seen before: The Leaf layer is indented below the Guide layer. This means that the Leaf layer is taking instructions from the guide layer. The Leaf layer contains your motion tween, and the guide layer will contain the path that the tween will follow. Before it can follow the path, however, you will have to draw one. That's coming up soon, so keep following along.

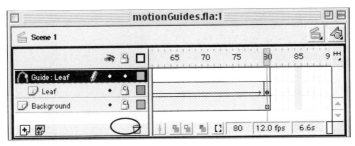

10. Lock the **Leaf** layer so that you don't accidentally put anything on it. You can do this by clicking on the small dot below the lock icon on the Leaf layer.

11. Select the **guide layer** by clicking once on the name of the layer. The layer should turn black.

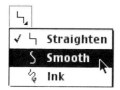

12. Select your **Pencil** tool and for the Pencil Mode option, choose **Smooth**. That way, when you draw the line for the leaf to follow, Flash will smooth out any irregularities for you automatically.

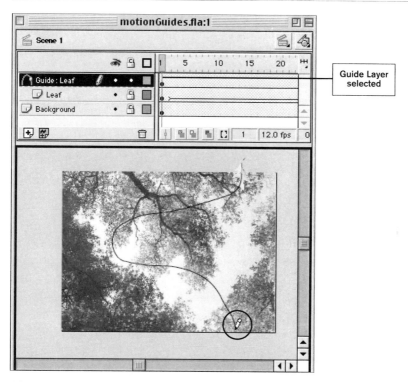

13. On the Stage, draw a curved line. It doesn't matter what color or stroke width you choose. Flash is only concerned with the *path* of the line.

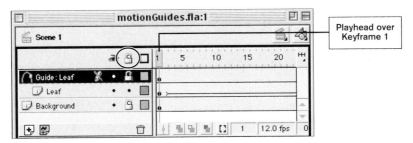

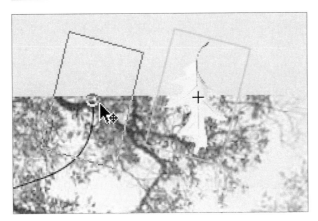

14. Make sure the **Playhead** is over **Keyframe 1**. Unlock the Leaf layer (so you can make changes to it) and lock the Guide layer (because you're done with it and you don't accidentally want to move or edit it).

15. Using the **Arrow** tool, click the little **plus** sign in the middle of the leaf instance—this is the centerpoint. Click and drag the **leaf** to the top point of the line that you drew in the Guide layer. When you get close to the line, the leaf will "snap" to it and turn into a small circle. This is where the leaf will start following the line.

Note: *It is very important that you grab the leaf symbol instance from the centerpoint in order for the motion guide to work properly. You will know if you have done this correctly if the centerpoint turns into a circle as shown in the picture above.*

16. Move the **Playhead** to **Frame 80**, the last keyframe of the animation.

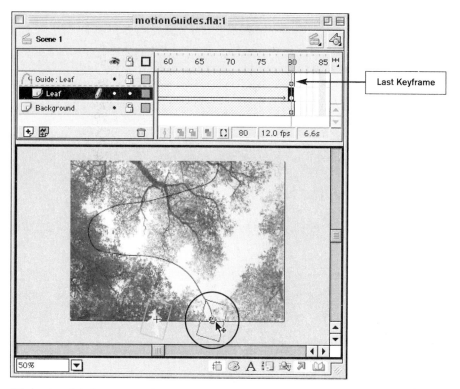

17. Again, click the centerpoint of the leaf symbol instance, and drag the leaf to the bottom point of the line that you drew on the Guide layer. This is where the leaf will stop following the line. That's it!

18. Preview your animation by pressing **Return/Enter** on your keyboard. Notice that the leaf now follows the line that you drew on the Guide layer! If you choose **Control > Test Movie**, you'll notice that now you don't see the line at all! That is because the contents of your motion guide layer will not be visually exported to the final .swf file, but your leaf will still continue to follow the path. When you choose **Test Movie**, Flash writes out a .swf file for you.

Wouldn't it be nice, however, if the leaf rotated in the direction of its movement, instead of always facing in the same direction? In other words, if the leaf is moving down, it should be pointing down, don't you think? You're going to do that next.

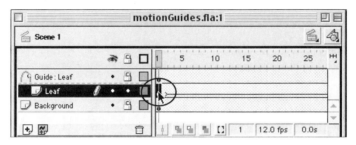

19. Click on **Keyframe 1** of the **Leaf** layer.

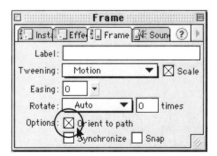

20. Open the **Frame** panel by choosing **Window > Panels > Frame**, or use the shortcut keys: **Cmd + F** (Mac) or **Ctrl + F** (Windows). Click on the **checkbox** next to **Orient to path** in the **Options** section of the **Frame** panel. This does as its name implies. Flash will do its best to orient the leaf to face the direction that the path is going.

21. Preview your animation again by pressing **Return/Enter** on your keyboard. Just by checking one checkbox, Flash now points the leaf symbol instance toward the direction the path is moving as if the wind was blowing it along. This is a great (and easy) way to add the visual effect that your graphic is actually following the path.

22. Save this file and close it. You won't be using it again.

5. ———————Motion Tweening Text

This exercise will show you how to create a motion tween using text. Unlike shape tweening where you have to break the text apart in order to create the animation, motion tweening requires that you use the whole text block to create the animation effect.

1. Open the file titled **mtnTwnTxtFinal.fla** in your **chap_08** folder. This file is a finished version of one you will create in this exercise.

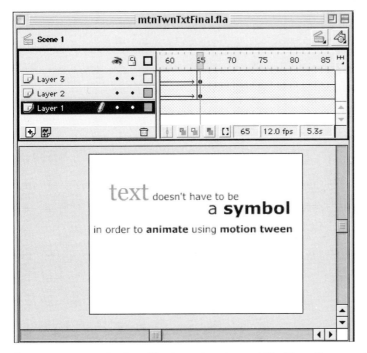

2. Choose **Control > Test Movie** to view the .swf file. You will create these same effects in this exercise.

3. Go ahead and close this file.

4. Choose **File > New** to open a blank document. Save this file as **mtnTwnTxt.fla inside the chap_08** folder on your hard drive.

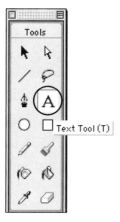

5. Select the **Text** tool, click anywhere on the Stage, and type the words **text doesn't have to be**.

6. Make sure the **Character** panel is open. If it's not, choose **Window > Panels > Character**.

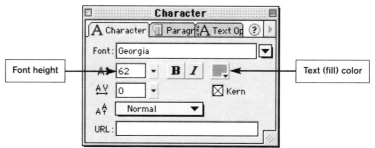

7. Highlight only the letters **text** in the text block. In the **Character** panel, choose **Font: Georgia**, **Font height: 62** and **Text (fill) color: Red**. If you don't have Georgia on your computer, you can use any other font you like.

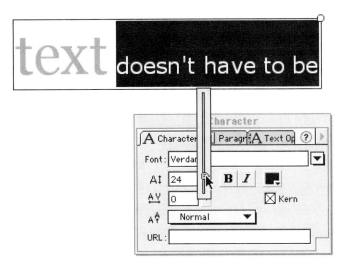

8. Select the remaining text **doesn't have to be**. In the **Character** panel, choose **Font: Verdana**, **Font height: 24** and **Text (fill) color: Black**.

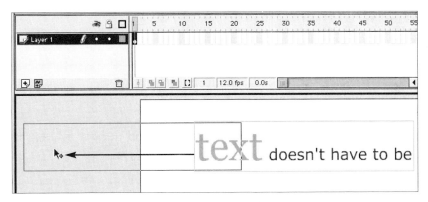

9. Select the **Arrow** tool and drag the text partially off the Stage in the upper-left corner. This will serve as the starting point of the motion tween.

10. On the Timeline, select **Frame 20** and press **F6** to add a keyframe to it.

11. Making sure that **Frame 20** is selected; drag the text block to the top-middle of the Stage. This will serve as the end point for the animation.

12. On the Timeline, click anywhere in between the two keyframes. This will highlight the first keyframe and all of the frames up until the last keyframe.

13. Make sure the **Frame** panel is open. If it's not, choose **Window > Panels > Frame**, or use the shortcut keys: **Cmd + F** (Mac) or **Ctrl + F** (Windows).

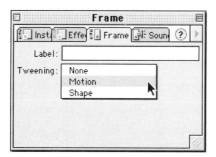

14. Now, turn on motion tweening by choosing **Motion** from the **Tweening** pull-down menu.

15. Preview the motion tween by pressing **Return/Enter** on the keyboard. The text will move from outside the top-left of the Stage to the top-middle of the Stage. You have just created your first motion tween using a text block. But wait, there's more!

In the next few steps you will add two new layers and two more motion tweens with more effects.

16. Lock **Layer 1** so that you don't accidentally modify that layer. You can do this by clicking once on the small dot below the lock icon.

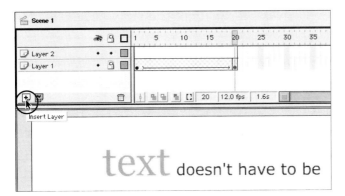

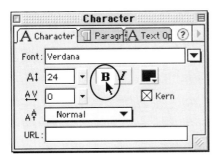

17. Add a new layer by clicking on the **Insert Layer** button.

18. Make sure you are on **Layer 2** and add a blank keyframe to **Frame 20** by pressing **F7** on your keyboard.

19. Select your **Text** tool, then click anywhere on the Stage and type the words **a symbol**.

20. Select all the text in the text block. In the **Character** panel (Window > Panels > Character if it's not already open), choose **Font: Verdana** and **Font height: 24**. Now select only the word **symbol** and click the **Bold** style button.

21. Select the **Arrow** tool and move the text block to just off of the right side of the Stage. This will be the starting point for this animation.

22. At **Frame 45** on **Layer 2**, press **F6** to add a keyframe to it. Move the text block to the middle of the Stage. This will be where the text stops.

Next you are going to add one more effect to the animation.

23. At **Frame 65** on **Layer 2**, press **F6** to add another keyframe at Frame 65.

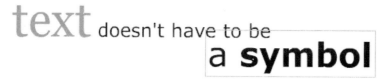

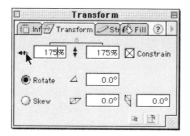

24. Making sure the **Transform** panel is open (if it's not, choose Window > Panels > Transform), select the text block. This time, check the **Constrain** box and enter **175%** in either the width or height field and press **Return**. (Flash will automatically duplicate the number you enter into the other field if your Constrain box is checked.) This will make the text field grow to 175% of its original size. All you have to do next is add the tween.

25. On the Timeline, click to the right of the Layer 2 name. This will highlight the entire range of frames up until the last keyframe.

26. If the **Frame** panel isn't open, choose **Window** > **Panels** > **Frame**, or use the shortcut keys: **Cmd** + **F** (Mac) or **Ctrl** + **F** (Windows) to open it. Turn on motion tweening by choosing **Motion** from the **Tweening** pull-down menu.

27. Test your animation! You should see the text block move from the right side of the Stage to the middle and then grow bigger.

Notice when you test your movie, the animation on Layer 1 disappears? You need to add frames to that layer so that it will be visible throughout your movie.

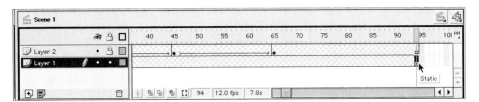

28. Lock **Layer 2** by clicking on the small dot below the lock icon, and unlock **Layer 1** by clicking on the lock symbol. On **Frame 65** on **Layer 1**, add frames by pressing **F5** on the keyboard. Test the animation again and now you should see all the contents on both layers throughout the movie.

29. Go ahead and lock **Layer 1**. Now you should have both layers 1 and 2 locked.

30. Add a new layer by clicking on the **Insert Layer** button. On this new layer–**Layer 3**–click on **Frame 45** and then press **F7**. This will add a blank keyframe to Frame 45.

31. Select the Text tool, and then click anywhere on the Stage and type the words **in order to animate using motion tween**.

32. Make sure the **Character** panel is open. If it's not, choose **Window** > **Panels** > **Character**.

33. Select all the text in the text block and choose **Font: Verdana** and **Font height: 24**. Make the words animate and motion tween bold by highlighting each word and choosing the **Bold** style.

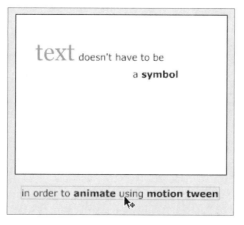

34. Select the **Arrow** tool and move the text block just off the Stage at the bottom. This will be the beginning point for the tween on this layer.

35. On the Timeline for **Layer 3**, add a keyframe to **Frame 65** by clicking on that frame and pressing **F6**. Move the text block to the middle of the Stage, under the previous text block with the words **a symbol**. This will serve as the end point for the animation on layer 3.

36. Click anywhere in between keyframes **45** and **65** to select the range of frames and add a motion tween by choosing **Motion** from the **Tweening** pull-down menu in the **Frame** panel.

37. Test your movie by pressing **Return/Enter** on your keyboard. You have created three different motion tweens using text blocks. In the next exercise you'll use text as a symbol to create even more effects.

38. Save and close this file. You won't be needing it any more.

6. _____Exploding Text

In the previous exercise, you made motion tweens using text blocks. In this exercise, you will create motion tweens using text again, but this time the text will be converted to a symbol first. With a symbol, you have more options to create effects in your motion tween than you have using a text block. While a text block can animate position and scale, a graphic symbol of text can animate position, scale, rotation, color, alpha, tint, and transformations.

1. Open the **boom.fla** file from the **chap_08** folder. This is a starter file that contains a brown background, and the frame rate has been set to 20 frames per second.

2. Using the **Text** tool from the Toolbox, click anywhere on the Stage and type the letter **B**.

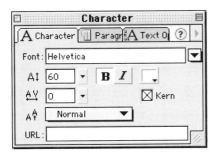

3. Highlight the **B** in the text block and in the **Character** panel (if it's not already open, choose Window > Panels > Character), choose **Font: Arial, Font height: 60, Text (fill) color: White**, and select the **Bold** option.

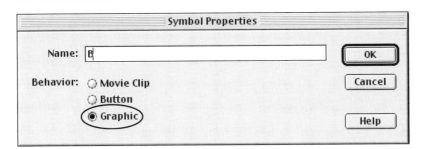

4. Switch to the **Arrow** tool and select the B. Choose **Insert > Convert to Symbol**. (Remember this from Chapter 7?) In the **Symbol Properties** dialog box, name the symbol **B** and choose **Behavior: Graphic**. Click **OK**.

5. Repeat steps 2, 3 and 4 two more times to make two more symbols: **O** and **M**. You can name the **O** text block **O** and the **M** text block **M** in the **Symbol Properties** dialog box.

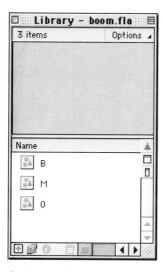

6. You should now have three graphic symbols titled **B**, **O**, and **M** in your Library. If the Library isn't open, choose **Window > Library, Cmd + L** (Mac) or **Ctrl + L** (Windows). These are the separate letters required to spell out the word "BOOM."

7. Press **Cmd + A** (Mac) or **Ctrl + A** and the press the **Delete** key to remove the three instances on your Stage.

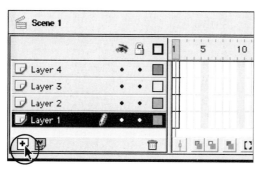

8. Create three new layers by clicking three times on the **Insert Layer** button.

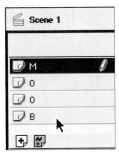

9. From the bottom up, rename the layers **B**, **O**, **O**, **M** by double-clicking on the layer name and typing the appropriate letter. Since these letters are going to be performing a separate animation at the same time, they need to be in their own separate layer.

10. Select the bottom-most layer, layer **B**.

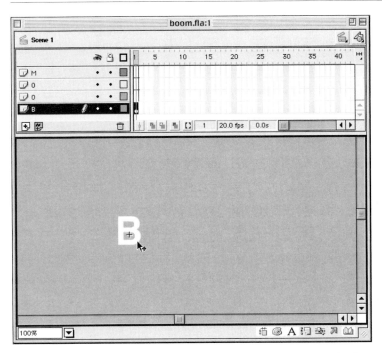

11. From the Library, drag an instance of the **B** symbol out onto the Stage.

12. Now select the next layer up, the first **O** layer. Repeat the same process that you did in the previous step, but this time drag the **O** symbol out onto the Stage, a little to the right of the **B** symbol instance. Alignment isn't too important at this point. In a few steps you will align all of the letters together.

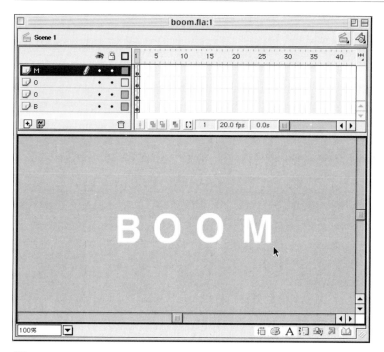

13. Repeat this process for the remaining two layers, putting the next **O** symbol instance in the next layer up, and the **M** symbol instance on the topmost **M** layer.

14. Select the four symbols on the Stage by holding down the **Shift** key and clicking on each one until all four are selected.

15. Open up the **Align** panel by choosing **Window > Panels > Align** or use the shortcut keys **Cmd + K** (Mac) or **Ctrl + K** (Windows).

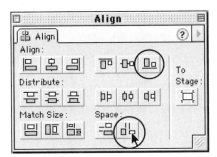

16. Align the bottom of all of the selected graphic symbols and space them evenly by pressing the **Align Bottom Edge** button, then the **Space Evenly Horizontally** button.

Now that they're aligned properly, it is time to animate them!

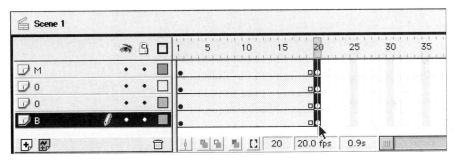

17. Add keyframes to **Frame 20** on all four layers by clicking and dragging down all four layers on Frame 20, and then pressing **F6** on the keyboard. The letters BOOM are going to sit on the Stage for one second (20 frames) and then start to animate.

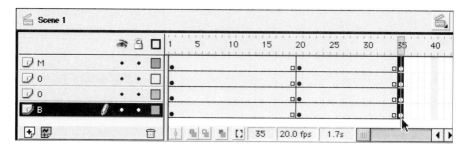

18. Add more keyframes to **Frame 35** on all four layers in the same way you did in the previous step. This is where the letters are going to finish their animation.

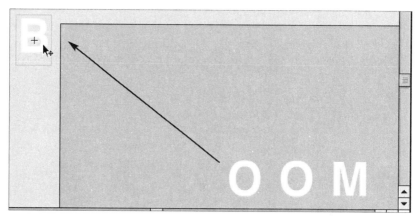

19. Making sure the **Playhead** is over **Frame 35**, click and drag the **B** symbol off the top-left side of your Stage onto the work area.

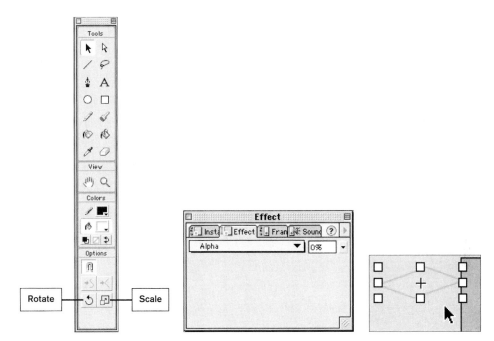

20. Using the **Rotate** and **Scale** tools on the Toolbox, rotate and scale the **B** symbol. The degree of the rotation and scale are completely up to you. Using the **Effect** panel, set its **Alpha** to **0%**. We recommend keeping the Alpha at 0% on the last keyframe. That way, the **B** will fade out completely as it gets blasted into outer space.

21. Modify the positions of the other graphic symbols on **Frame 35** as you did in the previous step; scaling, rotating, and adding an alpha effect to each one. Feel free to move, scale, and rotate each letter any way you want, but we recommend keeping the Alpha at 0%. In the screenshot above, we've selected all of them so you can see an example of the variety of positions you can choose.

22. Click anywhere between keyframes **20** and **35** on the **M** layer and add a motion tween by choosing **Motion** from the **Tweening** pull-down menu in the **Frame** panel. Repeat this process for the other three layers.

Now you're going to use a technique to make the explosion look more realistic.

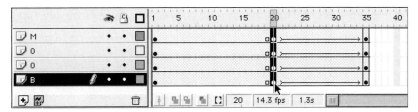

23. Hold down the **Cmd** (Mac) or **Ctrl** (PC) key and click and drag down to select **Keyframe 20** on all four layers.

*Note: In Flash 4, you could easily click and drag down (in a vertical line) to select keyframes on multiple layers. In Flash 5, if you try to simply click and drag down to select keyframes on multiple layers, you will end up having only one keyframe selected. However, if you hold down the **Cmd/Ctrl** key while you click and drag, you can select multiple keyframes all in one vertical line (on multiple layers).*

If you prefer the old style, you can turn on the Flash 4 "style" of keyframe selecting by choosing Edit > Preferences > Timeline Options: Flash 4 Selection Style.

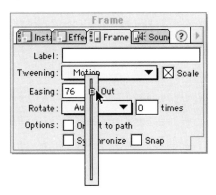

24. In the **Frame** panel (choose Window > Panels > Frame if it's not already open), drag the **Easing** slider up until it reads **76 Out**. Adding Easing to the motion tween will cause the animation to start off fast and then slow down as it nears the end of the animation.

25. Press **Return/Enter** on your keyboard a couple of times to preview it.

TIP | Easing In and Easing Out

The terms *Easing In* and *Easing Out* have to do with the speed of animation. By leaving Easing at its default of *none*, animation in Flash will produce linear motion. This means that all the frames will move at the same speed. Easing Out means that the animation will gradually slow to the last keyframe. Easing In means that the animation will gradually speed up to the last keyframe.

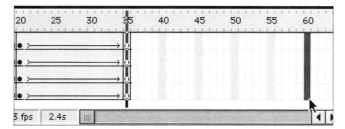

26. Select **Frame 60** on all four layers by clicking and dragging down on Frame 60.

27. Add frames on **Frame 60** on all four layers by pressing **F5** on your keyboard. Now the animation will pause for over a second before it loops and plays again.

28. That's it! Preview your movie by pressing **Cmd/Ctrl + Return**.

29. You can save and close this file. You will not need it again.

Text Motion Tweening Options and Limitations

As you might imagine, we have only scratched the surface and there are many additional options for creating animation using text blocks. As a reference tool, we have provided a list below listing the options and limitations of motion tweening.

What Motion Tweening Can Do

Symbol Instance

- Tween position
- Tween brightness
- Tween tint
- Tween alpha
- Tween scaling
- Tween rotation
- Tween skew

Grouped Object

- Tween position
- Tween scaling
- Tween rotation
- Tween skew
- Text Block (editable text)
- Tween position
- Tween scaling
- Tween rotation
- Tween skew

What Motion Tweening Can't Do

- Tween a shape
- Tween broken-apart text
- Tween multiple items on the same layer

9.
Bitmaps

| Benefits of Bitmaps |

| Importing and Compressing Bitmaps |

| Importing Bitmap Sequences | Bitmap Fills |

| Breaking Apart Bitmaps | Converting Bitmaps to Vectors |

| Basic Masking | Animated Masks | Fading Bitmaps |

| Cross Dissolve with Bitmaps |

chap_9

Flash 5
H•O•T CD-ROM

So far, you've mostly worked with vector images. However, as you get more comfortable in Flash, you'll want to use photos and other bitmapped images in your projects. This chapter concentrates on bitmap files and how Flash treats them differently from vectors. Although many people think Flash is simply a vector-editing and animation program, you will soon learn that Flash has some pretty impressive bitmap-editing features.

You will learn how to import bitmaps, how to optimize them, how to convert them to vectors, and how to create fills with them. You'll also learn the art of breaking apart bitmaps to edit or erase them, and how to create a static and animated mask of a bitmap.

Benefits of Bitmaps

Vector graphics are probably best known for their crisp appearance, small file size and flexibility in scaling. Their small, efficient file size makes your movie play faster and your visitors happier. However, vectors do have a few negative aspects. Complex vector artwork made up of many individual vector shapes can actually generate large file sizes. Also, many photographs do not look good as vector artwork. In these cases, you'll want to work with a bitmap file. Bitmap graphics (also known as raster graphics) are stored in the computer as a series of values, with each pixel taking a set amount of memory. Because each pixel is defined individually, this format is great for photographic images with complex details. This also means that bitmap graphics are typically larger than vector graphics.

As you create more projects using Flash, you may find that you want to use images created outside Flash in your movie. Some of these files will be imported to Flash as vectors, while others will be imported as bitmaps. Conveniently, Flash has the ability to import graphics of many different formats, including JPEG, GIF and–new to Flash 5–TIFF. Additionally, if you have QuickTime 4 or later installed on your machine, the list of files available for import increases even further. A chart of the file formats that can be imported into Flash is listed below.

File Types Supported by Flash					
Vector or Bitmap	**File Name**	**Extension**	**Mac**	**Windows**	**QuickTime 4 or later needed**
Vector	Adobe Illustrator 6.0 or earlier	eps, .ai	x	x	no
Vector	AutoCAD DXF	.dxf	x	x	no
Vector	Enhanced Windows MetaFile	.emf		x	no
Vector	Macromedia Freehand	.fh7, .ft7, fh8, .ft8, .fh9, .ft9	x	x	no
Vector	FutureSplash Player	.spl	x	x	no
Vector	Flash Player	.swf	x	x	no
					continues on next page

Vector or Bitmap	File Name	Extension	Mac	Windows	QuickTime 4 or later needed
Vector	Flash Player	.swf	X	X	no
Vector	Windows Metafile	.wmf		X	no
Bitmap	Bitmap	.bmp		X	no
Bitmap	GIF and animated GIF	.gif	X	X	no
Bitmap	JPEG	.jpg	X	X	no
Bitmap	PICT	.pct, .pic	X	X	no with Mac, yes with Windows
Bitmap	PNG	.png	X	X	no
Bitmap	MacPaint	.pntg	X	X	yes
Bitmap	Photoshop	.psd	X	X	yes
Bitmap	QuickTime Image	.qtif	X	X	yes
Bitmap	Silicon Graphics	.sai	X	X	yes
Bitmap	TGA	.tgf	X	X	yes
Bitmap	TIFF	.tif, .tiff	X	X	yes
Other	QuickTime movie	.mov	X	X	yes

File Types Supported by Flash *continued*

Note: *Flash will honor the transparency settings of graphics that can have a transparency applied such as .gif, .png and .pict files.*

I. ————————Importing and Compressing Bitmaps

This first exercise will teach you how to import a bitmap into Flash and then how to adjust the compression settings of the bitmap you just imported.

1. Copy the **chap_09** folder from the **Flash 5 H•O•T CD-ROM** to your hard drive. You must copy the files to your hard drive if you want to save changes to them.

2. Choose **File > New** to open a new document. Save the file as **import.fla** in the chap_09 folder.

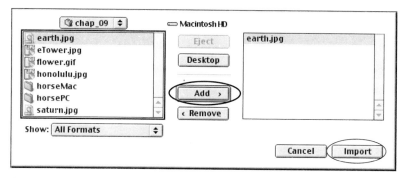

Import dialog box on the Macintosh.

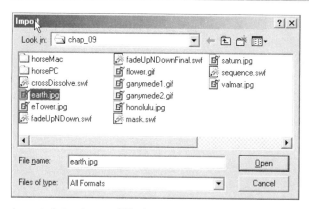

Import dialog box on Windows.

3. Choose **File > Import**, or press **Cmd + R** (Mac) or **Ctrl + R** (Windows). This will open the **Import** dialog box. Browse to the **earth.jpg** file located inside the **chap_09** folder. Select the file, click **Add** and click **Import** (Mac) or just click **Open** (Windows).

When you add a bitmap file to your project using the Import menu, you might wonder where the file goes. The file is automatically placed in three places: on the Stage, in the Library and in the Fill panel. This exercise will concentrate on the Stage and the Library. Later exercises will focus on the Fill panel.

4. Choose **Window > Library**, or **Cmd + L** (Mac) or **Ctrl + L** (Windows), to open the Library window.

5. Select the **earth.jpg** image inside the Library. Press the **Options** button and select **Properties** from the drop-down list. The **Bitmap Properties** dialog box will open.

You can also open the Bitmap Properties dialog box by either double-clicking on the image in the Library preview window or on the icon next to the image's name in the Library.

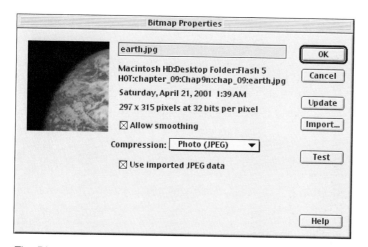

The Bitmap Properties dialog box is where you can set compression on individual images.

Bitmap Properties Dialog Box	
Preview window	Shows the current properties of the bitmap and allows you to preview any changes applied to the settings in the dialog box.
File Name	Displays the bitmap's Library item name. Clicking in the File Name field and typing a new name can change the bitmap's name.
Image path	Displays the path from where the image originated.
File information	Shows the date the bitmap was last modified, the file's dimensions, and the color depth.
Allow smoothing	Smoothes or dithers the image if this box is checked. If this box is unchecked, the image will appear aliased or jagged.
	continues on next page

Bitmap Properties Dialog Box *continued*	
Compression type	Allows you to choose between Photo (JPEG) or Lossless (PNG/GIF) for that particular bitmap in the Library. Photo compression is best used for complex bitmaps with many colors or gradations. Lossless compression is best used for bitmaps with fewer colors and simple shapes filled with single colors.
Use imported JPEG data (Use Document Default Quality)	Allows you to use the original compression settings and avoid double compression if this box is checked. If this box is not checked you can enter your own values—between 1 and 100—for the quality of the image.
Update	Allows you to update the bitmap image if it has been changed outside of Flash. It uses the image path to track the original image's location and will update the image selected in the Library with the file located in the original location.
Import	Enables you to change the actual file the image path points to. By choosing a new bitmap using the Import button, you will change the current image to the new file chosen, and all instances in the project file will reflect the new bitmap.
Test	Allows you to see the changes you make to the settings of the *Bitmap Properties* dialog box in the Preview window and displays the new compression information at the bottom of the dialog box.

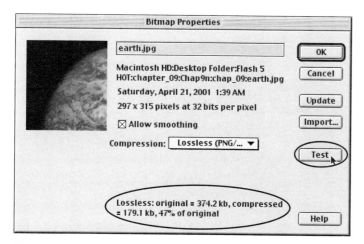

6. In the **Bitmap Properties** dialog box, choose **Compression: Lossless (PNG/GIF)** and click the **Test** button. Notice how the new compression information appears at the bottom of the dialog box? You have just changed the compression settings for the **earth.jpg** image. If you click **OK**, this setting will alter the bitmap in the Library and the instance on the Stage. However, don't close the dialog box just yet—you are going to make a couple more changes.

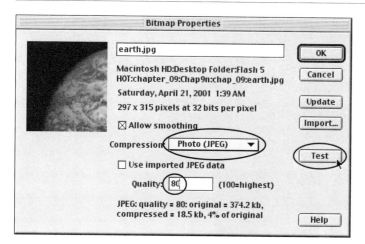

7. In the **Bitmap Properties** dialog box, change the compression settings back to JPEG by choosing **Compression: Photo (JPEG)**. Uncheck the **Use imported JPEG data box** and add your own quality setting by typing **Quality: 80** (100 is best, while 0 is worst). Click the **Test** button again. Notice how the new compression information appears at the bottom of the dialog box.

8. Click **OK** to keep the last settings you applied.

TIP | Compression Settings

One of the most important issues to keep in mind when working with bitmap files in Flash is that unless you tell it otherwise, Flash will always apply its own default compression settings to your bitmap graphics when the movie is exported from the project file. The graphics compression settings are available in two locations. You can set a single compression method and amount for every graphic in the project using the global *Publish Settings* (covered in Chapter 15) or you can use the *Bitmap Properties* dialog box to set and preview individual compression settings for each file. Any changes you make in the Bitmap Properties dialog box will affect the graphic in the Library and *all* the instances of the bitmap within the project file.

---

9. Save and close this file.

2. —————————Importing Bitmap Sequences

One way to create a "mock" video effect in Flash is to use a sequence of photographs in which each image is just slightly different from the previous image. When these images are placed in keyframes, one right after another, and you test the movie, it will appear as if the camera is rolling! The following exercise will demonstrate Flash's ability to create frame-by-frame animations (or mock video) by importing a series of bitmap graphics all at once.

1. Open **sequenceFinal.fla** in the **chap_09** folder.

2. You will see a series of images in Keyframes 1-10. Press **Return/Enter** on the keyboard to preview the movie. Notice how it seems as if you are watching a video of the horse running. You are going to create this animation sequence next.

3. Close the file.

4. Create a new document and save it as **sequence.fla** in the **chap_09** folder.

5. Choose **Modify > Movie** to change the movie's properties. Choose **Frame Rate: 22 fps** and select **black** for the background color. Click **OK**.

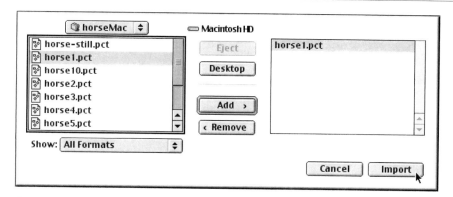

6. Choose **File > Import** or press **Cmd +R** (Mac) or **Ctrl +R** (Windows). In the **chap_09** folder, browse to the **horseMac** folder if you are using a Macintosh or **horsePC** folder if you are using Windows. Notice that there are ten numbered files named **horseX**. Select the file **horse1** and click **OK** (Mac) or **Open** (Windows).

The horseMac folder contains .pct images supported by Mac and supported by Windows only if you have QuickTime 4 or higher installed on your computer. The horsePC folder contains .bmp images only supported by Windows.

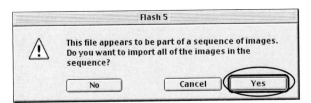

7. Flash will automatically detect that the image you are trying to import is part of a sequence of images, and you will be asked if you want to import the whole series of images. Click **Yes** so that all the images will be imported into Flash.

If you ever want to import a sequence of images as successive frames and have Flash recognize it as sequence, be sure to number the images in the order you want the sequence to appear, such as image01, image02, etc. Whenever Flash sees sequentially numbered images in the same folder, it will ask you if the images should all be imported at once in a sequence.

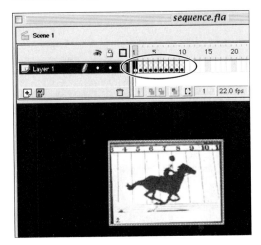

*When you click **Yes** in the last step, Flash will import all ten files in the sequence, place them on the Stage, and create a new keyframe for each in the Timeline. Pretty suave!*

8. Test the movie (**Control > Test Movie**). Notice that even though each frame holds a separate image, when you test the movie, it appears that you're watching video footage!

9. Go ahead and save and close this file. You will not need it in future exercises.

3. ————————Bitmap Fills

In the previous two exercises, you learned how to import bitmaps into Flash. This exercise will show you how to use a bitmap as a fill. This technique will allow you to paint with bitmap images, or fill a shape with them. It is useful for filling a single shape with a complex background, and it takes a lot less bandwidth than importing a big graphic to use as a masked shape fill (which you'll learn to do soon).

1. Choose **File > New** to open a new document. Save the file as **bitmapFills.fla** in the **chap_09** folder.

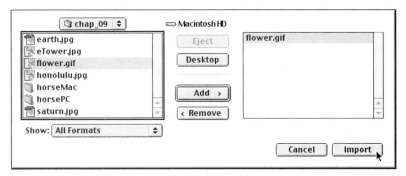

2. Choose **File > Import** or use the shortcut keys **Cmd + R** (Mac) **Ctrl + R** (Windows). In the **chap_09** folder, browse to the file named **flower.gif**. Double-click it to add the file to the import list and click **Import** (Mac) or just double-click to open (Windows). You will see the bitmap on your Stage.

As we explained in Exercise 1, each time you import a graphic file into Flash, the file is automatically placed in three locations: on the Stage, in the Library and in the Fill panel. The next steps will focus on the Fill panel.

3. Select the **flower** bitmap on the Stage and **delete** it. Although the instance will be removed from the Stage, the bitmap will still exist in the Library and in the Fill panel.

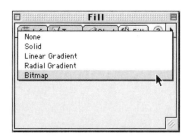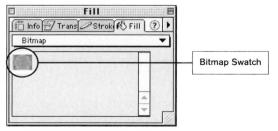

4. Choose **Window >Panels > Fill** to open the **Fill** panel. From the drop-down menu select **Bitmap**. You will see a thumbnail image of the bitmap you imported in the **Bitmap Swatches** panel.

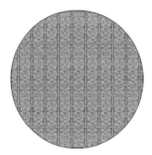

5. Select the **Oval** tool in the Toolbox and draw a circle on the Stage. Notice how the circle is filled with tiny images of the flower bitmap!

You can even alter the way the bitmap fill looks. The next steps will show you how.

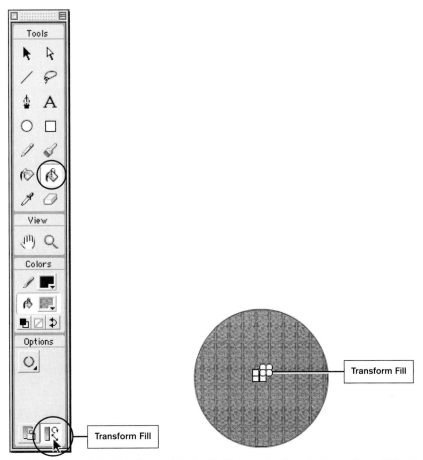

6. Click on the **Paint Bucket** tool in the Toolbox and select the **Transform Fill** option, located at the bottom of the Toolbox. Click in the center of the image to make the transform handles appear.

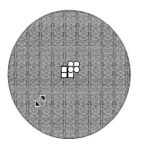
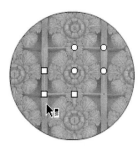

7. Grab one of the **squares** and drag it outward to change the scale of the bitmap fill.

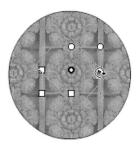
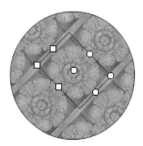

8. Select the **upper-right circle** and move it down to change the rotation of the bitmap fill.

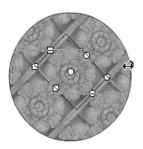
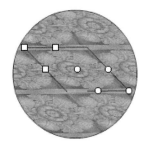

9. Drag the **upper-most circle** handle to the right to add a skew to the fill. Go ahead and play with the Transform Fill handles and modify the bitmap fill to your liking.

Not only can you create shapes that have bitmap fills, you can paint with bitmap fills, too.

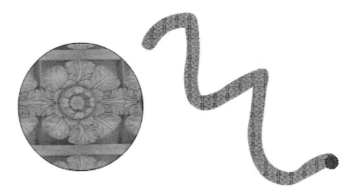

10. Select the **Brush** tool in the Toolbox and draw a shape on the Stage. As you can see, Flash not only offers the ability to import bitmaps, but it also allows you to use them in many creative ways.

11. Save and close this file.

4. ──────────Breaking Apart Bitmaps

When you import bitmaps into Flash, you are not limited to using the files as they exist in their original form. Flash offers a feature that allows you to convert the bitmap into one simple shape so that you can change the colors or even erase sections of the bitmap. The following exercise will teach you how to break apart bitmaps so you can modify areas of the bitmap with the drawing and painting tools.

1. Choose **File > New** to open a new document. Save the file as **breakApart.fla** in the **chap_09** folder.

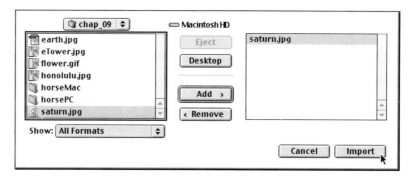

2. Choose **File > Import** or press **Cmd + R** (Mac) **Ctrl + R** (Windows). In the **chap_09** folder, browse to the file named **saturn.jpg**. Double-click it to add the file to the import list and click **Import** (Mac) or just double-click on it to open (Windows). You will see a photo of Saturn on your Stage.

Original saturn .jpg Bitmap

Broken apart saturn .jpg Bitmap

3. Select the **saturn.jpg** bitmap on the Stage and choose **Modify > Break Apart**. Click on a blank area of your Stage to deselect the bitmap.

Note: *Breaking apart a bitmap will affect only the instance on the Stage and not the original in the Library.*

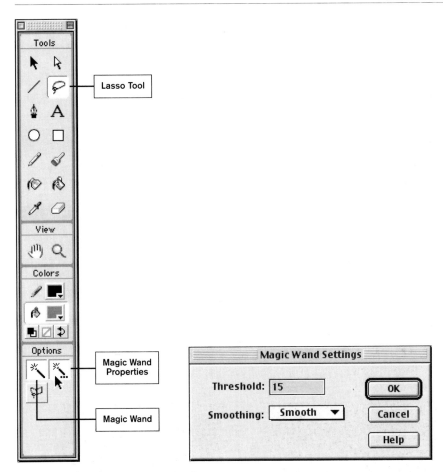

4. Select the **Lasso** tool in the Toolbox.

5. Open the **Magic Wand Properties** dialog box by clicking on the **Magic Wand Properties** button at the bottom of the Toolbox. Choose **Threshold: 15** and **Smoothing: Smooth**. This will set the range of similar colors within 15 pixels and the edge of the selection will be smooth. Click **OK**.

Note: *The Threshold setting determines how much the nearby pixels should match, colorwise, in order to be selected. You can enter any value in the threshold range from 0 to 200. A threshold of 0 will indicate that only the pixels that exactly match the first pixel color that you choose will be chosen. A threshold of 200 will select every pixel. The Smoothing setting defines the appearance of the edges of the bitmap.*

6. Click on the **Magic Wand** button in the Toolbox and move the cursor over the image. Click on a section of the bitmap to select a range of similar colors.

You will see the cursor change from the Lasso tool to the Magic Wand tool when the cursor is directly over the image.

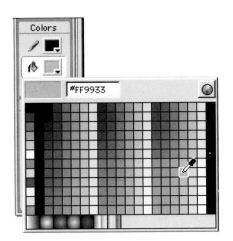

7. Click on the **Fill Color** option in the Toolbox to open the Fill Color picker and choose an orange color. As soon as you choose the color, the image on the Stage will be instantly updated to reflect the new color.

8. Repeat Steps 5 and 6 several times, selecting a different color each time.

9. Select the **Eraser** tool in the Toolbox and draw a line across the background of the image on the Stage. You have just removed part of the Saturn picture and separated it into two separate pieces.

10. With the **Eraser** tool still selected. Click on the **Faucet** option in the Toolbox and click on the black areas in the image. The faucet modifier allows you to obliterate an entire section of a fill (or a stroke) with one click!

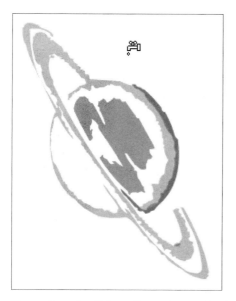

The end result will be a Saturn image that is significantly different from the original in the Library. This is a useful technique for creating a stylized image, or erasing parts of an image based on color.

---

11. Save and close this file.

---

5. ————————————**Converting Bitmaps to Vectors**

You can convert imported bitmaps into vector art by using the **Trace Bitmap** feature. You might want to do this to reduce the file size of a photographic image or to zoom into a photographic image during an animation (vectors scale when you magnify them, while bitmaps will get soft in focus when you enlarge them).

The Trace Bitmap feature traces the outlines and internal shapes of a bitmap graphic and creates a new set of vector shapes that simulate the appearance of the bitmap file. Trace Bitmap is not an exact science, though, and requires a little experimentation to get it just right. This exercise will teach you how to use this feature to turn a bitmap into a vector.

1. Create a new document (**File > New**) and save this file as **traceBitmap.fla** in the **chap_09** folder.

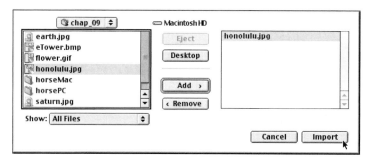

2. Choose **File > Import** or use the shortcut keys **Cmd + R** (Mac) **Ctrl + R** (Windows). In the **chap_09** folder, browse to the file named **honolulu.jpg**. Double-click it to add the file and click **Import** (Mac) or just double-click to open (Windows). You will see a photo of Honolulu on your Stage.

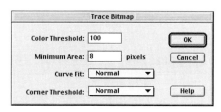

3. Select the image on the Stage and choose **Modify > Trace Bitmap**. This will open the **Trace Bitmap** dialog box.

Note: When you use the Trace Bitmap function, the changes will affect only the selected image on the Stage. The bitmap in the Library will remain unchanged.

Trace Bitmap Dialog Box Defined	
Color Threshold	Sets the amount of color that each pixel can vary before it is considered a different color. As the threshold value is increased, the number of colors in the image is decreased, and the resulting traced bitmap image will have fewer colors than the original. The Color Threshold range is 1-500.
Minimum Area	Determines the number of surrounding pixels to consider when calculating the color of a pixel. The Minimum Area range is 1-1000.
Curve Fit	Determines how smoothly the outlines in the traced shape are drawn and how closely they match the original image.
Corner Threshold	Determines whether to use sharp edges (Many corners) or smoother edges (Few corners).

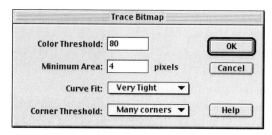

4. To produce the vector that closely resembles the original bitmap, decrease the settings in the **Color Threshold: 80** and in the **Minimum Area: 4**. For **Curve Fit: Very Tight** and for the **Corner Threshold** select **Many corners** to create a vector that has outlines with sharp edges that closely match the original bitmap. Click **OK**.

Be aware that the more detail a bitmap contains, and the lower your settings in the Bitmap dialog box, the longer it will take to convert the bitmap to a vector. This can increase the file size of the movie.

Bitmap   *Vector*

5. When the conversion process completes you will have an image of Honolulu that is composed of object vector fills. Click anywhere outside of the image to deselect it and you will see the vector shapes.

*By using the Undo function–**Cmd + Z** (Mac) or **Ctrl + Z** (Windows)–you can always return the vector art to the original bitmap version and try it again if you don't like how the new image turned out.*

Since you have transformed the bitmap image into a vector image, you can change and alter all of the shapes within the image just as you would any other vector image.

6. Pick an area of the image that you want to change, such as the dormant volcano Diamond Head in the background of the image. Click once on that vector shape to select it.

7. Using the **Fill** panel (Window > Panels > Fill), make the volcano erupt by choosing a **red** color from the drop-down color picker.

8. What would an erupting volcano be without a tidal wave? Move the cursor over the ocean edge and you will notice the shape of the cursor changing to indicate that you can move the line. Go ahead and click once to raise the ocean, simulating a tidal wave!

9. Try changing the colors and shapes of different parts of the vector image. Use can even use the **Ink Bottle** tool to add outlines to the shapes you select inside the image.

Note: *If the desired result of using the Trace Bitmap feature is to conserve file size, rather than match the original image as close as possible, choose a higher Color Threshold, higher Minimum Area, Smooth Curve Fit, and Few Corners. This will result in a decrease in final file size.*

10. Save and close this file. You won't be needing it anymore.

6. _____Basic Masking

Masking is another great technique that can be created using bitmaps. A mask is a special layer that defines what is visible on the layer below it. Only layers that are beneath the shapes in the mask layer will be visible. This exercise will teach you how to create a text mask that masks a bitmap background. You could also use a mask technique on vector art, but what fun would that be in the Bitmap chapter?

1. Create a new file and save it as **mask.fla** in the **chap_09** folder.

2. Choose **Modify > Movie** and enter **Frame Rate: 20** and select **Background Color: Black**.

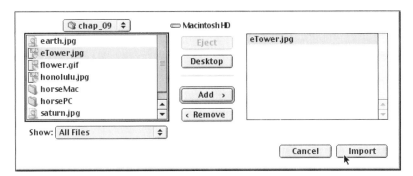

3. Choose **File > Import** and browse to the **eTower.jpg** file in the **chap_09** folder. Double-click the file to add it and then click **Import** (Mac) or just double-click to open (Windows). This will place the bitmap on the Stage.

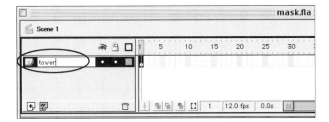

4. Double-click the **Layer 1** name and rename the layer: **tower**.

5. Click the **Insert Layer** icon to add a new layer above the **tower** layer. It's important that the new layer you create is positioned above the tower layer, so move it there by dragging it if it appeared below the tower layer.

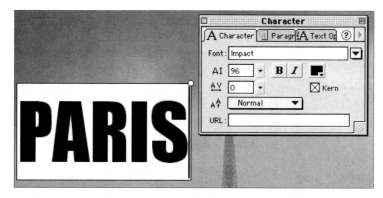

6. In the **Character** panel (Window > Panels > Character), choose **Font: Impact** and **Font Height: 96**. Make sure the new layer, **Layer 2,** is still selected and with the Text tool write the word: **PARIS** in capital letters in the middle of the Stage.

This text is going to end up as the mask for the bitmap. You can think of the text as a cookie cutter that will allow you to see what you cut out of the background image. Therefore, in order to take advantage of all the dough (the whole image you just imported) you will make the cookie cutter (the text block) larger.

7. Choose **Window > Panels > Transform** to open the **Transform** panel. It is best to use the Transform tool rather than the Scale tool because you can easily distort the text with the Scale tool.

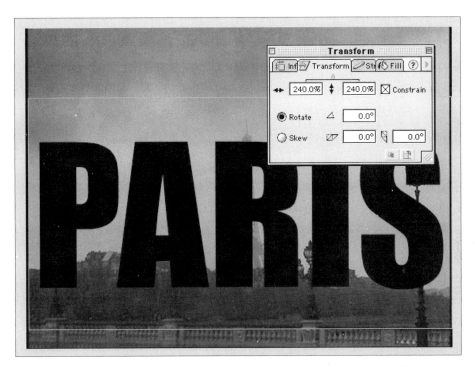

8. Select the text block on the Stage. In the **Transform** panel, make sure the Constrain box is selected and type **240.0%** in the width or height field. Press **Return/Enter** on the keyboard. The text block will transform to 240% of its original size.

In the following steps, you will turn this text block into a Mask layer next.

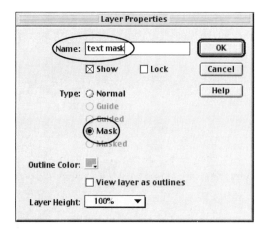

9. Make sure **Layer 2** is still selected and choose **Modify > Layer**. This will open the **Layer Properties** dialog box. Name this layer **text mask** and select **Type: Mask**. Click **OK**.

Up to this point, you have a mask layer ("text mask") with a defined mask area, although now you need to create the masked layer.

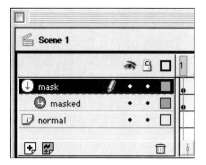

Note: *You can tell whether or not a layer is a mask or a masked layer by its icon. An unmasked (normal) layer has a standard layer icon: a white sheet of paper. A mask layer has a white circle with a purple arrow pointing down in it, and a masked layer displays an indented purple circle with a white arrow in it. Additionally, the lines that separate masked layers from the mask layer are dotted rather than solid.*

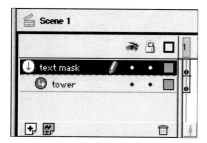

10. To make the **tower** layer become *masked* by the text mask layer, select the tower layer, choose **Modify > Layer** and select **Type: Masked** and click **OK**. You will see the icon for the **tower** layer change.

You can also select Option + Click (Mac) or Alt + Click (Windows) on the tower layer to turn it into a masked layer.

11. Choose **Control > Test Movie** to test the movie. You will see the bitmap showing through the text shapes.

You have just created your first mask! In the next exercise, you are going to animate the mask.

12. Save this file and keep this file open for the next exercise.

7. _____**Animated Masks**

In the previous exercise, you learned how to create a basic mask out of text. But, who says all masks have to be static? This exercise will teach you how to create a text mask that moves over a bitmap background.

1. You should still have the **mask.fla** file open from the previous exercise, but in case you accidentally closed it, choose **File > Open** and select the **mask.fla** file you saved in the **chap_09** folder on your hard drive.

2. Select the **tower** layer and click **Frame 40**. Press **F5** to add frames up to that frame. Click on the **lock** icon to lock this layer, so you don't accidentally select something on this layer.

3. Select the first keyframe on the **text mask** layer and move the text block off the Stage to the left. This will serve as the beginning of the mask animation.

4. With the **text mask** layer still selected, click **Frame 40** and press **F6** to add a keyframe to that frame. With Frame 40 still selected, move the text block off to the right side of the Stage. This will serve as the end point of the mask animation. You are going to add a motion tween next.

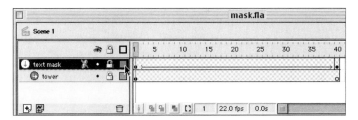

5. Select all of the frames in the **text mask** layer by clicking just to the right of the layer name. Choose **Window > Panels > Frame** to open the **Frame** panel. In the **Tweening** drop-down menu, select **Motion**.

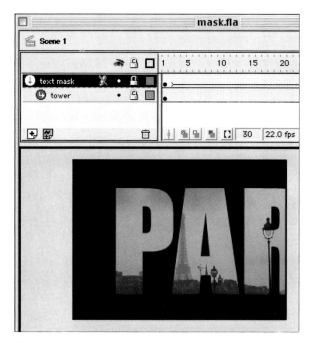

6. Click on the **lock** icon to lock the text mask layer. Notice that you can immediately see the masked image on the Stage.

7. Press **Return/Enter** to test your movie! Great job! You have now added a few steps to the basic mask exercise to create an animated mask.

8. Save and close this file.

_____Effects with Bitmaps: Fading Up and Down

When you are working with bitmaps, you can make them fade in from invisible to visible or vice versa. This handy technique can be accomplished by turning the bitmap into a symbol, creating a motion tween and applying an alpha to one of the symbols at the end or the beginning of the tween. You will learn how to do this in the following steps.

1. Open the **fadeUpNDownFinal.fla** file located inside the **chap_09** folder.

2. Choose **Control > Test Movie**. You will see the image of one of Jupiter's moons slowly disappear and then a portion of the moon reappear again. Next, you will create this effect.

3. Close this file.

4. Choose **File > New** to create a new document. Save this file as **fadeUpNDown.fla** in the **chap_09** folder on your hard drive.

5. Choose **Modify > Movie** and in the **Movie Properties** dialog box, type **500** in the width field and **500** in the height field. Select **black** for the background color of the movie and click **OK**.

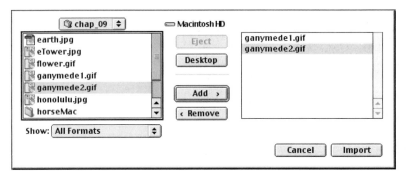

6. Import two bitmaps by choosing **File > Import**. In the **chap_09 folder**, browse to the **ganymede1** and **ganymede2** images. On the Mac, you can add both of them to the import list by double-clicking on each of them. Once they are added to the list, click **Import**. On Windows click on one, then shift-click on the second to select both, then click **Open**.

7. Although you imported both files, you will see only one image on the Stage. That's because the other image is behind it! Click anywhere off the Stage to deselect the images. Click on the top image and drag it to reveal the image underneath.

Note: When you import multiple images at once and they are not part of a recognized sequence, Flash will automatically stack all the images on top of each other in the same keyframe. Often, you will have to deselect all the images, click on the top image to select it, and then move it to access the other images underneath.

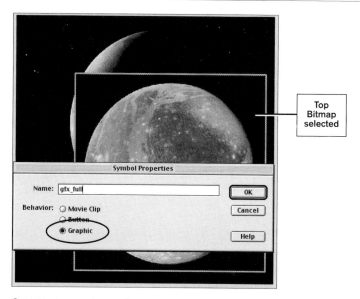

Top Bitmap selected

8. With the **top** image (the full moon) selected, choose **Insert > Convert to Symbol** (F8) to convert the bitmap to a symbol. Name the symbol **gfx_full** and select **Graphic** for the behavior and click **OK**.

Why convert the bitmap to a symbol? In a few steps you will be using alpha to create the fade effect and you can't apply an alpha effect to an object that is not a graphic or movie clip symbol (which you will lean about in Chapter 11).

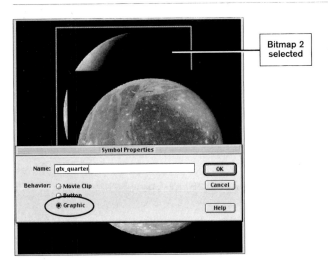

9. Click on the image behind the full moon to select it. Choose **Insert > Convert to Symbol** (**F8**) to convert the bitmap to a symbol. Name the symbol **gfx_quarter** and select **Graphic** for the behavior and click **OK**.

10. On the Stage, delete the **gfx_quarter** symbol. Although you have deleted it from the Stage, the symbol will still reside in the Library, and you will use it in a little later in this exercise.

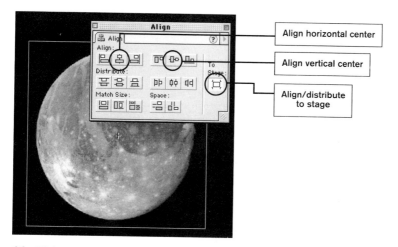

Align horizontal center

Align vertical center

Align/distribute
to stage

11. Click on the **gfx_full** instance on the Stage to select it. In the **Align** panel (**Cmd + K** or **Ctrl + K**), select the **Align/Distribute to Stage** button, which will apply all subsequent selections relative to the Stage. Select the **Align horizontal center** and **Align vertical center** to center the symbol instance on the Stage.

12. In the main Timeline, press **F6** on **Frame 20** to add a keyframe to that frame.

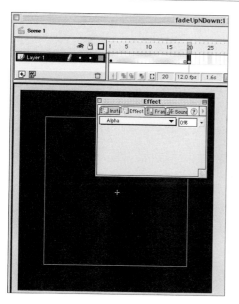

13. With the symbol instance in **Frame 20** selected, open the **Effect** panel (Window > Panels > Effect). Choose **Alpha** and move the slider to **0%** to make the moon invisible in Frame 20.

Now you have the full moon visible in Frame 1 and an invisible moon in Frame 20. All you have left to do is add the motion tween to animate the effect. You will do this next.

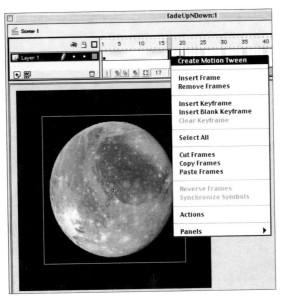

14. Select any frame between Frame 1 and 20 and press **Ctrl + Click** (Mac) or **Right-Click** (Windows) to access the drop-down menu. Choose **Create Motion Tween** to add the animation of the moon starting off visible and then turning invisible.

15. Press **Return/Enter** to test the movie. Notice how Jupiter's moon starts out visible and then vanishes. You have just created your first "fade down" animation!

You will create the "fade up" animation next.

16. Press **F7** on **Frame 30** to add a blank keyframe to that frame.

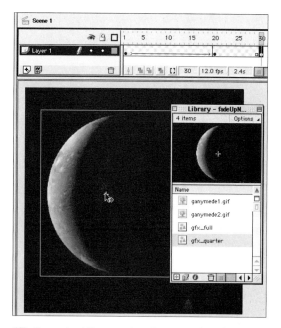

17. Open the Library using **Cmd + L** (Mac) or **Ctrl + L** (Windows). With Frame 30 selected, drag an instance of the **gfx_quarter** onto the Stage.

18. To make sure the fade-up animation is located in the same position as the fade-down animation you just created, select the symbol instance and apply the same settings in the Align panel that you did in Step 11: Select the **Align/Distribute to Stage** button and select the **Align horizontal center** and **Align vertical center** to center the symbol instance on the Stage.

The gxf_quarter symbol instance should now be located in the exact center of the Stage.

19. Press **F6** on **Frame 50** to add a keyframe to that frame.

20. This time, the animation should begin invisible and then "fade up" to a visible image, so select **Keyframe 30** and using the **Effect** panel, apply an **Alpha** of **0%** to the symbol instance just like you did in Step 13.

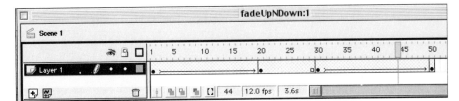

21. Select any frame between Frame 30 and 50 and press **Ctrl + Click** (Mac) or **Right-Click** (Windows) to access the drop-down menu. Choose **Create Motion Tween** to add the animation of the quarter moon starting off invisible and then turning visible. Your Timeline should look just like the picture above.

22. Click in **Frame 60** and press **F5** to extend the Timeline and length of the animation.

23. Choose **Control > Test Movie** to test the movie! You will see the image of Jupiter's moon fade down and then the image of the quarter moon fade up.

24. Save this file and keep it open for the next exercise.

9. _____Effects with Bitmaps: Cross Dissolve

In the previous exercise you created a fade animation. In this exercise you will be introduced to a technique that is often used in video and animation: the cross-dissolve effect. A cross dissolve occurs when one image fades out at the exact time that a replacement image fades in. This exercise also adds a few shortcut tips along the way, including how to duplicate and reverse frames.

1. You should still have the file open from the previous exercise. If you closed it, choose **File > Open** and browse to **fadeUpNDown.fla** that you saved in the **chap_09** folder on your hard drive.

2. Choose **Control > Save As**, name this file **crossDissolve.fla** and save it in the **chap_09** folder. This way, you will still have the file you created from the previous exercise and any changes you make will be saved in the **crossDissolve.fla** file.

3. Click on the **Insert Layer** icon to add a layer above the current layer.

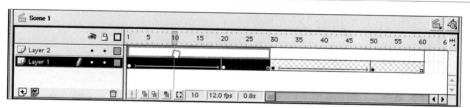

4. On **Layer 1**, click anywhere inside the first tween to select all the frames up to the next keyframe (Frame 30) and drag the frames to **Layer 2** as you see in the picture above.

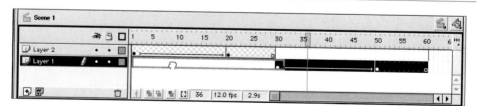

5. On **Layer 1**, move all the frames to the left by clicking inside the tween to select and then drag them.

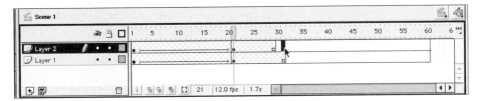

6. Click on **Frame 20** once and drag it to **Frame 21** so that both tweens end on the same frame. Click on **Frame 29** and move it to **Frame 31** as in the picture above, so the endframes of both layers are at the same frame.

Rather than having the fade-down animation occur first, and the fade up occurring next, you have altered the animation so both fades occur at the same time, creating the cross-dissolve effect.

7. Choose **Control > Test Movie** to test the movie! It will appear as if the full moon is transforming into the quarter moon.

Next, you will duplicate and reverse the frames to create the reverse effect. This technique creates a cross dissolve that fades in and then fades out.

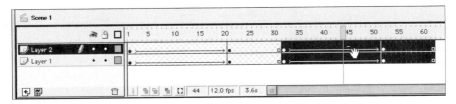

8. On **Layer 1**, click anywhere inside the tween to select all the frames. Hold down the **Shift** key and click anywhere inside the tween in **Layer 2** to select those frames as well. Hold down the **Option** key (Mac) or **Alt** key (Windows) and drag all the frames to **Frame 31**. You have just duplicated all the frames on both layers.

*If you release the **Option/Alt** key before you finish dragging the frames, you will move the frames rather than duplicate them. An indicator of whether you are copying or simply moving frames is on the hand cursor: If the hand is plain, you are moving frames. If the hand has a plus symbol on it, you are copying the frames.*

9. Press **Return/Enter** to test the animation again.

Notice how the animation smoothly changes from a full moon to a quarter moon, and then abruptly you see the full moon again? This is because you have duplicated the same animation so that the tween will automatically start over at Frame 31. You can create a smooth transition from the first tween to the second one by reversing the frames in the second set of tweens. You will do this next

10. Select from **Frame 31** to **62** on both layers (using the **Shift** key as you did in Step 8). Choose **Modify > Frames > Reverse**.

11. Choose **Control > Test Movie** to test your movie. This time, you should see a much smoother transition from the first cross-dissolve into the second one.

12. You can save and close this file.

MOVIE | crossfade.mov

To watch a movie of this exercise, open crossfade.mov from the Movies folder from the **H•O•T CD-ROM**.

Whew! You have conquered another chapter and quite a long one at that! Take a much-deserved break and get ready to learn about buttons next.

10.

Buttons

| Button States | Button Types | Rollover Buttons |

| Testing and Previewing Buttons |

| Rollover Buttons Modified |

| Duplicating and Aligning Buttons |

| Invisible Buttons | Adding Sound to Buttons |

chap_10

Flash 5
H•O•T CD-ROM

There are three types of symbols in Flash: graphic, button and movie clip symbols. You learned about graphic symbols in Chapter 7, and this chapter will introduce you to the button symbol. We'll get to movie clip symbols in the next chapter.

Buttons are a special type of symbol in Flash. They can include rollover states and even animated rollover states (which you'll learn about in Chapter 11, "*Movie Clips*"). What you might not realize is that buttons can be programmed to accept "actions" written in ActionScript (which you will learn about in Chapter 12). But before you can learn how to program the ActionScript for them, you have to learn how to create button symbols. Learning Flash involves putting a lot of puzzle pieces together, and button symbols are an extremely important part of the puzzle. In this chapter, we will give you a foundation to working with buttons, including how to create them, how to add sound to them, and how to test and preview them.

Button States

When you create or edit a button symbol, you will see that it has a different Timeline that displays four frames; **Up**, **Over**, **Down** and **Hit**. The first three keyframes of the button determine the appearance of the button during three different kinds of mouse interactions. The fourth keyframe, **Hit,** determines the clickable area of the button.

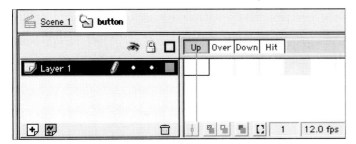

When you create a button symbol, Flash automatically adds a blank keyframe in the first frame–the Up state–of the button.

Button States Defined	
Up	The *Up* keyframe is what the button looks like when it is static and the mouse cursor is not over the shape defined in its *Hit* keyframe.
Over	The *Over* keyframe is what the button looks like when the user positions the mouse over the button. This is also referred to as the "rollover" state of the button.
Down	The *Down* keyframe defines what the button looks like when it is clicked. This state is usually seen for only a split second, but can be seen for longer periods of time if the user holds down the mouse button.
Hit	The *Hit* keyframe of the button is always invisible to the user. It defines the area of the button that is reactive to the mouse. This is what makes the button clickable.

Button Types

Fundamentally all button symbols are constructed alike. However, you can significantly change their appearance and behavior by altering what keyframes are used and what you put in those keyframes. The possibilities are nearly endless, but they will generally fall into these four categories:

Button Types	
Basic Buttons	A basic button has the same content in the *Up*, *Over* and *Down* keyframes. Users can click on it and it can contain actions, but it provides no visual feedback to the user's interaction with it.
Rollover Buttons	A rollover button has different content in the *Up* keyframe and *Over* keyframe (and sometimes *Down* keyframe). It gives visual feedback about the user's mouse position by changing when the cursor moves over it.
Animated Rollover Buttons	An animated rollover button is similar to a rollover button, but one or more of its keyframes (usually the *Over* keyframe) contains a movie clip instance. Whenever that keyframe is displayed, the movie clip animates. You will learn about animated rollover buttons and movie clips in the next chapter.
Invisible Buttons	Invisible buttons contain an empty keyframe in the *Up*, *Over* and *Down* slots and a populated keyframe in the *Hit* slot. This makes the button invisible to the user. Why not just use a shape with a transparent fill for the Up state? That would certainly work as an invisible button, but then it would be hard to see the instances of the button in your work area. When you build an invisible button with a Hit state, Flash displays the button as a translucent blue, which represents the hotspot of the button. This allows you to easily position and work with the button in the work area. You will learn how to make an invisible button in Exercise 3.

I. _____**Rollover Buttons**

This first exercise will teach you how to create a basic rollover button. You will see how the button's Timeline is different from that of the main Timeline and you will learn about the four different states of buttons.

1. Copy the **chap_10** folder, located on the **H•O•T CD-ROM**, to your hard drive. You need to have this folder on your hard drive in order to save files inside it.

2. Choose **File > New** to create a new blank movie and save this file as **rolloButton.fla** inside the **chap_10** folder.

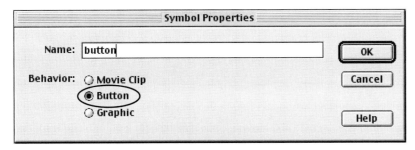

3. To create a button symbol, choose **Insert > New Symbol**. This will open the **Symbol Properties** dialog box. Name the symbol **button** and choose **Behavior: Button**. Click **OK**.

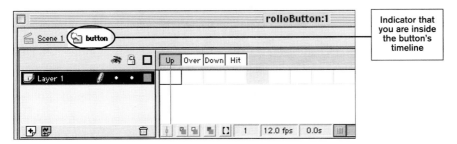

As soon as you click OK, you will see the button's Timeline. Button symbols have their own Timeline, which is independent of the main Timeline. This means that the finished button can be placed on the Stage, and even though it contains multiple button states, it will occupy only one frame in the Timeline. Notice there are four frames: Up, Over, Down and Hit. Buttons do not automatically "play" like the main Timeline. Rather, the button Timeline remains paused as the first keyframe (or Up state), showing only the content in the Up state until the cursor comes in contact with the button. The other keyframes in the button symbol (Over and Down) are shown only in reaction to the cursor position.

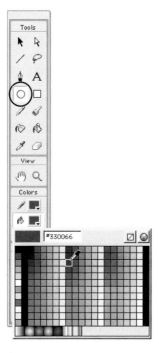

4. Select the **Oval** tool. Select a purple color for both the **Fill** and **Stroke** options.

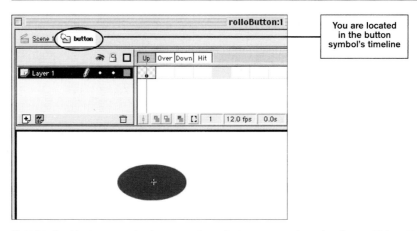

You are located in the button symbol's timeline

5. With the **Up** frame of the button selected, draw an **oval** on the Stage. This will serve as the Up state of the button before the user interacts with it.

You won't be able to see the difference between the shape's stroke and fill because they are the same color.

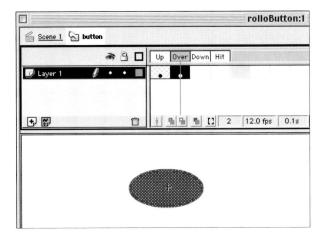

6. In the **Over** frame, press **F6** to add a keyframe.

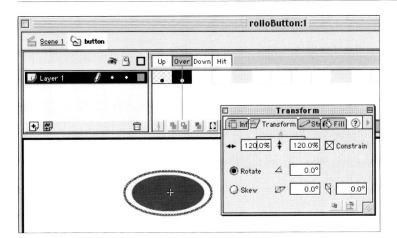

7. With the **Over** frame selected, use the **Arrow** tool and click on the outside of the oval to select the stroke around the oval. In the **Transform** panel (Window > Panels > Transform), make sure to select the **Constrain** box and then type **120.0%** in either the height or width fields. This will increase the size of the stroke. Now you will have different content in the **Up** and **Over** states of the button, indicating to the user that this is an interactive button.

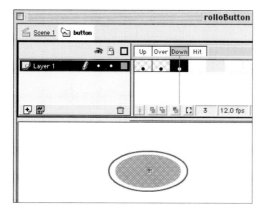

8. Press **F6** in the **Down** frame to add a keyframe to the Down state of the button. Select the solid oval shape, and with the **Paint Bucket** tool, change the fill color to one other than the original oval you created.

9. You can move the **Playhead** to see the different states of the button. Go ahead a click the **lock** icon to lock this layer so that you don't accidentally edit the content on it.

You aren't going to add the Hit state content just yet; in the next steps you are going to add text to your button first.

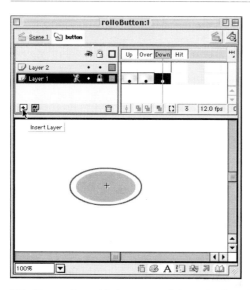

10. Choose **Insert > Layer** or click on the **Insert Layer** button to add a new layer to the button's Timeline.

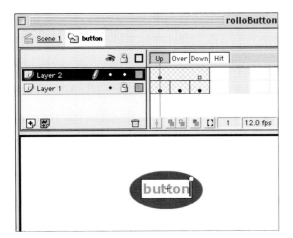

11. Select the **Up** frame on **Layer 2**. With the **Text** tool, type the word **button** with the color and font of your choice. This will automatically add the word **button** across the **Up, Over** and **Down** states.

12. Press **F6** in the **Over** frame to add a keyframe to the **Over** state of the button.

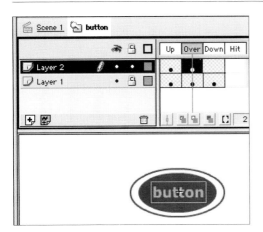

13. With the **Over** frame selected on **Layer 2**, select the **Paint Bucket** tool and change the text color.

14. Scrub the **Playhead** again to see the different states of the button.

To complete the button symbol, you need to define the Hit state of the button. We'll explain the importance of the Hit state and how to define it in the next exercise.

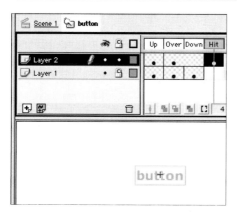

15. Press **F6** in the **Hit** frame on **Layer 2**. This will copy the content—the word "button"—from the last keyframe into the **Hit** frame.

You have just created your first button, but it's not ideal to define the Hit state using only text, which is sometimes difficult to click on. You will learn why in the next exercise.

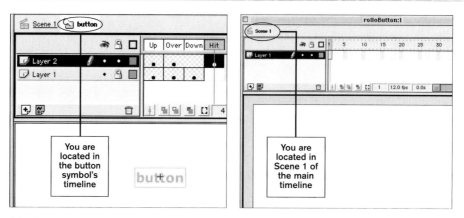

16. Click on the **Scene 1** tab to return to the **Scene 1** Timeline.

NOTE | Where's the button?

When you choose **Insert > New Symbol** (as you did in back in Step 3), Flash automatically places the new button symbol in the Library so you will not see the button on the Stage of the main Timeline. If you want to use the new button in your movie, you must drag an instance of the button onto the Stage. You will do this in the next exercise where you will learn how to test and preview buttons.

17. Save this file and keep it open for the next exercise where you will learn how to test the button.

2. _____Testing and Previewing Buttons

This exercise will show you how to test and preview the button you created in the previous exercise. In Flash, you can preview buttons three ways: in the Library, on the Stage and using **Test > Movie**. Testing and previewing is key to finding mistakes; in fact, you'll discover a problem with the Hit state of the button you created in the previous exercise by testing the button rollover in this exercise.

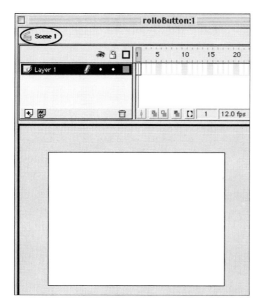

1. You should still have the file **rolloButton.fla** open from the previous exercise. If you don't, choose **File > Open** to open the **rolloButton.fla** file you saved inside the **chap_10** folder. You should be viewing Scene 1 on the main Timeline.

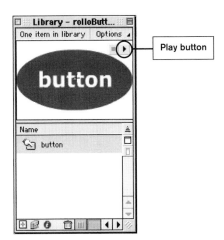

Play button

2. Choose **Window > Library** to open the Library window if it isn't already open. Click on the **button** symbol in the Library. Press the **Play** button on the controller in the **Preview** window to preview the button in the Library.

Notice the button will play one frame right after the next (Up, Over, Down and Hit). Although this will give you a very quick preview, it may not be very realistic. The following steps will teach you how to preview the button on the Stage.

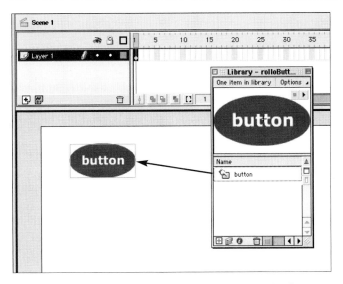

3. Drag an instance of the button you created onto the Stage.

4. Choose **Control > Enable Simple Buttons.** This will allow you to test the button right on the Stage.

---

5. Go ahead a move your mouse over the button to see the Over state. Click on the button to preview the Down state.

Notice that depending on where you click, the button may or may not work. This is because you used text in the Hit state and, therefore, the button will not be active until the mouse passes directly over the text itself as shown in the pictures above. This can confuse the end user, because the button will not work unless the user places the mouse cursor directly over the text. This is why using text to define the Hit state of your buttons is not a good idea. You will learn how to use a solid shape to define the Hit state in the next exercise. But first, you are going to learn one more way to preview the rollover button you created.

---

6. Choose **Control > Enable Simple Buttons** again to deselect this option. The button will not be active on the Stage anymore.

Note: *Although you can still select enabled buttons, it is easier to work with them if they are disabled. You can always enable the buttons again when you want to test their behavior on the Stage.*

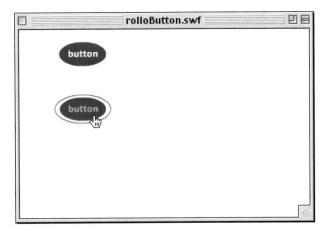

7. Choose **Control > Test Movie**. This will produce an .swf file (you'll learn more about this in Chapter 15, "*Publishing*") that will let you test any of the buttons on your Stage. This method of testing will yield the same visual results as choosing **Enable Simple Buttons**; it's just another way to test your work. Go ahead and move the mouse over the button and try to trigger the rollover state to see how it works. Again, you will notice that the text is difficult to click on even when you are right over the button.

NOTE | Hit Me!

The Hit state of the button has one objective: to define an area that will be active when the cursor comes in contact with it. Why not just copy the contents from the last keyframe into the Hit frame? For one reason, the Hit keyframe of the button is always invisible to the viewer, so detail isn't important here—a solid shape similar to a "shadow" of the button will work fine. Also, because the Hit keyframe defines the area of the button that is reactive to the mouse, it is important that it covers the entire area of the button that you want to be active. If the button is tiny and the hit area is small or smaller, it may be difficult for the user to interact with the button at all. For tiny buttons or buttons that are text-only, we suggest you use a solid shape slightly larger than the button's Up or Over states. You will do this in the next exercise.

---

8. Save this file and keep it open for the next exercise.

---

3. _____Rollover Buttons Modified

In the previous exercise you learned to test the button you created. This exercise will show you how to alter that button and create a solid shape for the Hit state of the button. In the steps that follow, you will learn the difference between using text to define the Hit state and using a solid shape to define the Hit state of the button.

1. You should still have the file **rolloButton.fla** open from the previous exercise. If you closed it, choose **File > Open** to open it again.

2. In the Library, **Cmd + L** (Mac) or **Ctrl + L** (Windows), double-click on the button symbol to open the button's Timeline.

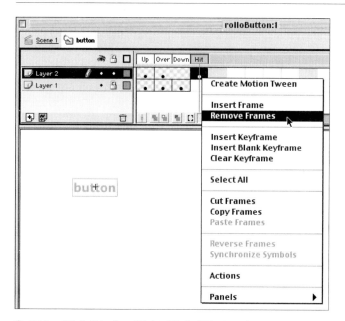

3. Ctrl + Click (Mac) or **Right-Click** (Windows) on the **Hit** frame in **Layer 2** to access the drop-down options. Choose **Remove Frames** to remove the keyframe in the Hit state of the button. You will be adding new content to define the hit area in the next few steps. Lock this layer so you don't accidentally edit the button text.

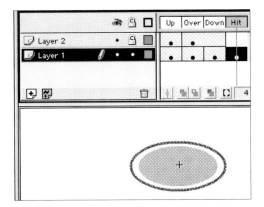

4. Unlock **Layer 1** and press **F6** in the **Hit** frame to add a keyframe to the **Hit** state of the button. As usual, adding a keyframe will copy the contents of the previous frame (the Down state) into the current frame (the Hit state).

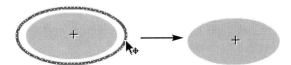

5. With the **Hit** frame still selected, click anywhere on the Stage to deselect the artwork. Click on the stroke to select it and press **Delete**. You will end up with a solid shape, and this will define the new **Hit** state for the **button symbol.** You have just modified the Hit state of your rollover button symbol!

6. Click on the **Scene 1** tab to leave the button symbol's Timeline and return to the main Timeline.

Notice the button instance that you placed on the Stage in the previous exercise. Since you modified the actual symbol itself in the last few steps, the button instance on the Stage will automatically be updated with the new Hit state.

NOTE | Understanding the Hit State

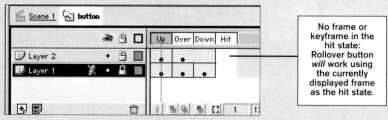

No frame or keyframe in the hit state: Rollover button *will* work using the currently displayed frame as the hit state.

If there is no frame or keyframe in the specified Hit state, then the Hit shape of the button is set by the currently displayed keyframe of the button. That means that if the Up and Over keyframes contain different shapes, then the Hit state will change when the user rolls over the button. This is not an ideal way to create buttons.

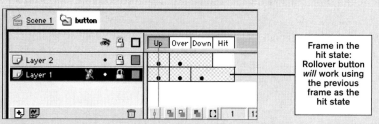

Frame in the hit state: Rollover button *will* work using the previous frame as the hit state

If there is a frame specified in the Hit state, it will automatically use the contents of the last set keyframe.

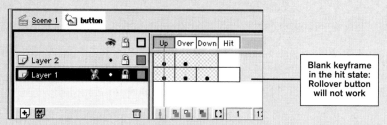

Blank keyframe in the hit state: Rollover button will not work

Setting a blank keyframe to the Hit state would result in the disabling of the rollover, since a Hit state is required to trigger the Over and Down states.

If the shape for the button is large enough for the Hit state, you don't have to create a keyframe in that frame or new artwork. In this exercise, however, the text was not an adequate shape or size for the user to access it and then trigger the rollover. The best method is to test your rollovers first, to ensure that the Hit state is the adequate shape for the job.

7. Choose **Control > Enable Simple Buttons** to test the button on the Stage. Move your mouse over the button to see the **Over** state and click on the button to preview the **Down** state. Notice how much easier it is to interact with the button now that you've changed the Hit state? This is because you defined the Hit state as a solid shape that's the same size as the Up state of the button. Therefore, as soon as you touch the edge of the oval shape, the Over state of the button will be triggered.

Button with text in the Hit frame

Button with a solid shape in the Hit frame.   *The new button is so much easier to trigger!*

8. Choose **Control > Enable Simple Buttons** again to deselect this option. The button will not be active on the Stage anymore.

9. Save this file and keep it open. You will be using it one more time in the next exercise.

4. _____Duplicating and Aligning Buttons

You have learned how to preview buttons and why the Hit state is important in the past three exercises. Now that you know how to make a rollover button, another handy skill is to make copies of the button in the Library. For example, you can change only the text in each copy of the button symbol to create a navigation bar in no time. This exercise will show you how to duplicate buttons in the Library and how to align them on the Stage.

1. You should still have the file **rolloButton.fla** open from the previous exercise. If you closed it, choose **File > Open** to open the **rolloButton.fla** file you saved inside the **chap_10** folder.

2. If the Library window is not open, choose **Window > Library** to open it. You will see the button in the Library.

3. With the button selected in the Library, click on the **Options** pull-down menu in the upper-right corner of the Library window. Choose **Duplicate** to make a copy of the button symbol you just created.

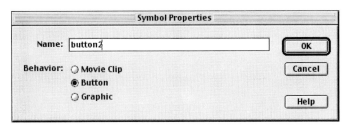

4. In the **Symbol Properties** dialog box, type **Name: button2** and make sure **Behavior: Button** is selected. Click **OK**. You have just made an exact duplicate of the button you previously created. Notice the new **button2** in the Library.

5. Double-click **button2** in the Library to open the button symbol's Timeline. Notice how the Timeline looks identical to the first button you created. Lock **Layer 1** so you don't accidentally edit anything on that layer.

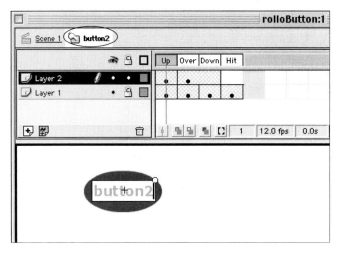

6. Click on **Layer 2**, **Frame 1**, the Up state of the button. Select the **Text** tool and type the number **2** after the word **button**.

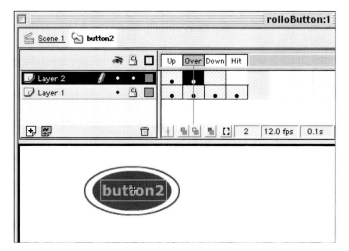

7. Click on **Frame 2**, **Layer 2** the **Over** state of the button, and with the **Text** tool, type in **2** after the word **button** in that keyframe.

8. Click on the **Scene 1** tab to leave the button symbols Timeline and return to the main Timeline.

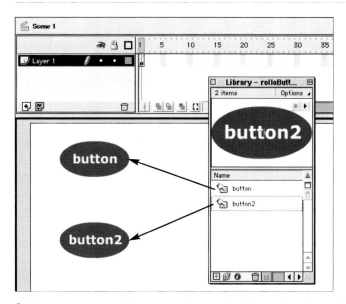

9. Drag an instance of the new button, **button2**, onto the Stage. Choose **Control > Enable Simple Buttons** and test it. When you are finished testing it, choose **Control > Enable Simple Buttons** again to deselect this feature.

10. Repeat Steps 3 through 7 and create two more duplicate buttons. Name them **button3** and **button4,** respectively.

11. Click on the **Scene 1** tab to leave the button symbol's Timeline and return to the main Timeline.

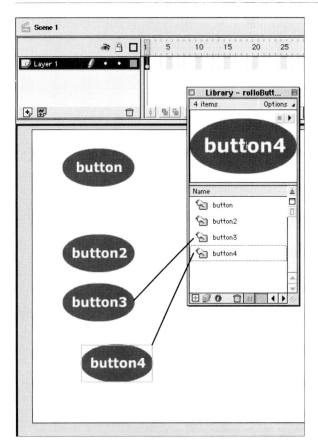

12. Drag **button3** and **button4** onto the Stage below buttons 1 and 2.

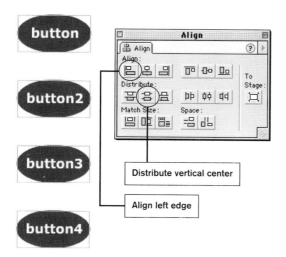

Distribute vertical center

Align left edge

13. Select **Cmd + A** (Mac) or **Ctrl + A** (Windows) to select all four buttons on the Stage. Open the **Align** panel (Window > Panels > Align) and select **Align left edge** and **Distribute vertical center** to make all the buttons aligned to the left and equally spaced. Make sure the **To Stage** option is not depressed.

14. Choose **Control > Test Movie** to test your rollover buttons. Rather than creating four separate buttons, one at a time, and creating all the artwork inside each button, you have streamlined the process. This simple navigation system was made easy by creating the artwork for only one button, duplicating it three more times, and changing only the text inside each button.

15. Save and close this file.

**Invisible Buttons**

In previous exercises, you learned about the importance of the Hit state for rollover buttons. The Hit state can also be used to create what are known as "invisible" buttons. This kind of button comes as an unexpected surprise, because there's no visible display of the button object until the end user passes over an invisible region.

1. Choose **File > Open** and browse to the **invisibleFinal.fla** file located inside the **chap_10** folder. This is the finished version of the movie you are going to create in this exercise.

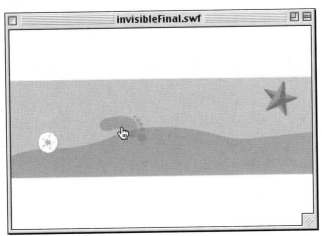

2. Choose **Control > Test Movie** to preview this movie. Move your cursor over the sand in the center of screen from left to right. Notice how the footprints magically appear. You will be creating this same effect next. When you are finished looking at this movie, close this file.

3. Choose **File > Open** and double-click on the **invisible.fla file** located inside the **chap_10** folder to open it. We created this file to get you started.

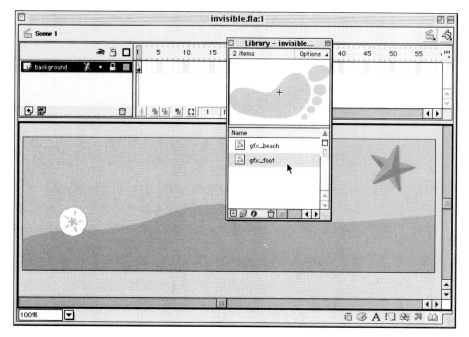

4. Notice that the file contains one layer with a background image on it. In the Library (Window > Library) you will see two graphic symbols: **gfx_beach** (the background) and **gfx_foot** (which you will be using to make the invisible button).

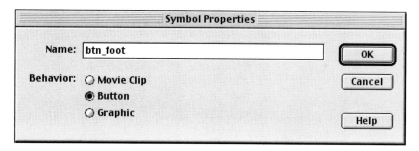

5. Choose **Insert > New Symbol**, **Cmd + F8** (Mac) or **Ctrl + F8** (Windows), to create a new button symbol. In the Symbol Properties dialog box, type **Name: btn_foot** and make sure **Behavior** is set to **Button**. Click **OK**.

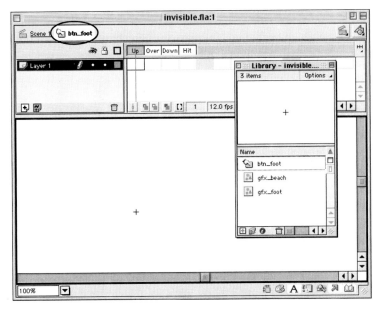

6. Notice that you are in the Timeline of the new button, **btn_foot**. You will create the invisible button next.

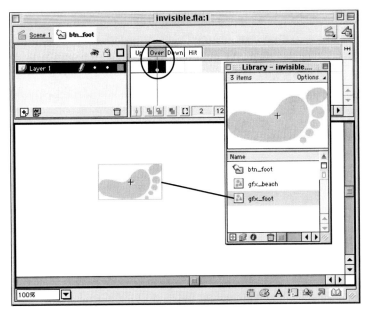

7. Press **F7** in the **Over** frame of the button symbol to add a blank keyframe. With the **Over** frame selected, drag an instance of the **gfx_foot** symbol onto the Stage.

Why not place the gfx_foot symbol in the Up frame? Because you are going to create an invisible button, the Up state needs to be empty so that the user will not know any button even exists until the mouse moves over the area that you will define in the hit state.

8. Press **F6** in the **Down** frame to add a keyframe, which will copy the contents of the previous frame into it.

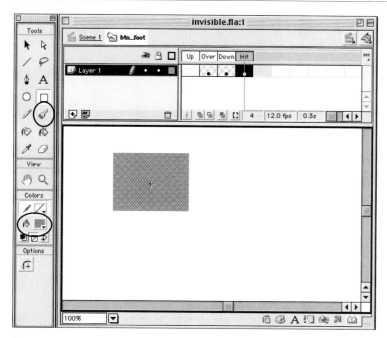

9. Press **F7** in the **Hit** frame to add a blank keyframe. Select the **Rectangle** tool and set the stroke color to **none**. Select any color you like for the fill color, and draw a rectangle a little larger than the foot.

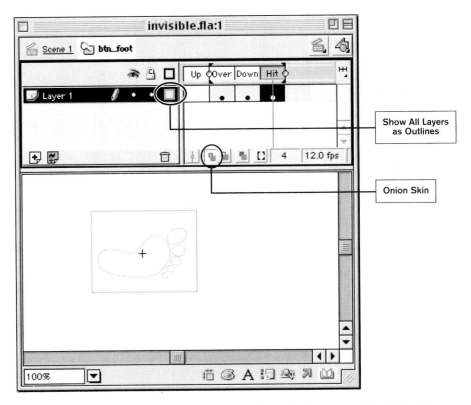

If you want to make sure your rectangle covers the entire foot, select the Onion Skin *button and select the* Show All Layers as Outlines *button. This will allow you to see all the frames at once and see the outlines of the frames at the same time. When you are through, don't forget to turn the buttons off by deselecting both of them.*

10. You have just created your first invisible button! Go ahead and scrub the **Playhead** to see the different states of the button.

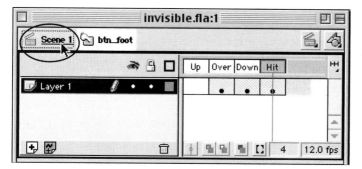

11. Click on the **Scene 1** button to return back to the main Timeline.

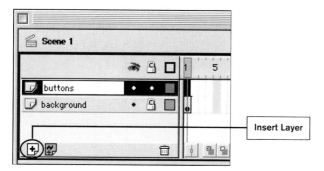

12. Click on the **Insert Layer** button to add a new layer. Name this layer **buttons**.

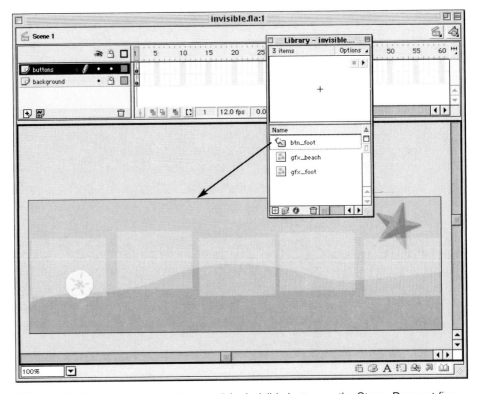

13. Now it's time to place the instances of the invisible button on the Stage. Drag out five instances of the **btn_foot** symbol. You don't have worry about the placement of the invisible buttons because you will align them in the next step.

Note: Any time you create an invisible button, the Up frame of the button is empty. To give you visual feedback that the button is located on the Stage, Flash will display the shape of the Hit frame in a transparent blue color.

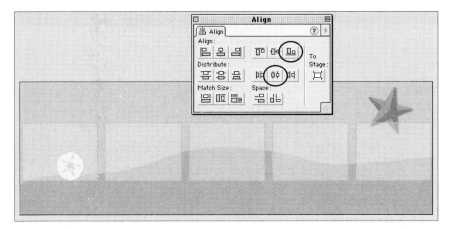

14. Select **Cmd + A** (Mac) or **Ctrl + A** (Windows) to select all the invisible buttons on the Stage. In the **Align** panel (Window > Panels > Align**),** click the **Align bottom edge** and the **Distribute horizontal center** buttons to align the invisible buttons.

15. Choose **Control > Test Movie** to test your movie. Notice how the footprints appear as you move the mouse across the sand. The only problem is they are all *right* footprints! You will fix this next.

16. Click on the button layer and select the second button and fourth button on the Stage. Press **Shift + Click** to select both buttons. Choose **Modify > Transform > Flip Vertical** to flip the two buttons over and create *left* footprints.

17. Test the movie again and you should see footprints (first right and then left) walking in the sand.

18. Save and close this file.

6. _____Adding Sound to Buttons

The different states of the buttons you create can each hold different sounds to give feedback to the user. This exercise will teach you how to add a simple sound to a button.

1. Choose **File > Open** and double-click on the **soundBtn.fla file** located inside the **chap_10** folder to open it. We created this file to get you started. Notice in the Library (Window > Library) there are two sound files and two button symbols named **soundOnOff1** and **soundOnOff2**.

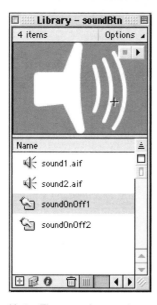

Note: The sounds were imported into this document the same way that external artwork is imported—using **File > Import**, or use the keyboard shortcut **Cmd + R** (Mac) or **Ctrl + R** (Windows). A list of supported sound formats in Flash is in Chapter 14, "*Sound*."

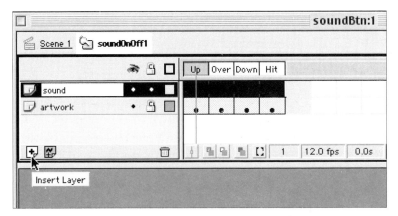

2. Double-click on the **soundOnOff1** button to open the button's Timeline. Click on the **Insert Layer** button to add a new layer. Name this layer **sound**.

3. Press **F7** on the **Over** frame in the sound layer to add a blank keyframe. You will be adding a sound to this frame.

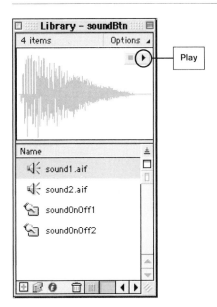

4. In the Library, select the **sound1.aif** file and preview the sound by clicking the **Play** button in the Library Preview window.

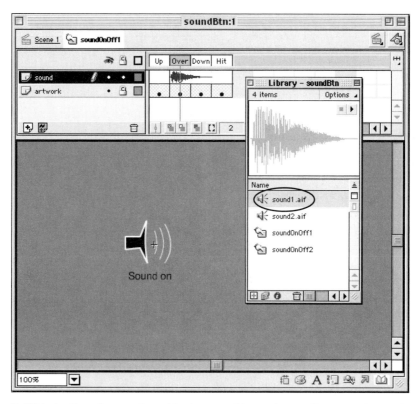

5. With the **Over** frame selected in the **sound** layer, drag an instance of **sound1** onto the Stage. That's it! You have just added a sound to the button.

*Note: You will not see a visual representation of the sound on the Stage. Instead, you will see sound waves appear in the **Over** frame of the Timeline.*

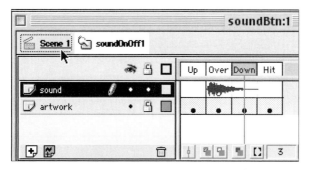

6. Click the **Scene 1** tab to return to the main Timeline.

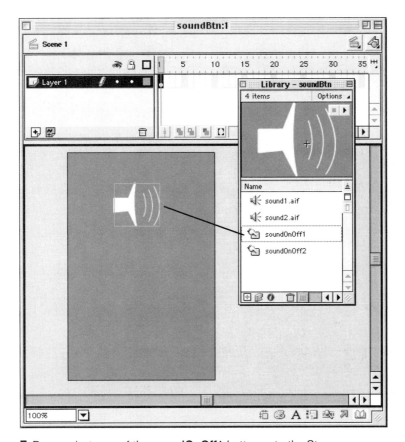

7. Drag an instance of the **soundOnOff1** button onto the Stage.

8. Choose **Control > Enable Simple Buttons.** This will allow you to test the button on the Stage. You should hear the sound play when you move the mouse over the button, because you added the sound to the **Over** state. When you are finished testing it, choose **Control > Enable Simple Buttons** again to deselect this feature.

You will add a sound to the Down state of the soundOnOff2 button next.

9. In the Library, double-click on the **soundOnOff2** button to open the button's Timeline. Click on the **Insert Layer** button to add a new layer. Name this layer **sound**.

10. Press **F7** on the **Down** frame in the sound layer to add a blank keyframe. You will be adding a sound to this frame.

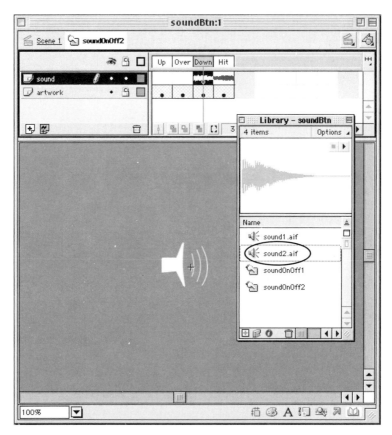

11. With the **Down** frame selected in the sound layer, drag an instance of **sound2** onto the Stage. Notice the sound waves appear in the Down state of the Timeline.

Tip: Adding a sound to the Hit keyframe will have no effect on the button.

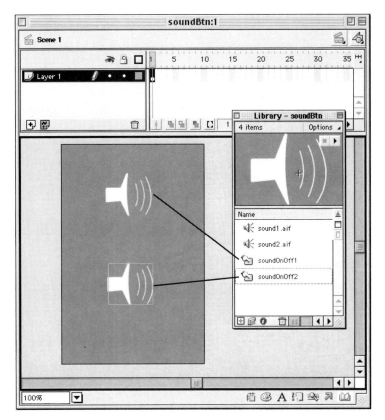

12. Click the **Scene 1** tab to return to the main Timeline and drag an instance of the **soundOnOff2** button onto the Stage. You now have two buttons on the Stage.

13. Press **Control > Test Movie** to test your buttons. Notice that the sound in the top button **(soundOnOff1)** will play when the mouse rolls over the button, and the sound in the bottom button **(soundOnOff2)** will play when you click on the button (because you placed the sound in the Down state).

You have just created buttons with sounds in a few short steps. You will be introduced to sound in greater detail in Chapter 14.

14. Save and close the file.

That's it! We hope this chapter gave you a good foundation to working with and under-standing the different button states and different kinds of buttons in Flash. The next chapter will introduce you to movie clips. Knowing how to make a movie clip will help you learn to make an animated button, so you'll get to add to your new button-making skills soon!

Movie Clips

| What is a Movie Clip? |
| Animated Graphic Symbol vs. Movie Clip Symbol |
| Modifying Movie Clip Instances |
| Creating a Movie Clip |
| Creating an Animated Rollover Button |

chap_11

Flash 5
H•O•T CD-ROM

Up to this point in the book, you've learned how to create both graphic and button symbols. At last, we'll introduce you to movie clip symbols and give you a solid understanding of how they are created and used, compared to—or in combination with—the other two types of symbols you already know.

Understanding movie clip symbols is key to producing interactive Flash movies later down the road. This is the last step in building a foundation that will prepare you for Chapter 12, *"ActionScripting Basics."* As you will see, the majority of ActionScripting requires a movie clip symbol, so don't underestimate the importance of this chapter.

What is a Movie Clip?

We saved movie clips as the last kind of symbol to describe, because they can be one of the hardest things to learn in Flash. For this reason, you'll need to learn a few new vocabulary terms and concepts just to understand what we're talking about! These terms follow:

Main Timeline: The term *main Timeline* refers to the Timeline of your entire project file, and controls how your project is viewed. Controlling the main Timeline can be done through Action-Scripting, which we will cover in Chapter 12. As you saw earlier, button and graphic symbols have their own Timelines. The Timeline of graphic (and animated graphic) symbols have a direct relationship to the main Timeline. This means that if the main Timeline is displaying the contents of Frame 5, you will see whatever is on Frame 5 of any graphic symbol on the Stage.

Timeline Independent: As we mentioned, graphic (and animated graphic) symbols have a direct relationship to that main Timeline. Button and movie clip instances do not have a direct relationship to the main Timeline. They are referred to as "timeline independent" objects. Why? Because they can function (play animation, sounds, etc.) regardless of what the main Timeline is doing. For example, if you have a movie clip that contains a bird flapping its wings, and you place this on the Stage, the bird will continue to flap its wings even if you tell the main Timeline to stop. As you can imagine, this behavior is what makes movie clips so powerful; the ability to have different animations and actions occur independent of the main Timeline.

Now that you have a better idea of what the main Timeline is and what the term "timeline independent" means, you are ready to understand movie clips.

Movie Clips: Movie clip symbols can contain multiple layers, graphic symbols, button symbols, animations, sounds, and ActionScripting. and operate independent of the main Timeline. Movie clip symbols can continue to play even if the main Timeline has stopped. They require only a single keyframe on the main Timeline to play. It's helpful to think of movie clips as movies nested in the main Timeline.

While movie clips are extremely powerful and flexible, they cannot be previewed by simply pressing **Return/Enter** as is done with button and graphic instances. Movie clips can only be previewed in the Library (out of context of the main movie), by selecting **Control > Test Movie**, or by publishing the final movie (which you will learn about in Chapter 15, "*Publishing*"). This is a very important point, because you will find yourself unable to view your work unless you remember this!

I. ───────────**Animated Graphic Symbol versus Movie Clip Symbol**

This first exercise will teach you the differences between animated graphic symbols and movie clip symbols. You'll see how the animated graphic symbol requires multiple frames in the main Timeline, while a movie clip does not. You will have the opportunity to learn first-hand why there has been so much focus on the independent timeline aspect of movie clips.

1. Copy the **chap_11** folder, located on the **HΣOΣT CD-ROM**, to your hard drive. You need to have this folder on your hard drive in order to save files inside it.

2. Open the **gfxVsMC.fla** file located inside the **chap_11** folder. We have created this file for you to get you started.

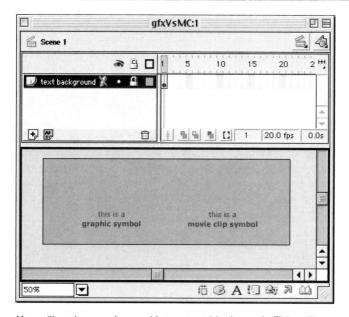

You will notice one layer with two text blocks on it. This will serve as the background layer for the movie.

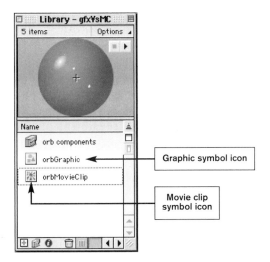

Graphic symbol icon

Movie clip
symbol icon

3. Press **Cmd + L** (Mac) or **Ctrl + L** (Windows) to open the Library if it isn't already open. The Library contains two symbols: a graphic symbol named **orbGraphic** and a movie clip symbol named **orbMovieClip**. Notice that the movie clip has its own distinct icon, different from the graphic symbol and from the button symbol.

NOTE | What's Up With the Briefcase Icon?

As you create movies with more and more items inside the Library, you will want a way to organize those items. Flash offers the capability to place library elements inside folders, which look like small briefcases, where you can store similar elements and even name the folders, to keep the Library neat and tidy. To create a folder in your Library, simply click on the **New Folder** button. At the bottom of the **Library** panel you can name the folder and drag library items in and out of folders. You will learn more about Library organization in Chapter 16, "*Deconstruction*."

Folder icon

New Folder
button

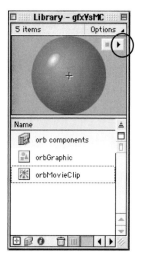

4. Select the **orbGraphic** and click the **Play** button in the Preview window to test the graphic symbol. Next, select **orbMovieClip** and click the **Play** button to test the movie clip symbol. Notice how the animations seem exactly the same?

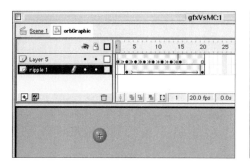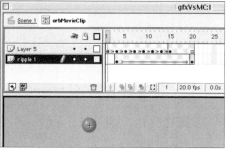

5. In the **Library**, double-click on the **orbGraphic** to open the graphic symbol's Timeline. When you are finished, double-click the **orbMovieClip** to view the movie clip's Timeline. You will see that the two symbols do, in fact, have the same elements in their Timelines. The only difference between the two symbols is that one is a movie clip and the other is a graphic symbol.

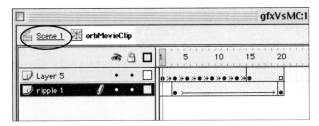

6. Click on the **Scene 1** tab in the upper-left corner to return to the main Timeline.

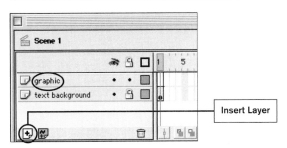

7. Click on the **Insert Layer** button to add a new layer to the main Timeline. Name the layer: **graphic**.

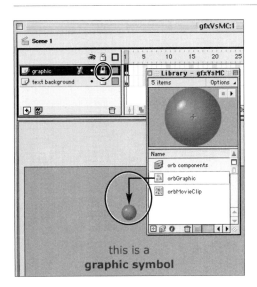

8. With the **graphic** layer selected, drag an instance of the **orbGraphic** onto the Stage above the **this is a graphic symbol** text to add the animated graphic symbol to the Timeline. When you are finished, lock the graphic layer so that you don't accidentally edit anything on that layer.

9. Click on the **Insert Layer** button to add a new layer above the **graphic** layer. Name the layer: **movie clip**.

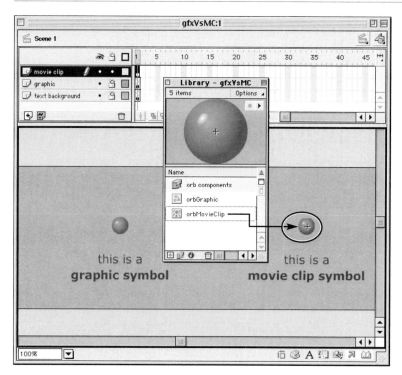

10. With the **movie clip** layer selected, drag an instance of the **orbMovieClip** onto the Stage and place it above the **this is a movie clip symbol** text to add the movie clip symbol to the Timeline.

11. Press **Return/Enter** to test the movie. Notice that nothing happens.

Why? When you press Return/Enter to test the movie, Flash will automatically move the Playhead across all the frames in the main Timeline of the movie. In this movie, you have only one frame so the Playhead has nowhere to go. Therefore, you will see both symbols in their static state only.

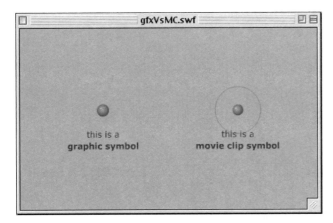

12. Choose **Control > Test Movie** to preview the movie. Notice, this time, the movie clip symbol plays and the graphic symbol does not. Why?

The main difference between an animated graphic symbol and a movie clip symbol is that the movie clip's Timeline is completely independent of the main movie's Timeline. So a movie clip's Timeline can play or stop regardless of how many frames the main Timeline contains. Animated graphic symbols, on the other hand, play in sync with main Timeline. The Timeline of an animated graphic symbol is tied to the main Timeline, and therefore at least the same number of frames in the graphic symbol's Timeline must exist in the main Timeline in order for the graphic symbol to play.

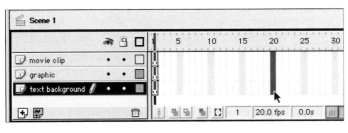

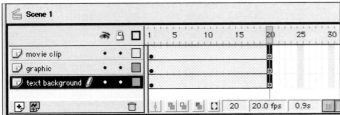

13. Back on the main Stage, unlock the layers on the main Timeline. Click and drag to select **Frame 20** in all three layers and press **F5** to add 20 frames to each layer in the main Timeline.

Why 20 frames? This is the same number of frames that exist in both the graphic symbol's Timeline and the movie clip's Timeline.

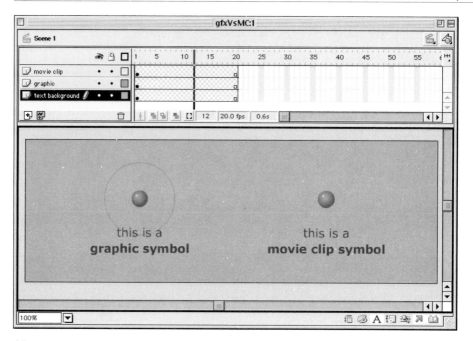

14. Press **Return/Enter** to test the movie. This time, the animated graphic symbol will play, although the movie clip symbol still will not play. This is because now there are enough frames in the main Timeline so that the animated graphic symbol can play. However, you will not be able to see the movie clip play on the Stage because in order to preview a movie clip, you must view it either in the Library or using **Control > Test Movie**. This is one of the "rules" of movie clips. They don't preview in Flash; you must choose **Control > Test Movie** to preview a movie clip.

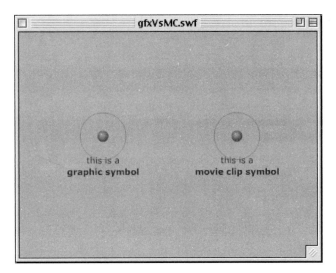

15. Choose **Control > Test Movie**. Now you will see both symbols animating.

To summarize, the animated graphic will play if there are enough frames in the main Timeline, but the movie clip will play regardless.

16. You can save and close this file.

NOTE | Why is Timeline Independence Important?

OK, now you probably understand that the movie clip can play in its entirety even though it only takes up one frame in the main Timeline, while the graphic symbol needed all 20 frames inserted into the main Timeline in order to play. You also probably understand that a movie clip cannot be previewed inside Flash, and that you must choose **Control > Test Movie** in order to see the movie clip play. Keep in mind that having a symbol be independent of the Timeline is extremely important when programming interactive presentations. ActionScripts, which you'll learn about in the next chapter, can refer to movie clips because they have the capacity to be "named" and referenced in scripts, while graphic symbols do not.

2. _____ Modifying Movie Clip Instances

Not only do movie clips have an independent Timeline from the main movie, but just like you did with graphic symbols, you can also apply effects to movie clip instances on the Stage. You have to create the movie clip only once and then you can change the attributes of each instance on the Stage to achieve very different visual effects. This exercise will show you how to alter the properties of a movie clip instance using the **Effect** and **Transform** panels.

1. Open the file named **modifyMC.fla** inside the **chap_11** folder. We have created this file for you to get you started.

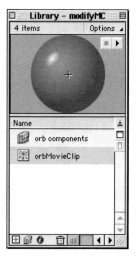

2. Press **Cmd + L** (Mac) or **Ctrl + L** (Windows) to open the Library if it's not already open. You will notice the same **orbMovieClip** you saw in the previous exercise.

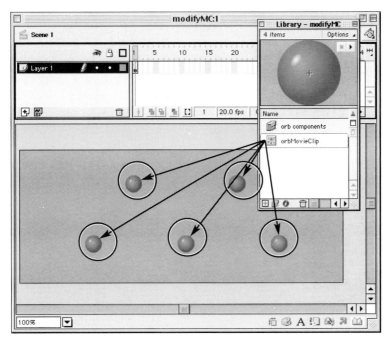

3. Drag out five instances of the **orbMovieClip** symbol onto the Stage, one at a time.

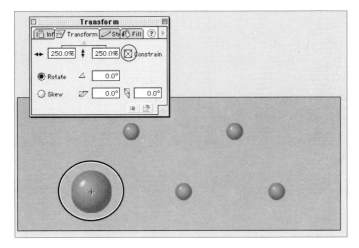

4. Select one of the movie clip instances and in the **Transform** panel (Window > Panels > Transform), make sure the **Constrain** box is checked and type **250.0%** in either the height or width field. This will increase the size of the movie clip instance 250%.

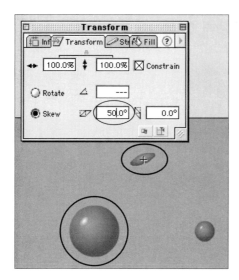

5. Select another movie clip instance on the Stage. Choose the **Skew** option, and in the **Skew Horizontally** field, type **50.0** to make that movie clip skew horizontally 50 degrees.

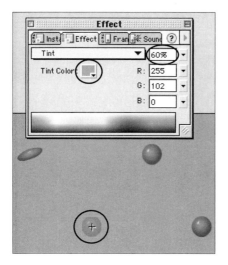

6. Choose **Window > Panels > Effect** to open the **Effect** panel. Select the third movie clip instance and in the **Effect** panel, choose **Tint** from the drop-down menu. For the tint color, select a shade of **orange** from the color bar. Use the slider to choose **60%** as the amount of tint used on the movie clip instance.

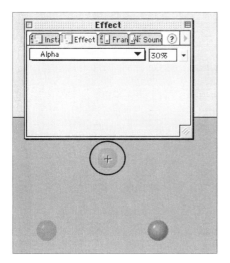

7. Select another movie clip instance, and in the **Effect** panel, choose **Alpha** from the drop-down menu. Type **30%** to change the transparency of the movie clip instance.

8. Select the last movie clip instance, and in the **Effect** panel, choose **Brightness** from the drop-down menu. Use the slider to choose **70%** for the brightness of the instance.

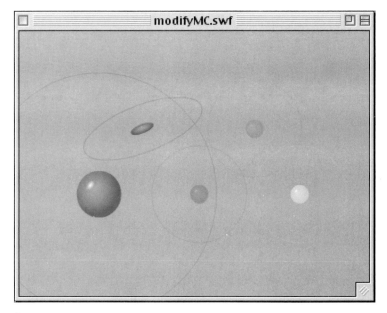

9. Choose **Control > Test Movie** to preview the changes you made. Notice how your modifications change each movie clip instance's appearance, although they each still animate. By adding transformations or effects to the instances on the Stage, you can change the appearance of the movie clip in just a few clicks of the mouse. The original movie clip, however, will remain unchanged in the Library.

10. Save and close this file.

3. ——————————Creating a Movie Clip

In the previous two exercises, you learned that movie clips have an independent Timeline from that of the main movie and that you can apply effects and transformations to movie clip instances on the Stage. The next step is to learn how to create movie clips. In Flash, movie clips often form the core of project design and interactivity. This exercise will start you off by showing you how to make a simple movie clip.

1. Choose **File > New** to create a new blank movie. Save the file as **movieClip.fla** inside the **chap_11** folder.

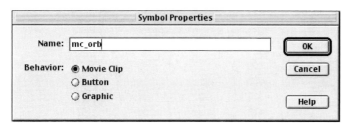

2. Choose **Insert > New Symbol** and type **Name: mc_orb** and make sure **Behavior: Movie Clip** is selected. Click **OK** when you are finished.

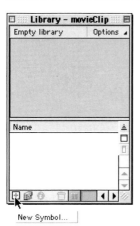

You can also create a new symbol several other ways: by choosing New Symbol from the Library Options menu in the upper-right corner of the Library, by clicking on the New Symbol button in the bottom-left corner of the Library, or by using the shortcut keys Cmd + F8 (Mac) or Ctrl + F8 (Windows).

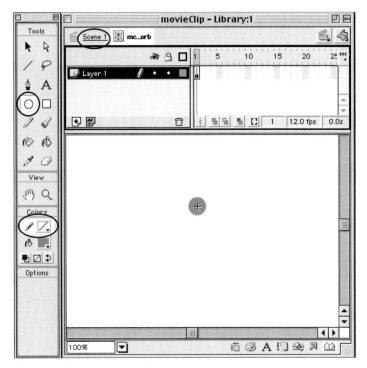

3. After you click **OK**, notice that you are inside the **mc_orb's** Timeline. Select the **Oval** tool and **turn off** the stroke and choose a fill color of your choice. Draw a small circle in the center of the Stage over the crosshair.

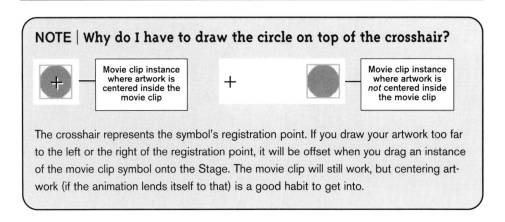

NOTE | Why do I have to draw the circle on top of the crosshair?

Movie clip instance where artwork is centered inside the movie clip

Movie clip instance where artwork is *not* centered inside the movie clip

The crosshair represents the symbol's registration point. If you draw your artwork too far to the left or the right of the registration point, it will be offset when you drag an instance of the movie clip symbol onto the Stage. The movie clip will still work, but centering artwork (if the animation lends itself to that) is a good habit to get into.

4. Press **F5** on **Frame 20** to add blank frames up to it. Lock this layer so you don't accidentally select something on it.

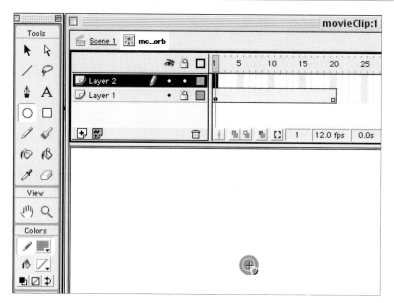

5. Click on the **Insert Layer** button to add a new layer to the movie clip symbol's Timeline. Using the **Oval** tool again, this time turn off the Fill and choose the same color you used in Layer 1 for the stroke. Draw a circle outline slightly smaller than the circle on Layer 1.

This shape will be used to create the ripple effect in the next few steps.

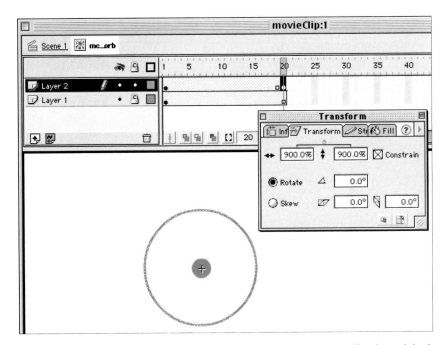

6. Press **F6** on **Frame 20** to add a keyframe to it. With Frame 20 still selected, in the **Transform** panel (Window > Panels > Transform), make sure the **Constrain** box is checked and type **900** in either the height or width field. This will increase the size of the circle outline to 900% of its original size.

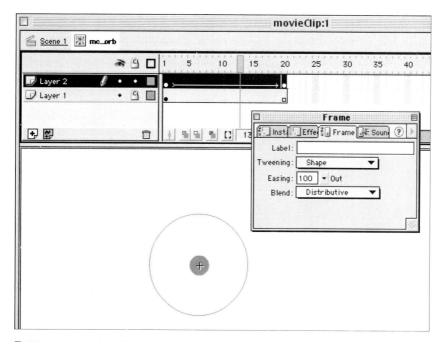

7. Click to the right of the **Layer 2** name to select all the frames on that layer. Press **Cmd + F** (Mac) or **Ctrl + F** (Windows) to open the **Frame** panel. Choose **Shape** from the **Tweening** pull-down menu and move the **Easing** slider up to **100**. This will make the ripple slow down as it becomes bigger. Scrub the **Playhead** to preview the ripple.

Notice how the ripple starts out small and grows larger but never disappears? This is because the last keyframe of the animation is the same color as the beginning. To make the illusion of the ripple disappearing into the background, you will need to change the color of the circle outline in the last keyframe to white.

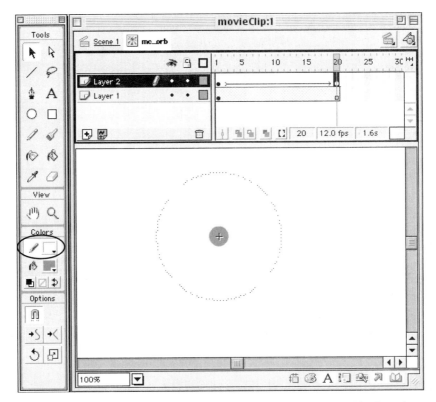

8. Select the artwork in the **last** keyframe on **Layer 2** and choose white from the stroke color picker (circled above). Scrub the **Playhead** again to preview the ripple. Much better!

You have just created your first movie clip! You will be able to test it in the next steps.

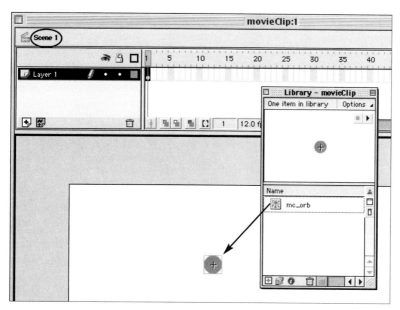

9. Click on the **Scene 1** tab in the upper-left corner of the Timeline to return to the main Timeline. Press **Cmd + L** (Mac) or **Ctrl + L** (Windows) to open the Library. Drag an instance of the movie clip onto the Stage.

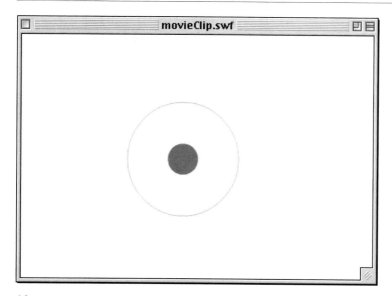

10. Choose **Control > Test Movie** to preview the movie clip you just made.

Notice how the movie clip plays although there is only one frame in the main Timeline. This is because the movie clip's Timeline is independent from the main Timeline. Movie clips need only one keyframe in the main Timeline in order to play, unlike animated graphic symbols, which you learned about in Exercise 1.

11. Save this file and keep the file open. You will need it for the next exercise.

4. ————————Creating an Animated Rollover Button

This exercise will demonstrate how to turn a normal rollover button into an animated rollover button by nesting a movie clip in the Over state of a button symbol. If you've been wondering why timeline independence is important, this example will drive the point home. As you've learned to create buttons in past chapters, there are only four frames in each button symbol–Up, Over, Down and Hit. The only way to put an animation into a single frame for one of these states is to use a symbol that can contain animation yet has an independent Timeline. The movie clip symbol is just that ticket.

1. To preview the animated button you are going to create in this exercise, open the **chap_11** folder you saved on your hard drive. If you are a Mac user, double-click on the file named **animButtonFinal Projector**. If you are a Windows user, double-click on the file named **animButtonFinal.exe**.

These are identical stand-alone projector files that Flash can create for you. You will learn about projector files in depth in Chapter 15, "Publishing."

2. Move the mouse over the button to see it animate. You will create this animated button in the following steps using a movie clip in the button's over state. When you are finished testing the button, click the upper-left corner of the Projector's window to close it.

3. You should still have the file open from the previous exercise. If you closed it, choose **File > Open** and browse to the file named **movieClip.fla** inside the **chap_11** folder. Choose **Open**.

4. Save this file as **animButton.fla** inside the **chap_11** folder.

5. You should see the movie clip instance from the previous exercise on the Stage. Move the movie clip to the left side of the Stage since you will not need it until the end of this exercise.

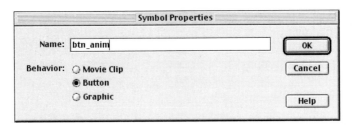

6. Lock **Layer 1** and click on the **Insert Layer** button to add a new layer. With **Frame 1** in **Layer 2** selected, create a new symbol by using the shortcut keys: **Cmd + F8** (Mac) or **Ctrl + F8** (Windows). This is another way to open the Symbol Properties dialog box. Name the symbol **btn_anim** and set its Behavior to **Button**. Click **OK**.

After you click OK, you will be inside the editing environment for the button symbol's Timeline.

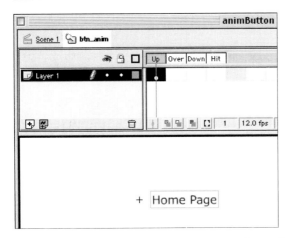

7. With the **Text** tool selected, type the words **Home Page** in the **Up** keyframe, just to the right of the crosshair registration point. You may select any font and font size you like using the **Character** panel (Window > Panels > Character). We used Verdana 16 in this example.

8. Press **F5** in the **Down** frame to add frames in the Over and Down states of the button. Double-click next to the **Layer 1** name and change the name of this layer to **text**. Lock this layer so the text block doesn't accidentally get edited as you add artwork to the button in the following steps.

9. Click on the **Insert Layer** button to add a new layer. Double-click next to the **Layer 2** name and change the name of this layer to **artwork**.

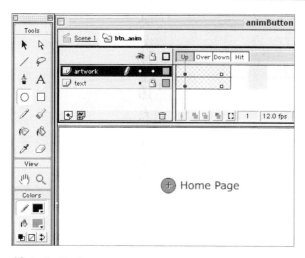

10. In the Toolbox, select the **Oval** tool and for the **Fill** color, select the same color you used for the movie clip you made in the previous exercise. You can add a stroke also if you wish. Select the **Up** frame and draw a circle about the same size as you did for the circle in the previous exercise. Position the circle in the center of the crosshair. This will serve as the Up state of the button.

11. Press **F7** in the **Over** frame to add a blank keyframe to the Over state of the button.

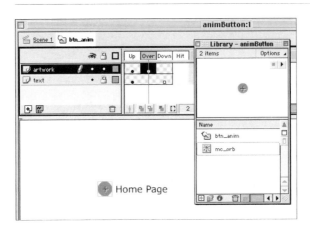

12. Press **Cmd + L** (Mac) or **Ctrl + L** (Windows) to open the Library. Notice the movie clip you created in the previous exercise and the button symbol you are creating now. With the **Over** state of the button selected, drag an instance of the **mc_orb** movie clip onto the Stage, just to the left of the text. You can line it up on the crosshair to make sure it is in the same position as the circle you drew in Step 10.

You have just added the movie clip you created in the previous exercise to the Over state of the button. You will add the Hit state to the button next to complete the exercise.

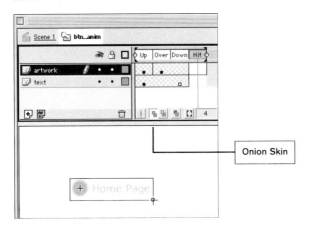

13. Press **F7** in the **Hit** frame to add a blank keyframe to the Hit state of the button. Select the **Rectangle** tool and draw a rectangle that covers the circle and the text. You may want to unlock the text layer and select the **Onion Skin button** to turn onion skinning on. This will help you make sure the rectangle covers the circle and the text.

*The rectangle will serve as the Hit state of the button so when the user's mouse touches
any part of the rectangle, the Over state will be triggered.*

14. You are finished with the button. Click on the **Scene 1** tab to return to the main Timeline.

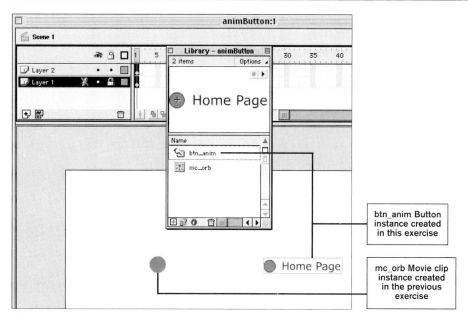

btn_anim Button
instance created
in this exercise

mc_orb Movie clip
instance created
in the previous
exercise

15. The Library should still be open, but in case it is not, press **Cmd + L** (Mac) or **Ctrl + L**
(Windows) to open it. Drag an instance of the **btn_anim** button symbol onto the Stage.

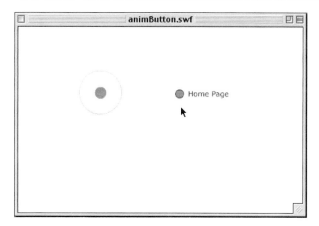

16. Choose **Control > Test Movie** to preview both symbols.

Notice how the movie clip continues to animate on its own, while the button waits for you to move the mouse over it in order for the animation to begin. By adding movie clips to different states of a button, you can take the rollover button to the next level by adding animation.

17. Save and close this file.

Congratulations! You have made it through an essential chapter. You now know how to create, modify, and nest movie clips inside buttons. In the next chapter you will use movie clips in more advanced ways. Make sure you are well rested before you take on the next chapter, "ActionScripting Basics," it's one of the most challenging chapters in the book.

TIP | Edit in Place Versus Edit in New Window

What if you want to make changes to the button symbol (or any symbol for that matter) after you have created it?

You have a choice between editing in a new window or editing in place.

Edit in New Window

You can edit the symbol in a new window by either double-clicking on the symbol's icon in the Library or you can press **Ctrl + Click** (Mac) or Right-Click (Windows) and choose **Edit in New Window** from the drop-down menu. This will take you into the Timeline of the symbol and you can make any changes you wish.

Edit in Place

You can also edit the symbol while still viewing other objects on the Stage. When you choose this mode, the other elements on the Stage are dimmed, which separates them from the symbol you are working with. To edit a symbol in place either double-click the instance on the Stage or press **Ctrl + Click** (Mac) or **Right-Click** (Windows) and choose **Edit in Place** from the drop-down menu.

12.

ActionScripting Basics

chap_12

Flash 5
H·O·T CD-ROM

So far, you've learned how to draw, mask, animate, and create symbols in Flash. The last step in learning how to make fully interactive presentations is how to add ActionScript to your projects. ActionScript is an internal programming language to Flash, similar to JavaScript. The good news is that you do not have to know JavaScript or be a programmer to add ActionScript to your movies. The Flash **Actions** panel assists you in writing this script so that it is not necessary to write the code from scratch.

Why is ActionScript important? On a basic level, ActionScript enables you to create buttons that control your movies, create pre-loaders, make slideshows with forward and back buttons, or link to other URLs on the Internet. This is the short list, and covers only some of the possibilities that ActionScripting offers. By the time you are finished with this chapter, you will have a solid understanding of how to add ActionScript to objects and frames and why you would choose one over the other. You will also learn many of the basic ActionScripts to apply in your own projects.

Working with ActionScript code is one of the most technically challenging aspects of Flash. We hope to give you a solid foundation on which to build later on your own.

The Actions Panel Defined

An **Action** is kind of like a Library element for ActionScripting. When you use one of the many actions that ship with Flash, it automatically writes the corresponding ActionScript code for you. The Actions panel is where you can create and edit **Object Actions** or **Frame Actions**, which you'll learn about in great detail later in this chapter. This panel has two modes, **Normal Mode** and **Expert Mode**. You will learn to work in Normal Mode, as Expert Mode is generally used by more advanced users.

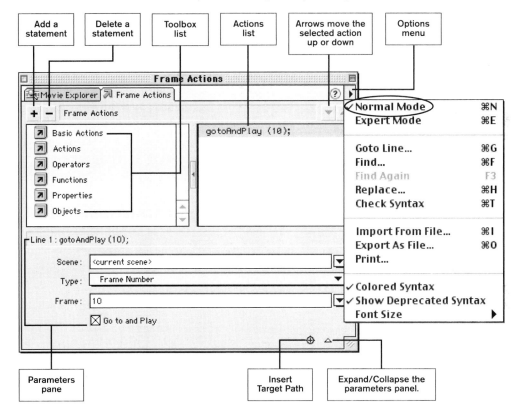

The Normal Mode includes the **Basic Actions Library**, the simplest actions in ActionScripting.

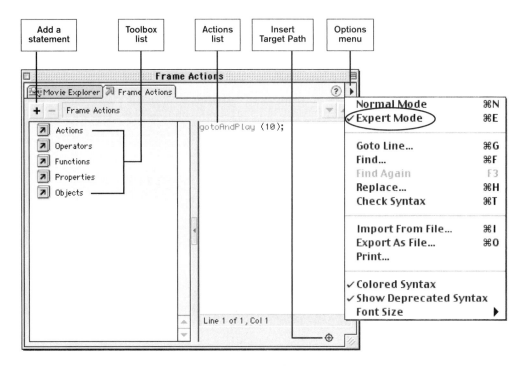

The Expert Mode allows you to type ActionScript code from scratch directly into the right side of the **Actions** panel. For this reason, it is used by intermediate to advanced Flash users who know how to hand-code actions. Because our book is targeted to beginners, there are no exercises to cover Expert Mode features. Once you're finished with this book, you will be better prepared to go deeper into ActionScripting.

Flash will save whichever mode is used to create the ActionScript, so if you need to go back and edit the actions later, the Actions panel will open up in the mode you used. Although you can toggle between the Normal and Expert modes using the **Options** arrow in the upper right corner of the Actions panel, we will use the Normal Mode for this book.

I. ————————Object Actions: Stop and Play

You've probably seen Flash movies in which you click a button and an animation plays. This exercise will teach you how to assign **Stop** and **Play** actions to button instances. You will learn how to apply actions to button symbol objects to achieve this effect.

1. Copy the **chap_12** folder, located on the **H•O•T CD-ROM**, to your hard drive. You need to have this folder on your hard drive in order to save files inside it.

2. Open the file called **stopAndPlayFinal.fla** located inside the **chap_12** folder. This is the finished version of the project you'll be building in this exercise.

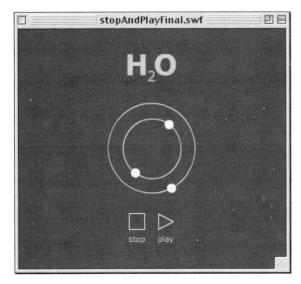

3. Choose **Control > Test Movie** to preview the movie. In the .swf file, press the **stop** button to stop the atoms from moving around the circle. Press the **play** button to set them in motion again. You will learn how to add the same functionality to this movie in the following steps.

4. When you are finished stopping and playing this movie, close the preview window and this file.

5. Open the **stopAndPlay.fla** file located inside the **chap_12** folder. This is an unfinished version of the movie you just previewed. It has everything built, except the ActionScript, which you will add in this exercise.

6. Choose **Control > Test Movie** to preview the movie. Click on the **stop** and **play** buttons.

Notice how nothing happens and the movie continues to play. Why? No actions have been added to these buttons yet, and therefore the buttons do not control the movie. You will learn to do this next.

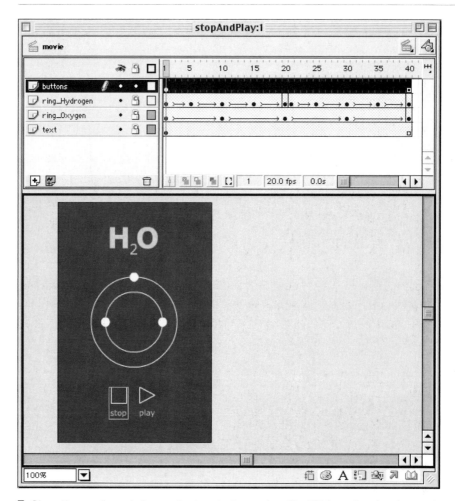

7. Close the preview window and return to the project file. Click on the **stop** button instance on the Stage to select it.

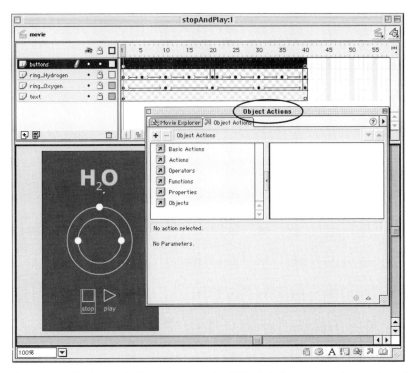

8. Choose **Window > Actions** to open the **Object Actions** panel. Notice how the top of the window reads *Object* Actions. Flash refers to the button instance that you selected as an object. Since you have selected the button instance, Flash knows to open the Object Actions panel, not the Frame Actions panel.

TIP | Actions Panel Shortcut

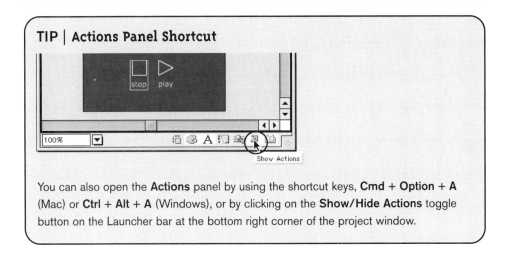

You can also open the **Actions** panel by using the shortcut keys, **Cmd + Option + A** (Mac) or **Ctrl + Alt + A** (Windows), or by clicking on the **Show/Hide Actions** toggle button on the Launcher bar at the bottom right corner of the project window.

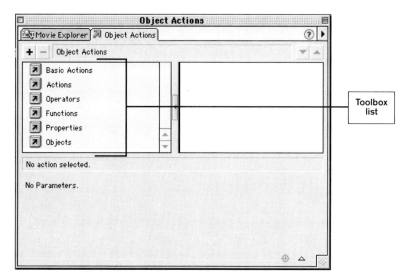

On the left-hand side of the Object Actions panel, you will see the Toolbox list that contains categories of actions.

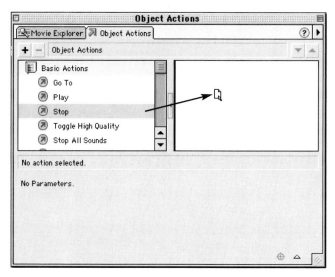

9. Click on the **Basic Actions** book to access a list of all the actions that fall under that category. Click the **Stop** action and drag it to the window on the right side of the **Actions** panel to add it to the list of actions. You have just added your first action to the project.

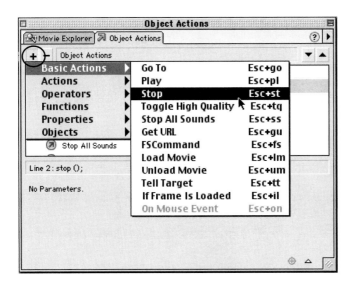

An action can also be added to the list by double-clicking on the desired action in the Toolbox list or by selecting the plus (+) button and choosing the action using the pull-down menus.

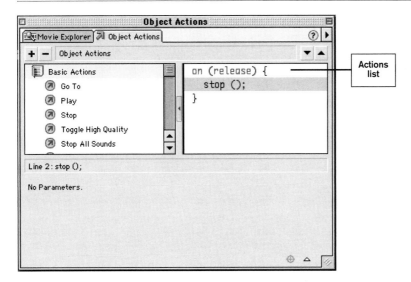

By dragging the Stop Action icon over to the right window in the Actions panel, ActionScript appeared in the window. This window on the right side of the Actions panel holds the Actions list and displays all the code for the actions that are applied to an object.

NOTE | Whoa! What's all the extra stuff in the Actions list?

You may have also noticed that when you added the **Stop** action, an **on (release)** event appeared above it in the Actions list, as well as some parentheses, braces and a semicolon. The **on (release) code** is added by default since you are adding an action to a *button* instance. Flash needs to know when to apply the Stop action and in this case, the default setting is for Flash to apply the Stop action *on release* or when the user releases the mouse. You will learn more about the On Mouse event in the next section after this exercise.

The **parentheses ( )** hold the parameters (called arguments) that apply to an action, the **braces { }** contain statements that should be grouped together and the **semicolon ;** marks an end of a statement. The good news is that you do not have to worry about writing these punctuation marks because in Normal Mode, Flash writes these for you; all you have to do is choose the action.

10. Choose **Control > Test Movie** and try out the **Stop** action you just added to the button instance. When you click on the **stop** button, the movie will stop!

When you add the Stop action to the button instance, Flash will wait until the user clicks and releases the mouse, because of the on (release) *event. When this happens, Flash will apply the Stop action and make the main movie Timeline stop. So, the action you just added to the button instance controls the Playhead in the main Timeline upon the click and release of the user's mouse.*

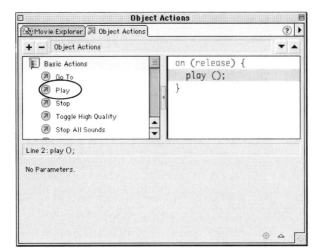

11. Close the preview window when you are finished. In the main Timeline, click on the **play** button instance on the Stage to select it. In the **Object Actions** panel, double-click on the **Play** action in the **Basic Actions** list to add it to the Actions list. You have just added a Play action to the button instance on the Stage.

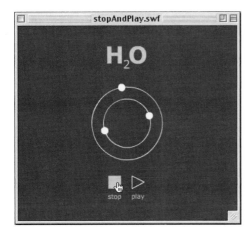

12. Choose **Control > Test Movie** and test the movie again. Click on the **stop** button to stop the movie. Click on the **play** button to make the movie play again!

Notice how the movie immediately plays as soon as the preview window opens? You'll learn to adjust this in the next exercise.

13. Save this file and keep it open for the next exercise.

2. _____Frame Actions: Stop

By default, the Timeline in the main movie will automatically begin to play until it reaches the last frame unless you tell it otherwise. You can keep a movie from playing automatically by adding an action to the Timeline to tell the movie to stop, before it begins to play. The movie will then start in a stopped position, and will not play until the button is pressed. In the last exercise, you learned how to add actions to *objects*. This exercise will teach you how to add actions to a *frame* in the Timeline.

1. You should still have the **stopAndPlay.fla** file open from the last exercise; if you've already closed it, open that file now.

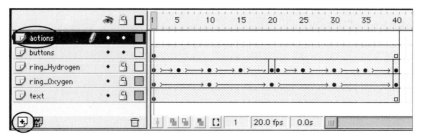

2. Click on the **Insert Layer** button to add a new layer to the Timeline, and name it **actions**.

3. Select **Frame 1** of the **actions** layer in the Timeline, which contains a blank keyframe. In the **Actions** panel, double-click on the **Stop** action to add it to the Actions list. Notice that the Actions panel no longer reads "Object Actions," but instead it reads "Frame Actions." This is a great feature, new to Flash 5, that gives you immediate feedback as to whether you are applying the action to an object or to a keyframe.

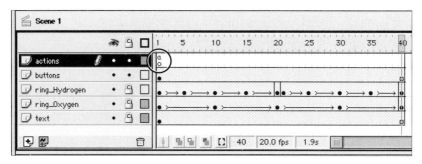

*Once you have added an action to a keyframe, the Timeline will display a small **a** inside the frame as further feedback that there is an action in the keyframe.*

NOTE | Adding a Layer for the Frame Action

We *strongly recommend* that you get in the habit of placing all frame actions on their own, separate layer in the Timeline. We also recommend that this layer is always located on top of all the other layers in your movie and that you consistently name it the same thing: **actions**. As the movies you create become more and more complex, it will be significantly easier to troubleshoot and debug a movie if you know you can always find the frame actions in the same place: on the first layer of the movie, on the layer named **actions**.

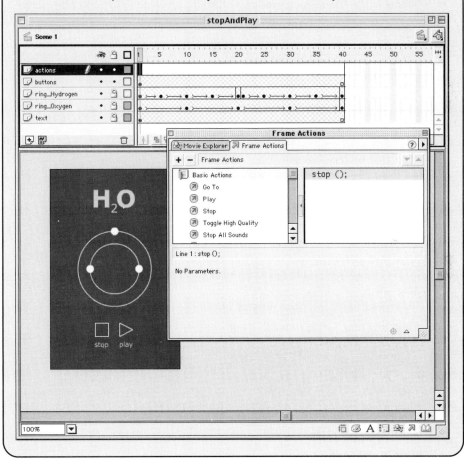

NOTE | Frame or Object Action Instruction

To add an action to a frame in a Timeline rather than to an object, you must place an action in a *keyframe*. To add an action to an object, as you did with the **stop** and **play** buttons, you must select the object and then add the action.

---

4. Test the movie again (**Control > Test Movie**). The movie will now begin in a static state, waiting for the user to click on the **play** button. Click on the **stop** and **play** buttons to control the animation.

You have many options in deciding how much control you give to users when they interact with your movie. By attaching actions the buttons (as you did in the first exercise), the main movie will immediately begin to play on its own until the user clicks on the stop button and from that point forward, the user is in control of the movie. By additionally adding the Stop action to the first keyframe of the main Timeline as you did in this exercise, the movie will not play at all until the user clicks on play, so in this case, the user has control of the movie as soon as the movie loads.

---

5. Save and close this file.

Interactivity and Actions: Events and Event Handlers

When a movie plays, any action that occurs (such as a user releasing the mouse on a button) is considered an **event** in Flash. The events fall into one of the following categories: mouse events, keyboard events, time-based events and—new to Flash 5—movie clip events. For every event, there must be something that manages the event. In Flash this is known as an **Event Handler**. You can think of the Event Handler as the event's agent since the Event Handler is in charge of the event. We will describe the three types of basic events below. You will learn movie clip events at a late time, once you have developed a stronger foundation in ActionScripting basics.

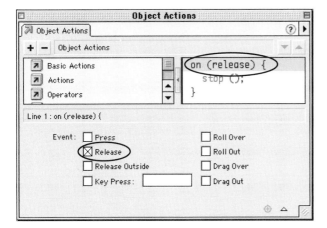

*When you add an action to an object in Flash, it will introduce an event. In the illustration above, the event is a **mouse** event. It states **on (release)**, meaning that when the user clicks the button, the action is triggered after the mouse has been clicked.*

Mouse Events

Mouse events occur when the user interacts with a button instance. When an action (such as "Stop") is added to a button instance, an **On Mouse** event will be automatically added, as you saw in Exercise 1. The default On Mouse event is **Release** (shown above). We will use this default in the exercises that follow.

A table defining each possible mouse event follows:

Mouse Events Defined	
Press	When the mouse is moved over the Hit area of the button, and the mouse is pressed.
Release	When the mouse is moved over the Hit area of the button, and the mouse is pressed and then let go.
Release Outside	When a Press occurs on the Hit state of a button, but the Release occurs outside of the Hit state.
Roll Over	When the mouse cursor moves over the Hit state of a button.
Roll Out	When the mouse cursor moves off the Hit state of a button.
Drag Over	When the mouse is pressed on the Hit state of a button, then rolls out of the Hit state, and re-enters the Hit state with the mouse still pressed.
Drag Out	When the mouse is pressed on the Hit state of a button, the mouse pointer rolls out of the Hit state with the mouse still pressed.

Keyboard Events

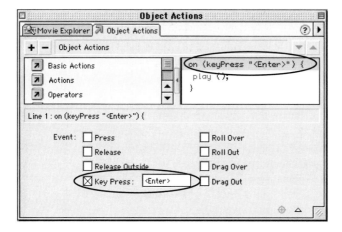

Keyboard events are similar to mouse events, except that they occur when the user presses a key on the keyboard rather than interacting with the mouse. For example, you might want to make a slide show move forward and backward by pressing the arrow keys on your keyboard instead of having physical buttons on your Stage. This kind of functionality is great when using Flash as a substitute for a PowerPoint presentation! To change the mouse event to a keyboard event, select the **Key Press** box (circled above). Press any key on the keyboard or type a letter into the **Key Press** field to assign a key press to the button. This example was created by pressing **Enter** on the keyboard. Flash will execute the Play action when the user presses the **Enter** key.

Note: If you assign a capital letter for a key press, the user *must* type in a *capital* letter. Likewise if you assign a lower-case letter, the user *must* type in a *lowercase* letter. Also, use caution when assigning a keyboard event to a movie that will be displayed on the Web: key presses will not be executed in a browser unless the user has already clicked inside the movie at some point. And further, your end users might not intuitively know to use their keyboard unless they are instructed to do so.

Time-based Events

Unlike mouse events and keyboard events, time-based events are located in keyframes as frame actions. Time-based events occur when the Playhead reaches a keyframe containing actions.

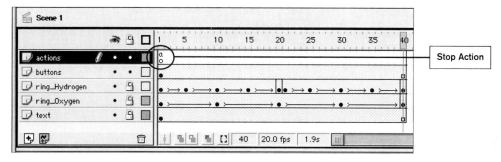

In the last exercise, you added a time-based event by adding the Stop action to the first keyframe. Time-based events can exist on the main Timeline or in any graphic or movie clip instance's Timeline.

3. _____Go To Frame Action (Slide Show)

In addition to the Stop and Play actions, you can be even more specific and add actions that tell the Playhead not just to play, but *exactly* where to go. This exercise will demonstrate how ActionScript can be used to create a Flash movie that can be navigated one frame at a time, similar to a slide show. You will learn a new action: the **Go To** action, which can be used to send the Playhead to a frame you specify.

1. Choose **File > Open** and select the file titled **slideShowFinal.fla** located inside the **chap_12** folder. Choose **Open**. This is the finished version of the slide show you are going to create.

2. Choose **Control > Test Movie** to preview the movie. Press the right arrow button instance to advance the slide show forward. Press the left arrow button instance to display the previous slide. You will be creating this same slide show in the steps that follow.

3. When you are finished, close the **slideShowFinal.fla file.**

4. Open the **slideShow.fla** file located inside the **chap_12** folder. This is an unfinished version of the movie you just previewed, containing only the slideshow images. You will add new layers, buttons, and the necessary ActionScripting in this exercise.

5. Choose **Control > Test Movie** to preview the movie. Notice how the frames go by very fast, one after another. This is because, by default, the movie will automatically play through the frames unless you tell it otherwise.

6. Close the preview window when you are finished. In the main Timeline, choose the **Insert Layer** button to add a new layer to the Timeline. Name the new layer: **actions**. Make sure the new layer is above the images layer. If it is not, click on the layer name and drag it above the images layer so that the actions layer is on top.

7. Select the first keyframe in the **actions** layer and open the **Actions** panel.

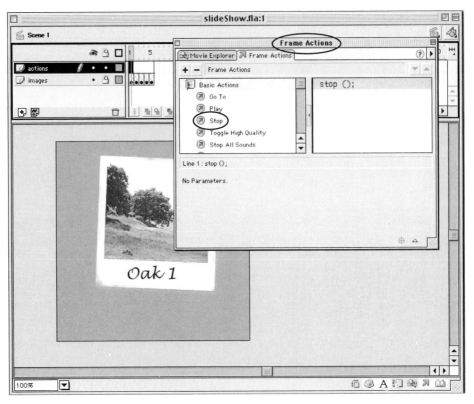

8. In the **Frame Actions** dialog box, open the **Basic Actions** list and double-click on **Stop** to add a Stop action to the **Actions** list window on the right side of the **Actions** panel. This will cause the movie to stop when it first appears on the screen.

Notice the Frame Actions title at the top of the Actions panel. This is an indication that you are adding an action to a frame, rather than an object.

9. Click on the **Insert Layer** button to add another new layer to the Timeline. Name the new layer: **control**.

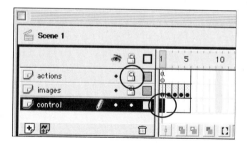

10. Lock the **actions** layer and select the first keyframe in the **control** layer. If it is not on the bottom already, move the **control** layer below the **images** layer by clicking on the layer name and dragging it below the images layer. The layer order should look like the picture above. You want your actions layer to remain on top. *Note: Windows users will not see a small circle in the keyframes that contain actions; only Macintosh users will see these.*

11. Open the **Library**, **Cmd + L** (Mac) or **Ctrl + L** (Windows). With **Frame 1** in the control layer still selected, drag an instance of **btn,next** and the **btn,previous** onto the **Stage**. Position them side-by-side. Select both of the button instances using **Cmd +A** (Mac) or **Ctrl + A** (Windows), then choose **Cmd + K** (Mac) or **Ctrl + K** (Windows) to open the **Align** panel and align the bottom edge of the buttons.

12. Click on the button instance on the right and make sure that **Actions** panel is still open. Choose **Window > Actions** to open it in case it is not. You will be adding actions to the button instance next...

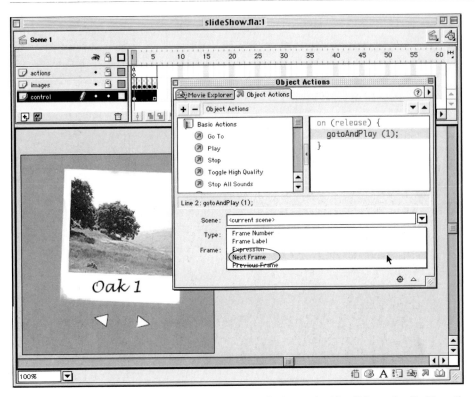

13. In the **Object Actions** dialog box, under **Basic Actions**, double-click on the **Go To** action to add it to the Actions list. Notice how once you add the **Go To** action; additional information appears at the bottom of the **Object Actions** panel. This is where you can change the parameters attached to the action. In the **Type** field, click on the arrow on the right to reveal the drop-down list. Select **Next Frame**.

When you are finished, your ActionScript should look like this:

```
on (release) {
  nextFrame ();
}
```

You have just added ActionScript to the right button. Now when the user clicks on this button and releases the mouse, the Playhead will advance to the next frame and stop.
Tip: *Part of the description in the nextFrame action will send the Playhead to the next frame and automatically* ***stop***, *so you do not need to add an additional Stop action.*

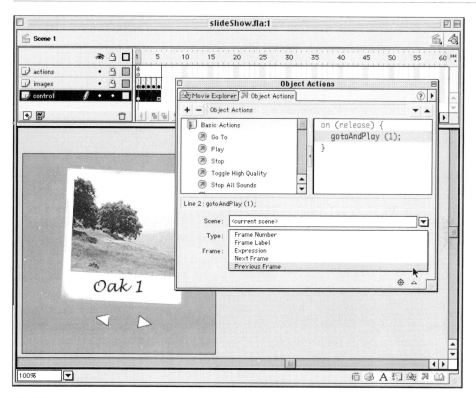

14. Click on the button instance on the left to select it. In the **Object Actions** dialog box, under **Basic Actions**, double-click on the **Go To** action to add it to the Actions list. In the **Type** field at the bottom of the **Object Actions** panel, click on the arrow on the right to reveal the drop-down list. Select **Previous Frame**.

When you are finished, your ActionScript should look like this:

```
on (release) {
  prevFrame ();
}
```

This time, you have just added ActionScript to the left button. Now when the user clicks on this button and releases the mouse, the Playhead will move to the previous frame and stop.

15. Choose **Control > Test Movie** to test your movie. Click on the right arrow button several times to advance the slide show to the next picture and click on the left arrow button to reveal the previous picture. Neat!

Notice when you continue to click on the right arrow, the side show stops at oak 5 (the last frame) and never starts over at Frame 1? Likewise, notice when you continue to click on the left arrow, the slide show stops at oak 1 (the first frame) and never loops to Frame 5? You can fix this to make the slide show loop back to the beginning or to the end by adding a few keyframes and changing some of the ActionScript, which you will do next.

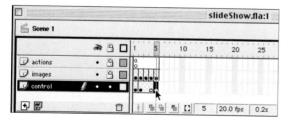

16. On the **control** layer, add keyframes to **Frame 2** and **5** using the **F6** key. Your control layer should look like the picture above. This will copy all the contents of Frame 1, including the actions attached to the buttons, to Frame 2 and Frame 5.

17. Move the **Playhead** so that it is over the **first** keyframe of the **control** layer. On the Stage, select the **left** button instance. (You may have to click off the Stage to deselect both buttons first and then select the left button.) You are going to change the ActionScript in this button next.

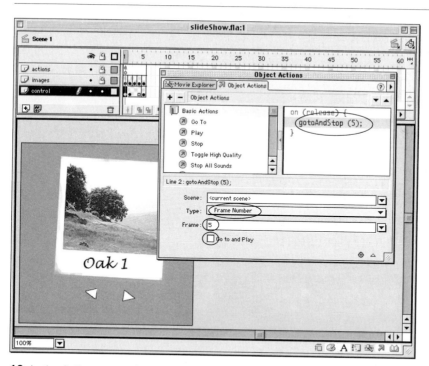

18. In the **Actions** panel (Window > Actions), select the line in the Actions list that reads **prevFrame ();**. This is the line you will be altering in the lower part of the panel. Click on the arrow to the right of the **Type** field to reveal the drop-down list. Choose **Frame Number** in the **Frame** field, and type **5**. Lastly, uncheck the box next to the words **Go To and Play.**

You have just changed the ActionScript on the left button instance appearing in the first keyframe of the movie. Instead of the script telling the Playhead to go to the previous frame (which it can't since this is Frame1, the first frame) you have now changed the script to tell Flash: When the user releases the mouse on this button in the first frame of the movie just go to Frame 5 and stop there!

19. Move the **Playhead** so that it is over the **last** keyframe of the **control** layer. On the Stage, select the **right** button instance. You are going to change the ActionScript in this button and then you are done!

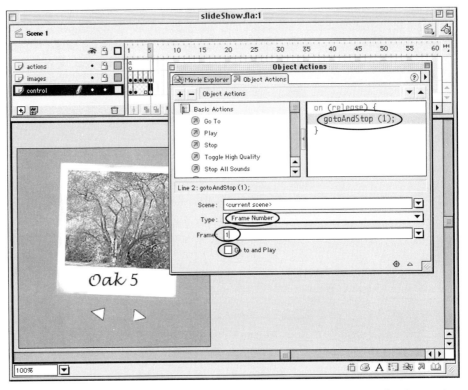

20. In the **Actions** panel (**Window > Actions**), select the line in the Actions list that reads **nextFrame ();**. This is the line you will be altering at the bottom of this pane. Click on the arrow to the right of the **Type** field to reveal the drop-down list. Choose **Frame Number**. In the **Frame** field, type **1**. Lastly, uncheck the box next to the words **Go To and Play.**

You have just changed the ActionScript on the right button instance appearing in the last keyframe of the movie. Instead of the script telling the Playhead to go to the next frame (which it can't since this is Frame 5, the last frame) you have now changed the script to tell Flash when the user releases the mouse on this button in the last frame of the movie just go to Frame 1 and stop there!

---

21. Test the movie again. This time, the movie should never be "stuck" on oak 1 or oak 5. Instead it should loop when either the first or last frame is reached.

---

22. When you are finished testing the movie, save and close this file.

_____On Mouse Event: Get URL

Not only can you use ActionScript to give users control over navigating within Flash movies, you can also use ActionScripting to open other Web sites from within a Flash movie. This exercise will introduce the **Get URL** action which is used to create links to other documents on the web. The Get URL action can also be used as an email link that will produce an email message. The following steps will teach you how to use the Get URL action to link to an external Web site and to generate a pre-addressed email message.

1. Choose **File > Open** and browse to the **getURL.fla** file located inside the **chap_12** folder. Select this file and choose **Open**. We have created this file to get you started.

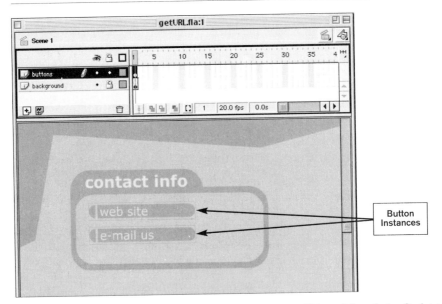

There are two button instances on the Stage. First, you will be adding ActionScript to the ***web site*** *button that will open up a Web site in a new browser window. In the next exercise, you will add ActionScript to the* ***e-mail us*** *button to create an email message.*

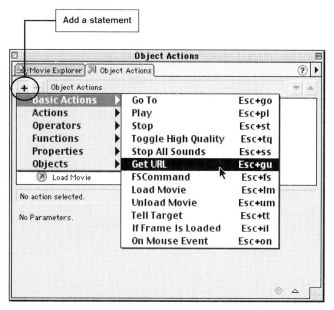

2. Select the **web site** button and choose **Window > Actions** to open the **Object Actions** panel. You have to select the button instance in order to be able to add actions to it. Click on the **Add Action (+)** button, choose **Basic Actions** and select **Get URL**.

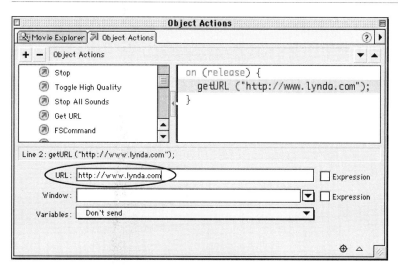

3. At the bottom of the **Object Actions** panel, type **http://www.lynda.com** in the **URL** field. This is an absolute link that will open the lynda.com Web site in a browser window when the user clicks on the **web site** button.

> ### TIP | Relative and Absolute Addresses
>
> The addresses that you use in a **Get URL** command can be either relative or absolute addresses. Relative addresses refer to local HTML files that are located in the same directory as the .swf file, such as **aboutus.html**. Absolute addresses refer to files located on other Web servers such as **http://www.macromedia.com**.

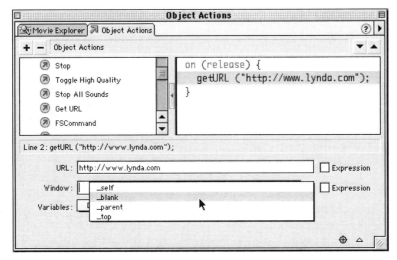

4. At the bottom of the **Object Actions** panel, select **_blank** in the **Window** field. This setting tells Flash to open the link you specified in Step 3 in a new browser window.

You have the ability to control the window or frame that displays the linked file by changing the parameters in the Window field. The table below explains each of the four options.

Get URL Window Parameter Options	
_blank	Opens the link up in a new browser window.
_self	Opens the link up in the same browser window that is occupied by the current Flash movie.
_parent	Opens the link in the parent window of the current window.
_top	Opens the link in the same browser window and removes any existing framesets.

5. The Variables option allows Flash to send variable values to a server. Leave the **Variables** option at the default setting since sending variables is beyond the scope of this exercise.

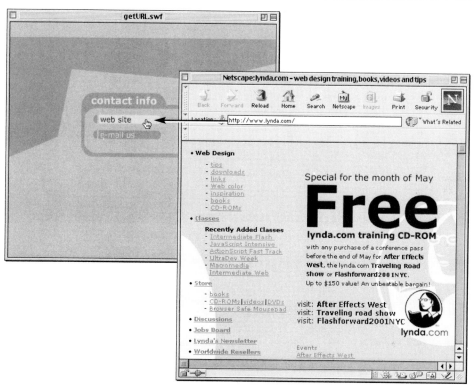

6. Press **Control > Test Movie** to preview the link you just created. When you use **Control > Test Movie**, the Get URL action will automatically launch your machine's default browser and load the Web address you specified into a new window.

Like an HREF tag in HTML, you can also use the Get URL action as an email link by adding "mailto" to an email address. In the steps that follow, you will add ActionScript to the second button to create an email link that will produce a pre-addressed email message.
`mailto:letters@lynda.com`

7. Back in the main movie, select the **e-mail us** button. In the **Object Actions** panel, click on the **Add Action (+)** button, choose **Basic Actions** and select **Get URL**.

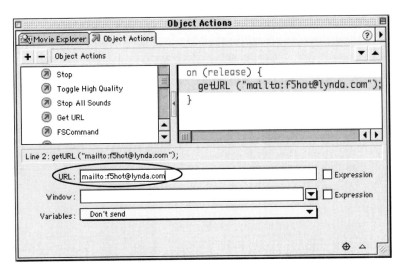

8. At the bottom of the **Object Actions** panel, type **mailto:f5hot@lynda.com** in the **URL** field. This will pre-address the email message to **f5hot@lynda.com** and open the message in a new window when the user clicks on the **e-mail us** button.

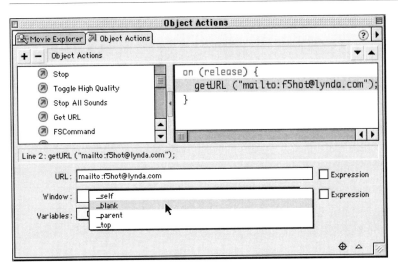

9. Select **_blank** in the **Window** field. This setting will tell Flash to open the email message in a new window, leaving the Flash movie still visible in the background. Leave the Variables option at the default setting.

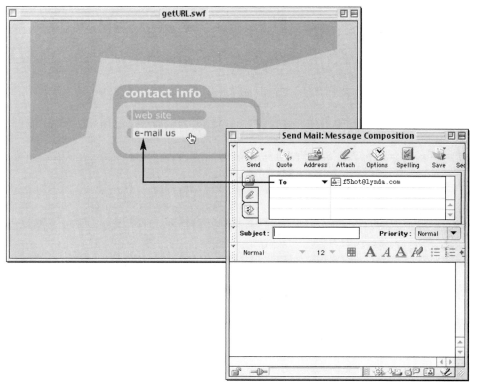

10. Press **Control > Test Movie** to test the email link. A new email message window will open when you click on the button!

11. Save and close this file.

5. _____Basic Drop-down Menu

There are many ways to create interactive menus in Flash. From scrolling menus to animated menus to draggable menus, all you need is a little creativity and a few bits of ActionScripting and you can develop all kinds of different navigation systems for your users. This exercise will start you on your way to creating interactive navigation schemes by teaching you how to develop a basic drop-down menu.

1. Open the file titled **menuFinal.fla** located inside the **chap_12** folder. This is the finished version of the menu you are going to create.

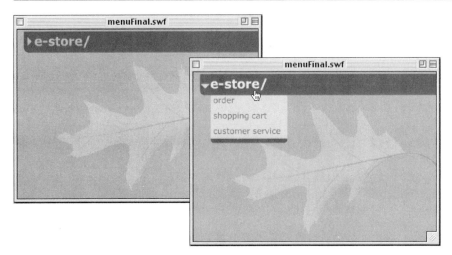

2. Choose **Control > Test Movie** to preview the movie. Click on the **e-store** button to reveal the drop-down menu. Click the button a second time to close the menu.

In this exercise, you will be adding frame labels and ActionScript to make this drop-down menu work. In the following exercise, you will add functionality to the buttons on the menu to make the buttons go to different scenes. You won't learn how to make scenes from scratch in this exercise, but you'll learn how to make scenes on your own in a later exercise.

3. When you are finished previewing the menu, close the **file.**

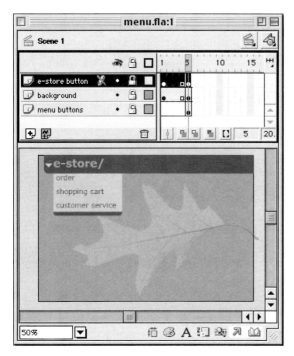

4. Open the **menu.fla** file located inside the **chap_12** folder. This is an unfinished version of the movie you just previewed containing everything you need to create a drop-down menu.

5. Choose **Control > Test Movie** to preview the movie. Notice how the menu flickers up and down uncontrollably. This is because no ActionScripting has been added to control the menu. You will add ActionScript to frames and objects in the steps that follow.

6. Click on the **Insert Layer** button to add a new layer to the Timeline. Name this layer: **labels**. Make sure the new layer is above all the other layers. If it is not, click on the layer name and drag it above all the other layers.

7. With the first keyframe selected in the **labels** layer, choose **Window > Panels > Frame**, or use the shortcut keys: **Cmd + F** (Mac) or **Ctrl + F** (Windows) to open the **Frame** panel.

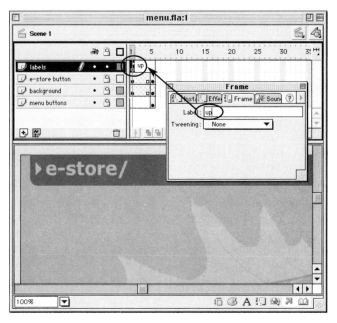

8. Type the name: **up** in the **Label** field of the panel. This will add the frame label: **up** to **Frame 1** where the menu is retracted or not present. As soon as you add the label name, notice the hollow circle and the flag in the Timeline. This is feedback to show you that a label exists on this frame.

NOTE | What is a Frame Label, Anyway?

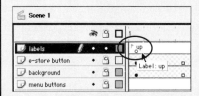

Frame labels identify a frame by a name, rather than a frame by a number. As you add and delete frames in the movie, the frame numbers will change and this can cause problems if you are referring to a frame number in your ActionScript. By referencing a frame label, if frames are added or deleted, the frame label will remain constant and Flash will be able to find the correct frame.

Frame labels are exported with the rest of the movie so it is a good idea to keep the frame labels short. Also, shorter frame labels are much easier to work with.

9. On the **labels** layer, select **Frame 5** and press **F7** to add a blank keyframe. In the **Frame** panel, type **down** in the **Label** field. This will add the frame label: **down** to **Frame 5**, where the menu is displayed or dropped "down."

10. Press the **Insert Layer** button to add another layer to your movie. Name this new layer: **actions**. Make sure the new layer is above the labels layer. If it is not, click on the layer name and drag it above all the other layers so that the actions layer is on top.

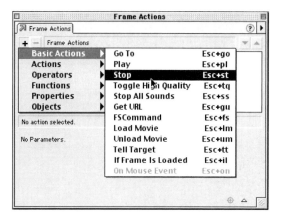

11. Select **Frame 1** in the **actions** layer and choose **Window > Actions** to open the **Frame Actions** panel. Click on the **Add Action (+)** button, choose **Basic Actions**, and select **Stop** to add a Stop action to the first keyframe. This action will tell the Playhead to stop on this frame.

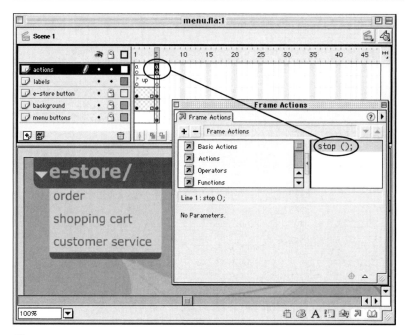

12. On the **actions** layer, press **F7** on **Frame 5** to add a blank keyframe. Click on the **Add Action (+)** button, choose **Basic Actions** and select **Stop** to add a Stop action on Keyframe 5. This action will tell the Playhead to stop on Frame 5 until another action tells Flash to do something else.

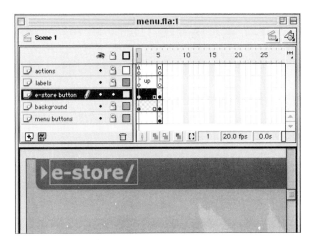

13. Lock the **actions** and **labels** layers and unlock the **e-store button** layer. Drag the Playhead to **Frame 1** and click on the **e-store** button instance on the Stage to select it. This is the button the user will click on to either display or hide the menu. You will add ActionScript to display the menu next.

14. With the button instance selected, choose **Window > Actions** to open the **Object Actions** panel. Click on the **Add Action (+)** button, choose **Basic Actions** and select **Go To** from the drop-down list.

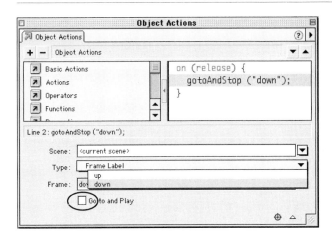

15. At the bottom of the **Object Actions** panel, leave the **Scene** field set to **<current scene>**. In the **Type** field select **Frame Label** from the drop-down menu. In the **Frame** field, select **down**. Make sure to uncheck the box next to **Go to and Play**. This ActionScript will tell Flash as soon as the user releases the mouse on this button, go to the frame label down and stop there.

16. Again, in the **e-store button** layer, drag the Playhead to **Frame 5** and click on the **e-store** button instance on the Stage. This is the button the user will click on to hide the menu. You will add this ActionScript next.

NOTE | Instances Can Have Different Actions

Each time you have a keyframe in the Timeline, the object on that keyframe is a different instance from that of the prior keyframe even if it is in the same exact location. Because each instance is unique, each instance can have different actions applied to it. Therefore, even though you added the ActionScript to the button on Frame 1, you can add a different ActionScript to the button on Frame 5.

17. In the **Object Actions** panel, click on the **Add Action (+)** button, choose **Basic Actions** and select **Go To** from the drop-down list.

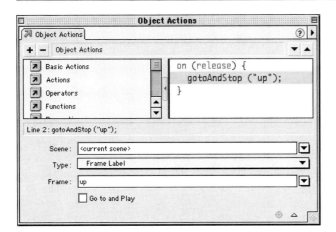

18. At the bottom of the **Object Actions** panel, leave the **Scene** field set to **<current scene>**. In the **Type** field select **Frame Label** from the drop-down menu. In the **Frame** field, select **up**. Make sure to uncheck the box next to **Go to and Play**. This ActionScript will tell Flash as soon as the user releases the mouse on this button, go to the frame label *up* and *stop* there.

19. Test the movie (**Control > Test Movie**). Click on the **e-store** button to reveal the drop-down menu. Click the button a second time to close the menu.

20. When you are finished, you can save and close this file. You will be using a similar file in the next exercise to make the buttons on the menu active.

What Are Scenes?

In Flash, you are not limited to the frames in the Timeline of the main movie. You can have several time-lines, which play one right after another. Flash calls these multiple timelines scenes. Scenes allow you to break up large projects into smaller manageable pieces. By default, Flash will play all the scenes in order, unless you use ActionScript to tell Flash otherwise. If no ActionScript is present in the main Timeline to stop the movie, the Playhead will continue on to the next scene and continue to play the frames until the end is reached or a Stop action is encountered. The Flash Player treats all the scenes in a movie as one long Timeline and therefore, if the first scene contains 30 frames and the second scene contains 20; Flash will see that as one Timeline of 50 consecutive frames and will play the scenes in the order that they appear in the Scene panel. The next exercise will teach you how to work with scenes.

6. _____Drop-down Menu Targeting Scenes

In the following exercise you will learn about scenes in Flash and how to target them using ActionScript. In the last exercise, you learned how to make a drop-down menu appear or retreat when the user clicks on a button. This exercise will take you up one level higher by teaching you how to use ActionScript to make the buttons on the drop-down menu go to scenes that you specify.

1. Open the file titled **gotoScenesFinal.fla** located inside the **chap_12** folder. This is the finished version of the file you are going to create. It is the similar to the file you created in the last exercise but this time, the buttons work and take you to a new scene when you click on them.

2. Choose **Control > Test Movie** to preview the movie. Click on the **e-store** button to reveal the drop-down menu and click on each of the buttons in the drop-down menu to move to the appropriate scene.

3. When you are finished previewing the menu, close the file.

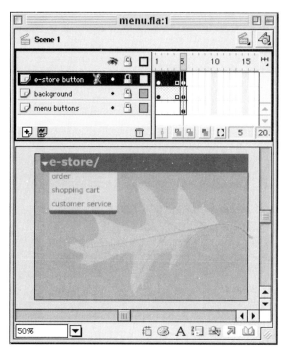

4. Open the **gotoScene.fla** file located inside the **chap_12** folder. This is an unfinished version of the movie that you just previewed, containing everything you learned in the last exercise, including three additional scenes.

5. Choose **Control > Test Movie** to preview the movie. Notice how the menu works just as it did in the last exercise, but the buttons don't go anywhere when you click on them. This is because there are no actions on the buttons telling them where to go. You will be adding ActionScript to the buttons in the steps that follow.

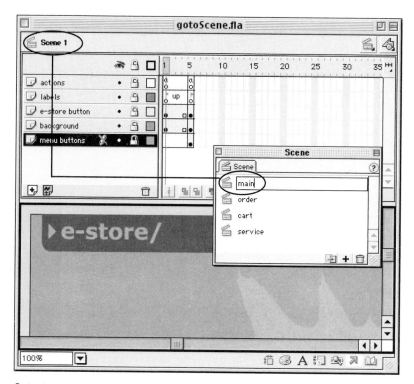

6. In the main Timeline, choose **Window > Panels > Scene** to open the **Scene Inspector**. You will see a list of the scenes in this movie that have been created for you. Double-click inside the **Scene 1** name and rename the scene: **main**. As soon as you hit **Return/Enter** on the keyboard, the name **Scene 1** will change to **main** in the Scene Inspector and also in the top left corner of the project window.

7. Click on the **Edit Scene** button in the upper-right-hand corner of the Timeline. A menu will appear with the list of scenes that have already been created for this project. From the menu, select the scene named **order**. This will take you into the Timeline of that scene. Notice how the scene name changed in the top left corner of the project window, the order scene is highlighted in the Scene Inspector and there is a checkmark next to the order scene drop-down menu from the Edit Scene button. These are all cues that tell you which scene you are currently inside within the project. Using the **Edit Scene** button, select the scenes named **cart** and **service** to also view their Timelines.

Note: You can't modify the scene names using the Edit Scene button (you would use the Scene Inspector for that as you did in Step 6), but you can use the Edit Scene button to move quickly to the Timeline of another scene.

8. Using the **Edit Scene** button again, choose the scene named **main** to return to the main Timeline.

Next, you will add the ActionScript to the buttons to tell Flash to go to a specific scene when the user clicks on a button.

9. Unlock the **menu buttons** layer and click on **Keyframe 5**. Notice the three buttons on the menu. Click on the Stage to the right of the menu to deselect the buttons.

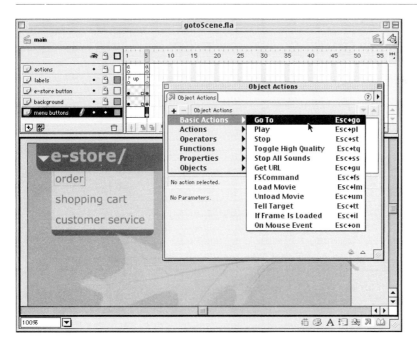

10. Select the **order** button by clicking on it. Choose **Window > Actions** to open the **Object Actions** panel. Click on the **Add Action (+)** button, choose **Basic Actions** and select **Go To**.

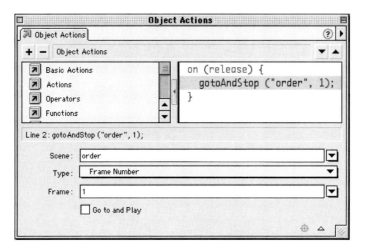

11. At the bottom of the **Object Actions** panel, choose **order** from the drop-down menu in the **Scene** field. Leave the **Type: Frame Number** and the **Frame: 1** fields at the defaults. Make sure to uncheck in the box next to **Go to and Play**. This ActionScript will tell Flash as soon as the user releases the mouse on the order button, go to the scene named order and stop there.

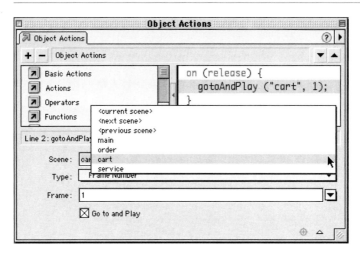

12. Repeat Steps 10 and 11 for the **shopping cart** button and the **customer service** button. The only differences are that, at the bottom of the **Object Actions** panel, choose **Scene: cart** for the shopping cart button and **Scene: service** for the customer service button.

You now have three buttons, each with ActionScript that instructs Flash to go to the appro-priate scene when the user releases the mouse on each button. You will add ActionScript in each of the scenes next.

13. Using the **Edit Scene** button again, choose the scene named **order** to open its Timeline.

14. Inside the **order** scene, click on the **Insert Layer** button to add a new layer to the Timeline. Name this layer: **actions**. Make sure the new layer is above all the other layers. If it isn't, click on the layer name and drag it above all the other layers so that you get in the habit of always placing the actions layer on the top.

15. Select **Frame 1** in the actions layer, choose **Window > Actions** to open the **Frame Actions** panel.

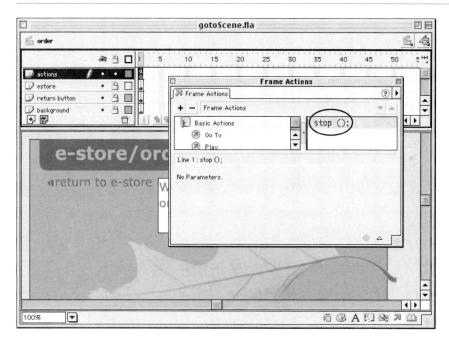

16. In the **Frame Actions** panel, open the **Basic Actions** list and double-click on **Stop** to add a Stop action to the **Actions** list window on the right side of the **Actions** panel. This will cause the movie to stop when the Playhead reaches the first frame in the order scene.

17. On the Timeline, unlock the **return button** layer. Select the **return** button on the Stage and in the **Actions** panel, open the **Basic Actions** list if it is not already open and double-click **Go To** to add an object action to the return button.

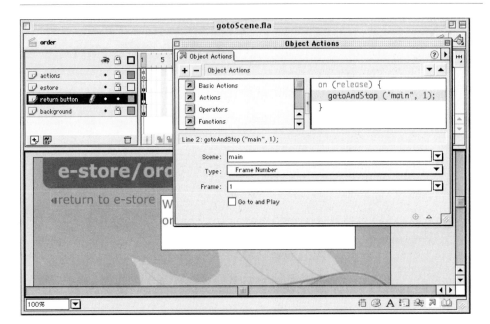

18. At the bottom of the **Object Actions** panel, choose **main** from the drop-down menu in the **Scene** field. You can leave the **Type: Frame Number** and the **Frame: 1** fields at the defaults. Make sure to uncheck the box next to **Go to** and **Play**. This ActionScript will tell Flash as soon as the user releases the mouse on the return to e-store button, go to the scene named main and stop there.

You will add actions to the cart scene and order scene next...

19. Using the **Edit Scenes** button, choose the cart scene. Inside that scene, click on the **Insert Layer** button to add a new layer to the Timeline. Name this layer: **actions**. Make sure the new layer is above all the other layers and if it is not, click on the layer name and drag it above all the other layers.

20. Select **Frame 1** in the **actions** layer. In the **Frame Actions** panel, open the **Basic Actions** list and double-click on **Stop** to add a Stop action to the **Actions** list window on the right side of the **Actions** panel. This will cause the movie to stop when the Playhead reaches the first frame in this scene.

21. On the Timeline, unlock the **return button** layer. Select the **return** button on the Stage and in the **Actions** panel, open the **Basic Actions** list (if it is not already open) and double-click on **Go To** to add an object action to the return button.

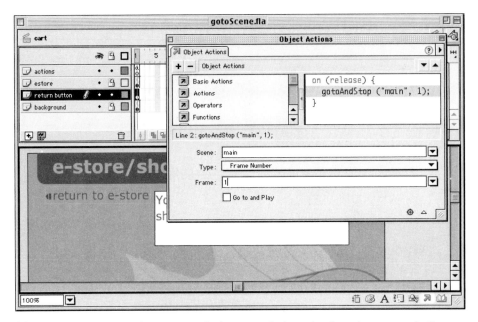

22. At the bottom of the **Actions** panel, choose **main** from the drop-down menu in the **Scene** field. Leave the **Type: Frame Number** and the **Frame: 1** fields at the defaults. Make sure to uncheck the box next to **Go to and Play**. This is the same ActionScript you added in Step 18. It will tell Flash as soon as the user releases the mouse on the return to e-store button, to go to the main scene and stop there.

You have one more scene to add actions to...

23. Using the **Edit Scenes** button, choose the **service** scene. Inside that scene, click on the **Insert Layer** button to add a new layer to the Timeline. Name this layer: **actions**. Make sure the new layer is above all the other layers and if it is not, click on the layer name and drag it above all the other layers.

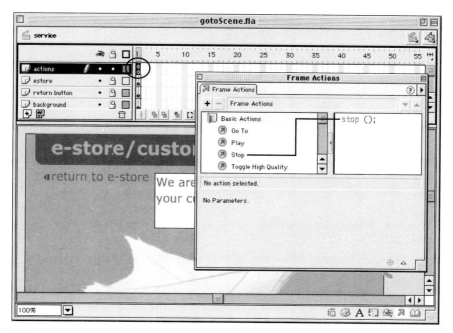

24. Select **Frame 1** of the **actions** layer. In the **Frame Actions** panel, open the **Basic Actions** list and double-click on **Stop** to add a Stop action to the **Actions** list window on the right side of the **Actions** panel. This will cause the movie to stop when the Playhead reaches the first frame in the service scene.

25. On the Timeline, unlock the **return button** layer. Select the **return** button on the Stage and in the **Actions** panel, double-click on **Go To** to add an object anchor to the return button.

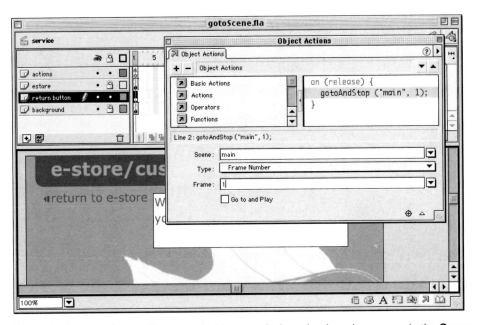

26. At the bottom of the **Actions** panel, choose **main** from the drop-down menu in the **Scene** field. You can leave the **Type**: **Frame Number** and the **Frame: 1** fields at the defaults. Make sure to uncheck the box next to **Go to and Play**. When the user releases the mouse on the return to e-store button, Flash will go to the main scene and stop there.

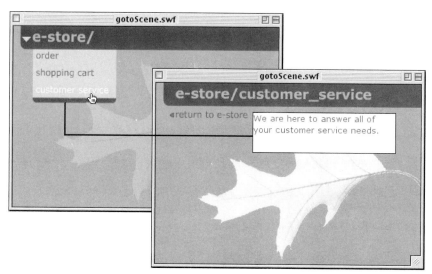

27. Press **Control > Test Movie** to test the movie! Click on each button to go to the appropriate scene. Click the **return to e-store** button to go back to the main menu. By using scenes, you can separate different sections of the project and target those sections on demand using ActionScript.

28. When you are finished testing the movie, save and close the file.

MOVIE | drop-down.mov

To learn more about creating drop-down menus, check out the **drop-down.mov** located in the **movies** folder on the **Flash 5 H•O•T CD-ROM**.

What is LoadMovie?

In earlier chapters, we described the difference between the project file (.fla) and the movie file (.swf). In this chapter, you will learn that a .swf file has the capability to load other .swf files into itself. This is a similar idea to links on an HTML page, which replace content with other HTML pages when clicked.

Why would you want to do this in Flash? If you have a large project with lots of graphics and navigation, it can take a long time to download all the content to the user's browser before they can access the finished result. If instead, you learn to structure your projects where many smaller movies get loaded on demand, it can create a better user experience for your audience than if they had to wait for the entire project to load.

This process is called Load Movie in Flash, because it requires the loadMovie action.

As you begin to stack .swf files on top of each other, their arrangement simulates layers. In Action-Scripting, the layers are called levels. The main Timeline (named Scene 1, by default) is always located at level 0 and when you load an additional movie, you can specify a level number for that movie such as 5 or 20. The number of levels is infinite, and as you load movies into different levels, any movies that are currently in different levels will still be visible and the movies that are loaded into higher levels will be placed in front of movies in lower levels. Again, this is similar to layers in the Timeline. You will learn to program the loadMovie action in the following exercise.

7. ————————Loading Movies

Loading multiple .swfs into the main .swf is an efficient way to present large Flash documents, because the visitor doesn't have to download the entire Flash movie. Instead, with the Load Movie ActionScript, multiple .swfs can be downloaded in the Flash Player on demand. This exercise will show you how this is done.

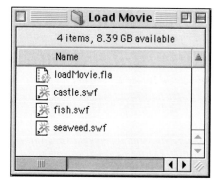

1. Browse to the **chap_12** folder on your hard drive. Browse to the folder titled **Load Movie.** Inside you will see three .swf files and one .fla file.

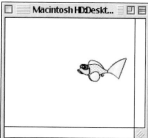

2. Double-click on each of the .swf files (**castle.swf, fish.swf** and **seaweed.swf**) to open and preview the animation inside them. These are the .swf files that you will be loading into a .fla file in the steps that follow.

3. Close the .swf files.

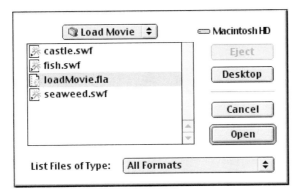

4. Open the file named **loadMovie.fla**, from the **Load Movie** folder located inside the **chap_12** folder. We have created this file to get you started.

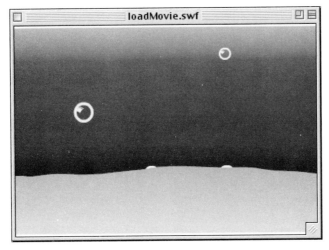

5. Choose **Control > Test Movie** to preview the movie. Notice that all you see is an ocean with random bubbles. This will serve as the main movie file. You will load the external movies (the .swf files that you previewed in Step 2) into levels above the main movie using the **Load Movie** action in the steps that follow.

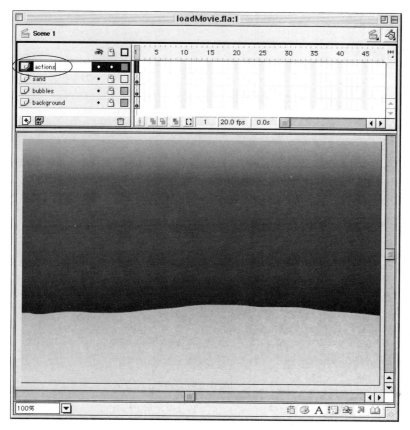

6. Close the preview window. In the main Timeline, click on the **Insert Layer** button to add a new layer to the Timeline. Name the new layer: **actions**. Make sure the new layer is above all the other layers and if it is not, click on the layer name and drag it above the other layers so that the actions layer is on top.

TIP | Why Add the Actions to a Frame Rather than an Object?

By adding the actions to a keyframe, the ActionScript will be executed as soon as the Playhead hits the keyframe with the action in it. In the following steps, you will add ActionScript to the very first keyframe in the Timeline. Therefore, as soon as the movie loads, the Playhead will trigger the first action immediately because it is located on the first keyframe. The ActionScript will then execute automatically as opposed to waiting for the user to click on a button.

Add a statement

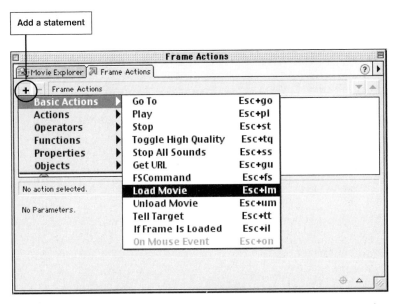

7. Select **Frame 1** of the **actions** layer and open the **Frame Actions** panel (Window > Actions). Click on the **Add Action (+)** button, choose **Basic Actions** and select **Load Movie**.

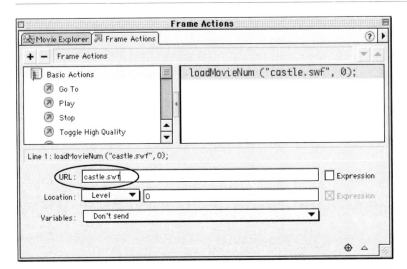

8. At the bottom of the **Actions** panel, type **castle.swf** in the **URL** field. This will tell Flash to load the **castle.swf** file into the main movie.

NOTE | Load Movie and Addressing

When you use the loadMovie ActionScript, the URL field at the bottom of the Frame Actions panel will specify the path to the file you are loading above the main movie. This path can be either relative or absolute. In this example, the relative path is used and therefore, all the .swf files you will be loading into levels above the main movie must be located in the same folder or directory as the main movie; otherwise Flash will not know where to find these files.

Use caution! Whenever you use a relative address for the loadMovie command, Flash will always look for the files in the same folder as the main project file.

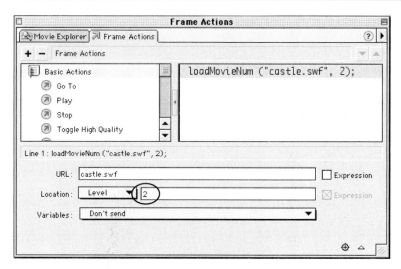

9. In the **Location:Level** field, type **2**. This will tell Flash to load the .swf file you specified (**castle.swf**) into level 2, above the main movie. Leave the **Variable** field at the default since variables are beyond the scope of this exercise.

10. Choose **Control > Test Movie** to test the ActionScript you added. You will now see a castle in the ocean! Notice how you added the castle but the main movie is still visible in the background. This is because you used the loadMovie ActionScript to load the castle into level 2, above the main movie that is located at level 0.

The main Timeline is always located at level 0 and as additional movies are loaded above it. Their corresponding level counts upward. Since there is no such thing as a negative level, you can't load movies below level 0. When you load movies into different levels, any movies that are currently in other levels will still be visible and the movies that are loaded into higher levels will be placed above movies in lower levels. Further, the loaded movies will have transparent Stages. So here, the ocean is at level 0 (the lowest level) and all other movies with their transparent backgrounds will stack above the ocean.

NOTE | The File Cabinet Analogy

As you begin to stack .swf files on top of each other, their arrangement simulates layers. In ActionScript, the layers are called levels. The concept of loading movies into layers can be a bit confusing, so we will use the likeness of a file cabinet to explain this more clearly.

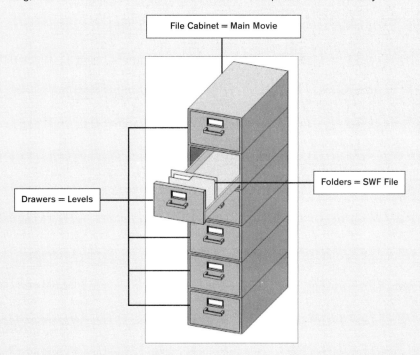

File Cabinet = Main Movie

Folders = SWF File

Drawers = Levels

Imagine a file cabinet. This file cabinet is an analogy to the main movie. Inside the cabinet, you have empty drawers, which are similar to levels within the main movie. Let's say that each drawer can only contain one thing, a folder, which is analogous to a .swf file. You can place one folder (.swf file) into any drawer (level) that you want to, but each drawer can only hold one folder. If you want to place a purple folder (.swf file) into a drawer (level 4) that already has a green folder (.swf file) in it, you have to take out the green folder first before you put the purple one in, because you can only have one folder (.swf file) in a drawer (level) at a time. However, if you have the green folder (.swf file) already in a drawer (level 4) you can add a blue folder (.swf file) to a drawer above it (level 5, for example). If you did this, you would have the file cabinet, a green folder in drawer 4 and a blue folder in drawer 5. Or, in Flash terminology you would have the main movie at level 0, with an .swf file loaded into level 4, above both the main movie and another .swf file loaded into level 5, above both the main movie and the .swf file in level 4.

11. In the main Timeline, make sure the first keyframe in the **actions** layer is still selected and open the **Frame Actions** panel (Window > Actions) if it is not already open. You are going to add an action to load another movie into a different level above the main movie next.

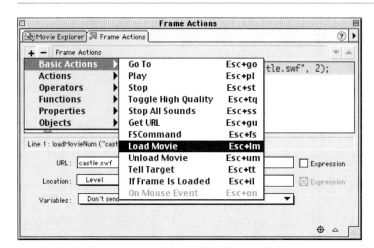

12. Click on the **Add Action (+)** button, choose **Basic Actions** and select **Load Movie**.

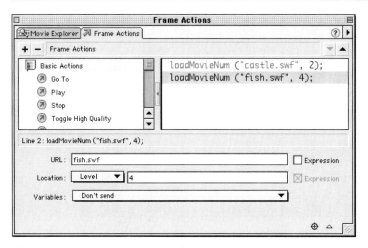

13. At the bottom of the **Actions** panel, type **fish.swf** in the **URL** field. In the **Location: Level** field, type **4**. This will tell Flash to load the **fish.swf** file into level 4, above the **castle.swf** in level 2, and above the main movie in level 0.

14. Choose **Control > Test Movie**. You will now see a fish swim in front of the castle and the ocean! Notice how you added the fish this time but the castle and the main movie are still visible in the background. This is because you used the loadMovie ActionScript to load the **fish.swf** into level 4, above the **castle.swf** in level 2 and above the main movie in level 0.

15. When you are finished previewing the file, close the window. You will load one more movie.

16. In the **Frame Actions** panel, click on the **Add Action (+)** button, choose **Basic Actions** and select **Load Movie**.

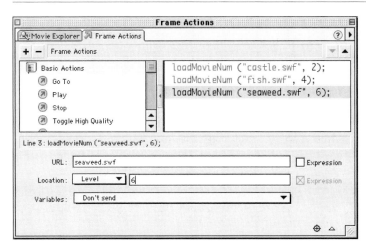

17. At the bottom of the **Actions** panel, type **seaweed.swf** in the **URL** field. In the **Location: Level** field, type **6**. This will tell Flash to load the **seaweed.swf** file into level **6**, above the **fish.swf** in level 4, above the **castle.swf** in level 2, and above the main movie in level 0.

TIP | Loading Into An Already Occupied Level

A movie doesn't have to be loaded into the next *empty* level; you can load a movie to any level you wish. However, if a movie is loaded into a level that is already occupied by another file, then the old file is kicked out and replaced by the new movie.

loadMovie.swf

18. Choose **Control > Test Movie**. You will now see seaweed in the forefront of the movie. Notice the fish swimming behind the seaweed but in front of the castle and the ocean bubbles! This is because you used the Load Movie action to load the **seaweed.swf** into level 6, above all the other .swf files.

If you don't care for the way the .swf files are stacked, you can easily switch their stacking order by changing the level number of one of the files. For example, lets say you want the fish to swim behind the castle and the seaweed. All you have to do is change the level where the fish.swf file will load, and specify a level that is lower than the level of the castle and the seaweed. You will do this next.

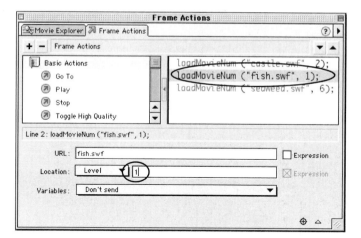

19. In the **Frame Actions** panel, click on the middle line of ActionScript to select the action that is loading the **fish.swf**. At the bottom of the **Actions** panel, change the **Location** field to **1**.

20. Test the movie using **Cmd + Return** (Mac) or **Ctrl + Enter** (Windows). Notice the fish is behind the castle and the seaweed now!

NOTE | Unloading Movies

In addition to loading movies into levels, you can unload them as well. Once a movie has been loaded into a level, there are two ways to remove it:

1. You can load a new movie into the same level by specifying the same level number. This will remove the movie that previously occupied that level and replace it with the new one. For example, if you have loaded a movie into level 20 and you load a new movie into that level, the old movie will be removed.

2. You can use the unloadMovie command, which will unload the movie you specify from the level you specify. This is generally the preferred method to unload movies, because loading a movie into the same level (#1, above) in order to unload the previous movie can cause hiccups in the transition from one movie to the next.

In summary, by using the Load Movie action, you can keep the main movie small and you can load additional movies into levels above the main movie as you wish or as they are needed.

21. Save and close this file.

What is a Preloader?

Flash is a streaming format, which means that the movie can begin playing before it is completely downloaded. In many cases, this is good because the user doesn't have to wait until the whole movie finishes loading in order to see the beginning of the movie. On the other hand, there are times when you may not want the movie to be seen until all the frames have been downloaded first—to assure smooth playback or synchronization with sound and the animation, for example. One method of achieving proper playback is using a preloader.

A preloader can exist in the very first frames of the movie, in the first scene of the movie or even at different points within the movie. The preloader uses ActionScript that detects whether the .swf file has finished downloading or not. Once the whole movie (or an amount you specify) has downloaded onto the user's machine, the movie will play. You can put different artwork or animation into your movie while the preloader is doing its detection work. The animation or artwork can keep users interested while they wait for a movie to download.

The following exercise will teach you how to create a simple preloader.

8. _____Preloader

As you build more complex projects in Flash you may find that the users will see the movie differently depending on their connection speed. Rather than allowing users to view a choppy animation or to click on a button that doesn't work yet because the movie is not completely downloaded, you can add a preloader to the movie. This will permit the movie to play, once all the necessary frames have downloaded. This exercise will teach you how to create a basic preloader so that you can control what your users see. As well, you will learn to make a new scene from scratch.

1. Open the **preloader.fla** located inside the **chap_12** folder. We have created this file to get you started.

2. Choose **Control > Test Movie** to preview the movie. This animation may seem familiar to you. It is the motion guide animation that you created in Chapter 8, "_Motion Tweening._" You will add a preloader to this movie in the following steps.

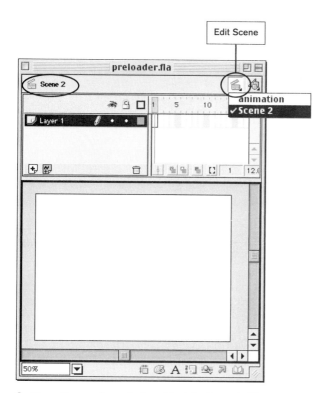

3. Close the preview window. Back in the main Timeline, choose **Insert > Scene** to add a new scene to the movie. This scene will hold the preloader that you will build in the following steps. Notice how Flash automatically places you inside the new scene's Timeline. Click on the **Edit Scene** button to see the list of the two scenes: the **animation** scene that was already created for you and the new scene you just added: **Scene 2**.

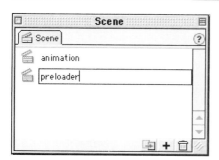

4. Open the **Scene Inspector** by choosing **Window > Panels > Scene**. Again notice the two scenes. Double-click inside the **Scene 2** name and rename the scene: **preloader**.

TIP | Creating Scenes

In addition to **Insert > Scene**, you can also add a new scene to the movie from the **Scene Inspector** by clicking on the **Add (+)** button at the bottom of the window. You can navigate from one scene to another by clicking on the names of the scenes in the **Scene Inspector**, or you can click on the **Edit Scene** button in the upper-right corner of the Timeline.

The order of the scenes listed in the Scene Inspector is the order in which they will play in the movie. When you have a preloader in the movie, the preloader needs to occur in the first scene. Therefore, you must move the preloader scene before the animation scene. You will do this next.

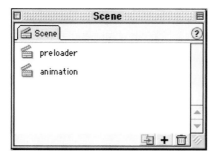

5. In the **Scene Inspector**, click on the **preloader** scene's name, and drag and drop it above the **animation** scene to make it first in the scene order. Your Scene Inspector should look like the picture above when you are finished.

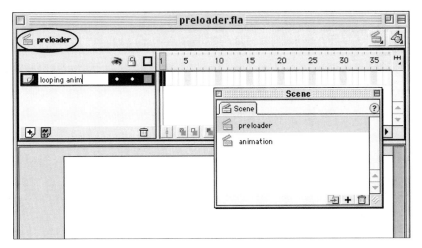

6. Make sure you are in the **preloader** scene by looking at the scene name in the top left corner of the window. It should read *preloader*. In case it does not, click on the **preloader** scene in the Scene Inspector window. In the main Timeline, double-click on the **Layer 1** name and rename it to **looping anim**.

7. Choose **Cmd + L** (Mac) or **Ctrl + L** (Windows) to open the **Library**. Double-click on the movie clip named **mc_loading** to open the movie clip's Timeline. Press **Return/Enter** to preview the frames in the movie clip. This will serve as the looping animation that will continue to play over and over until all the frames you specify are loaded.

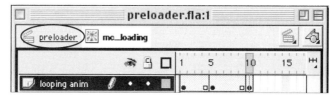

8. Click on the **preloader** button in the top left corner of the project file to return to the main Timeline in the **preloader** scene.

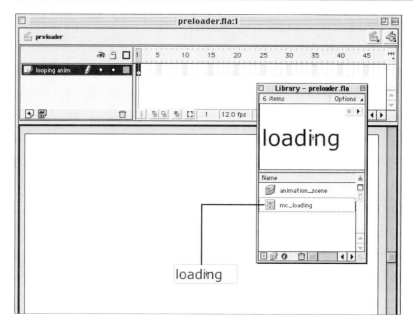

9. From the **Library**, drag an instance of the **mc_loading** movie clip onto the center of the Stage.

10. Press **F5** on **Frame 2** of the **looping anim** layer to add a frame to that layer. You will need only two frames on this layer for the preloader to work correctly. When you are finished, lock the looping anim layer.

11. Add a new layer above the looping anim layer and name it: **actions**.

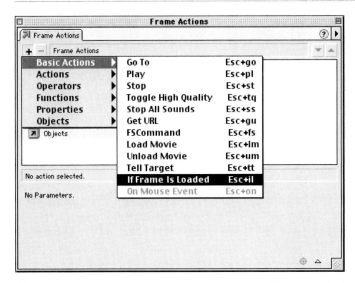

12. Select **Frame 1** in the actions layer and choose **Window > Actions** to open the **Frame Actions** panel. Click on the **Add Action (+)** button. Select **Basic Actions** and choose **If Frame is Loaded** from the drop-down list.

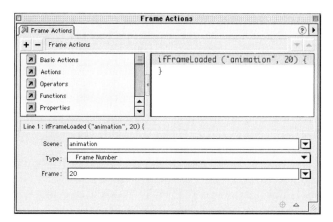

13. At the bottom of the **Actions** panel, select **animation** from the **Scene** field drop-down list. In the **Type** section, select **Frame Number**. In the **Frame** field, type **20**. The ActionScript you just created will tell Flash: If Frame 20 in the animation scene is loaded then something will happen. You will add the "something" in the next step.

14. With the **If Frame is Loaded** action selected in the **actions** window, click on the **Add Action (+)** button. Choose **Basic Actions** and select **Go To**.

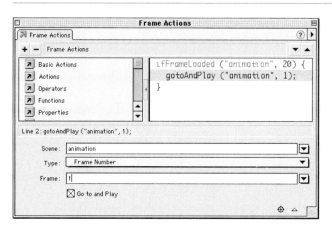

15. At the bottom of the **Actions** panel, select **animation** from the **Scene** field drop-down list. In the **Type** section, select **Frame Number**. Set the **Frame** field to **1**. Make sure there is a check in the box next to **Go to and Play** at the bottom of the **Frame Actions** window. This ActionScript will now tell Flash to check and see if Frame 20 in the animation scene has been downloaded, and if it has, then go ahead and play the animation scene from the beginning, starting at Frame 1.

You have just added ActionScript to have Flash to check to see if 20 frames from the ani-
mation scene have been downloaded to the user's system but what if the frames have not
downloaded yet? You need to add one more frame, which will cause this "check" command
to loop. You will do this next.

16. Select **Frame 2** in the **actions** layer on the Timeline and press **F7** to add a blank
keyframe. In the **Frame Actions** panel, click on the **Add Action (+)** button. Choose **Basic
Actions** and select **Go To**.

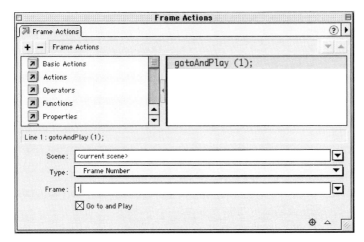

17. At the bottom of the **Actions** panel, leave the **Scene** field set to **<current scene>**. In the
Type section, select **Frame Number** and type **1** in the **Frame** field. Make sure there is a check
in the box next to **Go to and Play**. This ActionScript will tell Flash as soon as the Playhead hits
this frame, go back to Frame 1.

NOTE | What is Going On Behind the *Scenes*? (Pun Intended)

In Step 17, you added ActionScript to Frame 2 of the preloader scene so that once the Playhead reaches Frame 2, it will loop back to Frame 1 and perform a "check" to verify if Frame 20 of the animation scene has downloaded. If Frame 20 in the animation scene has not downloaded, the Playhead will move to Frame 2 of the preloader scene, which will send it back to Frame 1 to perform the check again. If Frame 20 of the animation scene has downloaded, the loop will be broken, and the Playhead will jump to the first frame of the animation scene and play the movie.

18. Select **Control > Test Movie** to preview the movie. You may not see the preloader!

Why? Frame 20 may load so fast that you can't even see the preloader in action. The next step will show you how to simulate the way the movie will appear on the Internet using the Bandwidth Profiler so that you can view the preloader hard at work.

NOTE | What is the Bandwidth Profiler?

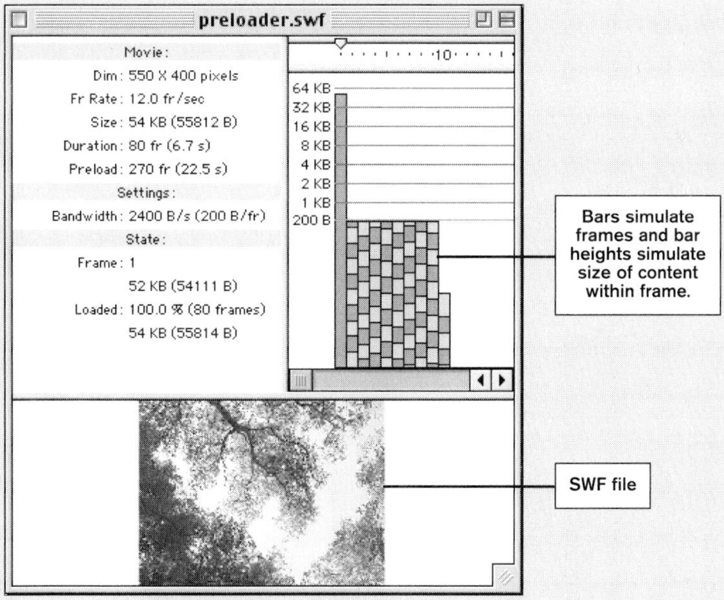
preloader.swf
Movie:
Dim: 550 X 400 pixels
Fr Rate: 12.0 fr/sec
Size: 54 KB (55812 B)
Duration: 80 fr (6.7 s)
Preload: 270 fr (22.5 s)
Settings:
Bandwidth: 2400 B/s (200 B/fr)
State:
Frame: 1
52 KB (54111 B)
Loaded: 100.0 % (80 frames)
54 KB (55814 B)
10
64 KB
32 KB
16 KB
8 KB
4 KB
2 KB
1 KB
200 B
Bars simulate frames and bar heights simulate size of content within frame.
SWF file

The Bandwidth Profiler is a feature in the Test Movie environment. It allows you to see how the movie streams based on different connection speeds. You can use the Bandwidth Profiler to simulate how a user would view your movie using a 28.8 kbps modem or a 56 kbps modem, for example. You can also use the Bandwidth Profiler to view the preloader before the movie plays.

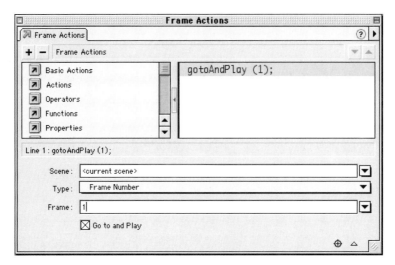

19. With the preview window open, select **View > Bandwidth Profiler**, then select **Debug > 28.8** to set the test a low bandwidth connection similar to a 28.8 modem dial-up connection. Choose **View > Show Streaming** to see your preloader work!

This allows you to see the movie as it would be streamed on a live 28.8 connection. Notice how the loading animation loops until Frame 20 is loaded, and then the animation scene begins.

20. Nice work, you have made your first preloader! Save and close this file.

The Toolbox List

The Toolbox list contains groups of actions that are organized into categories. Each category houses a list of actions that you can select from to build ActionScripts. Throughout this chapter, you have used the Basic Actions folder within the Toolbox. You might be wondering what the other folders contain, so we have provided a description of each category below.

ActionScript Categories Explained	
Basic Actions	Simplest form of actions. The Basic Actions list is only available in Normal mode, and it includes such actions as *Stop* and *Play*.
Actions	Includes the actions from the Basic Actions list and builds on that list to include more advanced actions such as *setProperty* and *set variable*.
Operators	Able to compare values, create mathematical equations and create combinations. Examples of *Operators* are *and*, *or* and == .
Functions	Combinations of ActionScript that are defined by the author. *Functions* perform frequently-used operations such as *GetProperty* and *updateAfterEvent*.
Properties	Characteristics of objects defined by Flash. Every object has *properties* and these properties can be retrieved and set such as rotation (*_rotation*) or alpha (*_alpha*).

The Basic Actions List

In this chapter you have been working with several of the basic actions within the Basic Actions list. The following table describes *all* the available actions in the Basic Actions drop-down list.

Basic Actions Defined	
Go To	Tells the Timeline to "go to" a particular frame number or to a frame label.
Play	Starts to play the Timeline from the current position of the Playhead. Telling a Timeline that is already playing to Play has no effect.
Stop	Stops play in the Timeline in which the action is located.
Toggle High Quality	Adjusts the entire movie's display quality, including the quality of symbol Timelines, by turning antialiasing on and off in the Flash Player. This action originated in Flash 2, and although it will work, this action is not recommended because Flash 5 offers better ways to work with the quality settings of the movie.
Stop All Sounds	Stops every sound that is currently playing when the action is evoked. The *stopAllSounds* action will not stop the Playhead.
Get URL	Creates a hypertext link and opens the URL in a browser window. This action is the same as an HREF tag in HTML. It is used to build links to other documents on the Web. *Get URL* can also send variables to the specified URL.
FSCommand	Controls the Flash player the movie is playing in. *FS Commands* invoke JavaScript functions from Flash. There are five built-in FS command statements in Flash 5, and they will be explained in Chapter 15, "*Publishing*."
Load Movie	Loads a Flash movie (the swf file) into another Flash movie. You learned about this in Exercise 7, "*Loading Movies*."
Unload Movie	Unloads a previously loaded movie.

Basic Actions Defined	
If Frame is Loaded	Checks to see whether a specific frame has been downloaded by the Flash plug-in or not. The *ifFrameLoaded* action is often used to begin playing an animation, such as a loading bar while the remainder of the movie is being downloaded in the background. Although this action will work, Flash 5 has introduced more advanced ways to determine if a frame has loaded, using the _framesloaded action, which allows you to use *if* or *else* statements.
On Mouse Event	Triggers an action by assigning a mouse event (such as release) or keystroke (such as *F2*).

That's a wrap on this chapter. We covered a lot of information in the exercises, and if anything isn't crystal clear, you can always go back and do a review. Take a well-deserved break and then get ready for the Text chapter, which comes next.

13.

Working with Text

| Text Box Types |
| Creating, Modifying and Formatting Text |
| Static Text | Dynamic Text |
| Input Text | Font Symbols |

chap_13

Flash 5
H•O•T CD-ROM

In the olden days of digital design (sarcasm intended, as digital design isn't really that old), a type tool was a type tool was a type tool. It set type, allowed you to change the font, and perhaps handled some spacing issues. Flash does that too, but it also has many type attributes that you've most likely never worked with.

Flash allows you to create three different types of text elements. *static* text, which is the default when you select the text tool, displays whatever text you type; *dynamic* text accepts and displays text from an outside source (such as a text file or a database file); and *input* text accepts and displays type entered by a user, such as entering a user name and password. In addition, you can even create font symbols to assist in rapidly updating multiple text blocks throughout a project file. You'll learn about these different types of text treatments with hands-on exercises to try them out.

Text Box Types

When you select the Text tool in Flash, you can create one of three different types of text boxes. Each of the text boxes has specific attributes and uses.

Label Text

Round handle indicates expandable Block Text. The text box will expand as text is entered.

By default, when you select the Text tool and click on the stage to begin typing, you create a **Label Text** box. A round handle at the top right corner of the box will appear as an indication you are creating a Label Text box. As you continue to type, you will notice that the it expands as you add characters. Be careful, though, because if you keep typing, the line of text will continue right off the stage and keep going and going! Therefore, with Label Text boxes, you need to make your own line breaks or returns. Label Text is often used when a small block of text is needed such as text within a navigation bar.

> **TIP | Zoom! Zoom! Zoom!**
>
> If, by accident, you do create a text block that continues off the stage, don't worry because you can choose **View > Work Area** and reduce the magnification to make the entire line of text visible. You can then force the text to wrap downward by placing the cursor inside the text block and adding your own line breaks or returns.

Block Text

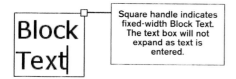

Square handle indicates fixed-width Block Text. The text box will not expand as text is entered.

Block Text boxes have a fixed width. As you type, your words will automatically be wrapped to the next line when they hit the end of the predetermined width of the box. To create a Block Text box, select the text tool and click anywhere on the stage. Move the cursor over the round handle (indicating that this is a Label Text box) and you will notice the cursor changes to a double-sided arrow. Drag the handle out to the desired width for the Block Text box and notice how the circle handle turns into a square handle when you release the mouse. You have just changed the Label Text box into a Block Text box. As you enter text, the words will automatically wrap to the next line, and the box will expand down as you add more text. Block Text boxes are often used for large amounts of text that need to fit into a specific area of an interface, for example.

TIP | Changing the Text Box

You can switch a text box from a Block Text box to a Label Text box and back again by simply double-clicking on the handle.

Editable Text

Editable Text

Circle handle indicates expandable dynamic or input Block Text.

Editable Text

Square handle indicates fixed-width dynamic or input Block Text.

Editable Text boxes are used for content that changes, such as password fields or for bringing in text from an external source. You can create Editable Text boxes by choosing Dynamic or Input Text in the Text Options panel (you will learn how to do this later in this chapter). By default, Editable Text boxes will extend horizontally (indicated by a circle handle at the bottom right of the text box) and you will need to add the line breaks. However, Editable Text boxes can be set to a fixed width (indicated by a square handle at the bottom right of the text box) by dragging out the handle. You will try this in two different exercises later in the chapter.

WARNING | Text in Flash and Search Engines

Whether you create label text, block text, or editable text in Flash, it is important to note that *unlike* HTML, Flash text is not searchable by search engines. Therefore, if you need key words within your movie to be seen by search engines, we suggest you add meta tags to the HTML document that the .swf file resides in. You will learn more about embedding .swf files in HTML documents in Chapter 15, "*Publishing*." For further information about meta tags, a good resource book is "*HMTL 4 for the World Wide Web Visual QuickStart Guide*," from Peachpit Press.

Creating, Modifying and Formatting Text

In Flash, you have a lot of control over the attributes of type. By using the **Character** panel and the **Paragraph** panel, you can change, preview and adjust text in a few easy clicks of the mouse. The next section will give you a close look at each of the panels.

Character Panel

To access this panel, the keyboard shortcut is **Cmd + T** (Mac) or **Ctrl + T** (Windows).

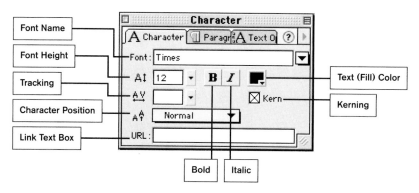

Character Panel Defined	
Font Name	Displays the name of the current font. Click the arrow to the right of the font name to view a list of all the available fonts. As you scroll through the font list, Flash displays a preview of what each font will look like.
Font Height (Size)	Displays the current font size. Click the arrow to the right of the font height field and use the slider to adjust the font size or type the desired size in the font height field.
Tracking (Space Between Characters)	Allows you to adjust the space between two or more characters. Click the arrow next to the tracking field and use the slider to increase or decrease the amount of space between characters.
Character Position (Baseline Shift)	*Normal*: Resets characters to the baseline. *Superscript*: Shifts characters above the baseline. *Subscript*: Shifts characters below the baseline.
	continued on next page

Character Panel Defined *continued*	
Link Text Box	Creates a hyperlink that is attached to selected text. In effect, this creates a button that will link to an internal or external HTML file, without needing to create a button symbol. Using this option will automatically add a dotted line under the linked text in the .fla file. However, take caution in that hyperlinks created using this feature will not carry any visual feedback (such as an underline) in the .swf file. When previewed in a browser however, the hand symbol will appear when the end user moves his or her mouse over the linked text.
Bold	Bolds the selected type.
Italic	Italicizes the selected type.
Kern	Checking this box will automatically use the font's built-in kerning (spacing between characters) information. (See sidebar below for more information on kerning.)
Text (Fill) Color	Allows you to change the color of the type by presenting you with a palette of available colors.

NOTE | To Kern or Not To Kern?

When font sets are created, the individual characters might look great all by themselves, but some letters don't look very good next to each other or they aren't spaced very well. To solve this issue, many fonts are created with additional instructions about spacing between specific characters. This is known as kerning information. Flash will not automatically add this special kerning information to your text unless you tell it to by checking the Kern checkbox in the Character panel. We recommend that you use this option, especially when typing paragraphs of text in order to achieve the best looking text Flash is capable of producing.

Paragraph Panel

To access this panel, the keyboard shortcut is **Shift + Cmd + T** (Mac) or **Shift + Ctrl + T** (Windows).

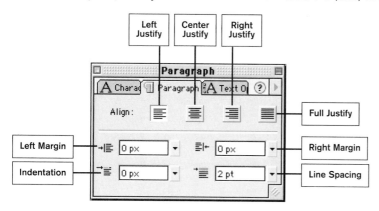

Paragraph Panel Defined	
Align	Controls how the selected text will be aligned: Left Justified, Center Justified, Right Justified or Full Justified.
Left Margin	Determines the amount of space between the characters and the left side of the text box. Click on the arrow to the right of the Left Margin field, and use the slider to change the margin space, defined in pixels. Even if text is center or right aligned, increasing the amount of space in the left margin will create the space you specify from the left side of the text box to the leftmost character within the text box.
Indentation	Controls the indent on the first line of a paragraph. Click on the arrow to the right of the Indentation field and use the slider to change the amount of indentation space, defined in pixels.
Line Spacing (Leading)	Controls the spacing between lines of type. Click on the arrow to the right of the Line Spacing field and use the slider to change the amount of space between lines, defined in points.
Right Margin	Determines the amount of space between the characters and the right side of the text box. Click on the arrow to the right of the Right Margin field and use the slider to change the margin space, defined in pixels.

Static Text

So far you've been had an in-depth look at the Character panel and the Paragraph panel. Next, you will be introduced to the **Text Options panel**. In the following section, we will explain the **Static Text** option that is the default behavior of any text box.

Text Options Panel: Static Text

Unfortunately, there is no keyboard shortcut for the **Text Options** panel but you can choose **Window > Panels > Text Options** to access this panel.

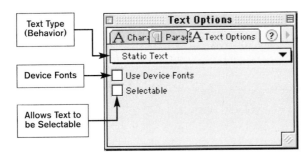

Text Options Panel: Static Text Defined	
Text Type (Text Behavior)	Allows you to choose from one of three behaviors (Static Text, Dynamic Text or Input Text) for the text box. Each *Text Type* has its own associated options that appear in the panel when that text behavior is selected. *Static Text* is the default behavior.
Device Fonts	If this box is *not checked*, Flash will embed font information for any fonts used within the text block. When the movie is exported, this font will appear antialiased (not jaggy).
	If this box *is* checked, Flash will prevent the font information from being embedded.
	(See the following section for further information on device fonts.)
Selectable	Allows a user to select text within a block and either copy it or cut it.

Embedded Fonts vs. Device Fonts

When you select a font for a text block, Flash automatically takes all the font information (description of how the font will look, aliasing or anti-aliasing, kerning, etc.) and embeds it in the exported movie. Often, this not only increases the file size of the movie but some fonts, although displayed in your project file, cannot be exported with the movie because Flash does not recognize the font's outline. You can select **View > Antialias Text** to preview the text and if it appears rough or jagged, this indicates a problem: the text will not be exported because Flash does not recognize the font outline.

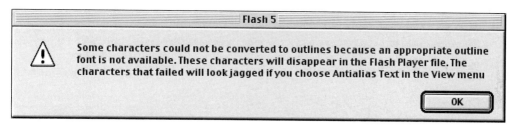

Another indication that Flash does not recognize the font's outline is when you get the error message above. You may be able to see the font on the stage, but when you try to test or publish the movie, you'll get this alert to let you know that the font may not be exported with your movie, and the text will disappear in the Flash Player file.

Device fonts were created as a way around this issue. They are special fonts that will not be embedded in the exported movie and therefore create a smaller file size. Rather than use an embedded font, the Flash Player displays the text using the closest match on the user's computer to the device font. Generally, at smaller type sizes, device fonts are sharper and easier to read.

The drawback to device fonts is that if a user doesn't have a font installed on his/her system that is similar to the device font, they might see text that looks nowhere near what it looks like on your machine. To combat this concern, Flash includes three built-in device fonts to help the results turn out more closely to what you expect:

• **sans**–similar to Helvetica or Arial

• **serif**–similar to Times Roman

• **typewriter**–similar to Courier

I. —————————**Working with Static Text**

When you add text to your Flash movie, it is important to be aware of what the end user will see when looking at the text on a live Web site. Often this will differ from what you see on your stage. There are features in the Text Options panel that give you more control over how the text will appear in a Web browser. This exercise will teach you the difference between embedded and device fonts. You will work with pre-developed static text blocks and then export the blocks of text using both options to see the difference between checking or not checking the device fonts box.

1. Copy the **chap_13** folder, located on the **H•O•T CD-ROM**, to your hard drive. You need to have this folder on your hard drive in order to save files inside it.

2. Open the **staticText.fla** file located inside the **chap_13** folder. We have created this file to get you started.

3. You will notice two text blocks side by side. Both of these text blocks have the exact same font. Click on the **left** text block to select it.

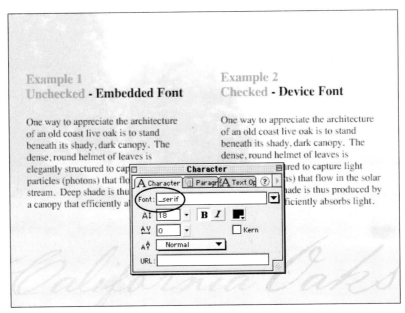

4. Open the character panel by selecting **Window > Panels > Character**. With the **left** block selected, notice the font setting applied to that text block: **Font:_serif**. Click on the **right** text block and you will notice the same font setting.

So far, nothing is different between these two blocks of text. In the following steps, you will modify the left block of text by using embedded type (the default), while making the right block of text use a device font.

5. Click on the left block of text to select it. In the same panel set (Character, Paragraph, Text Options), choose the **Text Options** tab to open the **Text Options** panel.

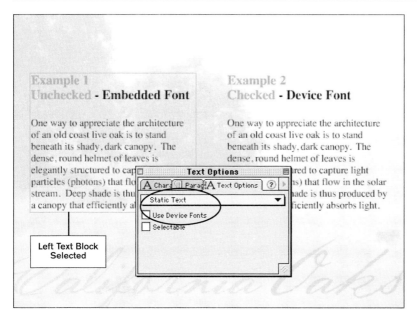

6. Make sure the left block of text is still selected and in the **Text Options** panel, notice how the **Use Device Fonts Box** is unchecked. This is the default setting when you create a static text block. In effect, it will create an embedded font.

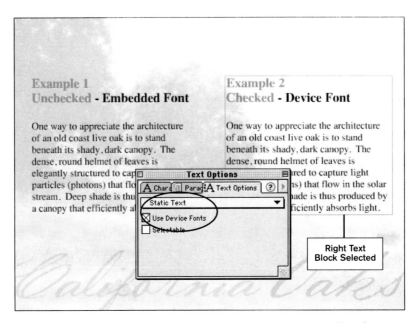

7. Click on the **right** block of text to select it on the stage. In the **Text Options** panel, check the **Use Device Fonts** box. When you preview this file, the right block of text will use the device fonts feature and the left block of text will not.

Example 1
Unchecked - Embedded Font

One way to appreciate the architecture
of an old coast live oak is to stand
beneath its shady, dark canopy. The
dense, round helmet of leaves is
elegantly structured to capture light
particles (photons) that flow in the solar
stream. Deep shade is thus produced by
a canopy that efficiently absorbs light.

Example 2
Checked - Device Font

One way to appreciate the architecture
of an old coast live oak is to stand
beneath its shady, dark canopy. The
dense, round helmet of leaves is
elegantly structured to capture light
particles (photons) that flow in the solar
stream. Deep shade is thus produced by
a canopy that efficiently absorbs light.

California Oaks

8. Choose **Control > Test Movie** to preview the movie. Notice how the Embedded Font text block on the left is fuzzier, whereas the text on the right is cleaner? This is because the text block on the right is using device fonts, which is a quick way to keep the file size down and allow the text to be readable even at smaller font sizes.

9. Save and close this file.

Character Attributes Gallery

We have included this section to give you a visual example of some of the features we introduced in the last exercise.

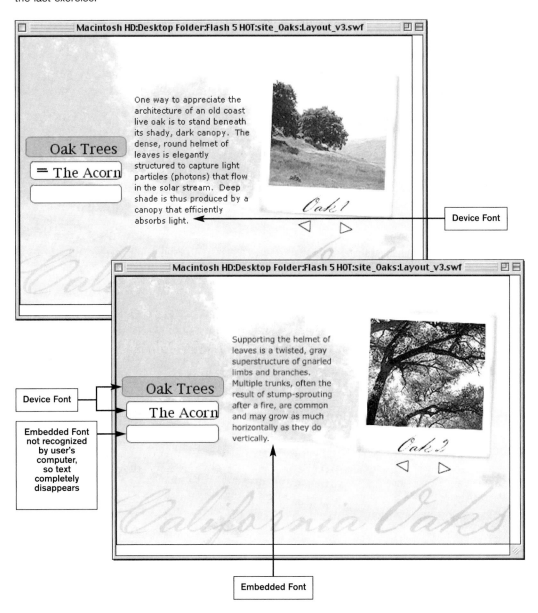

Dynamic Text

In the last section you learned about the Static Text option of the Text Options panel. Next, we will explain the **Dynamic Text** option. Dynamic text blocks allow you to import data into a SWF file from an outside source external to the Flash player (such as a text file or from a Web server). By making changes to the external file, Flash will automatically update the changes in the .swf without you even opening the Flash project file. This allows Flash to be a robust program for handling dynamic content. We will explain the settings for dynamic text next.

Text Options Panel: Dynamic Text

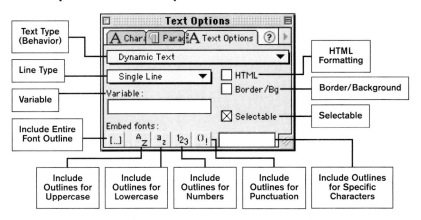

Text Options Panel: Dynamic Text Defined	
Text Type (Text Behavior)	Allows you to choose from one of three behaviors (*Static Text*, *Dynamic Text* or *Input Text*) for the text box. Each type has its own associated options that appear in the panel when that text behavior is selected. Dynamic text behavior has been chosen in the picture above.
Line Type	Allows you to set the text box to either *Single Line* (displaying the text in one line) or *Multiline* (displaying the text in multiple lines).
Variable	Enables you to assign a variable name (which must begin with a letter) to the dynamic text box. This is essential when you are working with dynamic data. (The name of the external variable needs to exactly match the variable name of the text box, as you will learn in Exercise 2.)

continued on next page

Text Options Panel: Dynamic Text Defined *continued*	
HTML	Checking this box enables Flash to interpret and preserve rich text formatting such as font, font style, hyperlink, paragraph, and additional text formatting with the appropriate HTML tags. See the Text Options Gallery section that follows this section.
Border/Background	Checking this box creates a border and background around the dynamic text box. If the box is unchecked, a dotted line will surround the text box in the .fla file, although when you publish the movie, there will be no border or background. See the Text Options Gallery section for a visual example of this.
Selectable	Checking this box allows the user to select the characters within the text box and cut and copy them.
Embed Fonts	Clicking on the buttons to select them allows you to choose which characters and/or numbers you wish to include when you publish the movie. • Embed all characters • Embed uppercase characters • Embed lowercase characters • Embed numbers • Embed punctuation Entering specific characters allows you to choose which characters and/or numbers you wish to include when you publish the movie. • Embed specified characters

---

NOTE | What is a Variable?

A variable is simply a container that holds information such as a name or number.

For example, if the following ActionScript is typed:

author=" Kymberlee";

The variable name (or container) is: **author** and everything after the equal sign is the value of the variable, which, in this example, is **Kymberlee**.

Text Options Gallery

We have included this section to give you a visual example of some of the new terms that will be introduced in this section.

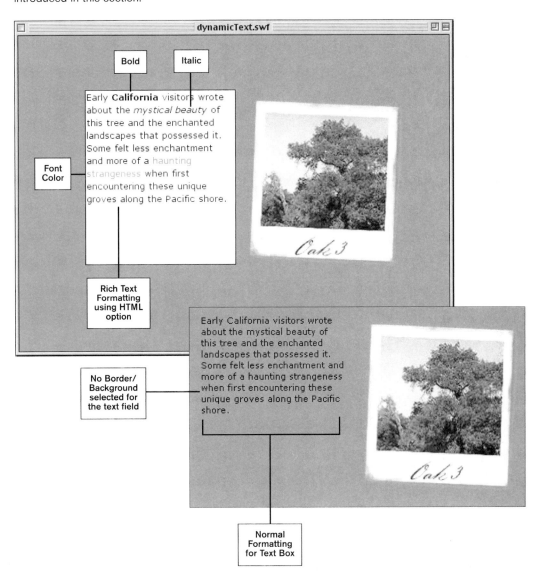

2. ———————————Working with Dynamic Text

Often times you may want to add functionality to your Flash movie, so that it displays current information such as news, weather reports, or company information that will get updated often. Flash allows
you to do this using a dynamic text field, a variable, and an external file that holds the text. The following exercise will take you through these steps and teach you how to load a pre-created .txt file right
into a dynamic text block.

1. Open the **textfile.txt** file located inside the **chap_13** folder by double-clicking on it. It will
open in the default text editor on your computer. We have created this file to get you started.

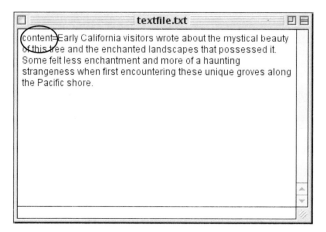

2. In order for Flash to recognize the information in this file, you need to give it a variable
name. Place your cursor at the very beginning of the paragraph and type **content=** , just as
you see in the picture above. You have now declared that the text within the text file will be
assigned to the variable name: **content**.

NOTE | URL–Encoded Text

When you use the Load Variables action (which you will add in Step 13) to load an external text file, the data in the file must be in a special format called **URL-encoded**. This format requires that each variable travel in a pair with its associated value. The variable and
the associated value are separated by the = symbol. In Step 2, above, the variable is
content and the associated value is all the text that immediately follows the = symbol.

3. Save and close the text file. Make sure you saved it in the **chap_13 folder,** because Flash will be referring to this file in later steps.

4. In Flash, open the **dynamicText.fla** file, which is located inside the **chap_13** folder.

5. You should see artwork on the right side of the stage. You will add the dynamic text box to the left of the image.

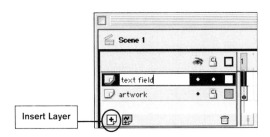

6. Add a new layer by clicking on the **Insert Layer** button and name this layer: **text field**.

7. Make sure the first keyframe in the new **text field** layer is selected. Using the **Text tool**, create a text box, just to the left of the artwork.

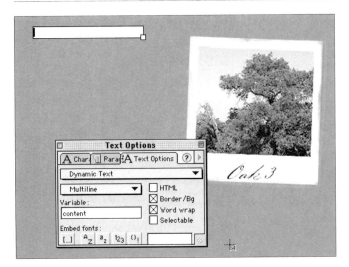

8. Open the text options panel by selecting **Window > Panels > Text Options**. Choose **Dynamic Text, Multiline, Border/Bg** and **Word Wrap**. Deselect the **Selectable** box (which is selected by default) because you will not want to allow the user to select the text in the movie. Lastly, enter the word **content** in the Variable field. This will be the variable name that is assigned to the text box and, as you will see in the next few steps, the same name that you assign to the external data, which will import inside a dynamic text box in this exercise.

9. Drag the dynamic text box handle out so that the size of the text box is slightly larger than the artwork.

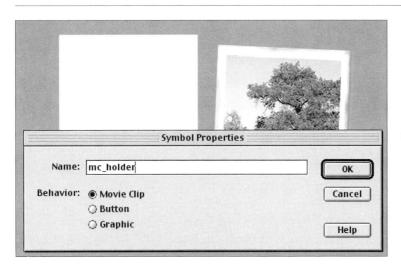

10. With the dynamic text box selected, choose **Insert > Convert to Symbol**. Select Behavior: **Movie Clip** and name the symbol: **mc_holder**.

This will place the dynamic text field you just made inside a movie clip. A movie symbol is necessary because this data will become a target in the ActionScript needed to bring in the dynamic text. A movie clip is the only kind of symbol that supports this type of targeting.

TIP | Loading External Data into a Project File

Whenever you load external data into Flash, you need to give Flash instructions about where to put it once it is loaded in. Although this exercise teaches you how to load variables using a text file, you also learned how to load external movies using the LoadMovie command in Chapter 12, "*ActionScript Basics*." You may notice that the steps involved in loading variables and loading movies are very similar. The options of where you load the data are limited to one of two locations: you can load the data (or movie) into a target or into a level.

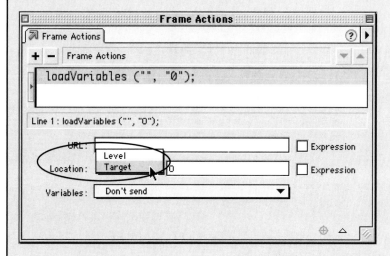

We covered levels when we showed you how to load movies in Chapter 12, "*Action-Scripting Basics*". For this exercise, you will load the data into a target. When you choose **Location > Target** (shown in the picture above), you are telling Flash: take a specified text file that resides outside your project and to place it into a target (or container). More specifically, you need give the target a name (this is case sensitive) to tell Flash where to place the external content.

Next, you will create a movie clip instance and give it a name. You will go though each step in the process.

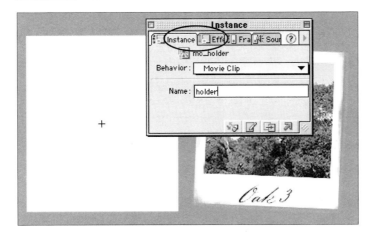

11. Name the instance of the **mc_holder** movie clip on the stage by choosing **Window >** **Panels > Instance** and type **holder** in the Name field. You need to name the instance because in the next step, you will load the text file into the holder movie clip. You are almost finished!

12. On the main timeline, choose the **Insert layer** button to add one last layer and name the layer: **actions**. Make sure the actions layer is above all other layers.

13. Select the first frame on the actions layer of the Timeline and choose **Window > Actions** to open the **Frame Actions** panel.

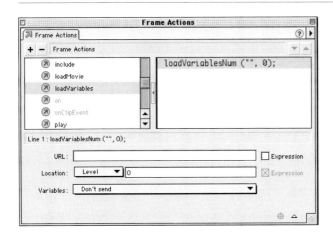

14. Inside the **Actions** drop-down list, double click on the **loadVariables** option.

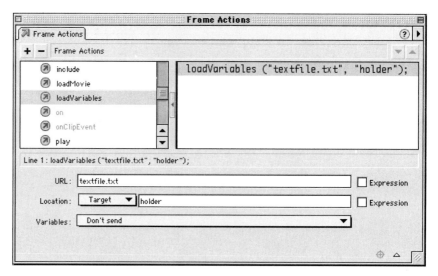

15. Type **URL: textfile.txt** (this is the text file you modified in the last exercise), choose **Target** from the **Location** drop-down list and type **holder** in the Location field. You have just told Flash to look for textfile.txt and load the variables from that file into the holder movie clip symbol instance. You assigned the variable name **content** to both the dynamic text field in the movie clip and to the text within the **textfile.txt**.

16. With the Frame Actions panel still open, choose **Basic Actions > Stop** to add a **Stop** action after the **loadVariables** action, so that your movie will stop at this frame and not continue into a loop.

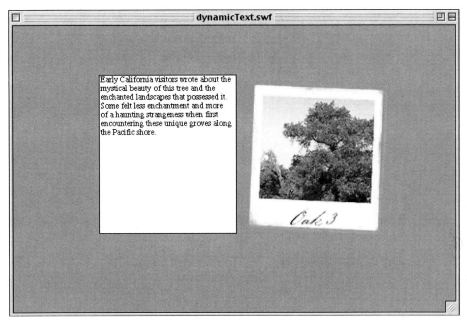

17. Choose **Control** > **Test Movie** to test your movie!

NOTE | **Changing character attributes**

The dynamic text field will take on all the character attributes that are set in the Character panel. You can quickly change the way the text is displayed in the .swf file by making some slight modifications to the text box using this panel. First, select the dynamic text field inside the mc_holder symbol. Then, go ahead and try changing the font name, the font height and the font color. You can even deselect the border/background option in the Text Options panel to remove the white background from the text. Test the movie again and you will see a completely different look for your text field!

18. Save the file and keep it open for the next exercise.

---

3. ———————————**Working with Dynamic Text and HTML**

In the last exercise you created a dynamic text field in your project file to display the data of an external text file. In this exercise, you will take it one step further and change one setting of the dynamic text field to allow Flash to recognize and preserve the HTML formatting applied to the content inside the external text field.

1. Open the **textfile.txt** file located inside the **chap_13** folder by double-clicking on it. This is the same file you worked on in the last exercise.

> **NOTE | Dynamic text HTML Support**
>
> Flash 5 supports the following HTML tags in Dynamic and Input text boxes:
>
> **<A>** = anchor, **<B>** = bold, **<FONT COLOR>** = font color, **<FONT FACE>** = typeface, **<FONT SIZE>** = font size, **<I>** = italic, **<P>** = paragraph, **<U>** = underline and **<a href="…">** = hyperlinks.

You will add some of these tags in the next few steps.

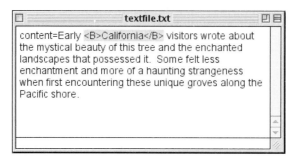

content=Early <B>California</B> visitors wrote about the mystical beauty of this tree and the enchanted landscapes that possessed it. Some felt less enchantment and more of a haunting strangeness when first encountering these unique groves along the Pacific shore.

2. Add **Bold** HTML tags around the word **California** so it should read: <B>California</B>.

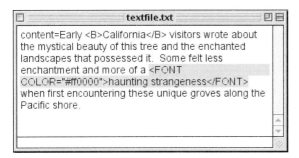

3. Add **Font Color** HTML tags around the words **haunting strangeness** so it should read: <FONT COLOR="#ff0000">haunting strangeness</FONT>.

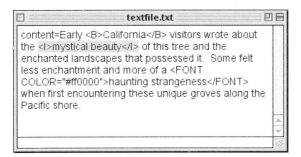

4. Add **Italic** HTML tags around the words **mystical beauty** so it should read: <I>mystical beauty</I>.

5. Save and close this file.

6. In case it isn't open from the last exercise, open the **dynamicText.fla** file located inside the **chap_13** folder.

All you need to do is change one setting and you will see the HTML-based text file loaded into the same dynamic text box.

7. From the main timeline, double click on the **mc_holder** symbol instance to open the **mc_holder** movie clip in its own timeline.

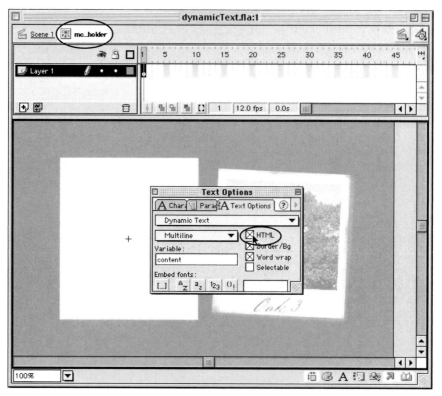

8. Select the **dynamic text** field on the stage, and in the **Text Options** panel, check the **HTML** box. This will allow the dynamic text block to interpret the HTML code and dynamically display any of the supported HTML tags within the external text file.

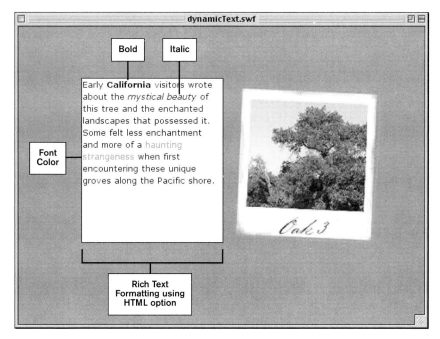

9. Test your movie! You will notice that Flash recognized all the HTML formatting you made in the text file!

---

10. You can save and close this file.

Input Text

In the following section, we will explain the **Input Text** option. This option is often used to capture information such as user names and passwords that the user will type in the input text field. The Input Text
settings are very similar to the Dynamic Text settings, with the exception that the password option in
the Line Type field has been added, along with the Maximum Character option where you can limit the
number of characters the user types in. The Input Text options are explained in detail below.

Text Options Panel: Input Text

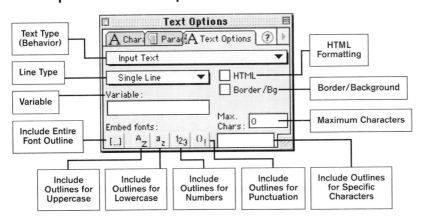

Text Options Panel: Input Text Defined	
Text Type (Text Behavior)	Allows you to choose from one of three behaviors (Static Text, Dynamic Text, or Input Text) for the text box. Each *Text Type* has its own associated options that appear in the panel when that text behavior is selected. *Input Text* behavior has been chosen in the picture above.
Line Display	Allows you to set the text box to either *Single Line* (displaying the text in one line), *Multiline* (displaying the text in multiple lines) or *Password* (automatically turns all characters into asterisks as they are typed in the field of either the .swf file or the executable).
Variable	Enables you to assign a variable name to the text box.
HTML	Checking this box enables Flash to interpret and preserve rich text formatting such as font, font style, hyperlink, paragraph, and additional text formatting with the appropriate HTML tags.

Text Options Panel: Input Text Defined	
Border/Bg	Checking this box creates a border and background around the dynamic text box. If the box is unchecked, a dotted line will surround the text box in the .fla file, although when you publish the movie, there will be no border or background.
Max Characters	Allows you to set the maximum number of characters that can be typed in the text box. The default is set to 0 meaning there is no maximum amount of characters. The user can type forever in this box, so entering in a value here is usually a good idea.
Embed Fonts	Clicking on the buttons to select them allows you to choose which characters and/or numbers you wish to include when you publish the movie. • Embed all characters • Embed uppercase characters • Embed lowercase characters • Embed numbers • Embed punctuation Entering specific characters allows you to choose which characters and/or numbers you wish to include when you publish the movie. • Embed specified characters

4. _____Input Text

Some projects that you develop in Flash will require the need for the user to enter a special code or password in order to gain access to a Web site. The following steps will show you how to use **input text** blocks and check if the user enters a correct username and password. This exercise will teach what input text is and how it differs from dynamic or static text.

1. Open the **inputText.fla** file located inside the **chap_13** folder.

2. You will notice one layer with a background image on it. Choose the **Insert Layer** button and add **five** new layers above the background layer. You will be adding content, actions, and labels to these layers in the next few steps.

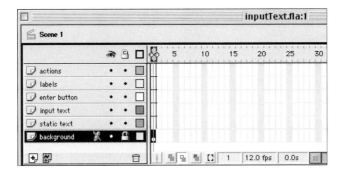

3. Name the layer above the background layer: **static text**. Continuing from bottom to top, name the remaining layers: **input text**, **enter button**, **labels** and **actions** respectively. Your layers should look like the picture above.

4. Select the **static text** layer and with the Text tool, add **three** static text boxes, one at a time, to the Stage. Make sure the **Text Type** option in the **Text Options** panel is set to **Static Text** for each text block.

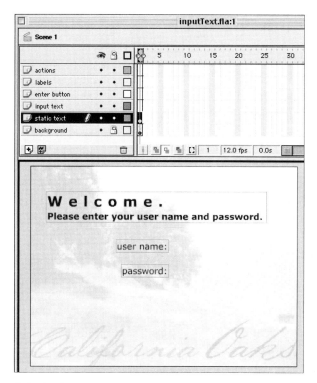

5. In the first text block add the text: **Welcome. Please enter your user name and password.** In the second block, add the text: **user name**. In the third block, add the text: **password**. Your stage should look similar to the picture above. Feel free to use any character attributes you wish for each of these static text boxes (font, font height, etc.).

6. Lock the **static text** layer to avoid editing anything on that layer by accident.

7. Click on the **input text** layer to select it. Using the **Text tool**, create a text box to the right of the **user name** text on the stage.

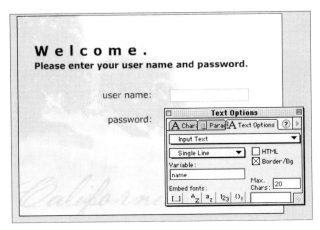

8. Choose **Windows > Panels > Text Options** to open the **Text Options** panel. Make sure the text box you just created is selected, and choose the following settings in the **Text Options** panel: **Input Text**, **Single Line**, Check **Border/Bg** and **Max Characters: 20**. In the **variable** field, type the word **name** to give this Input Text box the variable name: **name**. The Text Options panel should look just like the picture above.

9. Make sure you still have the **input text** layer selected and using the text tool, create a text box to the right of the **password** text on the stage.

10. With the text box selected that you just created, choose the following settings in the **Text Options** panel: **Input Text**, **Password**, check **Border/Bg** and Max Characters: **10**. In the **variable** field, type the word **password** to give this Input Text box the variable name: **password**. The Text Options panel should look just like the picture above.

You have just created two input text fields, which will allow users to enter their user name and password. In a few steps, you will add ActionScript to have Flash check to see if the user name and password are correct.

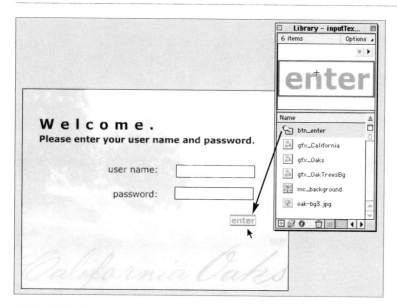

11. Lock the **input text** layer and select the **enter button** layer. Open the library (**Window > Library**) and with the **enter button** layer selected, drag an instance of the **btn_enter** symbol onto the stage. Next, lock the button layer so you don't accidentally edit anything.

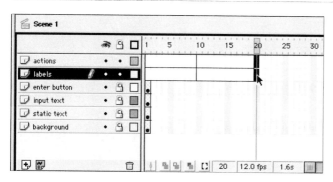

12. On the **labels** and **actions** layers, add a keyframe (F6) at **Frames 10** and **20**. Select the **labels** layer, and choose **Window > Panels > Frame** to open the **Frame** panel.

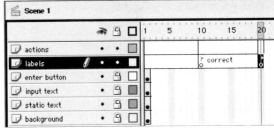

13. Select **Frame 10** on the **labels** layer and type **Label: correct** in the **Frame** panel. Select **Frame 20** on the **labels** layer and type **Label: incorrect** in the **Frame** panel.

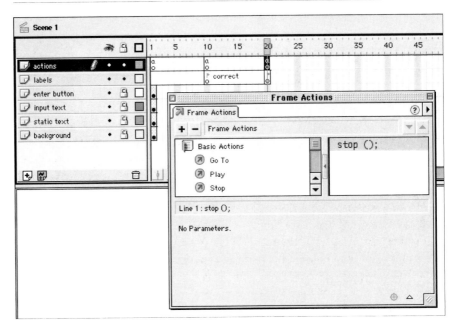

14. On the **actions** layer, add a **Stop** frame action (Window > Actions > Basic Actions > Stop) to **Frames 1, 10** and **20**.

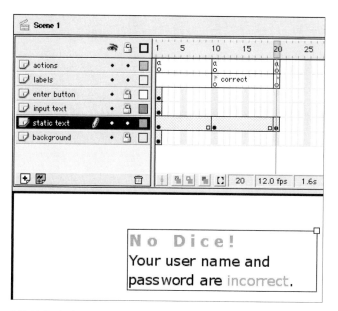

15. Unlock the **static text** layer and add a blank key frame (F7) to **Frames 10** and **20**. On **Frame 10** of the static text layer, create a static text box that reads: **Yippee. Your user name and password are correct**. On **Frame 20** of the static text layer, create a static text box that reads: **No dice. Your user name and password are incorrect**. Don't forget to select **Static Text** in the **Text Options** panel for both of these new text blocks. Feel free to adjust the settings of the Character panel, such as font name and font color.

You have just added messages that your movie will display depending on whether the user name and password are correct or not. You will add ActionScript shortly that will send the user to Frame 10 if the user name and password are correct and Frame 20 if they are incorrect.

16. Lock the **static text layer**. Unlock the **background** layer, and press **F5** on **Frame 20** to add frames up to this frame.

17. Unlock the **enter button** layer and click on the button to select it. Choose **Window > Actions** to open the **Object Actions** panel if it is not already open.

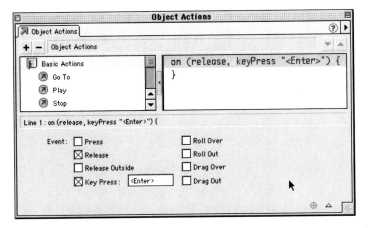

18. Choose **Basic Actions > On Mouse Event** and select the events **Release** and **Key Press: <Enter>**. This will tell Flash that when the user clicks on the button and releases the mouse, or presses Enter/Return on the keyboard, something is about to happen.

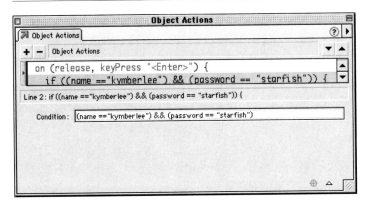

19. Choose **Actions > if** and type the following condition in the **Condition field**: (name == "kymberlee") && (password == "starfish"). Your Object Actions window should look similar to the picture above. This step tells Flash that if the user name is equivalent to kymberlee, and the password is equivalent to starfish, then do something. You will add the "something" in the next step...

TIP | Using the = or the == signs

In ActionScripting, when you use **name="kymberlee",** this means that name *becomes* kymberlee. When you use name == "kymberlee", this means that Flash will check for equivalency.

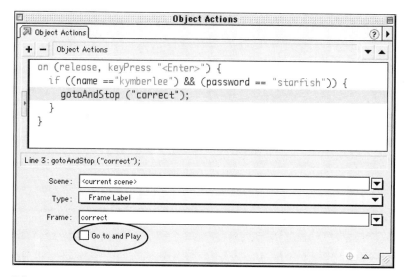

20. Choose **Basic Actions > Go To** and select **Type: Frame Label**, **Frame: correct** and uncheck the **Go To and Play** box. This will tell Flash that if the user name and password are correct, then go to the frame labeled "correct."

---

21. Choose **Actions > Else.** Then choose **Basic Actions > Go To** and select **Type: Frame Label**, **Frame: incorrect** and uncheck the **Go To and Play** box. This will tell Flash that if the user name and password are *not* correct, then go to the frame labeled "incorrect."

This is what your ActionScript should look like:

```
on (release, keyPress "<Enter>") {

   if ((name =="kymberlee") && (password == "starfish")) {

      gotoAndStop ("correct");

   } else {

      gotoAndStop ("incorrect");

   }

}
```

22. Select **Control > Test Movie** to preview.

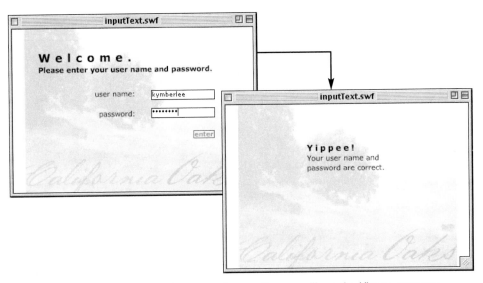

If you type in the user name and password correctly, you will get the Yippee message.

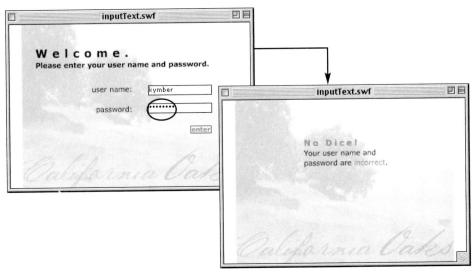

If you type in the user name and password incorrectly, you will get the No Dice message.

23. Save and close this file.

What is a Font Symbol?

Any time you have a project file where the same text formatting appears over and over throughout the movie, it is often a good idea to attach a **font symbol** to the text. A font symbol stores a specific font in the Library as a symbol. As well as storing a font, it can also include bold and/or italic-formatting attributes.

For example, imagine that you have the title of your company and tagline: "Acme Web Software: Your Web Development Superstore." Let's say this text is Verdana and italic, and appears more than 20 times throughout your Flash Web site. If you change your mind and decide that the font for that text should actually be Arial and bold, you would need to find every location where the title and tag line exist and change all 20 text fields, one at a time. How tedious!

Font symbols make this process much easier. By assigning a font symbol to that tile and tagline, all you have to do is change the font symbol once to Arial and bold, and all the text that has the font symbol attached to it will change instantly! What might have taken you 15 minutes or more will now take you less than one minute, although you can still charge your client for 15 and we won't tell ;).

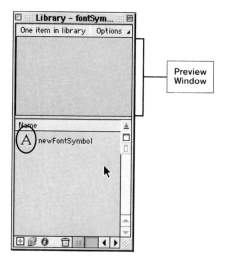

Font symbols appear different from other symbols in the Library—they have an A icon to the left of the symbol. Also, you will not see a preview of the font symbol in the Preview window of the Library as you do with other symbols.

The font symbol allows you to link text throughout the project without having to embed the font in the movie. These symbols allow you to update the text across your entire project. Rather than having to go into each text block to make a change to the font, you can simply change the font symbol and all the text will be instantly updated. If you're familiar with "styles" in Dreamweaver, Fireworks, or Photoshop, you might think of font symbols as styles for text formatting.

5.————————**Font Symbols**

In this exercise, you will create a font symbol and then update the style associated with it. You will also learn where to place the font once you create it.

1. Choose **Font > New** to open a new file in Flash. Name this file **fontSymbols.fla** and save it in the **chap_13** folder.

2. Open the **Library** (Window > Library). Click on the **Library Options** button in the upper right corner and choose **New Font** from the drop-down list.

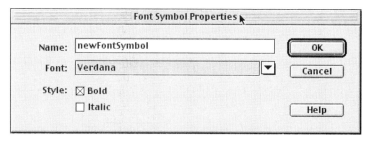

3. You will be presented with the **Font Symbol Properties** dialogue box. **Type Name: newFont Symbol, Font: Verdana** and **Style: Bold**. Press **OK**.

4. Look at the Library! If you closed it by accident, press **Cmd + L** (Mac) **or Ctrl + L** (Windows) to open it again. Flash has automatically added the newFontSymbol to the Library.

5. Choose **Window > Panels > Character** to open the **Character** panel. Notice anything different? Probably not at first.

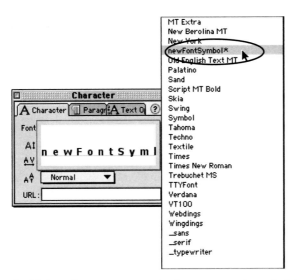

6. Click on the arrow next to the font name and scroll alphabetically until you see the **newFontSymbol**!

This newFontSymbol is stored in both the Library and the Character panel. You will notice a small asterisk next to the font symbol name in the font list. This is an indication that it is a font symbol rather than a normal font.

---

7. To apply this font symbol to text, all you need to do is to select this name in the **Character Options** panel and then choose the **Type** tool and type away. You can also select a block of text and choose the font symbol in the Character panel just as you would choose any other font for your text.

If you have text throughout your project file that uses the font symbol that you created and you decide you would rather use a different font, such as Helvetica, you can make one change to the font symbol and all the text will be dynamically updated.

8. To change the font symbol, select the font symbol from the **Library** and click on the **Library Options** button in the upper-right corner of the Library and choose **Properties** from the drop-down list.

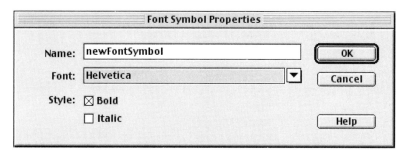

9. In the **Font Symbol Properties** dialogue box, select a new font, click **OK** and all the text that had the newFontSymbol applied to it will now be Helvetica and bold!

10. You can save and close this file.

You have successfully made it though the text chapter! Time to take a quick break and get amped up (pun intended) for the sound chapter next!

14.

Sound

| Importing Sounds | Compressing Sound |
| Creating Background Sound with Sound Effects |
| Controlling Sound with On/Off Buttons |
| Sound Synchronizing |

chap_14

Flash 5
H·O·T CD-ROM

In Flash, sound can be used for many purposes—
including narration, background soundtracks,
rollover noises, and to compliment animation
effects.

Older versions of Flash were limited
in handling sound compression. In
Flash 5, you can export and import
MP3 sounds as well. This is a wonderful improvement, because MP3
sound works on both Macintosh
and Windows platforms and allows
the file size to be small while the
sound quality is high.

This chapter will give you a solid
understanding of how to work with
sounds in Flash, including how to
import sounds and compress sound
files. You will learn how to change the
format of a sound using MP3 compression
settings, how to create background sounds,
and how to control sound using buttons. Lastly,
we will teach you how to synchronize sound to
a cartoon animation.

Importing Sounds

In this exercise, you will learn how to import sound files into Flash. The following steps will teach you which kinds of sounds can be imported into Flash and show you where the sound files go when you import them.

1. Copy the **chap_14** folder, located on the **H•O•T CD-ROM**, to your hard drive. You need to have this folder on your hard drive in order to save files inside it.

2. Choose **File > New** to open a new file. Save this file as **basicSound.fla.** inside the **chap_14** folder.

3. Choose **File > Import** and browse to the folder named **sounds_mac** if you are using a Macintosh, or **sounds_pc** if you are using a Windows machine. Notice the long list of sounds inside the folder that range from button sounds to business sounds to dance sounds.

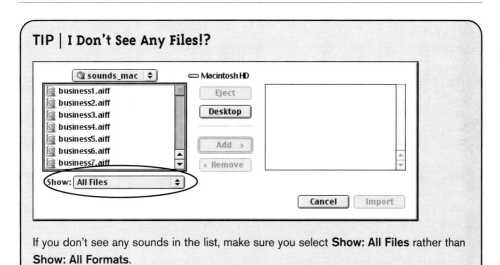

TIP | I Don't See Any Files!?

If you don't see any sounds in the list, make sure you select **Show: All Files** rather than **Show: All Formats**.

NOTE | What Kinds of Sounds Can I Import?

The sound file formats available for you to import are AIF format (Mac), WAV format (Windows), and, new to Flash 5, MP3 format. In Flash 4, you were able to export MP3 sound files but you could not import them. The added ability of importing MP3 sounds into Flash is a huge addition to Flash 5, because they are smaller than other sound formats, which makes them perfect for Web delivery.

---

4. To import the sound files:

- **Mac Users**: Click on the file named **business2.aiff, partyzone8.aiff,** and **urbangrooves4 .aiff** and click **Import**. The sound files will be imported into Flash.

- **Windows Users**: **Ctrl+Click** to select **business2.wav, partyzone8.wav,** and **urban grooves4.wav** and click **Open** to import the sounds into Flash.

TIP | Where Did the Sounds Go?

When you import an image, you will see the image on the Stage as soon as you click Import. Unlike importing an image, however, when you import sounds they will not be visible on the Stage. Instead, you must open the Library to view the sound files.

---

5. Choose **Window > Library** or use the shortcut keys **Cmd + L** (Mac) or **Ctrl + L** (Windows) to open the Library. You will see the all three sounds in the Library. Select each sound, one at a time and press the **Play** button to listen to each sound.

That's all there is to it! Importing sounds is the simple part. Working with them in the Timeline can be a bit more challenging. By the end of this chapter, you will have experience working with more challenging aspects of sound integration in Flash.

Note: *The sounds inside these folders were donated generously by Frank Bongers of* **soundshopper.com**. *Visit the soundshopper.com Web site for access to even more sounds to use in your Flash projects.*

6. Save this file and keep it open for the next exercise.

2. _____Compressing Sound

Now that you know how to import sounds into Flash, the next step is to learn how to compress them. Compressing sounds is especially important when you need to keep your file size down, because uncompressed sounds can increase your file size drastically. In this exercise you will learn how to control sound compression settings and how to alter one of the sounds using the MP3 compression settings and the Sound Properties dialog box.

1. You should have the file still open from the last exercise, but in case you closed it, open the **basicSound.fla** file located inside the **chap_14** folder.

2. If it is not already open, open the **Library** by choosing the shortcut keys **Cmd + L** (Mac) or **Ctrl + L** (Windows).

3. Click on the **business2** sound to select it. If you are on a Mac, the sound will be named business2.aiff, and if you are using a Windows machine, the sound will be named business2.wav. Click on the **Properties** button, located at the bottom of the **Library** panel, to open the **Sound Properties** dialog box.

> **NOTE | Sound Compression Movie-wide or Individual**
>
> In Flash, you have two general options for sound compression: you can set the movie-wide compression settings in the Publish Settings window or you can set the compression settings for each sound file individually in the Library. You will learn about the Publish Settings in the next chapter, but we recommend individually setting the compression setting to ensure the best fidelity and lowest file size of each sound.

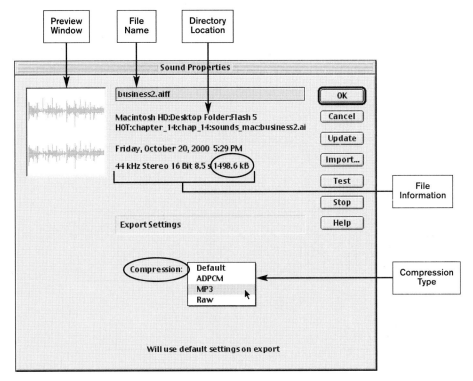

4. Notice how the sound is large at its default compression setting: 1498.6 kB. Click on the **Compression** option drop-down menu. You'll see four settings: Default, ADPCM, MP3 and Raw. Select **Compression: MP3**.

Sound Compression Defined	
ADPCM	This compression model is the "old" method of compression from Flash 3. It sets compression for 8-bit and 16-bit sound data. You may want to consider using this format if you need to author back to the Flash 3 plug-in.
MP3	This compression model can only be heard by users with the Flash 4 or Flash 5 plug-in, but it offers the best compression rates and sound fidelity.
Raw	This format will resample the file at the specified rate, but will not perform any compression.

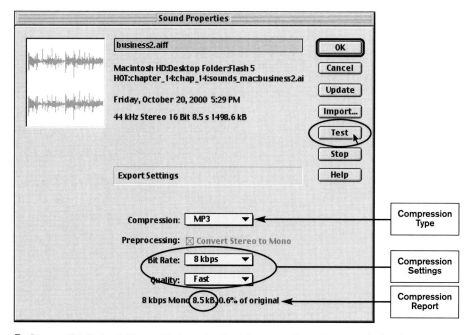

5. Choose **Bit Rate: 8 kbps**. Click on the **Test** button to hear the sound with the new compression applied. Notice how the file size drastically decreased to 8.5 kB from the original 1498.6 kB.

Note: The lower the bit rate, the lower the sound quality and the lower the file size. The higher the bit rate, the higher the sound quality and the larger the file size.

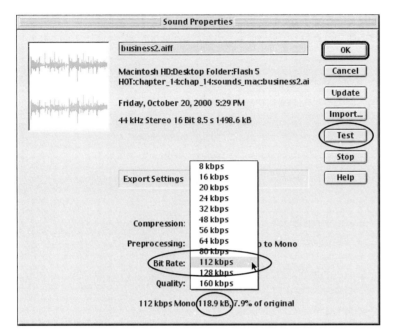

6. Choose **Bit Rate: 112 kbps** and click the **Test** button to hear the sound again. Notice how much better the sound quality is at 112 kbps. However, look at the file size: it has increased to 118.9 kB. Although this is smaller than the original (1498.6 kB) it is more than ten times the size of the 8 kbps bit rate.

7. Choose **Bit Rate: 24kbps** and click the **Test** button to preview the sound. Notice how the sound file sounds very good and the file size has dropped to 25.5 kB. *When you are working with sound files in Flash 5, you will find that you will want to test several bit-rate settings to find the one that has the lowest file size without sacrificing sound quality.*

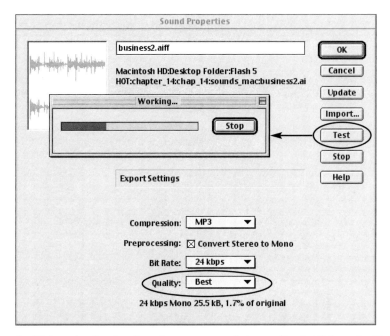

8. Click on the **Quality** drop-down menu and choose **Best**. Click on the **Test** button and notice that it takes much longer to convert the file to an MP3. The sound file will sound better and the file size will be the same, but the only trade-off is that it will take longer to convert the file. Not a bad price to pay for better sound.

To summarize, you will find that choosing the best compression settings is often a process of selecting and testing several different options before you settle on the best setting to meet your needs. We recommend using the MP3 compression settings wherever possible because of its superior compression capabilities. You have the best of both worlds using this compression: small file sizes with good sound quality.

9. Save and close this file.

3. _____Creating Background Sound with Sound Effects

As you develop certain projects in Flash, you may find that adding background sound that plays continuously will help the movie come to life. This exercise will show you how to create a background sound track for a movie, including how to fade the sound in and stop the sound in the Timeline.

1. Choose **File > Open** and browse to the file named: **bkgdSound.fla** inside the **chap_14 folder**. Click **Open** to open the file.

2. Choose **Control > Test Movie** to preview the movie. Look out! It's Jaws! When you are finished previewing the silent, yet terrifying animation, close this file. You will add the background sound to this movie in the steps that follow.

3. In the project file, choose **Cmd + L** (Mac) or **Ctrl + L** (Windows) to open the Library. Notice how there are movie clips and folders but no sounds... yet.

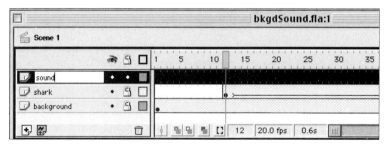

4. On the main Timeline, click on the **Insert Layer** button to add a new layer. Name the layer: **sound**.

TIP | Why am I making a new layer for the sound?

Ideally, like frame actions, sound files should be placed on their own separate layer. This will separate the sound from other artwork and animation, allowing you to view the wave-form (the picture of the sound) better and work with the sound more easily.

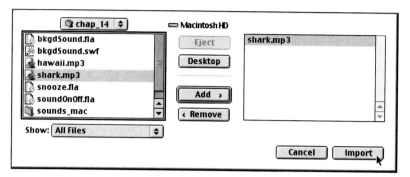

5. Choose **File > Import** and open the **chap_14** folder. Browse to the sound file named **shark.mp3** and **double-click** it to add it to the list. Click **Import**.

---

*MP3 sounds will work on both Macintosh and Windows machines, so no matter which platform you are using, choose the **shark.mp3** file.*

NOTE | Our Sounds for This Chapter

The sounds used in this exercise and the next two exercises are original sounds graciously contributed by Jamie McElhinney, a custom sound developer, who can be reached at **jsoundweb@excite.com**.

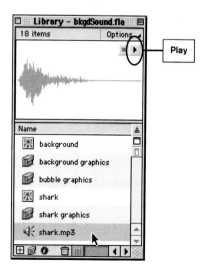

6. After you select **Import**, notice that the sound is added to the Library. Click on the **Play** button to test the sound. Scary! You will be adding this sound to the movie next.

> ## NOTE | When Sound Exists
>
> Although the sound file has been successfully imported into the Flash project file, it does not officially exist in the movie yet—it only exists in the Library. In order for it to be a part of the movie, you must add it to a keyframe in the Timeline.

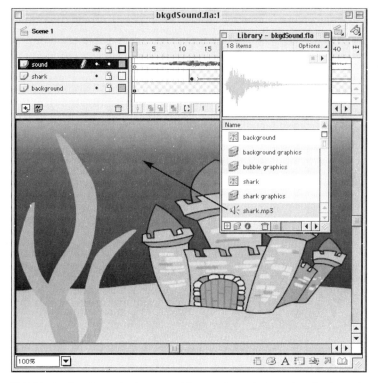

7. With the first frame in the **sound** layer selected, drag the **shark.mp3** out of the Library and drop it anywhere on the Stage. After you drop the sound, you will not see a representation of that sound anywhere on the Stage. However, the sound will appear in the Timeline in the form of a blue waveform. This is visual feedback to you that the sound is located there.

NOTE | Adding Sounds to Keyframes

Sound files must be tied to a keyframe. The simplest way to do this is to drag a sound symbol out of the Library and drop it onto the Stage at the point in your Timeline that you want it to start playing. Make sure that you have a keyframe at the point where you want your sound to begin, and that you have selected that keyframe. Otherwise, you will not be able to add the sound at all, or the sound will attach itself to the last keyframe prior to the location of the Playhead at the time you drag and drop.

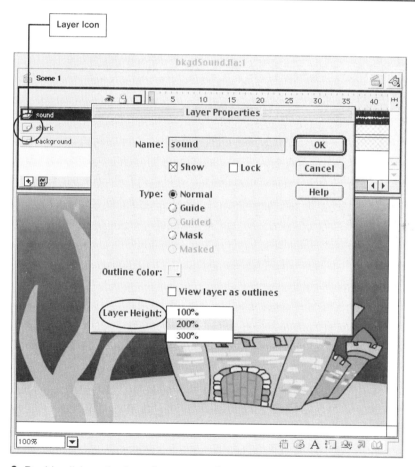

8. Double-click on the **layer** icon next to the **sound** layer's name. This will open the **Layer Properties** dialog box. From the **Layer Height** drop-down menu, choose **200%** and click **OK**.

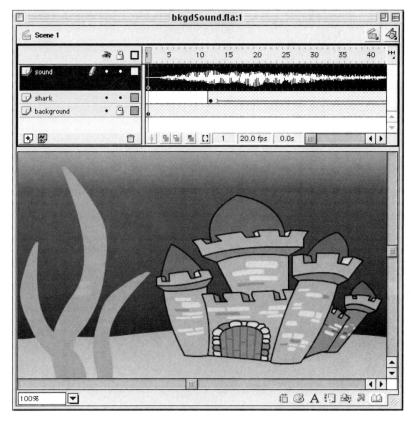

*Increasing the layer height allows you to view the waveform more easily. Notice how you can see the waveform in more detail now. **Tip:** You can also access the Layer Properties dialog box by choosing Modify > Layer.*

9. Choose **Control > Test Movie** to preview the movie with the new sound added. You will hear the sound play once and stop. This is okay, but you can do better by modifying the sound to make it fade in and loop. You will do this next.

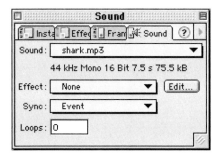

10. Back in the project file, click anywhere in the **sound** layer to select the sound and choose **Window > Panels > Sound** to open the **Sound** panel. This is where you control the behavior of the sound.

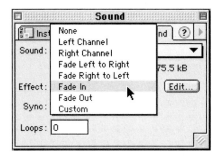

11. Click the **Effect** drop-down menu and choose **Fade In**. This will make the sound start out soft and gradually become louder.

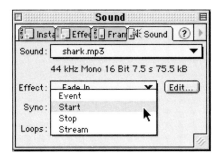

12. Click the **Sync** drop-down menu and choose **Start**. This setting is most often used for background sounds. Setting the **Sync** to **Start** will make the sound play independently, even if the Timeline stops.

You might wonder when to use a Start sound setting. This setting is used if you have a layer that has a sound that is already playing, and you don't want the new sound to begin until the currently playing sound has stopped. This prevents the sound from overlapping itself. For a detailed explanation of all the sound settings available to you, see the Sound Panel section complete with tables and pictures following this exercise.

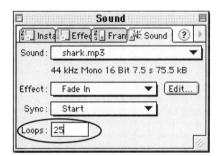

13. Type **Loops: 25**. This will make the sound repeat 25 times before it stops. It will not affect the overall file size, since Flash only downloads the file one time.

14. Choose **Control > Test Movie** to preview the movie again. Notice how the sound fades in and then repeats over and over, even when the shark is off the Stage. This is because the Start sound setting will play the sound even if the Timeline reaches the end.

15. Save and close this file.

The Sound Panel

After you place an instance of the sound in the Timeline, you can use the **Sound** panel to control the behavior of the sound.

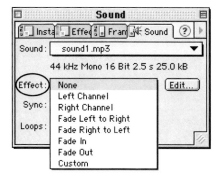

Effect

The **Effect** option in the **Sound** panel allows you to choose from a drop-down list of preset effects that you can apply to your sound. Choosing the **Custom** option will allow you to create your own sound effects.

Effect Options Explained	
Left Channel	Plays only the left channel of a stereo sound.
Right Channel	Plays only the right channel of a stereo sound.
Fade Left to Right	Creates a panning effect by playing a stereo sound from the left channel to the right channel (or left speaker to right speaker).
Fade Right to Left	Creates a panning effect by playing a stereo sound from the right channel to the left channel (or right speaker to left speaker).
Fade in	Makes the sound gradually become louder and louder as the sound begins to play.
Fade Out	Makes the sound gradually become softer and softer as the sound nears the end.
Custom	Allows you to create your own effects for the sound.

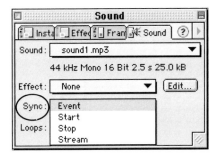

Sync

The **Sync** option in the **Sound** panel allows you to set the synchronization of the sound file in the movie. Each option controls the behavior of the sound in the Timeline and the Sync options are explained in the table below.

Sync Options Explained	
Event	Begins playing the sound when the Playhead reaches the frame that holds the sound in the Timeline. Event sounds will continue to play independently, even if the Timeline stops. If a different instance of the same sound is started, the sounds will overlap.
Start	Behaves similarly to the event sound, except that a second instance of the sound cannot be started until any currently playing instances have finished. This prevents the sound from overlapping itself.
Stop	Stops the indicated sound.
Stream	Forces the movie to keep pace with the sound. If the movie cannot download its frames fast enough to keep pace, Flash forces it to skip frames. Streaming sounds stop when the movie stops.

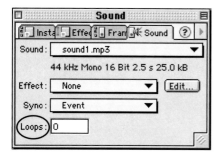

Loops

The **Loops** option in the **Sound** panel sets the number of times that the sound will repeat. There is no limit to the number of times the sound can loop. However, use caution when you have **Sync: Stream** selected in the **Sound** panel, because looping a streaming sound will cause Flash to add frames for each number of loops, thereby increasing file size significantly.

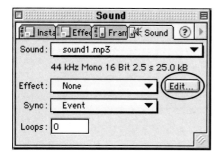

Edit button

When you click on the **Edit** button in the **Sound** panel, Flash will open the **Edit Envelope** window where you can edit your sound.

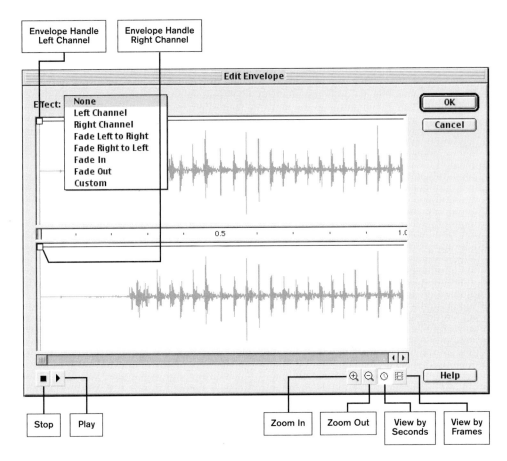

The Edit Envelope window

4. _____Controlling Sound with On/Off Buttons

There may be times when you have sound that you love in a movie, but certain users simply do not want to listen to it. This exercise will show you how to give them control of the sound in a movie using a sound off and a sound on button. You will be introduced to the **Edit Envelope** window, which can be used to customize effects applied to the sound files.

1. Choose **File > Open** and browse to the file named: **soundOnOffFinal.fla** inside the **chap_14** folder. Click **Open** to open the file.

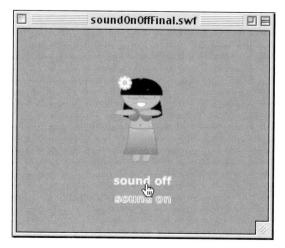

2. Choose **Control > Test Movie** to preview the movie. Click on the **sound off** button to stop the sound. Click on the **sound on** button to start it again. You will be creating this movie in the steps that follow. When you are finished, close this file.

3. Choose **File > Open** and browse to the file named: **soundOnOff.fla** inside the **chap_14** folder. Click **Open** to open the file. We have created this file to get you started.

4. In the project file, click on the **Insert Layer** button to add a new layer to the Timeline. Name the layer: **sound**.

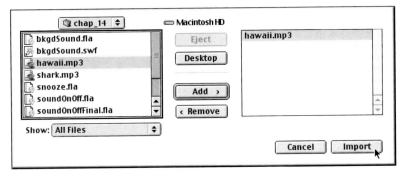

5. Choose **File > Import** and open the **chap_14** folder. Browse to the sound file named **hawaii.mp3** and double-click it to add it to the list. Click **Import**. **Note**: Windows users would click **Open**.

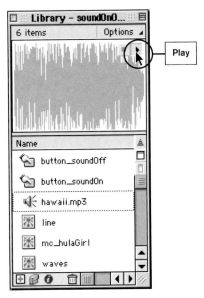

6. To open the **Library**, choose **Cmd + L** (Mac) or **Ctrl + L** (Windows). Notice the **hawaii.mp3** sound file in the Library. Press the **Play** button to test the sound file.

7. Select the first keyframe in the **sound** layer and drag the **hawaii.mp3** sound out of the Library and drop it anywhere on the Stage. Notice the blue waveform in the Timeline that serves as visual feedback that the sound is located there.

---

8. Click anywhere in the **sound** layer to select the sound and choose **Window > Panels > Sound** to open the **Sound** panel.

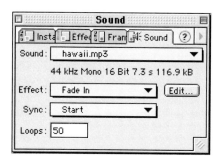

9. Choose the **Effect: Fade In** and **Sync: Start** options. Type **Loops: 50.** This will make the sound fade in, play independently of the Timeline and repeat 50 times.

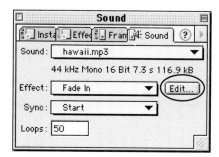

10. Click on the **Edit** button in the **Sound** panel. This will open the Edit Envelope window.

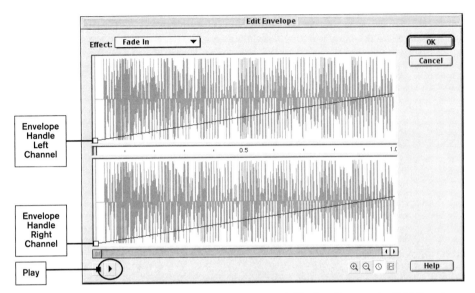

Envelope
Handle
Left
Channel

Envelope
Handle
Right
Channel

Play

When you click on the Edit button in the Sound panel, Flash will open the Edit Envelope window where you can edit your sound. Notice how the Effect shows the Fade In option. This effect was created when you selected it from the drop-down list in the Sound panel.

11. In the **Edit Envelope** window, click on the **Play** button to test the sound. Move the **Right Envelope** handle. This will change the way the sound fades into the right speaker. Click the **Play** button again to test it.

12. Move the **Left Envelope** handle. This will change the way the sound fades in the left speaker. Click the **Play** button again to test it.

13. When you are happy with the way your adjustments sound, click the **OK** button in the **Edit Envelope** window.

14. Choose **Control > Test Movie** to preview the movie. You will hear the sound play as the hula girl dances; however, although the buttons will animate when you roll over them, the buttons will not control the sound, yet. You will add ActionScripting to control the sound next.

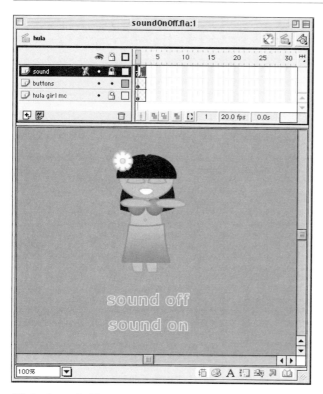

15. In the main Timeline, click on the **Lock** icon to lock the sound layer and unlock the buttons layer. Select the **sound off** button on the Stage. You have to select the button instance in order to be able to add actions to it.

16. Choose **Window > Actions** to open the **Object Actions** panel.

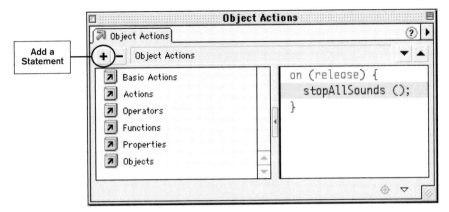

17. Click on the **Add Action** button **(+)**, choose **Actions** and select **stopAllSounds**. This action tells Flash: when the user releases the mouse, execute the **stopAllSounds** action, which will stop any sounds that are currently playing in the Timeline.

18. Choose **Control > Test Movie** to preview the movie again. Click the **sound off** button.

Notice how the sound immediately stops and begins to play immediately! Even though you have added ActionScript to tell all sounds to stop, the main Timeline is going to continue to loop by default. Each time it loops back to Frame 1, the sound will begin to play again. In order to fix this, you are going to add a Stop action to Frame 2 of the main Timeline. Why not Frame 1? Because, on Frame 1 the Timeline begins to play the sound, which is still the behavior you want when the movie plays. Also, notice that when you click the sound off button, the animation continues to play as well. This is because the stopAllSounds action only affects the sound, and not the animation, on the Timeline.

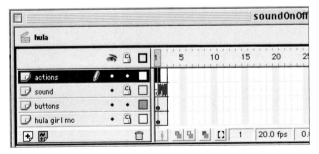

19. Add a new layer above the **sound** layer and name it **actions**.

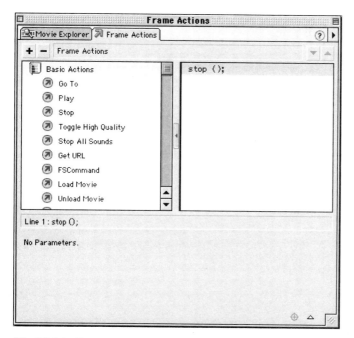

20. Click in **Frame 2** of the **actions** layer and press **F7** to add a blank keyframe. Select **Window > Actions** to open the **Frame Actions** dialog box. You can also double-click in Frame 2 to open the Frame Actions dialog box. Click the **Basic Actions** book and double-click on **Stop** to add that action to Frame 2.

21. Select **Control > Test Movie** again. Click the stop sound button. Notice that this time the sound stops playing. Close the preview window and return to Flash.

The following steps will show you how to make the play sound button work.

MOVIE | sound_handle.mov

To learn more about using buttons to control the sound, check out the **sound_handle.mov** located in the **movies** folder on the **Flash 5 H•O•T CD-ROM**.

22. Back in the project file, click the **sound on** button to select it. A thin blue line will appear around the button when it is selected.

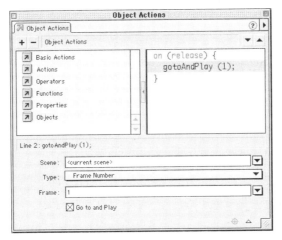

23. In the **Object Actions** panel, click on the **Add Action** button **(+)**, choose **Basic Actions** and select **gotoAnd Play**. This action tells Flash: when the user releases the mouse, go to Frame 1 and then play the movie. This will start the movie over from the beginning, and the sound and animation start over from Frame 1.

24. Choose **Control > Test Movie** to preview the movie one last time. Click the **sound off** button and then click the **sound on** button. Notice how the sound immediately stops when you click the sound off button and starts over again when you click the sound on button.

25. Save and close this file.

5. _____Sound Synchronizing

Sound in Flash can also be controlled so that it synchronizes with animation, such as narration or a sound effect that is synched with a character's movement. This exercise shows you how to use the streaming option so that your animation synchronizes with your sound files.

1. Choose **File > Open** and browse to the file named: **snoozeFinal.fla** inside the **chap_14** folder. Double-click the file to open it. This is a finished version of the file you are going to create.

2. Choose **Control > Test Movie** to preview the movie. Notice how the sound occurs in synchronization with the animation. When you are finished previewing the movie, close this file.

3. Open the file named: **snooze.fla** located inside the **chap_14** folder and select it. We have created this file to get you started.

4. You will see five layers in the main Timeline. Each holds different parts of the animation. Scrub the Playhead back and forth to see when the duck's jaw begins to open. In a few steps, you will be adding a snoring sound to the Timeline, and you'll decide where the snore sound should begin in the Timeline.

5. Press **Cmd + L** (Mac) or **Ctrl + L** (Windows) to open the **Library**. Notice how there are two sounds in the Library: **exhale.mp3** and **snore.mp3**.

6. Select the **exhale.mp3** button and press the **Play** button to test it. Then select the **snore.mp3** button and press the **Play** button to test that sound. You will be adding these sounds to the Timeline in the next few steps.

7. On the main Timeline, click on the **Insert Layer** button to add a new layer. Name the layer: **snore**.

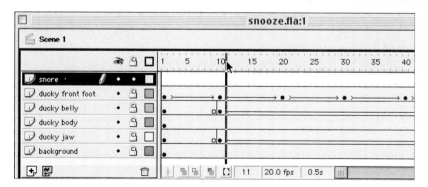

8. Scrub the **Playhead** back and forth again to pinpoint the spot when the duck's jaw begins to open. Notice that this happens at about Frame 11 and you will want to start the sound just before the jaw begins to drop, so Frame 10 is the right time to begin the snore sound.

9. On the **snore** layer, press **F6** on **Frame 10** to add a keyframe to that frame, because sound files must be tied to a keyframe.

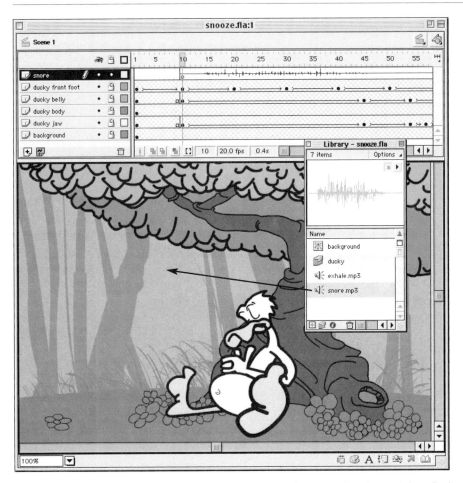

10. Drag an instance of the **snore.mp3** sound onto the Stage. Notice the waveform in the Timeline.

11. Choose **Control > Test Movie** to test the sound and the animation. Notice that the sound stops, but the jaw is still dropping. Although this does not look terrible, you can change one setting to make the sound and the jaw occur in unison.

12. In the project file, click on the sound in the Timeline to select it. Choose **Window > Panels > Sound** to open the **Sound** panel.

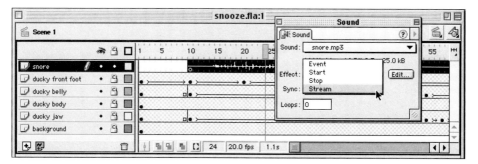

13. In the **Sound panel**, select **Sync: Stream.** The stream setting forces the movie to keep pace with the sound. If the movie cannot download its frames fast enough to keep pace, Flash forces it to skip frames.

14. Test the movie again to preview the changes. Notice that the sound and the jaw are now synchronized! This is a much more realistic animation effect.

TIP | Streaming and Looping

Be careful about setting your sound Sync to Stream and adding Loops. Unlike the Event and Start settings, when you use Stream, the file size will increase for each loop you specify. If you can avoid it, try not to loop sounds that are set to the Stream setting.

You will add the exhale.mp3 sound to the Timeline next...

15. Lock the **snore** layer so you don't accidentally edit the sound on that layer. Click on the **Insert Layer** button to add a new layer to the Timeline. Name the layer: **exhale**.

16. Scrub the **Playhead** back and forth to identify the spot when the duck's jaw begins to close. Notice that this happens at about Frame 46. You will want to start the exhale sound to start just before the jaw begins to close, so Frame 45 is the right time to begin the exhale sound.

17. On the **exhale** layer, press **F6** on **Frame 45** to add a keyframe.

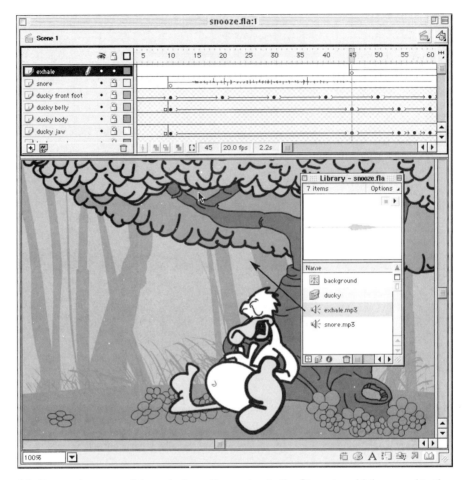

18. Drag an instance of the **exhale.mp3** sound onto the Stage to add the sound to the Timeline.

19. Click on the sound in the Timeline to select it. Choose **Window > Panels > Sound** to open the **Sound** panel in case it is not already open.

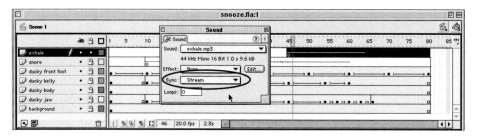

20. In the **Sound** panel, select **Sync: Stream.** This will force the movie to keep pace with the exhale sound. If the movie cannot download its frames fast enough to keep pace, it will skip frames to do so.

21. Test the movie again. Notice that the sounds and the animations of the jaw opening and closing are now harmonized! This is synchronization at its finest!

22. When you are finished, save and close this file.

Congratulations! You have conquered another chapter. You should feel comfortable working with sound in Flash and if you feel you need more practice, you can always review the exercises again. Next Stop: publishing all the hard work you've done!

15. Publishing

| Publish Settings | Flash and HTML |

| Creating Projectors |

| Modifying Projectors with FS Commands |

| More About Publish Settings |

| Optimizing Movies |

chap_15

Flash 5
H•O•T CD-ROM

Prior to this chapter, you tested your movies in Flash by choosing Control > Test Movie, in order to see your work and generate an .swf file. This chapter will show you how to publish your movies using the Publish settings instead. Testing and publishing are two different methods to produce an .swf file. You'll learn that publishing your site instead of testing offers many more options and control over the final output. As well, you'll learn how to generate an HTML file and a projector file from Flash. This chapter contains a reference guide that explains what all the publish settings do, so that you can try more advanced publish settings than what the exercises in this chapter cover.

We will conclude the chapter with a look at some tips and tricks for optimizing your movie.

What Types of Content Can Flash Publish?

In addition to the .swf file, Flash is able to export several different file formats. Here's a short table to describe some of the publishing options in Flash.

Flash Publishing Choices	
Web Delivery	If you plan to publish Web content, you will need to create minimal HTML to embed the Flash movie, as well as determine how the Flash movie will appear. You'll learn how to generate this HTML code in exercises provided in this chapter.
CD-ROM Delivery	If you want to use Flash on a CD-ROM, you can export a projector file. You'll learn to do this in exercises provided in this chapter.
Email Attachment	If you want to create a Flash movie as an email attachment, you would create a projector file. You'll learn to make a projector file in this chapter.
QuickTIme	It's possible to generate a Flash Track for QuickTime. This offers the opportunity to create Flash controllers or buttons for QuickTime content.
RealPlayer	Flash can also generate SMIL content for RealPlayer delivery. Settings for this type of publishing are included in the comprehensive charts at the end of this chapter.

I. ——————————**Flash and HTML**

This exercise will walk you through the Publish settings interface to learn how to create the necessary HTML files for Web delivery of Flash content. The following steps will show how the changes made in the Publish settings will effect the way your movie is viewed in a Web browser.

1. Copy the **chap_15** folder, located on the **H•O•T CD-ROM**, to your hard drive. You need to have this folder on your hard drive in order to save files inside it.

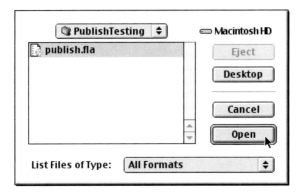

2. Open the file **publish.fla**, from the **folder** called **PublishTesting** located inside the **chap_15** folder.

3. Choose **Control > Test Movie** to preview the movie. This is the slide show movie you created in Chapter 12. Click the forward and back arrows to test it. Notice the title **publish.swf** at the top of the window:

4. Leave Flash for a moment and open the **chap_15** folder on your hard drive. Browse to the folder titled **PublishTesting.** Inside you will now see two files: one .fla file and one .swf file. By choosing Control > Test Movie, Flash created an SWF file in the folder as well.

5. Back in the project file, choose **File > Publish Preview > Default** or use the shortcut key: **F12**. This will trigger the Publish Preview command, which launches the default browser and displays an HTML page with the .swf file embedded inside it.

When you use the Publish Preview command, the Publish settings determine how Flash decides to publish the documents. You will work with the Publish settings in just a few steps.

> **WARNING** | **Publish Preview Versus Test Movie**
>
> The Publish Preview command, compared to using **Control > Test Movie**, gives you the most accurate indication of how your movie will look on the Internet. The **Control > Test Movie** command gives you a preview of the movie that will not always behave exactly the same as it will on a Web server. To be safe, use the Publish Preview or Publish commands to view the movie before you upload it live on the Internet.

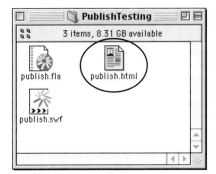

6. Open the **chap_15** folder on your hard drive. Browse again to the folder titled **PublishTesting** and open it. Inside you will now see *three* files: an .fla file, an .swf file and an HTML file. When you preview your movie in a browser, by choosing File > Publish Preview > Default, Flash will create an HTML file in the same folder you saved your .fla file in.

Notice also how all three files have the same name with the appropriate extension after it. By default, Flash names the additional files with the same name as the .fla file. You will change these names in the next few steps.

---

7. Back in the project file, select **File > Publish Settings**. This will open the Publish Settings window, which always opens to the Formats tab first.

The Formats tab is used to set which file formats will be created when you publish the movie. The other tabs will appear or disappear according to which boxes you check.

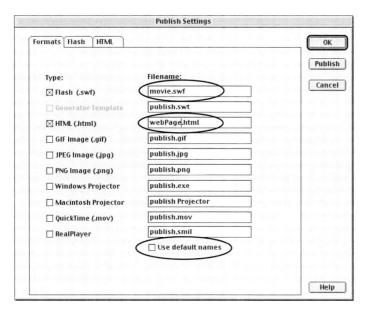

8. Make sure there are checks in the boxes next to the Format Types: **Flash** and **HTML**. Notice how all the **Filenames** are set to have the prefix called "publish?" This is because the **Use default names** box is checked. Uncheck the **Use default names** box and type **movie.swf** inside the **Flash Filename** field and type **webPage.html** inside the **HTML Filename** field.

9. Click the **Publish** button to publish these two files with the names you just gave them. Flash will create these new files and save them in the same folder as the original .fla file.

10. To make sure the new files have been published, open the **chap_15** folder on your hard drive. Browse to the **PublishTesting** folder and open it. Inside you will now see *five* files: the three files that were already there, each with the *publish* name and two new files named **webPage.html** and **movie.swf**.

Each time you click the Publish button in the Publish settings dialog box (or you use File > Publish), Flash writes and creates all of the files you have selected under the Formats tab in the Publish settings dialog box (in this case .swf and HTML). If you publish two or more times with the same settings, Flash will overwrite the existing files each time.

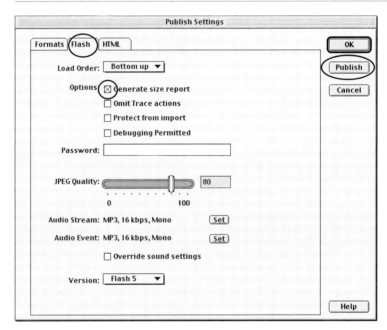

11. In the Publish settings dialog box, click on the **Flash** tab, which is next to the **Formats** tab. Place a check in the box next to **Generate size report**. Click the **Publish** button.

12. Open the **chap_15** folder on your hard drive. Browse to the **PublishTesting folder and open it**. Notice the new file: **movie.swf Report**.

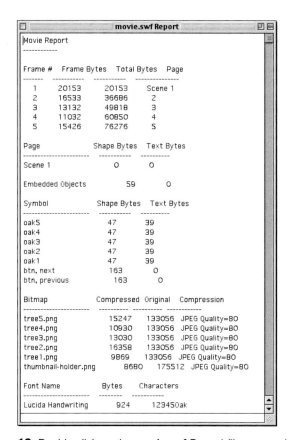

```
                    movie.swf Report

Movie Report
-----------

Frame #    Frame Bytes   Total Bytes    Page
-------    -----------   -----------    --------------
   1         20153          20153        Scene 1
   2         16533          36686        2
   3         13132          49818        3
   4         11032          60850        4
   5         15426          76276        5


Page                 Shape Bytes   Text Bytes
--------------------  -----------   ----------
Scene 1                    0            0

Embedded Objects          59            0

Symbol               Shape Bytes   Text Bytes
--------------------  -----------   ----------
oak5                      47           39
oak4                      47           39
oak3                      47           39
oak2                      47           39
oak1                      47           39
btn, next                163            0
btn, previous            163            0

Bitmap               Compressed  Original   Compression
--------------------  ----------  ----------  -----------
tree5.png               15247      133056    JPEG Quality=80
tree4.png               10930      133056    JPEG Quality=80
tree3.png               13030      133056    JPEG Quality=80
tree2.png               16358      133056    JPEG Quality=80
tree1.png                9869      133056    JPEG Quality=80
thumbnail-holder.png     8680      175512    JPEG Quality=80

Font Name             Bytes      Characters
--------------------  --------   -----------
Lucida Handwriting      924        123450ak
```

13. Double-click on the **movie.swf Report** file to open it. This is the Size Report file. Whenever you select *Generate size report*, Flash will create a special text file that gives a breakdown of the file size contributions of all of the symbols, fonts, and other elements in the movie. This is a handy tool to use when you want to know, frame by frame, how big the movie is and how many different elements are present in the movie.

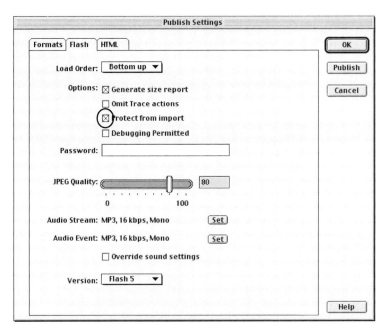

14. Back in the **Publish Settings** dialog box under the Flash tab, place a checkmark in the box next to **Protect from Import**. Checking this box prevents someone from importing your .swf movie file into Flash and converting it back to a project file.

Be aware that Protect from Import *is not 100% secure. You can still import a protected movie into a Macromedia Director movie and hackers can also use a utility called SWIFFER to break into any Flash movie. To be safe, don't put highly-sensitive information into Flash movies but do check the Protect from Import box to safeguard against at least the average person opening the SWF file.*

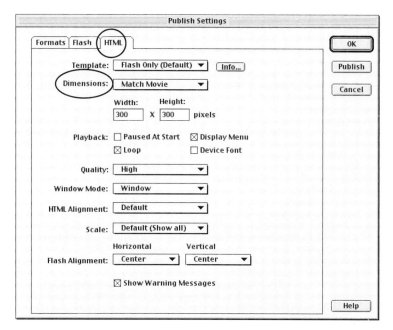

15. Click on the **HTML** tab. Notice how the **Dimensions** setting default is **Match Movie**. The Dimension setting determines the dimensions at which the Flash movie will be set in the HTML tags. This value can be in pixels or percentage of window size. As you will see in the next step, the Match Movie option will not allow the .swf file to scale.

16. In the **chap_15** folder on your hard drive, open the **PublishTesting** folder. Double-click on the file: **webPage.html** to open it. Resize the browser window by clicking and dragging the bottom right corner of the window. Notice the .swf file doesn't scale with the browser window and as you make the window smaller, the image becomes cut off. You will change the scalability restrictions by changing the Dimensions setting next.

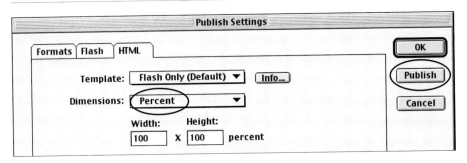

17. In the Publish settings of the **HTML** tab, choose **Dimensions: Percent**. Click **Publish**. This will replace the previous version of the **webPage.html** page.

*It is important that you remember to click the Publish button if you wish to preview the new settings you have created. Flash will only update the HTML doc with the new setting applied to it if you click the Publish button or choose **File > Publish**.*

18. To see the difference this makes, open the file **webPage.html** again. Try resizing the browser window by clicking and dragging the bottom right corner of the window. Notice how the .swf file scales this time! This is because the Percent setting allows the movie to fill the browser window 100% by 100%, so no matter how you resize it, the movie will scale and fit the entire browser window and will not be cut off.

> ### NOTE | Important Uploading Advice!
>
> Flash publishes the HTML file with the assumption that the .swf file will be located in the same folder as the HTML file, so when you upload the HTML file to a Web server, make sure you put both files in the same directory.

This exercise has taken you through many of the common Publish settings under the .swf tab and the HTML tab. For a more in-depth look at what each of the settings under these tabs can do, refer to the tables at the beginning of this chapter. Also, in Chapter 17, "Integration," you will learn how to control the .swf file inside an HTML document using Dreamweaver.

---

19. Save and close this file.

2. _____Creating Projectors

Have you ever received an attachment in an email that has the extension .exe or .hqx and when you opened it, it was a Flash movie that played right in its own window without a browser? If you have, you may be more familiar with projector files than you think. Projector files are often sent via email because they are stand-alone files that can play with or without the Flash plug-in on most computers! Projector files can also be distributed via floppy disks, CD-ROMs, or shown from your hard drive without a browser (as a great PowerPoint substitute!). This exercise will teach you how to create a projector file using the Publish settings dialog box.

1. Open the file called **projector.fla** located inside the **chap_15** folder. This is the project file from the background sound exercise you created in Chapter 14. You'll take that file one step further by turning it into a stand-alone projector file.

2. Choose **Control > Test Movie** to preview the movie. By choosing Control > Test Movie, Flash will create an SWF file and save it in the same folder as the FLA file.

3. Close the preview window and back in the project file, choose **File > Publish Settings**. This will open the Publish settings window.

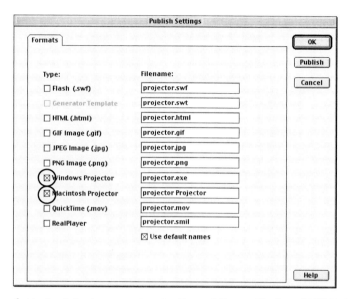

4. Uncheck the boxes next to the **Format Types: Flash** and **HTML**, because you will be working with projector files in this exercise. Check the boxes next to **Windows Projector** and **Macintosh Projector**.

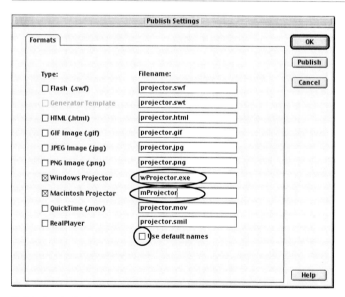

5. Uncheck the box next to **Use default names** and enter the names: **wProjector.exe** in the Windows Projector Filename field and **mProjector** in the Macintosh Projector Filename field. This will give your project files their own unique names. Click **Publish** when you are finished.

When you select Publish, Flash automatically saves the projector files to the same folder as your .fla file.

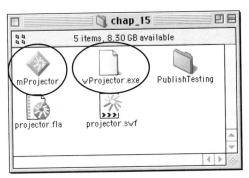

6. Open the **chap_15** folder on your hard drive. Inside you will see *four* files and one folder: the **PublishTesting** folder from Exercise 1, the original project file: **projector.fla**, the .swf file that was created when you chose Control > Test Movie in Step 2 of this exercise, and two new projector files named **mProjector** and **wProjector.exe**.

NOTE | Why do the icons of the two projector files look different?

Although you can *create* projectors for both Macintosh and Windows formats or either computer, you can't *open* a Windows projector on a Mac computer and likewise, you can't open a Mac projector on a Windows machine. The format that works on your machine will display the pink icon, while the icon for the format that doesn't work will look like a piece of paper.

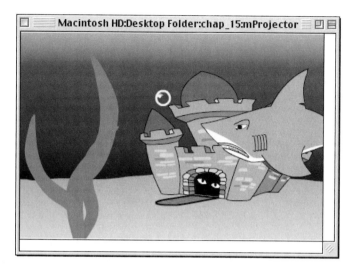

7. If you're on a Mac, double-click on the file named **mProjector** to open it. If you're using Windows, double-click on the file named **wProjector.exe** to open it. You have just created your first projector file. Notice the sound and animation play? This is because the projector file takes the entire movie, sound and all, and displays it in its own player.

When you create a projector file, Flash embeds the movie into its own stand-alone player, and this is why you can distribute projector files without having to worry about whether your audience has the Flash plug-in or not. Projector files will play by themselves, in their own container, as soon as they are opened!

NOTE | Why Aren't There Better Projector Publish Settings?

When you select the projector file types from the Formats tab in the Publish settings dialog box, no additional tabs become available for you to alter the settings. However, you can control the way your projectors behave using ActionScript and FS Commands. You will do this in the next exercise.

---

8. Save this file and keep it open for the next exercise.

3. ──────────**Modifying Projectors with FS Commands**

In the last exercise, you learned how to create a Projector file. This exercise will show you how to modify the original project file by adding ActionScript to control the stand-alone player. The following steps will teach you how to use FSCommands to force the movie to take up the full screen of the computer and to disable the menu so that users cannot right-click on the movie and see a list of menu items.

1. You should have the same file open from the last exercise. If you accidentally closed it, open the file named **projector.fla** from the **chap_15** folder. Save this file under a new name: **fsProjector.fla**.

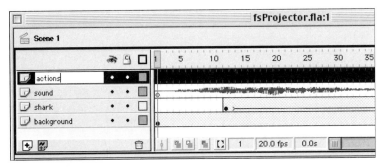

2. Select **Insert > Layer** to add a new layer to the movie. Name the new layer: **actions**. Make sure this layer is on the top of all the other layers.

3. Click on the first keyframe of the actions layer and choose **Window > Actions** to open the **Frame Actions** panel. You will add the ActionScript to control the stand-alone player in this keyframe next.

NOTE | FSCommands as Frame Actions

It is usually most effective to add the **FSCommands** that control the window behavior to one of the first keyframes in the movie. The reason is that this enables your commands to take effect immediately, as soon as the player opens.

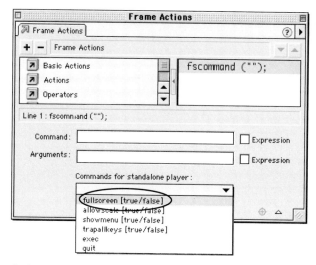

4. Click on the **Add (+) Action** button, select **Actions** and choose **FSCommand**. In the Parameters drop-down menu select **fullscreen [true/false]** in the **Commands for standalone player** field.

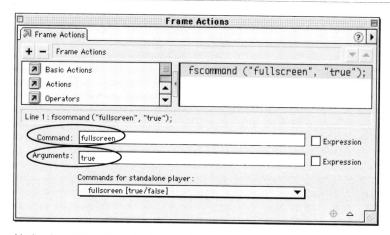

Notice how this automatically populates the Command and Arguments field. The fullscreen command makes the player take up the whole computer and prevents screen resizing when the argument is set to true.

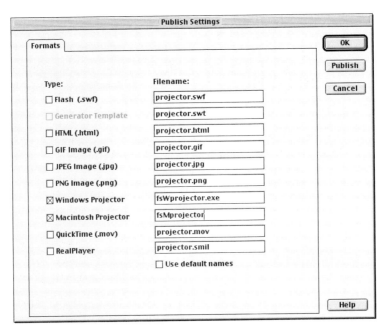

5. Choose **File > Publish Settings**. In the **Publish Settings** dialog box, rename the projector files: **fsWprojector.exe** and **fsMprojector**. This will allow Flash to publish two new files without replacing the old projector files you made in the last exercise. When you are finished, click **Publish** to publish the projectors with the FSCommands added.

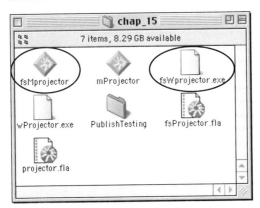

6. Open the **chap_15** folder on your hard drive. Inside you will see all the files you have created this far. If you are on a Mac, double-click on the file named **fsMProjector** to open it. If you are using Windows, double-click on the file named **fsWProjector**. Now the projector will launch full screen! To exit the full screen mode, simple press **Esc** on the keyboard.

What exactly are FSCommands?

FSCommands invoke JavaScript functions from Flash. They include a command that is similar to an instruction, and an argument that checks to see if the command should be allowed (true) or not (false). The table below describes the FSCommands for the stand-alone player.

FSCommands for the Stand-Alone Player Defined

Command	Argument	Function
fullscreen	true/false	Sets the movie to fill the full screen when set to true, and returns the movie to a normal window when set to false. Setting the movie to full screen without also setting allowscale to false will result in the movie changing scale in most cases.
allowscale	true/false	Enables or disables the user's ability to scale the player. It also prevents scaling that occurs from setting the movie to fullscreen.
howmenu	true/false	Enables right + click or Ctrl + click menu items when this command is set to true. When this command is set to false, it disables the user's ability to access the control menu.
trapallkeys	true/false	Enables the movie to capture keystrokes if set to true.
exec	path to application	Allows you to launch another application file on the local system. For this to work properly, you must know the correct path and name of the application. You must type the correct path and name of the application in the Arguments field. If you are calling a file in the same directory then all you need is the file name.
quit	none	Closes the projector.

7. In the project file, make sure that **Keyframe 1** is still selected. In the **Frame Actions** panel, click on the **Add (+) Action** button. Choose **Actions** and select **FSCommand**.

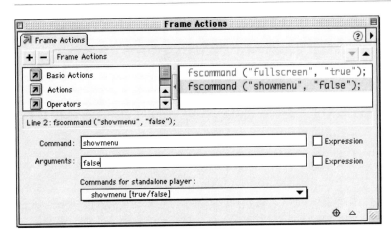

8. In the **Frame Actions** dialog box, select **showmenu (true/false)** in the **Commands for standalone player** field. This will auto-populate the Command and Arguments field. Change the **Arguments** field text to **false**. When the Arguments field is set to false, this command disables the user from being able to use **Ctrl + Click** (Mac) or **right-click** (Windows) to access the full list of menu items.

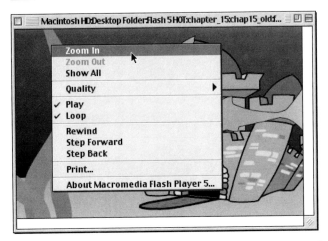

*While a projector is playing, the user can either **Ctrl + Click** (Mac) or **right-click** (Windows) to view a list of menu items. If the projector is set to full screen, you may not want to allow your users to zoom in or out or manipulate the way the movie is presented to them. By disabling the menu (showmenu = false) you can limit the control the users have.*

9. Select **File > Publish.** This will publish the changes you made (adding the new FSCommand) to the file formats that you specified in the Publish Settings dialog box.

10. Open the **chap_15** folder on your hard drive. If you are using a Macintosh, double-click on the projector file named **fsMprojector.** If you are using Windows, double-click on the file named **fsWprojector..** Try to **Ctrl + Click** (Mac) or **right-click** (Windows) to access the drop-down menu. You should not be able to do it! This is because you set the Argument to false in the Parameters pane, therefore preventing the user from seeing the menu and using any of the options within it.

11. When you are finished testing the projector, save and close this file.

More About Publish Settings

You've just completed three exercises that taught you firsthand how to use Publish settings. We're sure you noticed many settings that weren't covered in the exercises. Let this next section serve as a reference to you, should you want to publish other kinds of media from Flash such as GIF, JPEG, PNG, QuickTime or RealPlayer content.

The Publish settings are located under **File > Publish Settings**. You can change these settings at any point while developing or editing your project file (.fla). The Publish settings window is divided into a number of tabs.

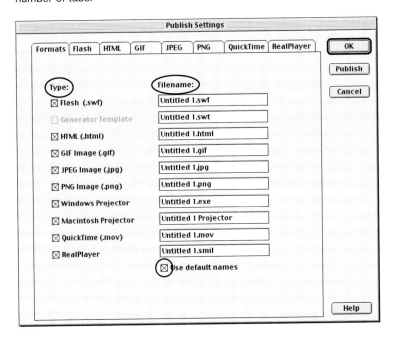

Formats Tab

The first tab is the Formats tab. It allows you to select the file formats that Flash will publish. As each format is selected, additional tabs will appear to the right of the Formats tab. The tabs hold settings (specific to the selected format) that can be modified. We will cover each of the format type options in detail below. The formats tab also allows you to modify the filename of each selected format that Flash will publish.

Filename

As you saw in Exercise 1, if the **Use default name** box is checked, all file formats you choose to create will have the same name as the original project file. If the **Use default name** box is unchecked, you can create a unique name for each of the file formats you select.

Type

In the Type section of the Formats tab, you can select the files you wish to publish. We will cover each of the settings in the pages that follow.

Flash Settings

The Flash tab contains all of the settings that will be used for the .swf file, which is the file you have been viewing when you choose **Control > Test Movie**. The .swf file is embedded in the HTML document so that the movie can be seen on the Web. A detailed description of each option under the Flash tab appears below.

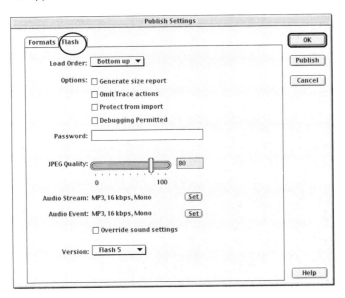

Flash Publishing Options	
Load Order	Sets whether the layers will be loaded from the top down or the bottom up. For example, *bottom up* means the lowest layer will be shown first, the second lowest next, etc. The reverse is true of *top down*. This loading setting only takes place when you have multiple elements loading in different layers in the same frame slot, and on a fast connection you may not ever see this happen. The frames (not layers) will always load in numeric order.
Generate Size Report	Checking this box will cause Flash to create a text file that contains detailed information about the size of all the elements in your movie. It will be published to the same directory as the rest of the files.
Omit Trace Actions	Blocks the Trace action from being exported with your movie. (The Trace action is a debugging tool. You should select this option if you are using Trace actions and are producing a final cut of your movie.)

Flash Publishing Options *continued*

Protect from Import	Prevents anyone from importing your .swf movie file into Flash and converting it back to a project file (.fla). This allows you to protect your work. However, you can still import a protected movie into a Macromedia Director movie. Additionally, the SWIFFER utility can break into any Flash movie, so to be on the safe side, don't put sensitive information into Flash movies.
Debugging Permitted	Activates the debugger and will allow the Flash movie to be debugged remotely.
Password	Allows you to set a password that others have to enter before they debug your movie. This can prevent unauthorized users from debugging a movie.
JPEG Quality	Allows you to set the default image quality export setting for all of the raster graphics in your movie. To retain greater control over your image fidelity and file size, we recommend that you bypass this setting and use the individual settings for each file in the Library instead.
Override Sound Settings	Checking this box allows you to force all sounds in the movie to use the settings here, instead of their own compression settings.
Audio Stream	Allows you to set separate audio compression types and settings for all sounds in the movie that have a *Stream Sync* type and have a compression type of Default. The *Audio Event* settings allow you to separately set the audio compression type and settings for all sounds in the movie that have a Start or Event Sync type whose compression type is set to Default. We recommend that you bypass both of these and use the individual settings in the Library instead.
Version	Allows you to export earlier formats of Flash .swf files. This is not very useful for publishing to the Web because Flash 5 movies will play with the Flash 4 plug-in, but the Flash 5 features won't work. When you export to Flash 4 the Flash 5 features are NOT converted, they are omitted. The real value of this feature is that it provides you the means to import work you did in Flash back to Flash 4. If you export to Flash 3, the animation and artwork created in Flash 5 will render OK although it will not recognize Flash 4 or 5 ActionScript or MP3 sound files.

HTML Settings

The HTML tab allows you to set values that determine how the HTML file is created for your movie. The HTML file is needed as a container to embed the .swf file if you plan to publish to the Web. By changing the settings under the HTML tab, you can change the appearance of your .swf when viewed from a browser. The available options are detailed below.

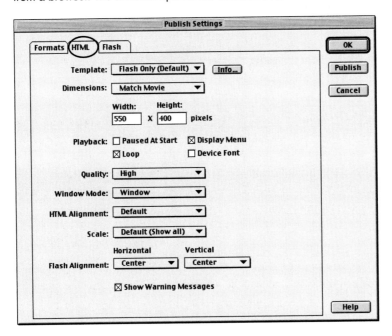

HTML Settings Options

Template	Allows you to choose from a list of pre-made HTML templates. Each of these templates were built to provide different types of support for the movie.
Dimensions	Allows you to set the dimensions which the Flash movie will be set to in the HTML tags. This value can be in pixels or percentage of window size. A setting of Match Movie will not allow the .swf file to scale in the browser. A percentage setting will allow the .swf content to scale if the user resizes the browser window.
Playback	Allows you to define how the movie will act in the browser. You can check *Paused at Start* to force the movie to start in a stopped position, without using a *Stop* action in the first keyframe. You can deselect the *Loop* checkbox to make the movie play only once. If you deselect the *Display Menu* option, then the Control menu will be disabled in the browser window. The *Device Font* box is an option that applies to a Flash movie playing on a Windows Flash Player. If this option is selected, it allows the movie to use the local antialiased system font on the user's system instead of the font(s) embedded in the movie.
Quality	Sets whether the movie will be played back with emphasis on graphics quality or playback speed. *High* emphasizes graphics quality over speed, whereas low emphasizes playback speed over appearance.
Window Mode	Determines how the movie interacts in a DHTML environment. This setting only has an effect on browsers that are utilizing absolute positioning and layering.
HTML Alignment	Sets the horizontal alignment of the Flash movie within the HTML page.
Scale	Determines how the Flash movie resizes within the movie window on the HTML page.
Flash Alignment	Determines how the movie is aligned within the Flash movie window. This determines how the movie will look if it is zoomed or cropped.
Show Warning Messages	Toggles whether or not the browser will display error messages that occur within the Object or Embed tags.

GIF Settings (.gif)

The GIF file format can be used to produce animated graphics and static graphics. For example, if you create a logo in Flash that you want to save to use in other applications, you can select the GIF file type under the Formats tab. The GIF settings are explained in detail below.

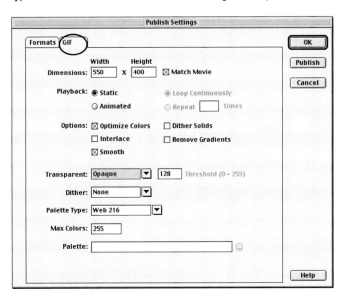

GIF Settings Options	
Dimensions	Allows you to set the size of the GIF by entering the width and height into the corresponding fields. Checking the Match Movie box will generate a GIF that has the same dimensions that were set in the Movie Properties dialog box in the project file.
Playback	Determines whether the GIF will be static or animated. If the *Static* box is checked, the first keyframe of the movie will be used as the GIF image. If you wish for a different keyframe to be used as the GIF image, you can add the label: *#Static* to the selected keyframe and Flash will export the labeled keyframe instead. If the *Animated* box is checked, Flash will export the whole project file as an animated GIF. If you want only a selection of frames to be exported, add these labels to the first and last keyframes: *#First* and *#Last*. If *Loop Continuously* is selected, the GIF will repeat the animation over and over. If *Repeat Times* is selected, you can manually enter the number of times you want the animated GIF to loop before it stops.

GIF Settings Options	
Options	*Optimize Colors:* Removes unused colors to decrease file size.
	Interlace: Causes the image to appear in stages as it is downloaded.
	Smooth: Causes the GIF to become antialiased, which can increase file size.
	Dither Solids: Matches colors as closely as possible that are not part of the 256-color palette by mixing similar colors.
	Remove Gradients: Changes all gradients to solid colors, thereby reducing file size.
Transparent	*Opaque:* Causes the background of the image to appear solid.
	Transparent: Causes the background of the image to appear invisible.
	Alpha: Controls the background and all shapes that have an alpha setting applied to them. Allows you to set the threshold so that all colors above the specified amount will be solid and all the colors that have an alpha setting below the specifed amount will be transparent.
Dither	*None:* Matches any color that is not within the 256-color palette with the closest color from within the 256 colors rather than using dithering.
	Ordered: Matches any color that is not within the 256-color palette using dithering from a pattern of colors.
	Diffusion: Matches any color that is not within the 256-color palette using dithering from a random pattern of colors. This creates the closest match of colors, but has the highest increase of file size from within these three options.
Palette Type	*Web 216:* Creates a GIF file using the 216 Web-safe colors.
	Adaptive: Creates a GIF file using only the Web-safe colors that were actually used within the GIF.
	Web Snap Adaptive: Creates a GIF file that substitutes Web-safe colors for any colors that are not Web safe but are a close match.
	Custom: Allows you to use a custom palette for the GIF file. When you select this option, the *Palette* option becomes active as well (see Palette, below).
Max Colors	Determines the maximum number of colors created within the palette when either the Adaptive or Web Snap Adaptive Options are selected.
Palette	Allows you to select your own custom color palette from your hard drive.

JPEG Settings (.jpeg)

The JPEG file format can be used for images that have more detail than GIF images generally do, such as photographs. Although JPEG images cannot be animated, they can have an unlimited number of colors, rather than having to fall within a specific color palette. The table below describes the available options for publishing a JPEG image.

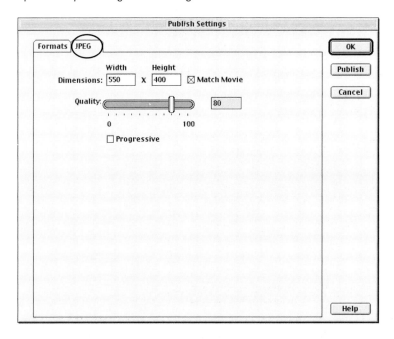

JPEG Settings Options	
Dimensions	Allows you to set the size of the JPEG by entering the width and height into the corresponding fields. If the Match Movie box is checked, the JPEG will have the same dimensions as the project file's Movie Properties settings.
Quality	Sets the amount of compression from 0 (lowest quality and smallest file size) to 100 (highest quality and largest file size).
Progressive	Allows the image to appear in stages as it is downloaded.

PNG Settings (.png)

The PNG file format can be used to produce static graphics. Similar to the GIF format, the PNG format supports transparency. The PNG settings, which are similar to the GIF settings, are explained in detail below.

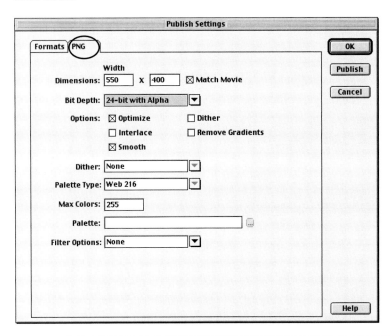

PNG Settings Options	
Dimensions	Allows you to set the size of the PNG by entering the width and height into the corresponding fields. Checking the Match Movie box will generate a PNG that has the same dimensions that were set in the Movie Properties dialog box in the project file.
Bit Depth	Sets the number of colors (bits per pixel) that will be used in the published file. As the bit depth increases, the file size increases as well. *8-bit:* Creates a 256-color image. *24-bit:* Creates an image using thousands of colors. *24-bit with Alpha:* Creates an image with thousands of colors and allows transparency.

continued on next page

PNG Settings Options *continued*	
Options	*Optimize Colors:* Removes unused colors to decrease file size. *Interlace:* Causes the image to appear in stages as it is downloaded. *Smooth:* Causes the PNG to become antialiased, which can increase file size. *Dither Solids:* Matches colors as close as possible that are not part of the 256-color palette by mixing similar colors. *Remove Gradients:* Changes all gradients to solid colors, thereby reducing file size.
Dither	*None:* Matches any color that is not within the 256-color palette with the closest color from within the 256 colors rather than using dithering. *Ordered:* Matches any color that is not within the 256-color palette using dithering from a regular pattern of colors. *Diffusion:* Matches any color that is not within the 256-color palette by dithering from a random pattern of colors, creating the closest match of colors, but with the highest increase of file size from within these three options.
Palette Type	*Web 216:* Creates a PNG file using the 216 Web-safe colors. *Adaptive:* Creates a PNG file using only the colors within the 256 colors that were actually used within the PNG. *Web Snap Adaptive:* Creates a PNG file that substitutes Web-safe colors for any colors that are not Web safe but are a close match. *Custom:* Allows you to use a custom palette for the GIF file. When you select this option, the Palette option becomes active as well (see Palette, below).
Max Colors	Determines the maximum amount of colors created within the palette when either the Adaptive or Web Snap Adaptive Options are selected.
Palette	Allows you to select your own custom color palette (in the ACT format) from your hard drive.
Filter Options	Allows you to choose a filtering method that produces an image at the best quality and smallest file size.

QuickTime

The QuickTime settings allow you publish the Flash project file as a QuickTime 4 movie (.mov). The layers of the Flash file will be converted to what is called the "Flash track" within the QuickTime Movie. Chapter 17, "*Integration*," will cover working with QuickTime in a step-by-step exercise. Below, the QuickTime tab options are explained in detail.

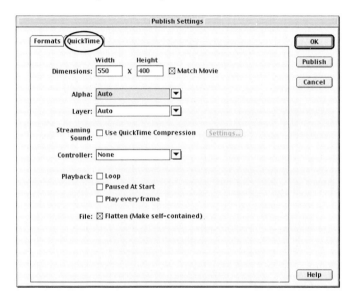

Flash Publishing Options	
Dimensions	Allows you to set the size of the QuickTime movie by entering the width and height into the corresponding fields. Checking the Match Movie box will generate a QuickTime movie that has the same dimensions that were set in the Movie Properties dialog box in the project file.
Alpha	Controls the transparency of the Flash track in the QuickTime movie. *Auto*: Makes the Flash track opaque if it is the only track in the QuickTime movie or if it is located on the bottom of the other tracks. Makes the Flash track transparent if it is located on the top of other tracks. *Alpha Transparent*: Makes the Flash track transparent. Other tracks below the Flash track will show through the Flash track. *Copy*: Makes the Flash track opaque. Tracks below the Flash track will be masked.

continued on next page

Flash Publishing Options *continued*	
Layer	Determines where the Flash track will reside relative to other tracks inside the QuickTime movie. *Top:* Positions the Flash track on top of all other tracks. *Bottom:* Positions the Flash track below all the other tracks. *Auto:* Positions the Flash track in front of the other tracks if Flash content is placed in front of QuickTime content in the Flash movie. Positions the Flash track behind the other tracks if Flash content is placed in back of QuickTime content in the Flash movie.
Streaming Sound	Allows you to convert all streaming audio in the Flash project file into a QuickTime sound track.
Controller	Specifies the type of QuickTime controller that will be used to play the QuickTime movie.
Playback	*Loop:* Makes the movie start over at the beginning once the end if reached if this box is selected. *Paused at Start:* Forces the movie to start paused if this box is checked. When the user clicks a button, the movie will play. *Play every frame:* Causes all sound to be disabled and plays each frame without skipping if this box is checked.
File	*Flatten* (Make Self-Contained): Combines Flash content and video content in one QuickTime movie if this box is checked. The Flash file and video file will be referenced externally if the box is not checked.

Real Player

The RealPlayer settings allow you to publish the Flash project file as one of the RealPlayer Formats: RealAudio, RealVideo or .swf files that are formatted for streaming playback. To publish an .swf file that is compatible with the RealPlayer, it can't have audio. A special .swf file is created that is called a **tuned file**. In the tuned file, all audio is deleted and the movie is resampled for streaming playback. Below, the RealPlayer tab options are explained in detail.

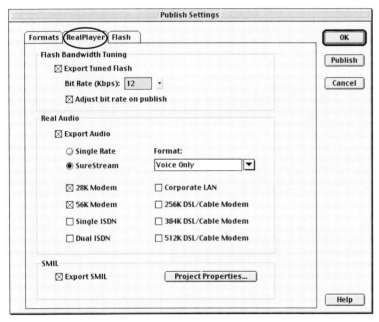

Real Player Publishing Options	
Flash Bandwidth	*Tuning Export Tuned Flash:* Includes the tuned (stripped of audio and resampled for streaming playback) Flash file with the published movie. *Bit Rate (Kbps):* Determines the bit rate for the tuned Flash file with a range from 1 to 100. *Adjust bit rate on publish:* Allows you to reset the bit rate when you publish the movie if this box is selected.
	continued on next page

Real Player Publishing Options *continued*	
Real Audio	*Export Audio:* Allows you to export streamed sound in the project file in RealAudio format. *Single Rate* streams sound for only one audience (or one connection speed for your users). *SureStream* streams sound for multiple target audiences (you can specify several connection speeds) switching to a lower bit rate during slower connection speeds. *Format: Voice Only* uses compression appropriate for voice sound where there is no background sound (such as narration). *Voice With Background Music* uses compression appropriate for voice sound where background sound is present. *Music* uses compression appropriate for mono music sound. *Music in Stereo* uses compression appropriate for stereo music sound.
SMIL	Exports a SMIL file with the published movie if this box is checked. The SMIL file synchronizes playback of the RealAudio stream and the tuned Flash file in the RealPlayer.

Projector files

Flash can also be used to produce stand-alone applications for Mac or Windows machines.

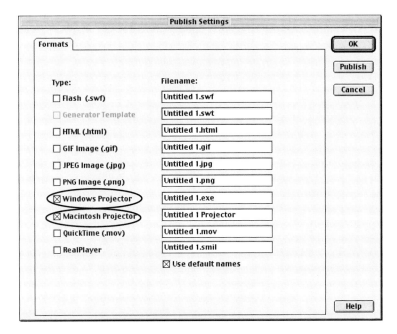

Although there are no additional settings to choose from in the Publish settings window, the **Windows Projector** and **Macintosh Projector** can be selected under the **Formats > Type** options. These projectors are self-contained files that can run on any computer, regardless of whether the user has the Flash Player installed or not. You learned about Projector files in depth in Exercise 3 earlier in this chapter.

Top Tips for Optimizing Movies

All movies in Flash are not created equal. You can, however, use a few tricks and follow some simple guidelines to reduce the file size and increase the playback performance of your movie. The section below will provide a list of helpful tips to generate the best performance of Flash files.

Use symbols. Any time you use artwork multiple times in your project file, turn the artwork into a symbol. This will allow the artwork to be downloaded only once and used over and over without having any significant impact on file size.

Use solid lines wherever possible. Try to avoid using the dashed, dotted, or jagged line styles. Each, dot, dash, or squiggle in these lines will be tracked as an independent object when the file is exported. The jagged line style is the worst of the three. Lines using the jagged style contribute more than 100 times more bytes to the files size of your movie than do plain lines.

Use alpha sparingly. The more alpha, or transparency, that you have in the movie, the slower the playback performance will be. Using alpha will not increase file size, but it can have a dramatic impact on playback performance. If you do use alpha, try not to have too many transparent elements stacked on top of each other.

Use gradients sparingly. Although their impact is not as serious as alpha, gradients can also slow down playback performance.

Use the Optimize command on your artwork. By selecting an object and using the **Modify > Optimize** command, you can reduce the file size of your movie.

Use vector graphics rather than bitmaps wherever possible. Vector graphics are usually significantly smaller than bitmaps, which can keep the file size down.

Be aware of complex objects in animation. The more complex your object is, the slower the playback performance will be.

Use device fonts where appropriate. By using device fonts, Flash will not embed the outlines for your movie's fonts as it does by default. Instead, Flash will display the font nearest to what the user's machine has and this will save file size.

Be cautious of looping streaming sound. When a sound Sync is set to Stream, it will play the sound at the same rate the animation is played. If you loop the streaming sound, Flash will multiply the file size by the number of times you loop the sound. This is because when the Sync is set to Stream and you specify a number of loops, Flash actually adds frames to the Timeline—so be careful of adding looping to streaming sound.

Turn layers into guide layers. To prevent unwanted content from being exported, convert unwanted layers into guide layers. For example, if you have artwork that you are only using for inspiration on a particular layer and you don't want to delete it but don't want that layer to end up in the movie, turn the layer that the content is on into a guide layer. Guide layers will not be exported with the final movie and this may save file size also.

Use the Load Movie command to keep file sizes small and display content only on demand. So rather than having one huge movie, you can create several smaller .swf files and load them into the main movie when the user requests the content by clicking on a button, for example.

Use the Generate Size Report feature to look at the breakdown of the .swf file, frame by frame. Here you can identify places where you may be able to reduce the file size by compressing an image further, for example, or you can spot a frame that is significantly larger than other frames.

Be aware of platform performance: Flash plays slightly faster (frames per second) on a Windows machine than it does on a Macintosh. Ideally, before you distribute Flash files or upload them to a live Web site, test the files on both a Mac and a Windows based machine to make sure the movie performs to your expectations on both platforms.

You have completed another chapter and should be ready to distribute your Flash movies all over the world! Before you do, you may want to hang on and finish the last two chapters, because we will cover some valuable information in the "Deconstruction" chapter next and in the last chapter, "Integration."

16.

Deconstruction

The Big Picture	Layer Management	Scene Management
Library Organization	Using the Movie Controller
The Movie Explorer	Setting Up the Basic Elements
Adding Buttons and Scenes	Instance Properties Panel
Swapping Background Symbols and Modifying Buttons
Modifying Scenes and Adding Actions	Printing

chap_16

Flash 5
H•O•T CD-ROM

After working through the exercises in the previous chapters, you're probably wondering how to pull all of the pieces together into one finished project file. This chapter will take you through a completed Web site, and we'll point out many elements in the site that you've learned within the exercises of this book. You will then have a chance to rebuild the site, using the many techniques that we've shown you here. We've included recommendations and tips so that you can learn from our workflow strategy. Additionally, we'll introduce several features within Flash that allow you to maximize your production efficiency, including the Movie Explorer and the Controller. Finally, you'll learn about the program's print capabilities, new to Flash 5.

I. _____The Big Picture

This exercise introduces you to the Oak Tree site that you will create in this chapter. Soon you will understand how to put many of the pieces together that you've learned in previous chapters to create a finished Web-based project.

1. Copy the **chap_16** folder, located on the **H•O•T CD-ROM**, to your hard drive. You need to have this folder on your hard drive in order to save files inside it.

2. Open the file named **siteComplete.fla** located inside the **chap_16** folder. We created this fully functional project file for you, using many of the techniques that you learned in this book. You will create this same project in just a few steps.

3. Choose **Control > Test Movie** to preview the movie. Notice the introduction of the leaf slowly falling down the screen. Does it look familiar? That is the same motion guide you created in chapter 8, "*Motion Tweening.*"

4. Click on each of the navigation buttons on the left side of the screen and investigate all the sections within the movie by clicking and testing the interactive elements. Notice how many of them look similar to smaller movies that you created in the preceding chapters of this book.

*We want you to explore this file to see how many of the pieces you recognize from your lessons thus far in this book. In later exercises of this chapter, you'll recreate this entire project file, piece by piece. When you are finished, close the preview window but leave the project (***siteComplete.fla***) open.*

Layer Management

You'll notice that the .fla file used in this chapter contains many more layers than other exercises you've tried in this book. For that reason, we've added extra material here to help you look deeper into how layers work.

Layers in Flash are similar to transparent sheets stacked on top of each other. Layers help you organize the content on the frames in the project file. For example, in Chapter 12, "*ActionScripting Basics*," you learned to get in the habit of adding an action layer on top of all other layers so that frame actions can always be found in the same place. In Chapter 14, "*Sound*," you learned to add a sound layer to the Timeline to keep the sounds consistently on the same layer and separate from others. Layers also play an important role in animation in Flash. For instance, if you want to tween multiple elements, then each element that is tweened must be on its own separate layer. By default, all movies in Flash have at least one layer, although you can add as many layers as you want to your movie.

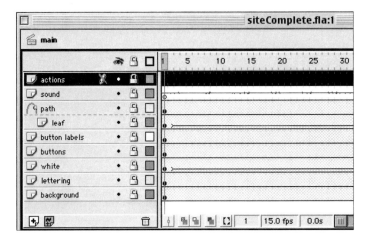

Adding and Removing Layers

You can add a new layer by choosing **Insert > Layer** or by clicking on the **Add Layer** button in the bottom left-hand corner of the Timeline. You can click on the **Add Guide Layer** button to add a guide layer. You can remove a layer by clicking on the **Delete Layer** button.

Types of Layers

Throughout this book you have worked with several kinds of layers in addition to a standard layer. There are three special types of layers: **mask**, **guide**, and **motion guide**.

Mask Layers

A mask layer is a special layer that defines what is visible on the layer below it. Only layers that are beneath the shapes in the mask layer will be visible.

Guide Layers

Guide layers come in two flavors: motion guide layers and guide layers. The difference between the two is that guide layers simply serve as a guide for you to layout images to trace in the project file. Motion guide layers serve as a path for an object to follow and have guided layers attached to it.

Both are special layer types that are not exported when the movie is published or tested, and therefore they will not add size to the .swf file. These layers are only visible in the development environment. Use caution: while artwork on a guide layer is not exported, actions *are* exported.

In the next exercise, you will see an example of both a motion guide layer and a guide layer in the **siteComplete.fla** project file.

2. _____ **Examining Scenes**

Scenes can be used to organize sections of content within the project file. You can use scenes to break up large projects into smaller manageable pieces. By default, Flash will play all the scenes in order unless you use ActionScript to tell Flash otherwise. If no ActionScripting is present in the main Timeline to stop the movie, the Playhead will continue on to the next scene and continue to play the frames until the end is reached or a Stop action is encountered. This exercise will point out certain scene attributes in the project file.

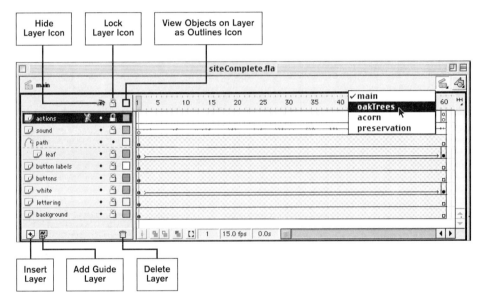

1. Click on the **Edit Scene** button in the top right of the **siteComplete.fla** file to reveal the four scenes within this project. Select the **oakTrees** scene to open that scene's Timeline.

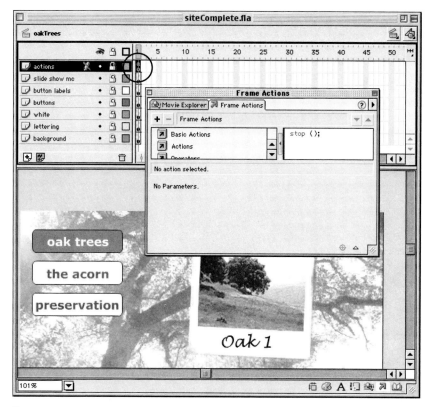

2. Select **Frame 1** in the **actions** layer and choose **Window > Actions** to open the **Actions** panel. Notice how there is a Stop action in the first keyframe on the actions layer. This will prevent Flash from playing one scene right after another.

3. Choose **Modify > Scene** to open the **Scene** panel and navigate through the available scenes. The Scene panel is where you can rename the scenes, change their order at any time, or select a scene to open the scene's Timeline. You can also access this same panel by choosing Window > Panels > Scene.

4. Click on the **acorn** scene in the Scene panel to open its Timeline. Notice another Stop action in the first keyframe of the actions layer. The purpose of this action is to cause Flash to stop as soon as the Playhead reaches this frame and wait until the user interacts with the buttons before it continues.

5. Leave this file open for the next exercise.

Library Organization

Through your production work on Flash projects, you will frequently use the Library for a variety of purposes including opening files, dragging sounds out to add them to the Timeline, renaming elements,
or finding elements within a project, to name a few. Since you will often use the Library, it is important
to keep it organized and consistent with naming schemes.

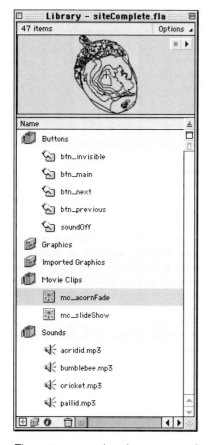 

These two examples show an organized Library on the left, and a disorganized Library on the right.
Would you rather search for a button symbol in the Library on the left, which has consistently named
elements, or the Library on the right, which is disorganized and uses many different naming schemes,
as well as inconsistently placed items in the folders?

In addition to helping your efficiency, organizing your Library can also help other individuals who may be working on the project with you. There are several basic "Library etiquette" guidelines to keep in mind:

- Be consistent in your naming conventions. There is no "right way" to name the items within your project file but once you decide on a structure to follow, stick to it. Since the Library sorts elements alphabetically, we recommend using prefixes at the beginning of the item name, such as **btn,home** or **mc,fallingLeaf**. Again, there is no perfect way to name your elements. Instead, consistency is what matters.

- Choose brief descriptive names such as **btn, main menu** rather than a series of letters such as **btn, MM**. This way, when you look for the button at a later point, you can find it a lot easier knowing that you have given it an accurate descriptive name.

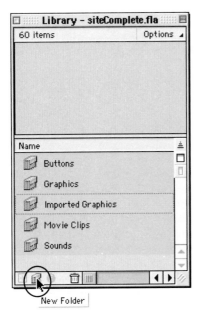

- Use folders to organize the Library elements and stay consistent with the folder names. You can create a folder by clicking on the New Folder icon shown in the picture above. Short descriptive names will help you navigate through the Library faster and you will know what to expect inside each folder even before you open it.

3. ————————Investigating the Library

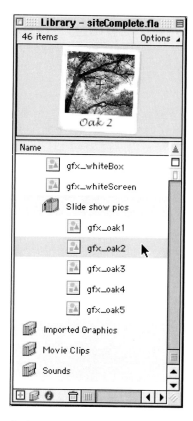

1. Open the Library, **Cmd + L** (Mac) or **Ctrl + L** (Windows), and double-click on the folders to view the elements inside them. Notice how all the elements are named consistently and located in the corresponding folders. Double-click on any Library item that intrigues you to either open the symbol's Timeline or open the Properties dialog box to learn more about the element.

2. Continue to click around, expand and collapse the folders and examine other elements inside the Library. When you are finished recreating this project file in the exercises that follow, your Library should look very similar to the Library you are investigating now.

3. When you are finished, leave this file open for the next exercise.

4. _____Using the Movie Controller

In addition to previewing your work using **Control > Test Movie**, you can use the Controller to test the movie right inside the authoring environment. The Controller is similar to a VCR or DVD remote in that you can play the movie, rewind, or stop it at any point. This exercise will teach you how to work with the Controller.

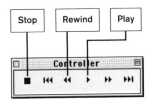

1. To open the Controller, choose **Window > Toolbars > Controller**. In the Scene panel, select the main scene to open its Timeline. Click on the Controller's **Play** button to test this scene right on the Stage.

2. Click on the **Step Back One Frame** button to rewind the movie one frame.

3. Click on the **Go to End** button to fast-forward to the last frame in the scene. Using the Controller can help speed up your production time by allowing you to preview the movie right inside the authoring environment. This is a quick way to test a movie.

Caution: Not all parts of the project will preview properly using the Controller. For example, as you use the Controller in the editing environment (the .fla file), you will see the motion guide for the leaf as you preview the movie. However, if you view the .swf file using Test Movie or Publish command you won't see the motion guide. For this reason, always make sure you test the movie using the Publish command before you finalize the final version of the movie. As you learned in Chapter 15, "Publishing," using this command will produce the most realistic view of what the file will look like on the Web.

NOTE | The Controller and Scenes

The Controller will only work and control the current scene that you are in. It will not jump to the next scene if there are multiple scenes in the movie.

4. When you are finished, leave this file open for the next exercise.

5. —————————The Movie Explorer

New to Flash 5, the Movie Explorer is a handy tool that provides you with a visual representation of every aspect of the project file, organized into a hierarchical structure. Just about every element within the project can be viewed and located using the Movie Explorer, including graphic symbols, button symbols, movie clip symbols, text, ActionScripts, frames and scenes. This exercise will introduce you to the basic features of the Movie Explorer while looking at the **siteComplete.fla** project file.

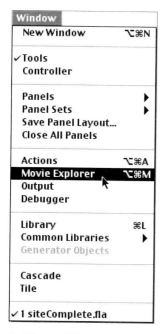

1. Choose **Window > Movie Explorer** to open the Movie Explorer.

TIP | Why use the Movie Explorer?

The Movie Explorer can be used for many different purposes. It acts as a detective that displays a map, which is customized to what you instruct it to show. For example, the Movie Explorer can be used to search and display all the text within a movie that uses the Verdana font. It can also be used to list all the graphic symbols, or even sounds within a scene. Additionally, it can be used to locate a particular element when you know its name but not its location. The following steps will take you through some of these examples.

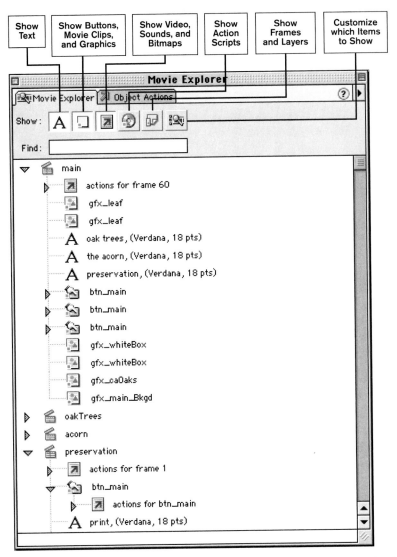

By default, the Movie Explorer will open displaying all text, buttons, movie clips, graphics and ActionScripts. However, you have control over what the Movie Explorer shows by selecting display categories.

2. Click on the icons next to **Show** to select the elements to be displayed. Once you have selected the categories you want to see, you can expand and collapse the folders within the window to reveal or hide the contents inside.

The Movie Explorer also allows you to search for an item by name, including font names, symbols, ActionScript, and frame numbers. You'll search for a specific item next.

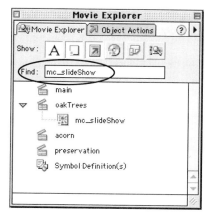

3. In the **Find** field, type the item name: **mc_slideshow** to search for an element within the project file. When Flash finds it, it will be displayed in the window.

CAUTION | Finding Files in the Movie Explorer

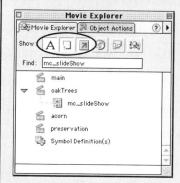

When you use the **Find** feature in the Movie Explorer, Flash will search all the categories currently selected, not all categories in the project file.

If, for example, you are searching for a movie clip, make sure you have the second button (**Show Buttons, Movie Clips and Graphics**) selected. Otherwise, the Movie Explorer will not find the item you are searching for. When you open the Movie Explorer for the first time, by default, the first three buttons (including the **Show Buttons, Movie Clips and Graphics** category circled above) are selected for you.

The Movie Explorer will also reveal ActionScript applied to frames and objects within the project file. You will see this next.

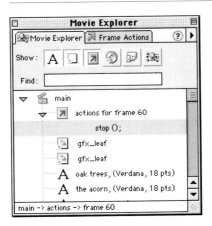

4. Click on the arrow next to the **actions for frame 60** text to reveal more elements related to that object. In this case, the Movie Explorer will reveal the actual ActionScript–the **Stop** action.

TIP | Viewing the Full Path

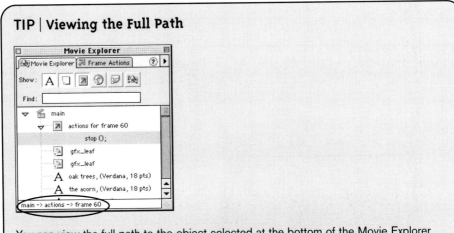

You can view the full path to the object selected at the bottom of the Movie Explorer window. Also, if the layer is not locked in the project file, Flash will select the element on the Stage when you select the element in the Movie Explorer.

5. When you are finished investigating the Movie Explorer, close the file. You will rebuild this project file in the exercises that follow.

6. _____ Recreating the Oak Tree Project

After investigating the complete project file in the first few exercises, it is now time to recreate the project. This exercise will teach you how to set up the base layers for the movie using shortcuts to maximize your production efficiency. In the following steps, you will recreate the basic elements common to all four scenes in the **siteComplete.fla** project file.

1. Open the file named **newSite.fla** inside the **Chapter_16** folder on your hard drive.

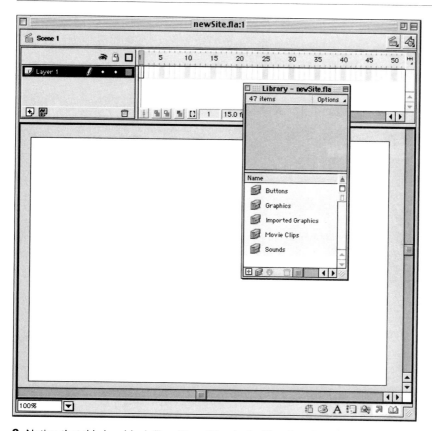

2. Notice that this is a blank file with nothing in the Timeline. Press **Cmd + L** (Mac) or **Ctrl + L** (Windows) to open the **Library**. Double-click on the folders to expand or contract them. All the elements you need to build the Web site are located in the Library, and in the following exercises, we will show you how to use these items to recreate the whole project file.

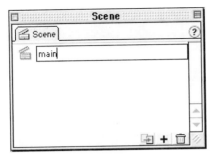

3. Choose **Modify > Scene** to open the Scene Inspector. Rename scene 1 **main**.

4. In the **main scene's** Timeline, double-click on the **Layer 1** name and rename it **background**.

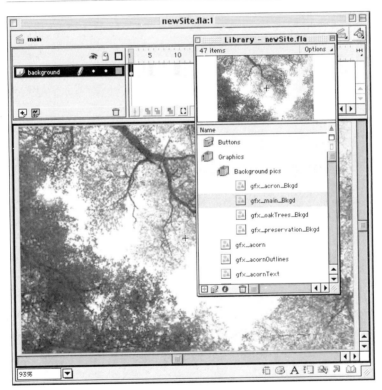

5. In the **Library**, double-click on the **Graphics** folder to expand it and double-click on the **Background pics** folder to reveal the graphic symbols inside. Drag an instance of the **gfx_main_Bkgd graphic symbol** onto the Stage.

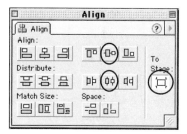

6. Using the **Align** panel, **Cmd + K** (Mac) or **Ctrl + K** (Windows), position the **gfx_main_ Bkgd graphic symbol** so it is centered on the Stage.

The Stage dimensions and the symbol dimensions are the same size. This is not a coincidence—we created the background symbols at a specific size and used the movie properties to match the movie dimensions to the size of the background images. This is a good work-flow—to plan the size of the movie and make the movie dimensions match so that you don't have to resize the images later and lose image quality.

7. Lock the **background** layer and click on the **Insert Layer** button to add a new layer to the Timeline. Name this layer **lettering**.

8. In the **Library**, locate the graphic symbol named **gfx_caOaks** inside the **Graphics** folder. Drag an instance of the **gfx_caOaks graphic symbol** onto the Stage and position it near the bottom of the Stage.

9. Use the **Transform** panel to decrease the instance's size to **80%** of the original. Use the **Effect** panel to add a tint to the instance by selecting **Tint** from the drop-down menu and typing **57** in the **R** field. If you need a brush up on how to work with these panels, refer to Chapter 7, Exercises 5 and 6.

10. Lock the **lettering** layer and click on the **Insert Layer** button to add a new layer to the Timeline. Name this layer **white**.

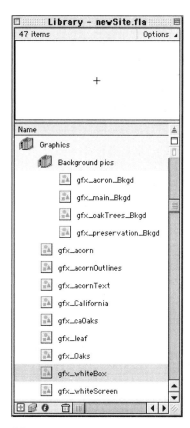

11. In the **Library**, inside the **Graphics** folder, locate the graphic symbol named **gfx_whiteBox**. Drag an instance of it onto the Stage.

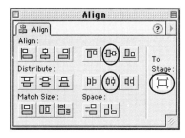

12. Using the **Align** panel, **Cmd + K** (Mac) or **Ctrl + K** (Windows), position the **gfx_ whiteBox** graphic symbol so it is centered on the Stage. You will add a motion tween and alpha effect next to make the white box change from invisible to slightly visible, and to give the background image more of a screened-back appearance.

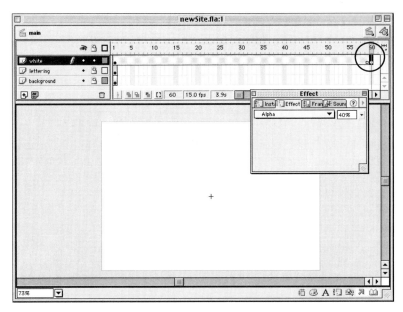

13. Press **F6** on **Frame 60** of the **white** layer to add a keyframe to it. Using the **Effect** panel, choose **Alpha** and move the slider to **40%**.

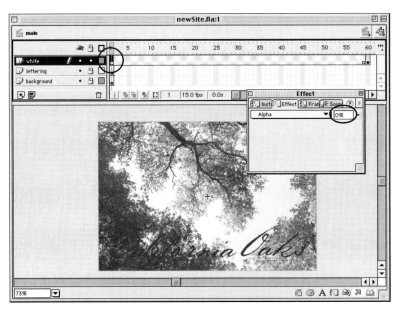

14. Click on **Keyframe 1** in the **white** layer and apply an alpha of **0%** to the instance of the **gfx_whiteBox** symbol.

15. Using the **Frame** panel, add a motion tween between the two keyframes. If you need a brush up on creating motion tweens, refer to Chapter 8, "*Motion Tweening*."

16. Select **Frame 60** on the **lettering** and **background** layers and press **F5** to add keyframes up to Frame 60 in both layers.

17. Use the **Controller** (Window > Toolbars > Controller) to test the animation on the Stage. Notice how the **gfx_whiteBox** instance starts out invisible, and then gradually ends up with an alpha of 40% in the last keyframe, creating a softened effect over the background layer.

18. Save the file and keep in open for the next exercise.

7.———————————**Adding Buttons and Scenes**

This exercise will walk you through setting up buttons, adding scenes and adding ActionScript to the buttons. In the following steps, you will recreate the more basic elements common to all four scenes in the **siteComplete.fla** project file.

1. Lock the **white** layer and click on the **Insert Layer** button to add a new layer to the Timeline. Name this layer **buttons**.

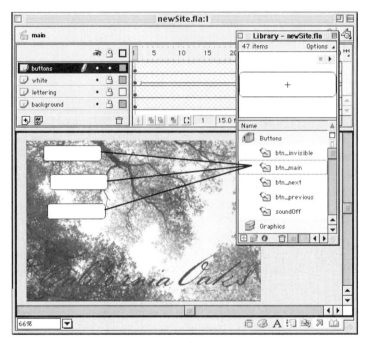

2. In the **Library**, locate the button symbol named **btn_main** inside the **Buttons** folder. Drag three instances of the btn_main symbol onto the Stage and position them near the upper-left quadrant of the Stage as shown in the picture above.

3. Press **Cmd + A** (Mac) or **Ctrl + A** (Windows) to select all three buttons at once on the Stage. This is the shortcut key for "select all." Because other layers are locked, only the button objects will become selected. Use the **Align** panel, **Cmd + K** (Mac) or **Ctrl + K** (Windows), to space all three buttons evenly.

You have just created this navigation system for the movie using three instances of only one button. Rather than create a different button symbol for each button, it's more efficient to create a generic button only once and use several instances of the it on the Stage. Then you can add distinctive text on top of each button in a different layer to differentiate between them.

4. Lock the **buttons** layer. Click on the **Insert Layer** button to add a new layer to the Timeline and name this layer **button labels**.

5. Using the **Text** tool, create three labels for the buttons by typing the words on top of the buttons: **oak trees**, the **acorn** and **preservation** respectively.

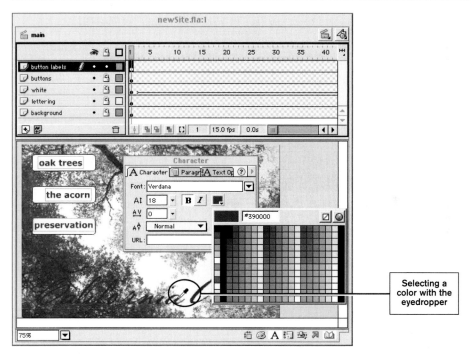

Selecting a color with the eyedropper

6. In the **Character** panel, **Cmd + T** (Mac) or **Ctrl + T** (Windows), choose **Font: Verdana**, **Font Height: 18** and select the **Bold** button. Choose the **Font Color** button, and once the **Swatches** panel opens, move your cursor outside of the panel as shown above. The cursor will change to an **eyedropper**, and you can click anywhere in on the lettering at the bottom of the Stage (shown in the picture above). This will change the font color of the button labels to match the color of the California Oaks text at the bottom of the Stage.

7. Press **Cmd + A** (Mac) or **Ctrl + A** (Windows) to select all three button labels at once on the Stage. Use the **Align** panel, **Cmd + K** (Mac) or **Ctrl + K** (Windows), to space all three button labels evenly. Now, to the user, these will look just like normal buttons, even though the buttons and the labels are on separate layers.

8. Lock the **button labels** layer and choose **Modify > Scene** to open the **Scene** panel.

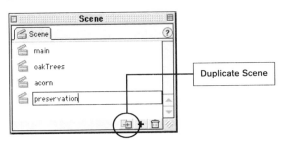

9. Click on the **Duplicate Scene** button three times to make three copies of the **main** scene. Rename each of the new scenes **oakTrees**, **acorn** and **preservation**, respectively. The movie will now have a total of four scenes with the exact same layers, layer names, and artwork.

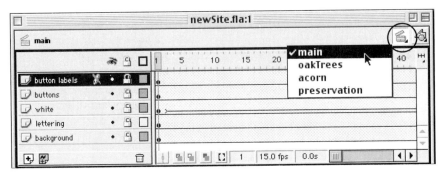

10. In the Timeline, click on the **Edit Scene** button to look at the menu, which should include the new scene names you just created. If you choose any of these scene names, you'll see that all the layers that were in the main scene are now in the other three scenes. Return to **main** when you are finished looking.

NOTE | Why did I need to follow this workflow?

Although there are many ways to recreate the **siteComplete.fla** file, we have found that this is one of the most efficient ways to do it. If you know that several sections within a project will have similar elements, then you can cut down your production time by making the element once and duplicating it several times. You have seen this with the button instances in Step 2 and again with the scenes in Step 9. So rather than creating all these layers from scratch in each scene, you can duplicate and rename them. This is a quick way to get all the basic elements you need for each scene in place. You will add ActionScript to the buttons next.

11. Unlock the **buttons** layer and select the **first** button.

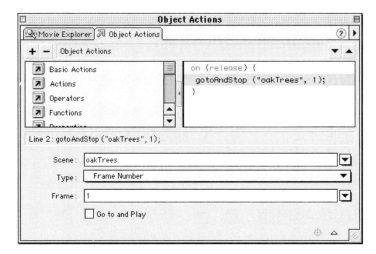

12. Choose **Window > Actions** to open the **Object Actions** panel. From **the Basic Actions** list, choose **Go To** and in the **Scene** field at the bottom of the **Actions** panel, choose **oakTrees**. Click on the box next to **Go to and Play** to deselect it, making the ActionScript read **gotoAndStop**. Your ActionScript should look like the picture above.

This ActionScript will tell Flash that when a user clicks and releases the top button, go to the oakTrees scene and stop there on Frame 1. If you feel like you need a brush up on your ActionScripting, see Chapter 12.

13. Repeat Step 12 on the **middle** and **bottom** button to add ActionScripting to each of these button instances. Make sure to select **Scene: acorn** for the middle button and select **Scene: preservation** for the bottom button.

14. Click anywhere in the **buttons** layer to select everything on that layer. Choose **Edit > Copy Frames** to copy the frames in this layer.

15. Click on the **Edit Scene** button in the Timeline and choose **oakTrees** to open its Timeline. Unlock the **buttons** layer, select the first keyframe and choose **Edit > Paste Frames**. This will paste the buttons with the ActionScripting intact into the **buttons** layer for that scene.

TIP | Pasting Frames

When you paste frames into a frame that already contains content, Flash will overwrite the old content with the new content. You will not end up with duplicate buttons in the same layer using this method. Instead, Flash will erase the old buttons before it places the new ones there. You might wonder, why not create the ActionScripting for each button, one at a time, in each scene? It is much more efficient to create the ActionScripting once and then simply copy the frames into each of the scenes.

---

16. Repeat Step 15 in the two remaining scenes to paste the frames from the button layer in the main Timeline into each scene's Timeline. When you are finished with this step, you will have four scenes, each with artwork, buttons and ActionScripting.

17. Save the file and keep it open for the next exercise.

8. ——————Swapping Symbols and Modifying Button Behavior

This exercise will show you how to use the **Instance** panel to swap symbols and to change the behavior of several button instances. In the following steps, you will work with each scene except the main scene to alter its appearance.

1. In the Timeline, click on the **Edit Scene** button and choose the **oakTrees** scene.

2. Choose **Cmd + I** (Mac) or **Ctrl + I** (Windows) to open the **Instance** panel.

3. In the **oakTrees** Timeline, unlock the **background** layer and select the first frame to select the **gfx_main_Bkgd** symbol instance on the Stage.

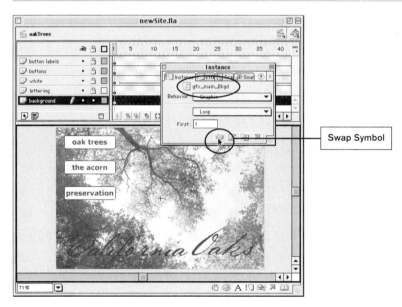

4. In the **Instance** panel, click on the **Swap Symbol** button. You will use the Swap Symbol feature to change the background image to a different image in the Library.

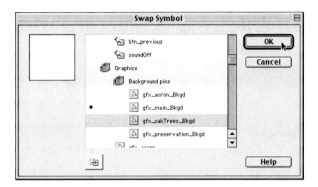

5. From the **Swap Symbol** window that appears, click on the **gfx_oakTrees_Bkgd** symbol and click **OK**. This will swap the **gfx_main_Bkgd** symbol instance on the Stage with the new **gfx_oakTrees_Bkgd** symbol instance. Notice the black dot next to the symbol icon in the Swap Symbol window represents the symbol that is currently on the Stage. **Tip:** You can also double-click on the new image that you want to use, rather than selecting the image and then clicking on the OK button.

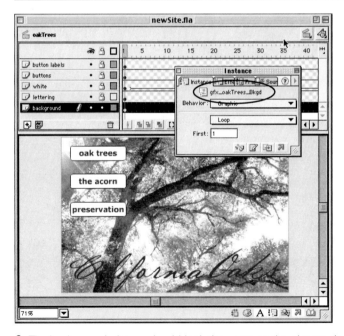

6. The background picture should look the same as the picture above. In the **Instance** panel, notice the name of the instance is updated as well. The Swap Symbols feature is a great way to quickly change the look of a scene by substituting one image for another one. Lock the **background** layer.

7. Click on the **Edit Scenes** button in the Timeline and choose **acorn** to open the acorn scene.

8. In the **acorn** scene, repeat Steps 3, 4 and 5 to swap the background symbol instance with the symbol named **gfx_acorn_Bkgd**. This will change the background image in the acorn scene.

9. When you are finished, lock the **background** layer.

10. Click on the **Edit Scenes** button in the Timeline and choose **preservation** to open the **preservation** scene's Timeline.

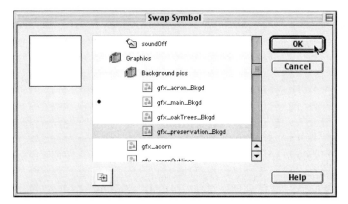

11. In the **preservation** scene, repeat Steps 3, 4 and 5 to swap the **background** symbol instance with the symbol named **gfx_preservation_Bkgd**. This will change the background image in the preservation scene.

12. When you are finished, lock the **background** layer in the **preservation** scene.

Using the Swap Symbol feature on the Instance panel, you have created three different scene backgrounds in a few clicks of the mouse! The artwork changed, but it remained in the same perfect position as the original. This is another great strategy for keeping artwork registered in the same position, but changing the content.

13. You should still be in the **preservation** scene. Unlock the **button** layer and select the bottom button that has the text label **preservation**. Make sure that you select the button, not the text label!

14. Next to the **Instance** panel, click on the **Effect** tab to open the **Effect** panel.

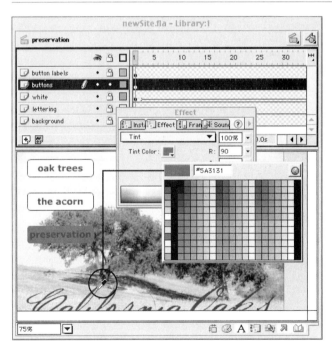

15. Choose **Tint** from the drop-down menu and using the eyedropper, click on the lettering at the bottom of the Stage to match the color.

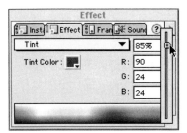

16. Move the slider down to make the **Tint: 85%**. This will make this button different from the other two buttons. It serves as an identity label to let users know they are in the preservation section of the Web site.

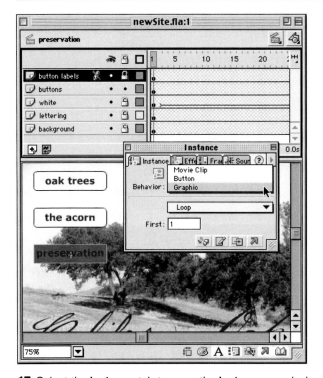

17. Select the **Instance** tab to open the **Instance** panel, choose **Graphic** from the **Behavior** drop-down menu. This will change the symbol instance behavior from that of an interactive button to that of a graphic that just remains stationary on the Stage. The original symbol in the Library will remain unchanged.

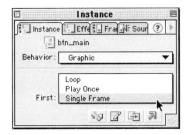

18. Click on the drop-down menu next under the Behavior setting and choose **Single Frame**. This is important to make sure the graphic doesn't loop and instead it remains static at one frame.

By changing the behavior of the button to a graphic symbol, the user will no longer be able to click on this button. You may be thinking, why am I doing this? The reason is for good user-interface design. When users are inside the preservation scene, there is no need to click on the preservation button because they are already in that location. However, you'll want to visually reinforce the user's location. In the next steps, you will change the color of the text label for this "button turned graphic."

---

19. Lock the **button** layer and unlock the **button labels** layer.

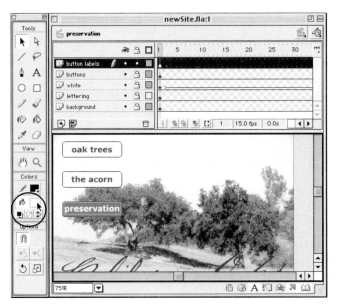

20. Select the **preservation** label text and choose **white** from the Fill Color in the Toolbox to change the text to white.

---

21. Repeat Steps 15 through 20 in the **acorn** scene and **oakTrees** scene. In the acorn scene, change only the behavior, tint, and text color for the **acorn** button. Likewise, in the oakTrees scene, change only the behavior, tint and text color for the **oak trees** button.
Tip: You can always refer to the **siteComplete.fla** file to see how the finished product looks.

22. When you're finished, save the file and keep it open for the next exercise.

Instance Properties Panel

Once you place an instance of a symbol on the Stage, you can modify the behavior of a symbol instance, or switch that instance out for another one rather quickly. The **Instance** panel allows you to make changes to any symbol instances on the Stage.

Changing the Behavior of a Symbol

There are three behavior settings in the Instance panel: **Graphic**, **Button** or **Movie Clip**. You can define the behavior for an instance by selecting one of the three options from the drop-down list. For example, if you decide that a graphic symbol instance should behave like a button (so that you can add ActionScripting to it), you can change its behavior by choosing *Button Behavior* from the drop-down list. Changing the behavior of an instance using the Instance panel allows the original symbol to remain unaltered, and saves you time by eliminating the need to create another symbol from scratch. You will do just this in the next exercise.

The **Graphic Behavior** has a Play Mode option section, allowing you to define how its Timeline will work in relation to the Timeline that contains it.

The **Button Behavior** setting lets you choose among three Track options. These options help you define how the button instance will work when it is in a pop-up menu.

The **Movie Clip Behavior** has a field called *Name* where you can type in a name for this instance. Naming an instance will come in handy when you expand on your ActionScripting skills. You can use the name to give commands to this instance.

The options in the lower portion of the Instance panel will change, depending on which behavior you have assigned to the symbol. In the following exercise, you will change the behavior of several button symbols.

Instance Panel Button Options

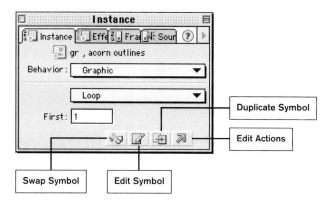

Duplicate Symbol

Edit Actions

Swap Symbol

Edit Symbol

At the bottom of the Instance panel, there are four buttons from which you can modify the instance further: **Swap Symbol**, **Edit Symbol**, **Duplicate Symbol** and **Edit Actions**. You will learn to use the Swap Symbol button in the next exercise. A description of each button at the bottom of the Instance panel follows.

Instance Panel Button Options Explained	
The Swap Symbol button	Allows you to change the symbol that is used for this instance and replace it with another symbol from the Library.
The Edit Symbol button	Opens the symbol's timeline so that you can edit the symbol.
The Duplicate Symbol button	Makes a copy of the symbol in the Library.

9. _____Cleaning Up the Scenes and Adding Stop Actions

This short exercise will show you how to delete multiple frames on multiple layers all at one time to remove unnecessary frames. You will add a Stop action to each of the Timelines in each of the scenes to keep Flash from playing one scene right after another.

1. Using the **Edit Scenes** button, select the **oakTrees** scene to open that scene's Timeline. Notice how there are 60 frames.

In this scene, the only reason there are 60 frames is due to the tween of the white box. That layer is the only one that has another keyframe past Frame 1. This effect was ideal for the opening scene of the movie, but it would be overkill to make the users sit though a fade in each scene. Therefore, in the following steps, you will take the tween out and simply add an alpha on the first keyframe of the white layer.

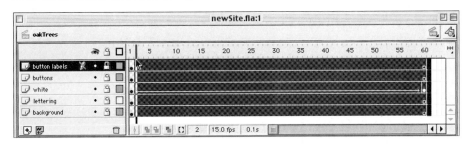

2. Start at the **background** layer, **Frame 61** and click and drag diagonally to the left, to **Frame 2** in the **button labels** layer to select that group of frames.

3. Ctrl + Click (Mac) or **Right Click** (Windows) to access the drop-down contextual menu. Choose **Remove Frames** to remove all the frames from **Frame 2** forward from the Timeline.

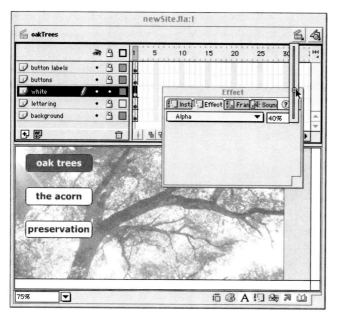

4. Unlock the **white** layer and using the **Effects** panel, use the slider to change the **Alpha** to **40%**. This will fade the background out to the same degree that the motion tween stopped at in the **main** scene, Frame 60.

5. Lock the **white** layer of this scene.

6. Repeat Steps 1 through 5 inside the **acorn** and **preservation** scenes to delete the unnecessary frames and add 40% alpha to the white box on the **white** layer in those scenes.

7. When you are finished, open the **preservation** layer's Timeline. You will add the Stop action to the Timeline next.

8. Click on the **Insert Layer** button to add a new layer to the Timeline. Name this layer: **actions**. Make sure this layer is on top of all the other layers to stay consistent.

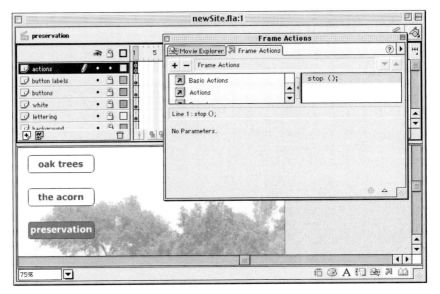

9. Select the first frame and using the **Frame Actions** panel (**Window > Actions**), add a **Stop** action to the first frame. This will stop the Playhead at Frame 1. If you need a brush up on ActionScripting, refer to Chapter 12, "*ActionScripting Basics.*"

10. Select the actions layer and choose **Edit > Copy Frames**. Next, rather than repeating these steps in each scene, you will paste the frame with the Stop action already in place into the other scenes.

11. Open the **acorn** scene's Timeline.

12. Click on the **Insert Layer** button to add a new layer to the Timeline. Name this layer: **actions**. Make sure this layer is on top.

13. With the first frame selected, choose **Edit > Paste Frames**. This will paste the frame with the Stop action into the actions layer of the acorn scene.

14. Repeat Steps 12 and 13 in the **acorn** and **main** scene's Timeline to add **Stop** actions to both of those scenes.

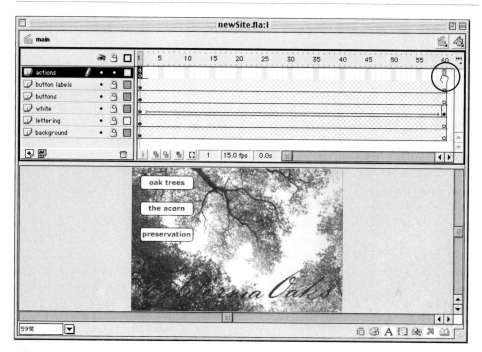

15. In the **main** scene's Timeline, click and drag the first keyframe in the **actions** layer to **Frame 60**. You need to do this because you don't want the Playhead to stop until it has reached the last frame in this scene, Frame 60.

16. When you are finished, choose **Control > Test Movie** to preview the movie at this stage! Click the buttons to test the scenes. Notice how the background of each scene is different, and that the button of the scene you are in is not clickable, but is a different color. You will add content to each scene in the following exercises.

If any element of the movie is not working properly, you can reread the steps to trouble-shoot the problem or refer to the finished file, siteComplete.fla, to compare to your file.

17. When you are finished, save this file and keep it open for the next exercise.

IO. _____Finishing the Main Scene

To complete the main scene, you will create a guide layer to make the falling leaf animation and add a sound layer.

1. Open the main scene and insert a new layer under the actions layer. Name the layer: **path**. This will be the motion guide layer that the leaf follows as you saw in the **siteComplete.fla** file.

2. Select the **Pencil** tool (or press **Y** on the keyboard) and draw a path for the leaf to follow.

In Chapter 8, "Motion Tweening," you created this same animation of the leaf falling in the Motion Guide exercise. We encourage you to revisit that exercise if you need a brush up on creating motion guides, as the steps that follow will be brief.

3. Change this layer into a guide layer.

4. Add a layer to the Timeline that will be the guided layer and name this layer: **leaf**.

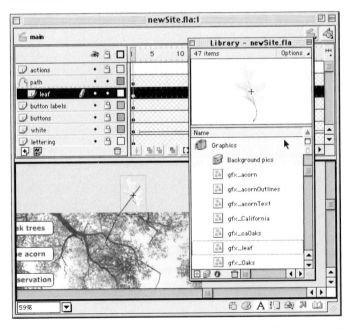

5. Drag an instance of the **gfx_leaf** symbol from the **Library** onto the leaf layer and make sure it snaps to the **guide** layer.

6. Add the ending keyframe for the end-point of the leaf and add a tween to finish the animation effect.

You can also refer to the siteComplete.fla to see the finished version of the motion guide animation.

7. Add a new layer below the actions layer and name this layer **sound**.

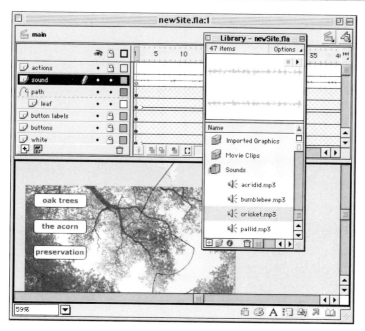

8. With the first frame selected in the **sound** layer, drag an instance of the **cricket.mp3** from the Library onto the Stage.

9. Select the **sound** waveform in the Timeline and choose **Window > Panels > Sound** to open the **Sound** panel.

10. Select **Stream** from the **Sync** drop-down menu. This will make the sound and the leaf animation keep pace with each other.

11. Choose **Control > Test Movie** to preview the changes and additions you made to the main scene in this exercise.

12. Save the file and keep it open for the next exercise. You'll work with the oakTrees scene next.

II. ——————————Finishing the OakTrees Scene

In this exercise, you will create a slide show just as you did in the ActionScripting chapter. However, in this exercise, you will create the slide show inside a movie clip and then you will add the movie clip to the scene.

1. Open the oakTrees scene and in the Timeline, insert a new layer under the actions layer. Name the layer: **slide show mc**. This layer will hold the movie clip of the slide show you will create in the next few steps.

2. In the Library, expand the **Movie Clips** folder and double-click on the **mc_slideshow** to open the movie clip symbol.

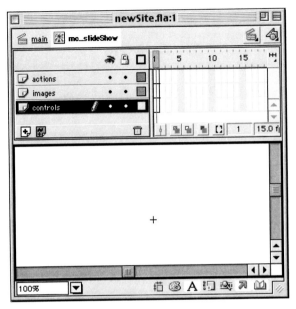

Notice the three layers named actions, images and controls. We have created this movie clip symbol to get you started.

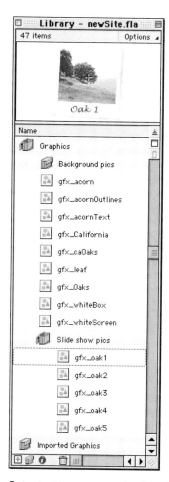

3. In the Library, open the **Graphics** folder and locate the subfolder named **Slide show pics**. Open that folder and notice five graphic symbols. These will be the slide show images.

4. In the images layer, drag the **gfx_oak1** symbol into **Keyframe 1**, and center it on the Stage so that the center crosshair of the symbol matches the center crosshair of the Stage. **Note**: You can also use the Info panel to set the X and Y coordinates to 0, 0.

5. After you have lined up the crosshairs, press **F6** in **Frames 2**, **3**, **4** and **5** to add a keyframe to each of these frames.

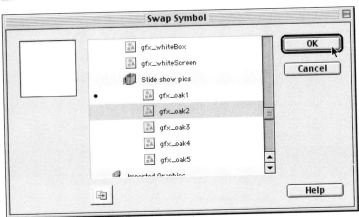

6. Select the instance in **Frame 2** and using the **Instance** panel, swap the symbol in Frame 2 with **gfx_oak2** symbol. This will change the **gfx_oak1** symbol to the **gfx_oak2** symbol in that frame.

7. Repeat Step 6 for **Keyframes 3**, **4** and **5** to swap each symbol with the corresponding oak image, **gfx_oak3**, **gfx_oak4** and **gfx_oak5** respectively. When you are finished, you should have a different oak tree image in each of the keyframes.

NOTE | Swap Symbols with Bitmap Sequences

If you import a series of bitmap images, as you did in Exercise 2 of Chapter 9, "*Bitmaps*." the sequence of images will appear in your Timeline in perfect registration, and with keyframes. This exercise is different however, because you are not importing the artwork it's already in your Library. If each of the images of the oak trees were in your Library as bitmaps, but not as symbols, you would not be able to use the swap symbol feature and instead, you would have to spend a lot of time trying to align each image perfectly in position with the last keyframe. The swap symbols feature allows you to position the art-work (which has been imported and then turned into a symbol) only once, copy it four more times, and swap out the artwork in one frame for a different image with a few clicks of the mouse. If you ever do this on your own—aligning several images on different keyframes like you did here—convert those images to symbols and use this swap symbol technique. It beats aligning each image frame-by-frame!

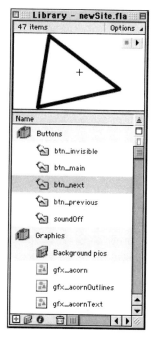

8. On the **control** layer, drag out the button symbols named **btn_next** and **btn_previous**, located in the **Buttons** folder in the Library. Add the ActionScript to each of the buttons to make Flash either advance to the next frame to go to the previous frame. Review Chapter 12, "*ActionScripting Basics*," if you need a refresher on how this is done.

If you need a brush-up on creating a slide show, we encourage you to review the Slide Show exercise inside Chapter 12, "ActionScripting Basics." You can also take a look at the siteComplete.fla file to view the finished slide show.

9. Complete the slide show by adding the **Stop** action to the first keyframe in the **actions** layer and pressing **F5** in **Frame 5** to add frames between the two of them.

When you are finished, your movie clip symbol Timeline should look like the picture above.

10. Return to the **OakTrees** Timeline and select the first frame of the slide show mc layer. Drag an instance of the completed **mc_slideshow** movie clip onto the Stage and position it to the right of the buttons, above the lettering at the bottom of the Stage, similar to the picture above.

11. Choose **Control > Test Movie** to preview the changes and additions you made to the oakTrees scene in this exercise.

12. Save the file and keep it open for the next exercise.

12. _____Finishing the Acorn Scene

In this exercise, you will add text and a white screen background behind the text so that it is readable. You will also create a page title and add a movie clip animation to the Timeline.

1. Open the acorn scene and insert a new layer under the actions layer. Name the layer: **white screen**.

---

2. In the Library, locate the symbol named **gfx_whiteBox** in the **Graphics** folder. Drag an instance of the symbol onto the Stage.

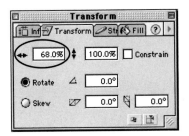

3. Using the **Transform** panel, change the **width** to **68%**. **Note**: Make sure the constrain checkbox is *not* checked.

4. Position the **gfx_ whiteBox** on the right side of the Stage using the **Alignment** panel as shown in the picture above. This white screen will cover a little more than half the movie, so that the text you are about to add will be more legible and not have to compete with the background image.

5. With the **gfx_whiteBox** instance selected on the Stage, use the **Effects** panel to add an **Alpha** of **65%** to the graphic symbol.

6. Lock the white screen layer and add a new layer above it. Name this new layer: **paragraph**.

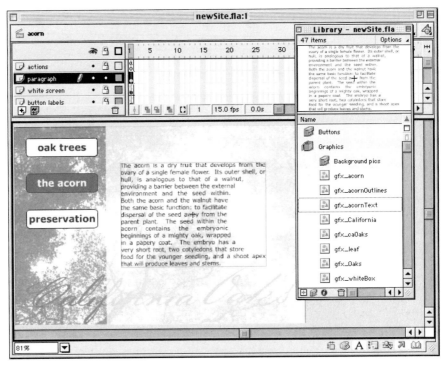

7. In the Library, locate the symbol named **gfx_acornText** in the **Graphics** folder. Drag an instance of the symbol onto the Stage and position it as shown in the picture above.

This text was originally created in an outside program, imported in Flash and turned into a symbol. The same text layout effect can be created in programs such as Freehand or Illustrator and then imported into Flash. Notice that the right side of the paragraph is curved? You can't easily create curved paragraphs like this in Flash.

8. Lock the **paragraph** layer and add a new layer above it. Name this new layer: **title**.

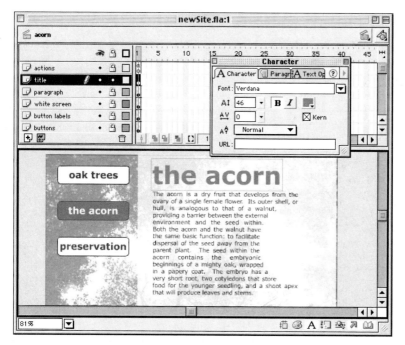

9. Using the **Text** tool, type the words: **the acorn** above the text paragraph. In the **Character** panel, choose **Font: Verdana**, **Font Height: 46**, click the **Bold** button and choose an olive color from the color picker.

10. Lock the title layer and add a new layer above it. Name this new layer: **acorn anim**.

11. In the Library, locate the **mc_acornFade** inside the **Movie Clips** folder and double-click on it to open the movie clip's Timeline.

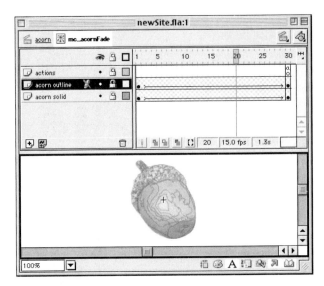

This movie clip consists of two motion tweens and a Stop action of the last keyframe.

12. At the top of the Timeline, click on the **acorn** scene name to return to the its Timeline and select the first frame in the **acorn anim** layer.

13. Drag an instance of the **mc_acornFade** movie clip onto the Stage and position it just to the right of the text. This will add a dynamic element to this portion of the movie.

14. Choose **Control > Test Movie** to preview the new additions to the movie.

15. When you are finished, save the file and keep it open for the next exercise. You will work with the preservation scene next.

13. _____Finishing the Preservation Scene

In this exercise, you will copy and paste frames from the previous scene to maximize your production efficiency. In the following steps, we will also teach you how to add an invisible button to launch a Web site.

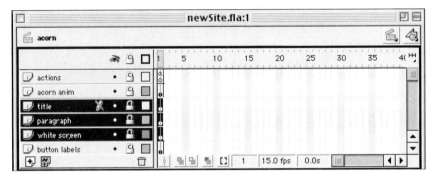

1. Make sure you are still in the **acorn** scene and select the **title**, **paragraph** and **white screen** layers. Choose **Edit > Copy Frames** to copy all the contents in the frames of those three layers.

---

2. Using the **Edit Scenes** button, choose the **preservation** scene. In the Timeline under the **actions** layer, add a new layer.

Select the first frame of the new layer and choose **Edit > Paste Frames**. Flash will paste the clipboard contents into three new layers. Even though you only added one new layer, Flash will automatically add two more layers to accommodate the layers you chose when you selected Edit > Copy Frames.

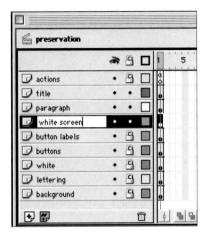

3. Name the appropriate layers **title**, **paragraph** and **white screen** respectively. When you are finished, lock the white screen and the title layers. The content that you just pasted will be for the acorn section, but that's okay for now. You'll be swapping that out soon!

4. Select the first frame of the **paragraph** layer to select the graphic symbol instance on the Stage. In the **Instance** panel, click on the **Swap Symbol** button.

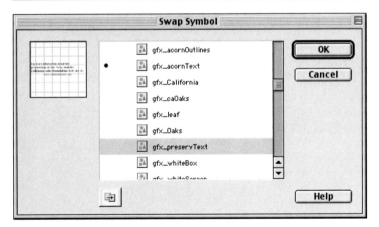

5. In the **Swap Symbol** dialog box, double-click on the **gfx_preservText** symbol to switch the paragraph with the new text.

6. In the **Library**, locate the **btn_invisible** button symbol in the **Buttons** folder. If you remember from Chapter 12, an invisible button only contains artwork in the Hit state. This makes it invisible to the end user, but still has actions attached to it. Drag an instance of it onto the Stage over the red lettering. Use the **Scale** tool to increase the width of the button so that the invisible button covers all the red text.

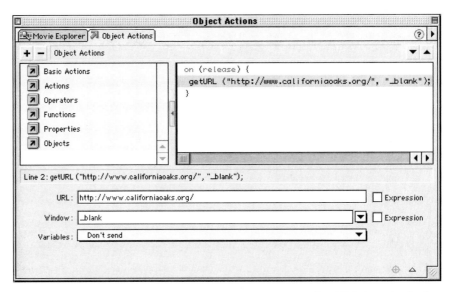

7. With the **btn_invisible** selected, choose **Basic Actions > Get URL** from the **Actions** panel, and type in the address: **http://www.californiaoaks.org** in the URL field. Select **Window**: **_blank** in the next field. This will launch the California Oaks Web site in a separate window. Leave the **Variables** field alone.

8. Lock the **paragraph** layer and unlock the **title** layer. Select the first keyframe and using the **Text** tool, change the text to read: **preservation**.

By using the Paste Frames feature, the title will end up in the same exact location as the acorn scene's title. So rather than trying to guess exactly where the title was in the last scene, the Paste Frames feature allows you to simply modify the text itself and the alignment will remain the same as long as you do not move the text box.

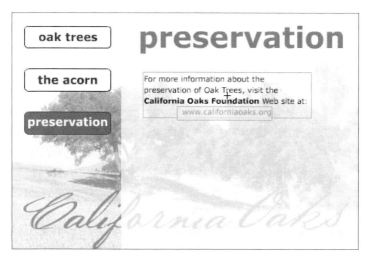

9. Unlock the **paragraph** layer and click in the first keyframe to select all the content in that frame. Move the paragraph higher on the Stage so that the page layout looks better.

10. Choose **Control > Test Movie!** Test the invisible button to see if it works... **Note**: you must be connected to the Internet to access the URL in a browser.

11. When you are finished, save the file and keep it open for the final exercises on printing.

Printing from the Project File

Printing capabilities are new to Flash 5. There are two environments from which you can print: the project file (.fla) and the Flash Player. In the project file, you can choose to print all frames in the movie or the first frame of each scene, for example. In the Flash Player, you can specify which frames will be printable by a *user* viewing the movie. This exercise will show you how to set up the parameters and print a section of the movie from inside the project file. Then, the following exercise will show you how to allow your users to print from the Flash Player.

1. The project file should still be open and if not, choose **File > Open** to open **newsite.fla**. Select **File > Print Margins** (Mac) or **File > Page Setup** (Windows) to open the corresponding dialog box.

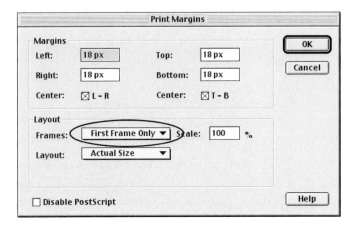

Macintosh and Windows dialog boxes differ slightly although the Layout options (circled above) are the same. The picture above is from a Macintosh.

2. From the **Frames** option in the **Layout** section of the dialog box, choose **First Frame Only** to print the first frame in each scene.

The other option, All Frames, will print all the frames in the movie.

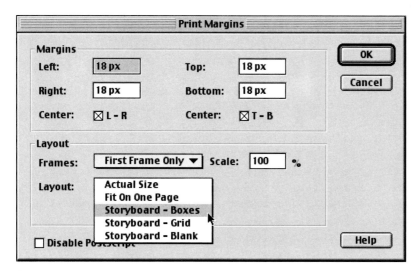

3. From the **Layout** drop-down menu choose **Storyboard-Boxes**. This will determine how you want the frames to appear on the page.

4. After you are finished setting up the options, click **OK**.

Layout Settings

The Layout settings will allow you to select from five options, which are described in the table below.

Printing Layout Options Explained	
Actual Size	Prints the frame at full size.
Fit On One Page	Increases or decreases the size of the each frame so that it fills the print area of the page.
Storyboard-Boxes	Prints multiple thumbnails on one page and creates a rectangle around each thumbnail.
Storyboard-Grid	Prints multiple thumbnails inside a grid on each page.
Storyboard Blank	Prints multiple thumbnails on one page and prints only the artwork inside each thumbnail.

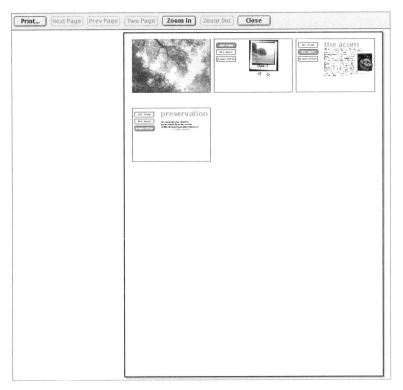

5. Choose **File > Print Preview** to preview how the printed page will look based on the settings you selected in the steps above.

6. Choose **Print** from the **Print Preview** window to print the first frames of each scene from the project file.

CAUTION | Problems with Postscript

There have been reported problems printing Flash files on a PostScript printer. If your printer is not capable of printing PostScript, make sure you select the **Disable PostScript** in the Print Margins dialog box (Mac) or in Preferences (Windows). You can visit **http://www.macromedia.com/support/flash/** for more detailed information on how to troubleshoot PostScript printer issues.

---

7. You have just printed your first document from inside Flash! Save the file and leave it open for the next exercise.

15. ————————Printing from the Flash Player

In addition to printing files from within the project file, you can specify which frames will be printable by users viewing the movie in the Flash Player. This exercise will teach you how to add ActionScripting to a button and set up the printing parameters for your users.

1. In the project file, click on the **Edit Scenes** button to access the drop-down list. Choose **preservation** to open the preservation scene's Timeline.

2. Add a new layer to the Timeline below the actions layer and name this layer: **label**.

3. With the first frame selected in the **Label** layer, open the **Frame** panel, **Window > Panels > Frame**.

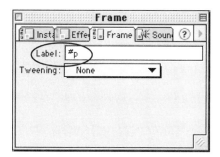

4. Type **#p** in the **Label** field of the **Frame** panel to define that keyframe as printable.

NOTE | Printing from the Contextual Menu

You can permit your users to access the Print command from the drop-down contextual menu. The contextual menu will appear in the Flash Player when a user on a Mac chooses **Ctrl + Click** or a Windows user right-clicks on the movie.

By default, the Print option in the contextual menu will print every frame in the movie. However, you can change this by labeling certain keyframes as printable in the project file (as you did in Step 4) and thus restricting the users to print only the frames you specify.

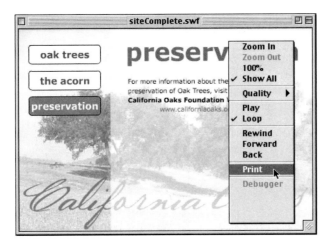

5. Choose **Control > Test Movie**, **Ctrl + Click** (Mac) or **Right-Click** (Windows) on the movie to access the drop-down contextual menu. Choose **Print** to print the frame you labeled in Step 4.

After you have defined a keyframe as printable, when a user accesses the drop-down menu and chooses Print, Flash will print only the frames labeled as #p. **Note:** When you add the #p label to a frame, you must attach the label to a keyframe, not a frame.

In addition to allowing access to the drop-down menu, you can also allow the user to print frames within the movie by attaching ActionScript to a button that will print the frames you specify. To do this, you must first create the printable frame labels as you did in the steps above and then you can create the button, which you will do in the steps that follow.

6. Lock the **label** layer and add another new layer to the Timeline below the label layer and name this layer **print button**.

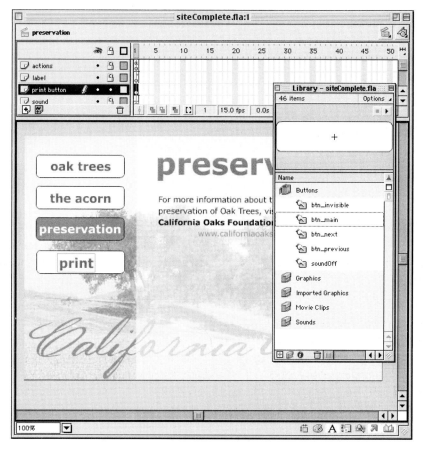

7. Drag an instance of the **btn_main** button onto the Stage under the preservation button. With the text tool, add the label **print** on top of the button.

8. Select the button (make sure you don't select the text) and choose **Window > Actions** to open the **Object Actions** panel.

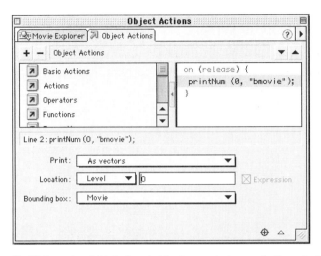

9. Click on the **Add Action** (+) button and choose **Actions > Print**. You can leave the specifications in the lower part of the **Actions** panel at their default settings. Adding this ActionScript will give the user the ability to click on the button to print the keyframes you have specified.

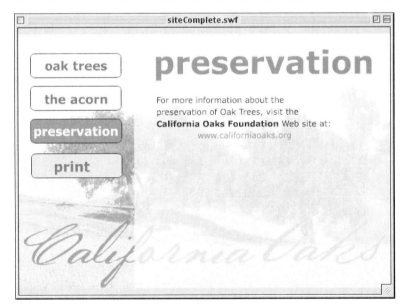

10. Choose **Control > Test Movie** and test the print button by clicking on it in the preview window! Your printer will print the frame you labeled with the #p.

11. When you are finished, save and close the file.

You have conquered another chapter! You should now have a more solid understanding of how the different pieces within this book come together to make a whole. Now there is only one more important chapter left: Chapter 17, "Integration."

I7.

Integration

| Bringing Fireworks Content Into Flash |
| Editing PNG Files in Flash |
| Importing FreeHand Content as Keyframes |
| Importing FreeHand Content as Scenes |
| Dreamweaver | QuickTime | Illustrator

chap_17

Flash 5
H•O•T CD-ROM

Though many designers work exclusively in Flash, the program doesn't have to be used like an island unto itself. There are many opportunities to combine other tools with it. The following hands-on exercises show how to use Fireworks, Dreamweaver, FreeHand, Illustrator and QuickTime with Flash. Keep in mind that in order to try these exercises, you must have these programs installed on your system. If you don't own this software, save this chapter for another time. You never know when you'll be adding new programs to your system, or working for someone else who has them.

I. _____Bringing Fireworks Content Into Flash

There will be times when you'll want to bring in images into Flash from other applications. This is especially true of images you can't create from scratch in Flash, such as those that contain bevels or glows.
While you can use applications other than Fireworks (such as Photoshop or PaintShop Pro), the
advantage to using Fireworks is that colors and text remain editable objects in Flash. Alternatively,
you can import a flattened (bitmap)image, which is necessary if you want to preserve any bevels
and/or glows contained in the original Fireworks artwork. The following exercise will take you through
some basic techniques for importing Firework's .png files, as both editable and flattened objects.

1. Copy the **chap_17** folder, located on the **H•O•T CD-ROM**, to your hard drive. You need to
have this folder on your hard drive in order to save files inside it.

2. Choose **File > New** to create a new blank document. Save this file as **integrate.fla** inside
the **chap_17** folder.

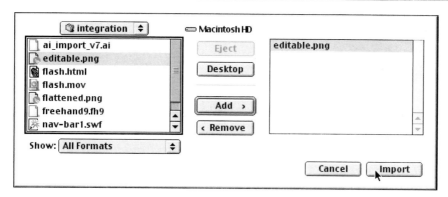

3. Select **File > Import**. Browse to the **chap_17** folder and locate the **editable.png** file.
Select this file and click the **Add** button. Click **Import**. Windows users would click **Open**.

4. Flash will automatically detect that you are trying to import a Fireworks .png file. The **Fireworks PNG Import Settings** dialog box will open.

5. Make sure the **Import Editable Objects** radio button and all of the checkboxes beneath it are selected, and click **OK**. The options in this dialog box allow you to determine if the imported .png files will contain editable objects such as images, text and/or guides, or if the .png files will be imported as a flattened image with nothing editable.

Note: Importing a .png file with editable objects allows all the vector information to remain as vector information and even allows text to be editable. However, you will lose bitmap effects, such as bevels and glows.

6. Using the **Arrow** tool on the Stage, double-click inside the block of text and type in "**about us**." See how easy this is to edit and change?

Note: By default, when importing a .png file as Editable Objects, Flash may move your text to the bottom of your artwork, even if the text of the original .png was centered. However, this should not be of major concern to you because the text is editable, and you can move your text block to any location you wish!

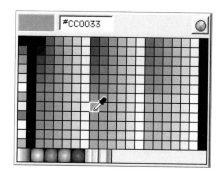

7. Click to select the **background** of the shape, and change the fill by selecting a new color from the **Fill** color panel. Make sure the shape is selected before you choose a new color.

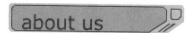

Your artwork should look just like the picture above.

You just learned how to import Fireworks .png files as editable objects, which allows you to modify object attributes such as the type and object color. In the next part of this exercise, you will learn how to import Fireworks documents as flattened images. Importing flattened .png files allows you to retain effects like bevels and glows; however, you lose the ability to edit the object as a vector because it is imported as a bitmap graphic.

8. Choose **File > Import** to open the **Import File** dialog box. Browse to the **chap_17** folder and locate the **flattened.png** file. Select this file, click the **Add** button, and then choose **Import**. Windows users would click **Open**.

9. Flash will automatically detect that you are trying to import a Fireworks .png file, and the **Fireworks PNG Import Settings** dialog box will appear again. This time, choose **Flatten Image** and click **OK**. This file is identical to the one that you imported in the first part of this exercise. However, because you are now importing the file as a flattened image, you will see a noticeable difference in the image's appearance.

Note: This file was created inside Fireworks with a transparent background and saved as a .png. If you follow this method of creating and saving from Fireworks, the transparency properties will remain intact when you import the file into Flash.

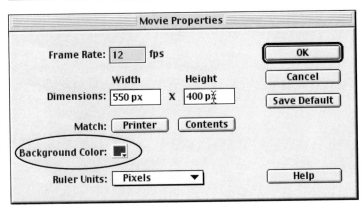

10. Press **Cmd + M** (Mac) or **Ctrl +M** (Windows) to access the movie properties. Select a dark background color and choose **OK**. Changing the background color of the Stage helps demonstrate that the transparency of this file has been preserved.

Notice how Flash honored the transparency in both graphics. While importing .png files as editable objects loses some bitmap effects, and importing as flattened image loses the ability to edit the objects, neither method loses the transparency.

You have just learned how to import artwork into Flash as either editable or flattened objects. Next, you will learn how to modify those files using Fireworks from right inside Flash. Keep this file open for the next exercise.

2.————————Editing PNG Files in Flash

In this exercise, you will learn how to modify a Fireworks .png file directly within Flash. The difference between this exercise and the previous one is that Flash will allow you to modify the flattened image in Fireworks without you ever having to leave Flash to do it!

Note: You must have Fireworks 4 installed in order to complete this exercise. We have included a trial-version of Fireworks 4 on the Flash 5 H*O*T CD-ROM. It is located inside the **software** folder on the CD-ROM.

1. Select the **flattened.png** bitmap image you just imported from Fireworks and open your Library by pressing **Cmd + L** (Mac) or **Ctrl + L** (Windows). Now, highlight the item in your Library.

2. From the **Options** menu in the upper-right corner of your **Library** window choose **Edit with Fireworks 4**. This will automatically open **flattened.png** in the Fireworks program.

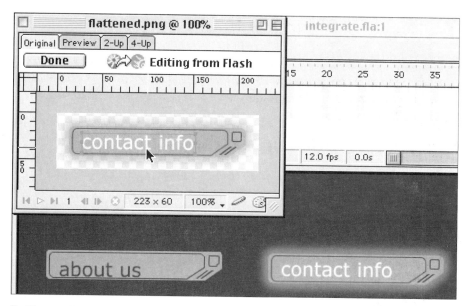

3. Change the text of the object in Fireworks 4 by double-clicking on the text, which will open the **Text Editor.** Type **contact info**, select a new color and click **OK**.

4. In Fireworks, choose **File > Update** and then go back to Flash and you will see that your file has been instantly updated!

5. Save and close the file; you won't need it for future exercises.

3. _____Importing FreeHand Content as Keyframes

As the creator of both Flash and FreeHand, Macromedia has strengthened the compatibility between the two programs with the release of Flash 5. Flash allows you to import FreeHand 7, 8 or 9 files and turn them into a Flash Web site with a few easy steps. The next exercise will show you how.

1. In Flash, open a new document and save it inside the **chap_17** folder as **freehand_ keyframes.fla**. Select **File > Import**.

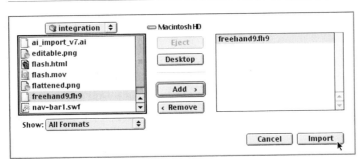

2. Locate the integration folder and add the **freehand9.fh9** file to your list on the right side of the window by clicking the **Add** button. Then click the **Import** button.

Tip: *If you import a FreeHand 9 file that contains symbols into Flash, it will automatically add those symbols to the Library.*

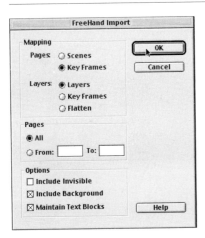

3. Flash will automatically detect that you are trying to import a FreeHand file and will open the **FreeHand Import** dialog box. Choose **Key Frames** in the **Mapping Pages** section of the dialog box and click **OK**.

The FreeHand Import Dialog Box

The FreeHand Import dialog box appears whenever you import FreeHand files into Flash 5. The settings allow you to have control over the specific aspects of your file. See the chart below for an explanation of its features:

FreeHand Import Dialog Box	
Setting	**Description**
Mapping Pages	This option controls how FreeHand document pages are imported into Flash 5. If you select *Scenes*, each page will be transformed into a scene in Flash. If you select *Key Frames*, each page in your FreeHand file will be transformed into a keyframe. You can choose the method that you prefer.
Mapping Layers	This option controls how individual layers are imported into Flash from your FreeHand file. Selecting *Layers* allows the layers in your FreeHand file to remain as layers when imported into Flash. Selecting *Key Frames* allows Flash to convert the layers into keyframes. Selecting *Flatten* will convert multiple layers in FreeHand into one layer in Flash.
Pages	This option allows you to either import all pages from your FreeHand file or specify a range of pages to import into Flash.
Options Include Invisible	If this box is checked, Flash will include all hidden layers from your FreeHand document.
Options Include Background	If this box is checked, the background layer in your FreeHand file will be included during import.
Options Maintain Text Blocks	If this box is checked, Flash will preserve the text blocks in your FreeHand file so that they will remain editable in Flash after you import your FreeHand file.

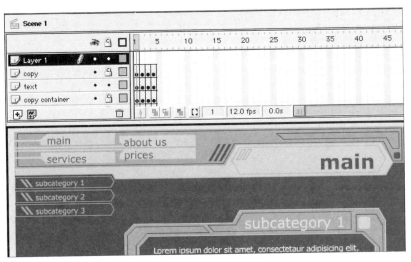

After you clicked OK in Step 3 above, notice how Flash brought in all the pages from the FreeHand file and placed the content onto separate keyframes.

4. On the Timeline, click on **keyframes 1**, **2**, **3** and **4** (or scrub the Playhead) to see the content Flash imported as separate keyframes. Can you imagine how easy it would be to mock up a Web site inside FreeHand and simply import it into Flash? This is truly powerful integration!

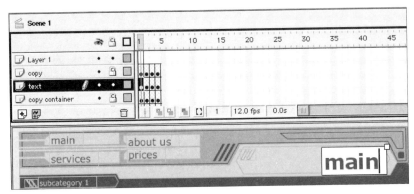

5. When you import FreeHand pages as keyframes, all your text will still be editable as long as the **Options > Maintain Text Blocks** box is checked in the **FreeHand Import** dialog box. Click in **Keyframe 1** on your text layer. Double-click in the text box that reads **main** and notice that it is editable!

Note: *If the* Maintain Text Blocks *option is not checked in the* FreeHand Import *dialog box, the text in your FreeHand document will be converted to groups when imported into Flash and will not be editable as text.*

6. Select **File > Save** and then close this file.

4. _____**Importing FreeHand Content as Scenes**

In this exercise, you'll get a chance to bring the Freehand content in as scenes instead of as keyframes. There is an ongoing debate within the Flash developer community as to whether it is better project management to use scenes or keyframes to organize sections of a Flash project. As you become more and more proficient in Flash development, you will ultimately choose the style that works best for you. In the meantime, since there is not only one "correct" way to import content from FreeHand into Flash, we want to show you both methods.

1. Select **File > New** to create a new document. Save this document as **freehand_scenes.fla** inside the **chap_17** folder. Choose **File > Import.**

2. Choose the same FreeHand file (**freehand9.fh9**) and add it to your list on the right side of the window by clicking the **Add** button. Then click the **Import** button. Windows users will click open.

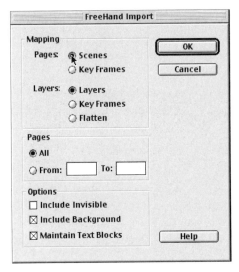

3. In the **FreeHand Import** dialog box that comes up, choose to have all the pages brought in as scenes by clicking on the **Scenes** button in the **Mapping Pages** section and click **OK**.

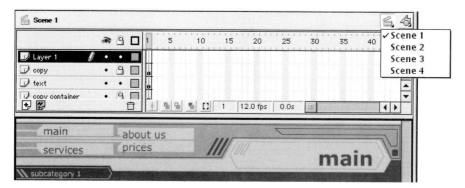

4. Click on the **Edit Scenes** icon in the upper-right corner of the Timeline to reveal that Flash has imported the content from the FreeHand file as four separate scenes! Now click on a different scene to see the content within that scene. It's really easy to import a FreeHand file into Flash and transform each page into a separate scene.

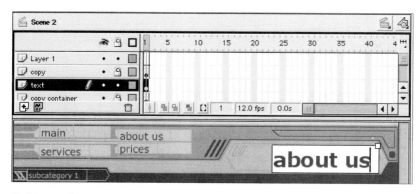

5. Choose **Scene 2** using the **Edit Scenes** icon and click in **Keyframe 1** on the text layer. Double-click in the text box that reads **about us** and you'll see that the text is editable. Just as with importing FreeHand pages as keyframes, when you import FreeHand pages as scenes, your text will still be editable as long as the **Options > Maintain Text Blocks** box was checked in the FreeHand Import dialog box.

You can also drag your FreeHand file directly onto the Stage in Flash.

6. Select **File > Save** to save the changes you made to this file. Close this file.

TIP | Learning More About FreeHand

If you are interested in learning more about Freehand, here is a list of learning resources and support sites:

`http://www.macromedia.com/support/freehand/`

`http://www.freehandsource.com/`

`http://www.ruku.com/tutorials/freehand9.html`

`http://www.elementk.com/CourseCatalog/course_syllabus.asp?CourseID=1335&CourseType=4`

5. —————————**Dreamweaver and Flash**

Many designers create content that is a combination of HTML and Flash. This next exercise shows how to combine HTML and Flash using Dreamweaver. You might wonder why not just use the publishing features of Flash for your HTML? That's fine for simple pages that contain only Flash, but Dreamweaver offers more control if you plan to integrate Flash with HTML. After you import a .swf file into Dreamweaver, you can alter many attributes of your Flash file, such as size and positioning. You can even insert Flash content inside frames, tables or layers within a Dreamweaver HTML document. Actually, the process is quite simple and the following exercise will show you how.

1. Choose **File > Open** and located the **nav-bar1.fla** file inside the **chap_17** folder.

2. Test the movie (Control > Test Movie) to produce the .swf file you will need in later steps in this exercise. Test the buttons to observe that they turn green when you roll over them.

3. Close the file when you are finished previewing it.

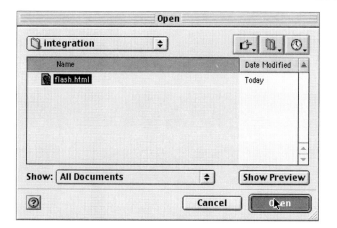

4. Open Dreamweaver and choose **File > Open** and select the **flash.html** file from the **chap_17** folder.

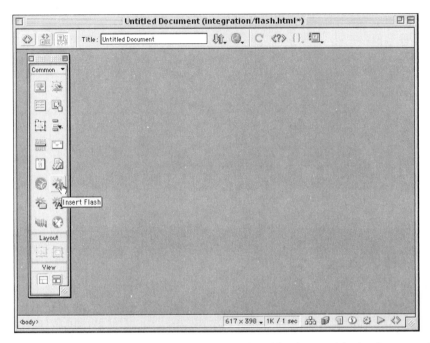

5. You will see a document that simply has a colored background. In the **Common Objects** panel, click on the **Insert Flash** icon (shown above).

6. Browse to the **Integration** folder and locate the **nav-bar1.swf** file and click **Open**. Make sure you choose the **.swf** file and not the .fla file!

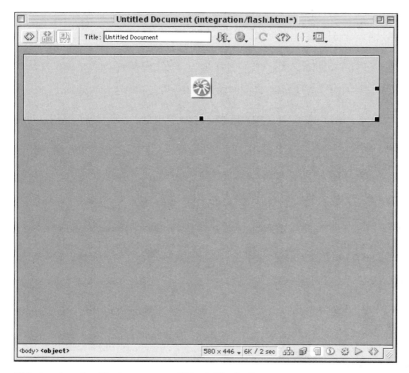

This is what the Flash content will look like in Dreamweaver.

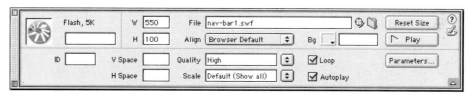

7. In the **Property Inspector**, notice the green **Play** arrow on the right side. Clicking on the arrow allows you to preview the Flash file right on the screen inside Dreamweaver. Go ahead and click it. You can even check the rollover functionality of the links to make sure they turn green when you roll your mouse over them.

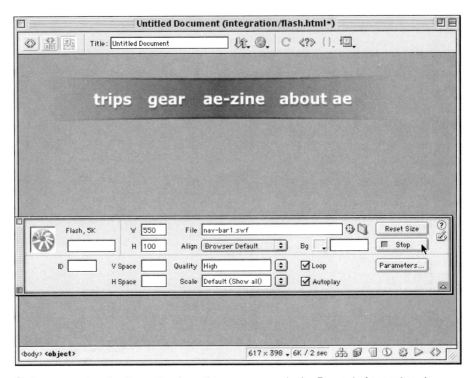

8. As you preview the file, notice how the green arrow in the **Property Inspector** changes to a red square. Once you've previewed the file, click the red square to return to your work environment.

Note: The Property Inspector is an easy way to assign attribute tags, the background color, how the content is going to be aligned or how the movie will scale, and plenty of other useful properties. Dreamweaver offers a lot of control over how the content is displayed.

6. _____**QuickTime**

In the following steps, you will learn about the integration between Apple QuickTime and Macromedia Flash. This exercise will show you how to add a custom Flash interface to a QuickTime movie. You need to have a current version of QuickTime to complete this exercise. We have included the full version of Apple QuickTime 5 on the **H•O•T CD-ROM**. It is located inside the software folder.

1. Choose **File > New** and save this file as **quicktime_test.fla** inside the **chap_17** folder. Choose **File > Import**.

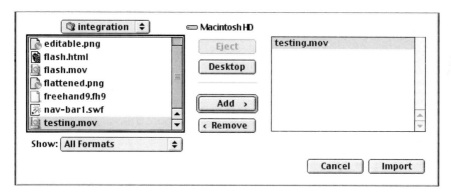

2. Locate the file called **testing.mov** file from the **chap_17** folder, add it and click **Import**.

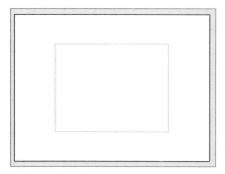

Note: When you import a QuickTime movie into Flash, the movie will be added to the center of the Stage as a transparent box with a turquoise outline.

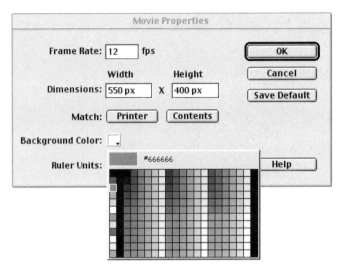

3. Because the QuickTime movie has a white background that matches the Stage, select **Modify > Movie** and in the **Movie Properties** window, change the background color to something other than white so you can see the movie's outline.

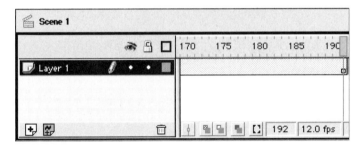

4. Next, you must extend the Timeline of the layer with the QuickTime content so that it is the same length as the movie. Unfortunately, there is no way to measure how long your movie is ahead of time, so you will have to guess by pressing the **F5** key at different points in your Timeline. Use this key until you see a blue box (explained next) with lines in it, which indicates that there is no more content. For this exercise, we have already counted the frames for you. Go to **Frame 192** and press **F5** on your keyboard to add frames that will make your Flash file exactly as long as the QuickTime movie.

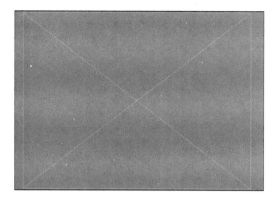

Note: *If you extend the frames too far, you will get a blue box with lines through it, which symbolizes that the movie does not occupy that space.*

5. Double-click on **Layer 1** and rename the layer **quicktime**.

6. Scrub through the movie with your **Playhead** to see the QuickTime content playing.

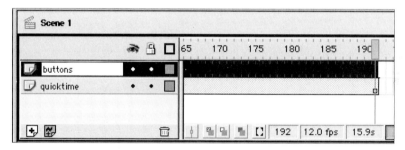

7. Add a new layer and name it **buttons**. You will add two buttons to the bottom of your QuickTime movie that will stop and play the movie.

8. Choose **Window > Common Libraries > Buttons.** Locate the **Play** and **Stop** buttons in the **(circle) Button Set** in the Library.

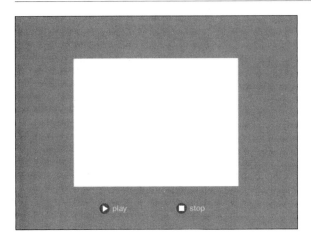

9. Make sure **Frame 1** in your **buttons** layer is selected and drag an instance of each on to the Stage, placing them towards the bottom of the movie. In the following steps, one button will tell the movie to play and the other will tell the movie to stop.

Tip: To align your buttons, make sure both buttons are selected and press Cmd + K *(Mac) or* Ctrl + K *(Windows) to access the Align window.*

10. Select the first button and choose **Control + Click** (Mac) or **Right+ Click** (Windows) to select **Actions** from the contextual menu.

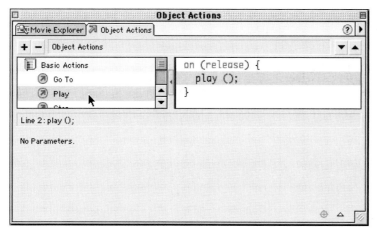

11. In the **Object Actions** panel, click the **Basic Actions** icon and double-click on **Play**. The code will appear to the right of the window in the Actions list. Close the **Object Actions** panel.

12. Now, select the **stop** button and **Control+Click (**Mac) or **Right-Click** (Windows) to select **Actions** from the contextual menu.

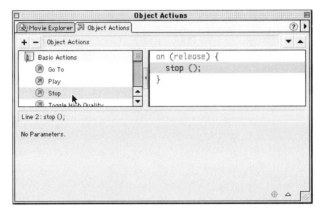

13. From the **Object Actions** panel, open the **Basic Actions** icon and double-click on **Stop**. The code will appear to the right of the panel in the actions list. Close the **Object Actions** panel. You are almost done!

14. Choose **File > Export Movie**.

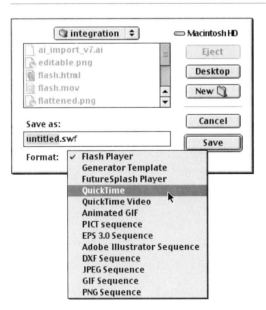

15. From the **Export Movie** dialog box, select **QuickTime** as the file format. Although you will notice many file format options here, the only way to view the QuickTime content is to save the file in the QuickTime format. Don't save the file just yet, because you will be naming your movie in the next step. **Note:** You can't import a QuickTime file and export out a .swf file because your QuickTime movie simply will not play as a .swf.

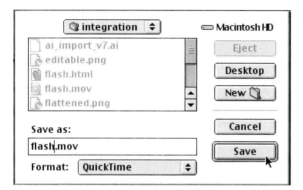

16. Name your file as **flash.mov** and choose **Save,** then put it inside the **chap_17** folder.

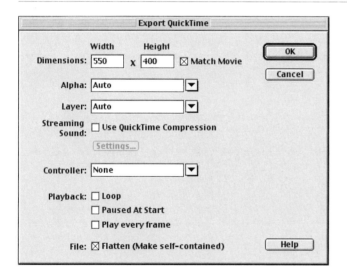

Note: QuickTime uses "tracks" to separate and store different forms of multimedia. In version 4 of QuickTime, the Flash track was added.

The QuickTime Dialog Box

The following chart explains all of the QuickTime features.

QuickTime Dialog Box	
Setting	**Description**
Dimensions	This option controls the size of the movie. If the *Match Movie* box is checked, a QuickTime movie will be created that will have the same dimensions as the those you set in *your Movie Properties* dialog box.
Alpha	This option controls transparency of Flash background on top of QuickTime. The *Auto* option sets the Flash track to transparent if the Flash track appears over the other tracks, and opaque if it is at the bottom or the only track in the movie. *Alpha Transparent* makes the Flash track transparent so you can see content under it. *Copy* sets the Flash track to opaque.
Layer	This option controls where Flash plays in the stacking order of QuickTime tracks. *Top* places the Flash track on top of all other tracks. *Bottom* places the Flash track below other tracks in the QuickTime movie. *Auto* detects where the Flash content is located and places the Flash track on top if it has been positioned in front of an imported QuickTime movie.
Streaming Sound	If this box is checked, Flash will export streaming sound to a QuickTime sound track.
Controller	This option allows you to choose which QuickTime controller will be used to play back your exported QuickTime movie.
Playback	This option allows you to choose how your movie is played. *Loop* will play your movie from start to finish and will keep playing over and over. *Pause At Start* will not play your movie until a button is pressed within your movie to initiate it, or until the play button is pressed on the QuickTime control panel. *Play every frame* will allow every frame to be viewed, no matter the effect on playback, and all sound will be disabled in the exported QuickTime movie if this option is selected.
File	If this box is checked, Flash content will be combined with the imported video content into a single QuickTime file.

17. You will be presented with the **Export QuickTime** dialog box. Most of these options are going to work just fine at their default settings, so simply click **OK**.

After you clicked OK in the last step, Flash exported this file as a QuickTime movie. To check the results, go to the chap_17 folder and double-click on the file titled flash.mov *to open your file inside the QuickTime movie player.*

You can easily play and stop your movie using the buttons you've just created. As you can see, it's not that difficult to create your own custom Flash controller for QuickTime content.

18. When you're done, close the **flash.mov** file. Save and close the **quicktime_test.fla** file.

7.————————**Illustrator Files Into Flash**

Many people are more comfortable using programs other than Flash that also offer vector drawing tools. Of them, Adobe Illustrator is quite popular; however techniques for working between Flash and Illustrator are not that easy to find. This exercise will walk you through a few different processes, and requires that you have Illustrator 9.0.

> **1.** Open Illustrator 9.0. From Illustrator, open the file **flash4hot.ai.** located in the **chap_17** folder.

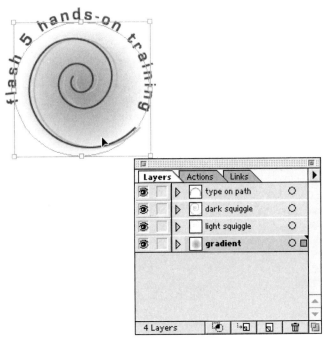

This file contains multiple layers, as well as shapes that would be difficult to create in Flash. As well, Flash does not allow you to create text along a path, such as the text shown in this document. For these reasons, creating this artwork in Illustrator is preferable over Flash.

2. Choose **Edit > Select All.** This selects all the shapes on the screen. Choose **Edit > Copy** to place this file in the memory of your computer. It is now ready to paste into Flash.

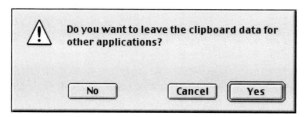

3. Open Flash. If you don't have enough computer memory to have Flash and Illustrator open at the same time, quit Illustrator. A dialog box might appear asking if you want to leave the clipboard data for other applications. Choose **Yes** so the information you just copied is stored after you quit. **Note:** If you have both programs open, you won't be asked to respond to this question.

4. In Flash, choose **File > New** and save the file as **illustrator_test.fla** inside the **chap_17** folder. Choose **Modify > Movie…** and change the **Background** to **white**, if it's set to a different color.

5. Choose **Edit > Paste**. The image from Illustrator will be pasted to the center of your Stage. Color information from the gradient as well as layer information will be lost. If you click on it, the objects will be grouped so that you can't access each individual artwork component.

6. Delete this artwork. There is a better way!

7. Open or return to Illustrator. This time, choose **File > Save As**. Change the format to Illustrator EPS, and name the new file **flash4hot.eps**.

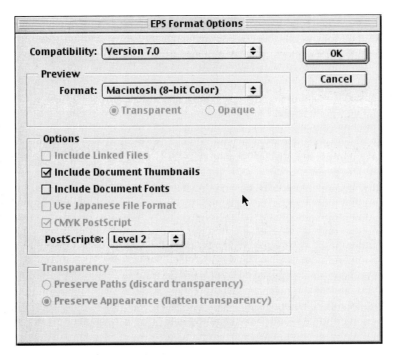

8. The **EPS Format Options** dialog box will open. Set **Compatibility: Version 7.0**. Choose **OK**. Flash understands Version 7.0 .eps files better than more current versions of Illustrator.

9. Return to Flash and choose **File > Import**, browse to the file you just saved named **flash5hot.eps** and press **Add**. When this file is added, it appears on the right side of the dialog box. Press **Import**.

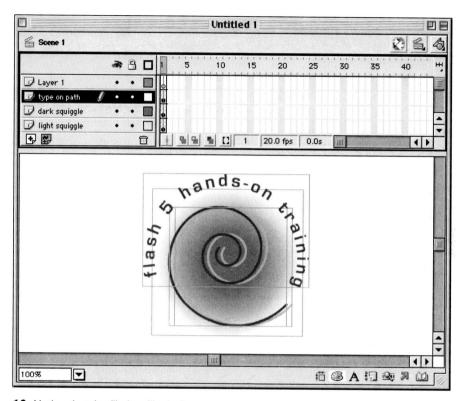

10. Notice that the file is still missing some of its color information, but this time it brought in each layer from Illustrator! This is a better way to work than copying and pasting, especially if you want to retain the layer names and information from Illustrator. You could always recreate or recolor one layer if you needed to. Still, there's another way to get the file into Flash with the proper color information.

11. Return to Illustrator. This time, choose **File > Export**. The Export dialog box will appear. Change the field for **Format: Flash (SWF)**, name the file **flash4hot.swf**, and click **Export** (Mac) or **Save** (Windows).

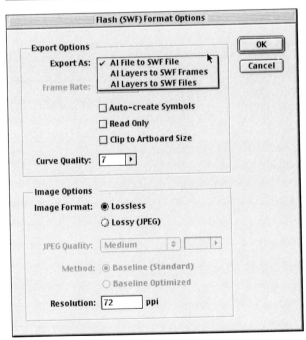

12. In the **Export As** field, choose **AI File to SWF File**. This will create a single .swf file. Press **OK**.

Flash (SWF) Format Options Explained

Export Options	Menu Choices	Description
Export As:	AI File to SWF File	This will group all the objects into a single .swf file.
	AI Layers to SWF Frames	This will create an animation based on layer information. Each layer will import into Flash as a separate frame.
	AI Layers to SWF Files	This will export each layer as a separate .swf file.
Auto-Create Symbols		This will create each object as its own symbol. You'll see the symbols appear with default names (symbol 1, etc.) inside Flash 5.
Read Only		Creates a protected .swf movie that cannot be imported into Flash.
Clip to Artboard Size		Trims the canvas size to fit the artwork.
Curve Quality		Settings from 1–10, with 1 representing the lowest quality.
Image Format	Lossless	Lossless is best for images that have solid colors.
	Lossy (JPEG)	Lossy is best for images that have gradations.
Resolution		Use the default setting of 72 ppi. Even if you change this setting, Flash will only recognize 72 ppi.

13. Return to Flash. Turn off all the layers in the document. Create a new layer and name it **swf**. With that layer selected, choose **File > Import**. Locate the **flash5hot.swf** file and click **Add**. It will appear in the list to the right. Press **Import**.

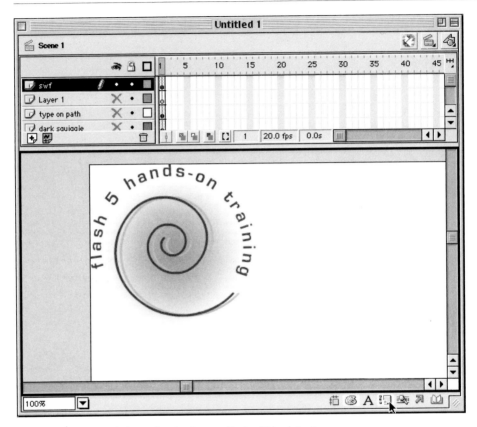

This time, the color information in the gradient will be intact.

In summary, you can see that there are three ways to bring the Illustrator document into Flash: pasting, importing as EPS or importing as .swf. You've seen the tradeoffs for each method, which will help you make an educated decision the next time you want to work with Illustrator and Flash together.

Illustrator to Flash Techniques

Method	Pros	Cons
Pasting	It's the fastest and easiest way to get Illustrator files into Flash	You might loose some color information, and your Illustrator layers won't be preserved
Importing EPS (Version 7)	Preserves layer information and layer names	You might lose some color information
Importing SWF	Preserves color information	You will lose layer information

14. Save and close this file.

You did it! Congratulations. We really hope this book helped to get you up to speed with Flash quickly, and that you now feel better prepared to create your own animated and interactive projects. We wish you the best of luck on all of your future creations!

Troubleshooting FAQ

| Appendix A |

H·O·T

Flash 5

If you run into any problems while following the exercises in this book, you might find the answer in this troubleshooting guide. This document will be maintained and updated at this book's companion Web site: `http://www.lynda.com/ products/books/fl5hot`.

If you don't find what you're looking for here or there, please send an email to:

`fl5faq@lynda.com.`

If you have a question related to Flash, but unrelated to a specific step in an exercise in this book, visit the Flash site at: `http://www. macromedia.com/support/flash/` or call their tech-support hotline at 415.252.9080.

Q: On the Macintosh, why can't I see any .fla files when I choose File > Open?

A: If the .fla file was created on a PC, you might experience a problem seeing those files when you choose **File > Open** from within Flash on a Macintosh. You can correct this by changing **List Files of Type** option to **All Files**.

Q: My Toolbox has disappeared. What should I do?

A: If your Toolbox has vanished, you can easily make it reappear again. Choose **Window > Tools** to show/hide the Toolbox. Chapter 2, *"The Flash Interface,"* explains the Toolbox in detail.

Q: All of my panels have disappeared. What should I do?

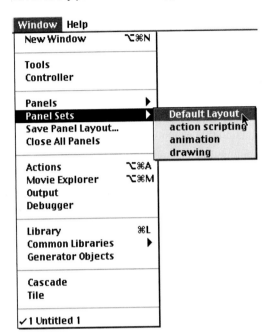

A: If you lose your panels, or if you don't like their arrangement, you can revert them back to their default positions by choosing **Window > Panel Sets > Default Layout**. This will cause all of the panels to reappear in their default positions on the screen. This is especially helpful when someone else has undocked and changed the combination of your panels. In Chapter 2, *"The Flash Interface,"* each of the panels is described in detail.

Q: When I test my movie it always looks larger than it is supposed to. Why?

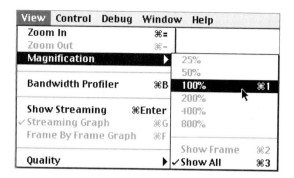

A: When you choose **Test > Movie**, Flash will open a preview window to display your .swf file. This preview window is not displayed at 100% by default. With the preview window open, press **Cmd + 1** (Mac) or **Ctrl + 1** (Windows) to ensure that you are previewing your movie at the proper magnification. You can also choose **View > Magnification > 100%**.

Q: Why does Flash create extra files when I press F12?

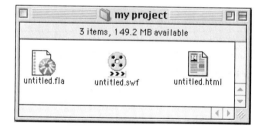

A: Pressing **F12** is a shortcut for *Publish Preview*. This means that Flash will publish an .swf file and an HTML file when you press this key. These files will be created in the same directory as the .fla file. If you want to preview your movie without publishing any other files, choose **Control > Test Movie** and only the .swf file will be created. In Chapter 15, *"Publishing,"* the publish features are explained in detail.

Q: I tried to create my own shape tween but it won't work, and the Timeline has a broken line. What does that mean?

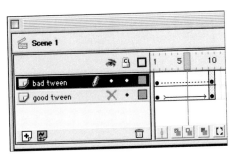

A: You cannot create a shape tween using symbols, groups, or text blocks (text that hasn't been broken apart). A solid line with an arrow indicates that the tween is working properly. This is a good tween. A dashed line in the Timeline indicates there is a problem with the tween. This is a bad tween. Make sure you are only using objects that work with shape tween. In Chapter 6, *"Shape Tweening,"* you will find a detailed list of what objects can be used to create shape tweens.

Q: Why do all of the objects on my stage appear faded?

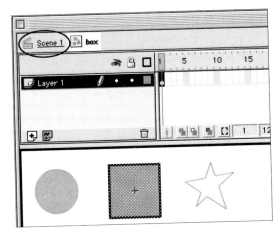

A: This occurs when you double-click on an instance or right-click on one and choose **Edit in Place**. This is a quick way to make changes to a symbol without having to access the Library, however it can be confusing if that's not what you intended to do. Click on the **Scene 1** tab to exit this editing mode and return to the main Timeline.

Q: I tried to create my own motion tween, but it won't work. And the Timeline has a broken line. What does that mean?

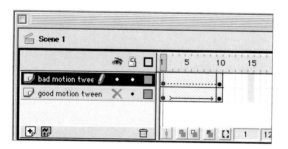

A: You cannot create a motion tween using shapes or broken-apart text. A solid line with an arrow indicates that the tween is working properly. This is a good tween. A dashed line in the Timeline indicates there is a problem with the tween. This is a bad tween. Make sure you are only using objects that work with motion tweens. In Chapter 8, *"Motion Tweening,"* you will find a detailed list of what objects can be used to create motion tweens.

Q: I tried to motion tween multiple objects, but it's not working. What could be wrong?

A: Motion tweening multiple objects requires that each different object exist on a separate layer. If you have all the objects on a single layer, the tween will not behave as expected. Also, make sure you are trying to tween objects that are capable of being motion tweened. Objects such as shapes and broken apart text cannot be motion tweened.

Q: Why won't my movie clips play when I press the play button on the Controller?

A: You can't preview your movie clips on the Stage within the Flash-authoring environment. Movie clips can only be previewed in the Library or by selecting **Control > Test Movie** or pressing **F12** to preview the movie clip in a browser.

Flash Resources

| Appendix B |

There are lots of great resources for Flash users. You have ample choices between a variety of newsgroups, conferences, and third-party Web sites that can really help you get the most out of Flash. This appendix lists some of the best resources for developing your Flash skills.

H•O•T

Flash 5

Macromedia Exchange for Flash

http://www.macromedia.com/exchange/flash/

Macromedia has set up a section of its Web site, designed to be a portal for Flash users, called the **Macromedia Flash Exchange**. There you'll find hundreds of free extensions written by third-party users and developers that can help you build new features into your Web site. These features are not part of the Flash product that installs from Macromedia, but can be downloaded when you need them. Many of these extensions have features that normally would require an advanced level of ActionScripting. For example, some of these behaviors can give you the ability to password-protect areas of your site, create pop-up menus, scroll bars, complex text effects, etc.

The Macromedia site is not just for developers, but for any Flash user who wants to take Flash to the next level. If you are a developer, this is a great place to learn how to write your own behaviors to share with the rest of the Flash community.

Macromedia Discussion Groups

Macromedia has set up several discussion boards (newsgroups) for Flash. This is a great place to ask questions and get help from thousands of Flash users. The newsgroup is composed of beginning to advanced users, so you should have no problem finding the type of help you need, regardless of your experience with the program. Garo is a participant, as well as many other Flash authors. In order to access these newsgroups, you will need a newsgroup reader, such as Microsoft Outlook or Free Agent.

Flash

Forum for technical issues related to creating dynamic Web content using Flash, Aftershock for Flash, and the Flash Player Java Edition.

news://forums.macromedia.com/macromedia.flash

Flash Site Design

Online forum for design feedback on your Flash animations. Dedicated to the discussion of Flash design, and animation principles and practices. Other issues not specific to the Flash tools, yet important to Flash designers can also be discussed here.

news://forums.macromedia.com/macromedia.flash.sitedesign

Flash Handhelds

Forum for technical issues related to creating Flash content for handheld devices, such as the PocketPC.

news://forums.macromedia.com/macromedia.flash.handhelds

Third-Party Flash Web Sites

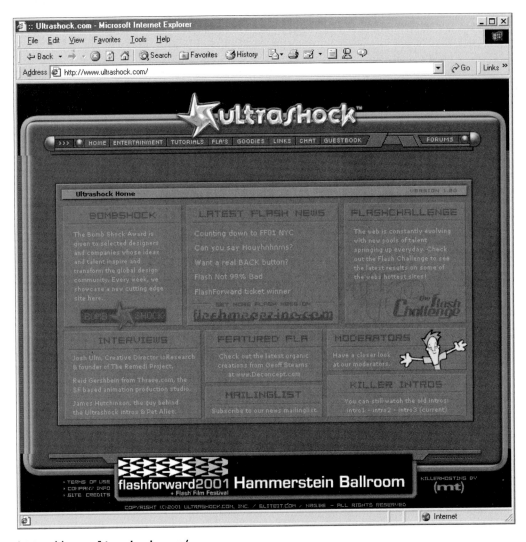

http://www.ultrashock.com/

http://virtual-fx.net/

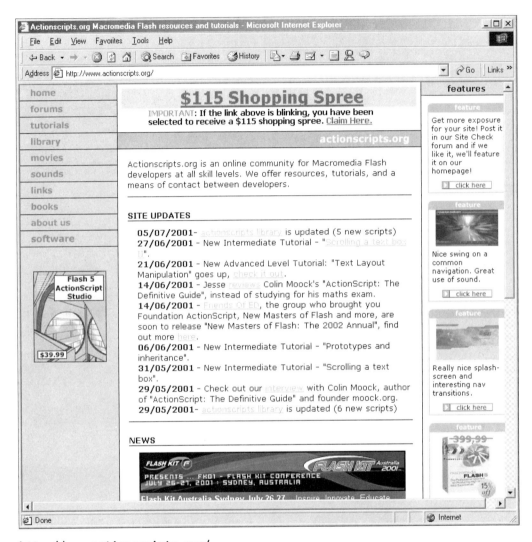

http://www.actionscripts.org/

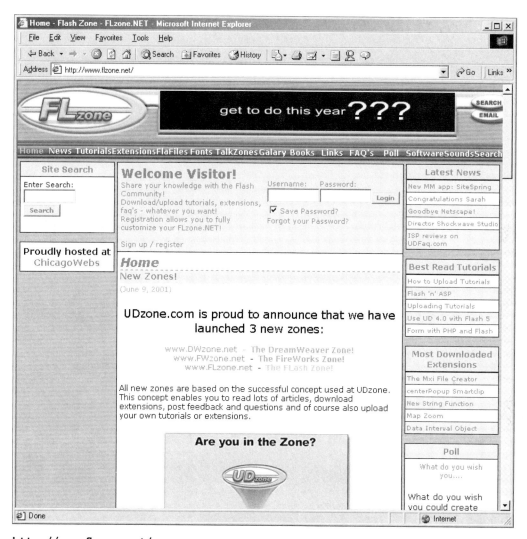

http://www.flzone.net/

http://flashmove.com/

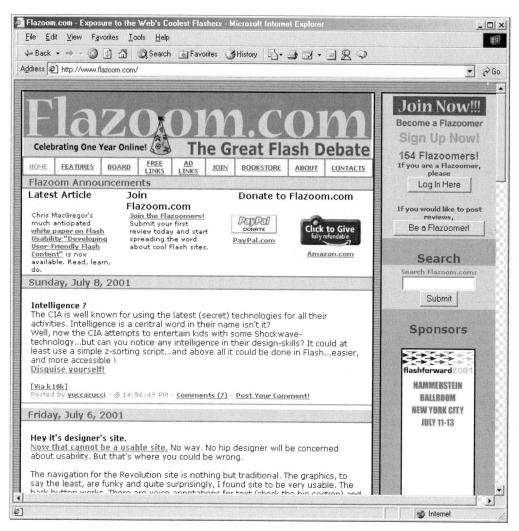

http://flazoom.com/

Flashforward 2001

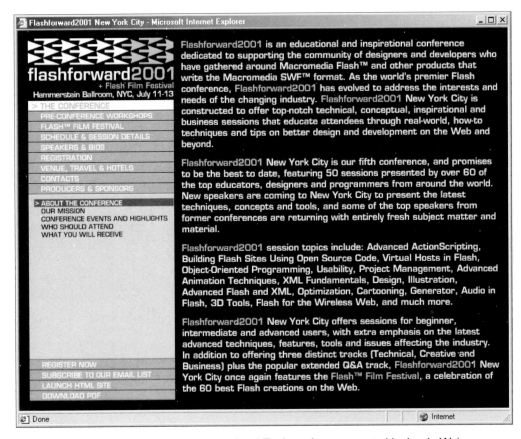

Flashforward 2001 is an international educational Flash conference created by Lynda Weinman of lynda.com and Stewart McBride of United Digital Artists, and sponsored by Macromedia. It's a great conference to attend, once you know Flash and want to take your skills to a new level. The best Flash developers and designers in the world present their technical and artistic work in an educational setting. You can learn more about Flashforward and its offerings by visiting http://www.flashforward2001.com

Forward Society

http://www.forwardsociety.com

An association for digital artists and Flash developers that offers discounts on Flash events, classes, seminars, and CD-ROMS.

CD-ROMs from Lynda.com

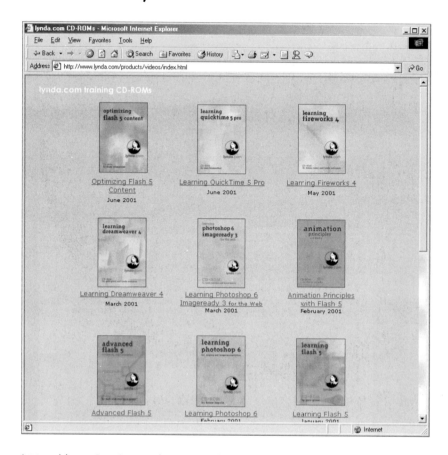

`http://www.lynda.com/products/videos/index.html`

- *Learning Flash 5*
- *Intermediate Flash 5*
- *Advanced Flash 5: Introduction to ActionScripting*
- *Flash 5 Optimization Content*
- *Animation Principles with Flash 5*

CDs from Flashforward

`http://www.lynda.com/products/videos/index.html`

- *Getting to the Source Behind Radiskull and Devil Doll* with Joe Sparks
- *Advanced Flash 5 Action Script* with Sam Wan
- *A Guide to User Friendly Flash* with Chris MacGregor

Technical Support

| Appendix C |

H·O·T
_____
Flash 5

Macromedia Technical Support

`http://www.macromedia.com/support/`

415.252.9080

If you're having problems with Flash, please contact Macromedia Technical Support at the number listed above. They can help you with typical problems, such as: the trial version has expired on your computer or your computer crashes when you try to launch the application. Please note that lynda.com cannot help troubleshoot technical problems with Flash.

Peachpit Press

`customer_service@peachpit.com`

If your book has a defective CD-ROM, please contact the customer service department at the above email address. We do not have extra CDs at lynda.com, so they must be requested directly from the publisher.

lynda.com

We have created a companion Web site for this book, which can be found at:

http://www.lynda.com/books/fl5hot/

Any errors in the book will be posted to the Web site, and it's always a good idea to check there for up-to-date information. We encourage and welcome your comments and error reports to **fl5faq@lynda.com**. Both Kymberlee and Garo receive these emails.

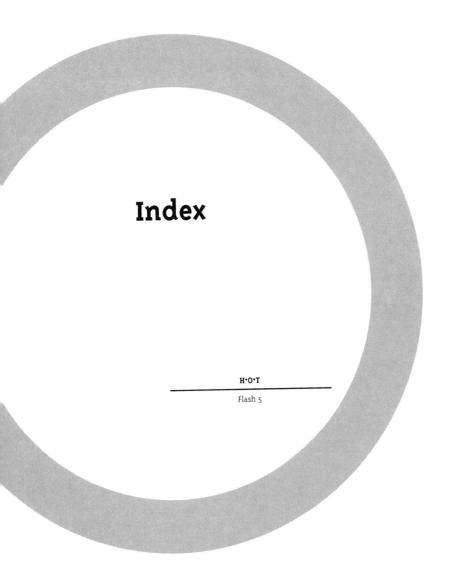

Index

H•O•T

Flash 5

Symbols

() (parentheses), 402
{} (braces), 402
+ (plus sign), 200
; (semicolon), 402
= (equal), 512
== (double equal), 512

A

absolute addresses, 422
acorn scene, 646-52
.act files, 45
actions
 adding, to button instance, 402,
 406, 414
 adding, to keyframe, 451
 adding to list of, 400-401
 applying to button symbol objects,
 397
 categories, 400
 defined, 395
 frame, 395, 404-9
 FSCommand, 474, 573, 576
 Get URL, 420-25, 474, 656
 Go To, 410-19, 474, 513
 If Frame is Loaded, 467, 468, 475
 instances, 432
 keyframes containing, 413
 layer, 411, 442, 444, 451, 467
 list, 395, 396
 Load Movie, 448, 450, 474, 595
 Load Variables, 492, 497
 object, 395, 397-403
 On Mouse Event, 475, 512
 Operators, 473
 Play, 403, 474
 Print, 664
 Properties, 473
 Stop, 397-403, 474, 498, 634
 Stop All Sounds, 474, 546
 Toggle High Quality, 474
 Unload Movie, 474
ActionScript(s), 394-475
 adding, to left button, 416
 adding, to right button, 414-15
 code, typing directly, 396
 code, working with, 394
 defined, 11, 394
 display in Movie Explorer, 610
 importance of, 394
 JavaScript and, 11
 levels, 448
 looping, 416-17
 movie clips and, 373
 naming conventions and, 198
 testing, 416, 419, 454

Actions list, 395, 396, 442, 473, 497
Actions panel, 394, 395-96
 Actions list, 395, 396, 442
 Add a statement button, 395, 396
 Basic Actions Library, 395
 Delete a statement button, 395
 Expand/Collapse parameters panel
 button, 395
 Expert Mode, 395, 396
 Functions, 473
 illustrated, 395
 Insert Target Path button, 395, 396
 keyboard shortcut, 399
 list, 395, 396, 473
 modes, toggling between, 396
 Normal Mode, 395
 opening, 399
 operators, 473
 Options menu, 395, 396
 Parameters pane, 395
 Properties, 473
 See also Frame Actions panel;
  Object Actions panel; panels
addressing, 422
 absolute, 422
 Load Movie and, 453
 relative, 422, 453
.ai file format, 283
AIF format, 522
aligning
 buttons, 349, 413, 618, 688
 graphic symbols, 275
 invisible buttons, 356-57
 text, 481
Align panel, 647
 Align Bottom Edge button, 275, 357
 Align/Distribute to Stage button,
 319, 321
 Align Horizontal Center button,
 319, 321
 Align Left Edge button, 349
 Align Vertical Center button, 319,
 321
 Distribute Horizontal Center button,
 357
 Distribute Vertical Center button,
 349
 illustrated, 275
 keyboard shortcut, 275, 319, 613,
 618
 opening, 275, 319, 613, 618
 Space Evenly Horizontally button,
 275
 To Stage option, 349
 See also panels
allowscale FSCommand, 575

alpha effect, 223, 238, 277
 applying, 318, 321, 616, 647
 movie clip instance, 377
 setting, 616, 633
 use of, 594
 See also transparency
anchor points
 adding, 83
 converting, 84-85
 corner, 84-85
 creating, 73
 creation indicator, 83
 cursor over, 81
 curve, 84-85
 deleting, 85
 as hollow points, 75
 illustrated, 81
 as solid points, 75
 square, 74
animated glows, 175-78
animated_gradient2.fla file, 175
animated_gradient.fla file, 171
animated gradients, 171-74
animated graphic symbols, 231-37
 changing starting frames of, 235
 main Timeline and, 371
 movie clips vs., 366-73
 number of frames and, 231
 Timeline, 234
 See also graphic symbols; symbols
animated masks, 314-15
animated rollover buttons, 387-92
 creating, 387-92
 defined, 328
 with nested movie clip, 387
 previewing, 387, 391
 See also buttons
animation
 basics, 110-53
 capabilities, learning, 110
 fade-down, 316-20
 fade-up, 320-22
 frame-by-frame, 232
 frame-by-frame, with keyframes,
 118-23
 looping, 124, 128, 147, 416-17, 465
 pausing, 280
 playback time calculation, 137
 playing, 135
 previewing, 121, 123, 139, 142,
 143, 148
 scaling to size of window, 150
 slowing down, 139
 timing, controlling, 139
 twinkle, 233
animButtonFinal.exe file, 387
animButtonFinalProjector file, 387
animButton.fla file, 387

TIFF file format, 283, 284
time-based events, 409
Timeline, 15-18
  Add Guide Layer button, 258, 598
  Add Layer button, 598
  animated graphic symbol, 234
  black dots, 141
  blank keyframe, 111
  blue waveform, 532, 637
  broken line, 162
  button, 329, 340, 359
  Current Frame, 111
  Current Scene readout, 15
  defined, 13
  Delete Layer button, 18, 598
  docking, 17
  drop-down menu
    Create Motion Tween command, 320, 322
    Remove Frames command, 340
  Edit Multiple Frames button, 251
  Edit Scene button, 16, 438, 441, 442, 444, 463, 600
  Edit Symbol List button, 16
  Elapsed Time, 111
  Frame Rate, 111
  Frame View menu, 16, 111
  graphic symbol, 232, 239
  gray bar, 251, 252
  green-shaded, 161
  as the heart of Flash, 15, 110
  Hide Layer button, 18
  hollow square, 141
  illustrated, 13, 111
  independence, 365, 371, 373, 386
  Insert Layer button, 258, 267, 272, 309, 323
  keyframes, 111
  Layer Controls, 15, 18
  Layer Name, 18
  layers, 111
  light gray frames, 141
  Lock icon, 18, 190, 207
  main, 215, 216, 234, 239, 365
  Modify Onion Markers button, 129
  movie clip, 368, 371
  Onion Skin button, 126, 354, 390
  Outline View button, 18
  Playhead, 15, 111, 121, 123, 129, 430
  playing from current position, 474
  Preview view, 122
  scene, 239, 438, 441, 600
  Show All Layers as Outlines button, 354
  sounds in, 532
  Status Bar, 16

stopping play from current position, 474
symbol location, 201
undocking, 17
vocabulary, 239
white frame, 141
tints, 220-22
  colors, 221
  movie clip instances, 376
  percentage, 222, 376
  selecting, 221, 376
  symbol, 220-21
Toggle High Quality action, 474
Toolbox
  Arrow tool, 33, 35, 46, 49, 51, 62, 68
  Brush tool, 55, 90-93, 119-20, 131
  defined, 20
  disappeared, 703
  docking, 21
  Eraser tool, 55, 132-34
  Fill Color swatch, 172, 301
  illustrated, 20
  Ink Bottle tool, 55, 68-71, 214
  Lasso tool, 299, 300
  Line tool, 55, 201-2
  Oval tool, 55, 86-87
  Paint Bucket tool, 37, 55, 94, 97-98, 171-74
  Pencil tool, 55, 57-61, 636
  Pen tool, 55, 72-78
  Rectangle tool, 55, 87-89, 181
  Subselect tool, 75, 79, 80, 84
  Text tool, 264
  tool tips, 20
Trace Bitmap dialog box
  Color Threshold option, 306
  Corner Threshold option, 306
  Curve Fit option, 306
  illustrated, 305
  Many corners option, 306
  Minimum Area option, 306
  opening, 305
traceBitmap.fla file, 305
tracking, 480
transform handles
  dragging, 296
  showing, 295
Transform panel, 176-77, 226-29, 614
  Constrain checkbox, 176, 226, 268, 311, 331, 375
  defined, 22, 197
  for exact numeric changes, 227
  Height field, 177, 226, 268, 331, 375
  illustrated, 22
  opening, 176, 226
  Rotate button, 227

Skew Horizontally field, 376
Skew option, 376
Width field, 177, 226, 268, 331, 375
  See also panels
transparency, 36
  graphic symbol, 277, 278
  instances, 223
  movie clip instance, 377
  settings, 284, 633
  use of, 594
  See also alpha effect
transparent gradients, 50
trapallkeys FSCommand, 575
troubleshooting FAQ, 702-7
  can't see .fla files, 703
  disappeared panels, 704
  extra file creation, 705
  faded objects, 706
  motion tween creation failure, 707
  motion tweening multiple objects, 707
  movie clips won't play, 707
  online resources, 702
  shape tween creation failure, 706
  tested movie too large, 705
  Timeline broken line, 706, 707
  Toolbox has disappeared, 703
tweening
  defined, 155
  See also motion tweening; shape tweening
twinkle animation, 233

U

Undo function, 307
ungrouping objects, 108
unloading movies, 460
Unload Movie action, 474
unlocking layers, 190, 192, 194, 341, 390, 439
  background, 511, 623
  button labels, 628
  buttons, 621
  enter button layer, 511
  paragraph, 657
  static text, 511
  See also layers; locking layers
Up state, 329, 346
  adding text to, 333
  defined, 327
  frame, 330, 333, 389
  invisible buttons and, 353
  keyframe, 327, 342, 388
  See also button states
URL=encoded text, 492